THE BIG BOOK OF HOME LEARNING
Volume Four: Afterschooling & Extras

Also by Mary Pride:

The Way Home
All the Way Home
Schoolproof
The Child Abuse Industry

With Paul deParrie:

Unholy Sacrifices of the New Age
Ancient Empires of the New Age

THE BIG BOOK OF HOME LEARNING

Volume Four: Afterschooling & Extras

Mary Pride

Crossway Books • Wheaton, Illinois
A Division of Good News Publishers

The Big Book of Home Learning: Volume 4.

Copyright © 1990 by Mary Pride.
Published by Crossway Books, a division of
Good News Publishers, 1300 Crescent Street, Wheaton, Illinois 60187.

Cover Design by Mark Schramm.
Interior Design by Mark Schramm and Mary Pride, based on the
original concept by Karen L. Mulder.
Layout by Bill Pride and Mary Pride.
Cover illustration by Guy Wolek.

First printing, 1990.

Printed in the United States of America

Library of Congress Cataloging-in-Publication Data
Pride, Mary
    Big book of home learning / Mary Pride
        v.   cm.
    Includes bibliographic references.
    Contents: v. 1. Getting started — v. 2. Preschool and elementary —
v. 3. Teen and adult — v. 4. Afterschooling and extras.
    1. Home schooling—United States.   2. Home schooling—United
States—Curricula.   3. Education—United States—Parent
participation.   4. Child rearing—United States   I. Title.
LC40.P75 1990   649'.68 ' 0973—dc20   89-81254
ISBN 0-89107-551-8 (v. 4)

99	98	97	96	95	94	93								
15	14	13	12	11	10	9	8	7	6	5	4	3		

TABLE OF CONTENTS

INTRODUCTION

I've had it. I'm finished. Kaput!

If anyone feels like asking me, "How did you ever put together four huge volumes like this while taking care of your family and home business and having a baby?" the answer is easy.

You miss your deadline by months and collapse!

I thank my good friends, like Pam Lancaster, who invited our children over for several fun-filled days of unit studies and learning to sew, and the Lord, who kept me from appearing in the local paper as, "Author dead; found slumped over keyboard."

If I didn't love finding about all these great new educational items, there's no way you'd get me to ever consider putting out a book like this. No way at all.

But (this is the part that always gets me) there *are* tons of fantastic educational resources out there, with more coming out every minute. For far too long there has simply been no way for everyday people like you and me to find this great stuff. And there's been no way for the people who invent, or who'd like to invent, great products to get the word out to us.

That is why every parent and teacher in this land should be thankful for the home schooling movement. Quite apart from home schooling's contributions to general educational excellence, home schoolers have done something that has never been done before. They (we) have huddled together long enough to be discovered and identified as A Market. So now, for the first time, educational suppliers are aware of a new group of people who might be interested in their products:

Parents!

We're talking *real* education, too, not flash cards. Parents are discovering we can add some meat to Johnny's curriculum, regardless of what happens at the next school board meeting. Johnny can learn Latin, and sign language, and guitar, and oil painting, and more—all at home! He can stretch his mind with any of an increasing number of colorful, high-interest books that take the "yawn" out of subjects like history. And if any of Johnny's school subjects are giving him premature gray hairs, masses of great supplemental and drill products are available, too—some even on computer!

ADVANTAGES OF AFTERSCHOOLING

Before you get out the old family Chevy and start toting Johnny around to dozens of afterschool activities, consider the advantages of afterschooling at home:

- Less stress
- Less money
- No time wasted commuting
- And last but not least, more family togetherness!

Family members of all ages can play computer games together, watch how-to videos together, work together on hobbies and crafts. The six-year-old can learn oil painting along with a sixty-year-old. Mom and Dad can enjoy building with blocks right along with the baby. Brother and sister can stump each other with riddles and brainteasers.

At home you also now have access to a far wider range of enrichment options than you can find in your local community. How many of us ever have the chance to study painting with dozens of great art teachers? How many are familiar with the history of art and music? How many are fluent in Latin, or Greek, or Hebrew . . . or French, or German, or Russian? How many can draw really well, or knit, or weave, or read music, or compose music, or play an instrument well? And when your child needs extra help in academics, or more advanced academic stimulation, where can you find patient, *individualized* tutoring that doesn't cost thousands of dollars?

The answers to all these questions are right in this book. Today a family living in the frozen wilds of Alaska can offer its children a greater variety of enrichment options than were available to rich New Yorkers twenty years ago. All the educational enrichment you will ever need is now in print, on disks, on videotape. You and your children can learn from the greatest experts in any field, in the privacy of your home.

If, that is, you know where to find them. That is where *The Big Book of Home Learning* comes in. For the last four years I've been tracking down the best and brightest educational resources you can use at home today. In the three other volumes of this series you will find resources for getting started with home education and resources for teaching and learning all the basic academic subjects at home. This volume is dedicated to the "fun stuff"—things you learn because you *want* to, not because you *have* to. (Not that you can't enjoy math or grammar for their own sake—but that's another story!)

So if you or anyone in your family always wanted to learn to paint with acrylics "someday" . . . or to play the piano . . . or to brush up on French . . . or just plain to have a lot of good mentally-stimulating fun . . . now is the time to start! Have fun with these reviews. Pick out items that your family will enjoy. Bask in the knowledge that all these options are at your fingertips.

Education is one of the very best investments you can ever make. And home education is the best educational investment. Here are the tools to help you make the most of it!

HOW TO USE THIS BOOK

You know how to read a resource book. Just turn to the section that interests you and browse through the reviews until something pops out at you from the text.

Well, guess what?

You can do the same thing with this book!

The editors and I have, however, incorporated a few innovative features that, we hope, will make each volume of *The Big Book of Home Learning* more useful than the average resource book.

If you'll flip to the Index of Suppliers you can see that it is more than just names with addresses attached. We're added all sorts of helpful information: toll-free telephone numbers for ordering, fax numbers, best times of day to call, methods of payment allowed, refund policy, whether or not the supplier has a free brochure or catalog and what it costs if it *isn't* free, plus a brief description of the supplier's product line.

It is easy to find the address of any given company. Instead of searching through a chapter to find the company, as you have to when full addresses are given in the text, just flip to the index.

What all this means is that you can relax and enjoy *The Big Book of Home Learning* without having to write down reams of information about every product that interests you. Just jot down the name of the supplier, the name of the item, and its price on a handy index card or Post-It™. When you get your whole list together, then you can turn to the index and highlight or underline the companies you intend to contact. Stick the card you were taking notes on in the index and go your merry way. When you are ready to sit down and send away for catalogs, or to call up and order, all the addresses are in one convenient location and you have all the item names and prices handy, too. And you can always find any item whose review you want to reread by turning to the General Index.

The information in *The Big Book of Home Learning* is as current and up-to-date as we could possibly make it. After the reviews were written, both they and the index information were sent back to the suppliers for verification. Even so, *it is always wise to write or call the supplier to check on prices before ordering*. The prices in this book are included to help you compare different products for value and are not permanently guaranteed. Prices go up and down. Both you and the supplier will feel better if the supplier does not have to return your order because the check you enclosed was not for the right amount.

The four volumes of this third edition of *The Big Book of Home Learning* are not only bigger than the two volumes of the previous edition; we hope they are better as well. Over some product reviews you will see the heading, "**NEW****." This means you are looking at a new review, not necessarily a new product. We decided to highlight the new reviews in this way, so that readers of previous editions can immediately turn to the new items. Products that have undergone significant revision are also highlighted as "updated" or "improved." Product reviews that are essentially the same, except for new prices, have no special headings. All prices and reviews have been updated, and the Suppliers' Index now includes fax numbers and foreign suppliers. We have several hundred new suppliers and over a thousand new products reviewed. All this is laid out in a way that should make it easy for you to instantly find the resources you need in any school or afterschool subject area.

And the best news of all—the products themselves are better! I keep telling you, people, that education suppliers are listening to you! This edition includes products that are better, more colorful, more educationally sound, simpler to use, and even (sometimes) cheaper than ever before.

So if you need to learn more about education, to set up a home education program (whether home school or afterschool), or to find out what's happening in packaged home schooling curriculum—turn to Volume One.

If you are looking for resources for a preschooler or elementary-level child in the basic school subjects—turn to Volume Two. (A quick note: Many of these resources are great for older people, too!)

If you need more advanced resources at the junior high, high school, or adult level—turn to Volume Three. (Most home-taught children are ready for this in their preteens.)

And if you are looking for the resources to round out your family's education, and want to have some fun—you're in the right place right now!

All four volumes have been designed for the everyday, normal reader. I'm assuming that you are no more interested in boring textbooks and tedious worksheets than I am. So you'll find lots of posters, videos, and make-it-yourself kits throughout each volume, along with the better traditional resources, including some revived classics from yesteryear. Simply reading about what's available in all these areas is an education in itself. Not to mention how it can spice up your gift shopping list!

One last note. This book would not have been possible without the active cooperation of many of the companies listed. Those who supplied me with samples and free catalogs bravely ran the risks of review, and I have not hesitated to point out their products' warts. I would like them to feel they gained more than a critical going-over by their generosity. Both the publisher and I would be grateful if you would mention *The Big Book of Home Learning* when you contact a supplier whose product is mentioned here.

ART

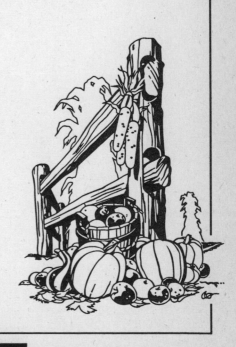

CHAPTER ONE

DRAWING AND PAINTING FOR THE REST OF US

I s art just a pastime for special people with enormous talent?

Not in my book!

Here's the proposition:

Every person reading this book can learn to draw.

"Hey, not me! No way! I can't even draw a straight line!"

Well, first of all, *drawing* is not *drafting*. You can always use a ruler or a computer to draw a straight line. Drawing is about making curved lines and wiggly lines and crosshatching and such until the final result looks like something. Drafting is about defining the outlines of manmade structures—and I don't know any mechanical designers who try to produce straight lines freehand, either!

Second, and far more important, is the fact that, rare cases aside, most people need to be *taught* to draw—and almost none of us have received this training. The reason? Somehow the idea has taken hold in art instruction circles that the way for people to learn art is for each of us to make "five thousand mistakes" on our own. Then, after we've made all these mistakes, the talented will emerge and the rest of us will sink back into the dregs. This is the way the schools teach reading, and it of course produces the same sorry results.

Contrast this with the ancient and honorable apprenticeship system. There the would-be artist worked under the direction of a master in his craft. At first the apprentice spent most of his time doing mechanical tasks: rehairing brushes, mixing paints, and so on. During this phase he was learning to handle the physical tools of his art. Then the master would let him try some small exercises, and if the apprentice was successful he would perhaps get to contribute a minor part to one of the master's own projects. In time, he would learn most of the master's techniques (canny masters kept some back!) and would be ready to try something new on his own.

At each step the apprentice was taught the skills he needed. He saw all the stages artwork goes through; he saw the finished result; he heard the master criticize his efforts and make suggestions for improvement. He did *not* blunder about making five thousand mistakes, as the master wanted a productive apprentice, not a nitwit.

As someone who has never been accused of possessing great artistic talent, I am here to tell you that today you can start learning to produce really nice drawings, even if you never have before.

Over the last few years a number of really fun and easy-to-follow drawing programs have been developed. These all follow the time-tested method of introducing skills one at a time, rather than mindlessly urging the student to be "creative." Below you will also find a number of excellent resources that introduce you to other media and techniques besides drawing. Then, since the best artistic inspiration comes from seeing what others have done before, Chapter 2 tours sources for teaching art history. Chapter 3 shows you where to get the supplies you need, and Chapter 4 introduces programs and suppliers for crafts that do not generally fall under the "fine arts" label.

So when your local school or college decides to junk the art department so they can afford to Astroturf the football field, it won't mean the death of Western civilization as we have known it. Should Congress even finally decide to defund the National Endowment for the Arts, the pillars of civilization need not crumble. While "real" artists churn out works like crosses suspended in vials of urine (a work taking no technical skill whatsoever to produce), the rest of us can be learning to step up to a blackboard and draw a recognizable dog or daisy or funny picture of Uncle Fred.

Art is, or should be, mainly for bringing joy into the world. Joy to the maker and joy to the beholder. If you want to get depressed, watch the evening news. If you want to get happy, learn to draw!

INTRODUCTION TO ART VIA DRAWING

UPDATED**
Audio-Visual Drawing Program

Drawing Textbook, $5. By the same author: *Drawing in Three Dimensions, Art Elements, Cute Animals, Things for Sports, Scenery, Flowers and Trees, Land Vehicles, Water Vehicles, Best Book on Drawing People*, $5.00 each; *Free-hand Sketching*, $6.50. Add $1 postage to book orders. *Self-Study Drawing Course* (37 booklets) $99 postpaid. Individual booklets, $3.50. Free sampler lesson.

It is being overly generous to say that 5 percent of our college graduates know how to draw. There is no successful drawing program in our public schools and educators know it . . .

If you will evaluate our public-school art program, do not ask the art supervisor. The reply would probably sound much like the weavers' description of their goods in the tale, *The Emperor's New Clothes*. Instead, ask yourselves and your neighbors because you are the products of the public-school art program and NO EDUCATIONAL PROGRAM IS BETTER THAN THE PRODUCT IT TURNS OUT . . .

Many art supervisors and teachers maintain that there is no "right" and "wrong" in drawing . . . In a drawing program where there is no right and wrong and no rules, the children have nothing tangible to grasp and nothing to take home. They do not learn the right way; they do not learn the wrong way; they do not learn . .
.
One of the main objectives of today's public-school art program is "Free Expression (creative self expression)." We know that people who do not know how to draw cannot express themselves freely . . .

So says Bruce McIntyre, a veteran public school art instructor who also put in a decade as a a Walt Disney artist in the era when Disney's art was really something. His first book, aptly named *Drawing Textbook*, explains in crystalline detail why public school (and most private school) art programs fail to produce students who can draw. His analysis of what went wrong is combined with a stirring call to achieve drawing literacy in our day, and takes up the first 13 pages of the book. Find out why the ability to communicate visually makes such a difference, and the one approach to art instruction that provides it. Then you and your children can tackle the 222 graduated exercises that make up the rest of the book! These start with simple stuff—a birthday cake, a TV set—and progress along merrily introducing the Seven Laws of Perspective (surface, size, surface lines, overlapping, shading, density, and foreshortening) and other goodies until by lesson 58 you're drawing realistic skyscrapers, by lesson 94 you're getting down on paper a twisted candle that would make the Hildebrandt brothers proud, and by the last lesson you can draw *anything!*

Once you've finished *Drawing Textbook, Drawing in Three Dimensions* gives you 12 "clubs" (actually, 12 timed drawing exercises of increasing difficulty) and a more in-depth explanation of each drawing principle—plus tips on how to make your drawings more attractive by adding tapering, texture, repetition, S curves, variety, color, value, and distribution. This is an updated and improved version of Bruce's original *Big Easel II* book. *Art Elements* takes up the theme of how to make your drawings more attractive, with more input on the "25 elements of art," including those mentioned above. From here on in, it's merely a matter of adding to your visual vocabulary with his supplementary books, such as *Cute Animals, Things for Sports, Scenery,* and *Flowers and Trees.* Each of these shows how to apply the seven elements of drawing to a particular class of objects.

Freehand Sketching is the book for teens and adults. It covers the same basic seven principles of drawing, plus info on positioning and aligning.

The only problem with this series is the poor reproduction (photocopy or mimeo quality), which makes some drawing details hard to follow.

Based on the *Drawing Textbook,* Bruce McIntyre's *Self-Study Drawing Course* is a set of 37 lesson booklets, each containing six drawing lessons. Or, for those who prefer video, the same program is available as the *California Easel TV Series*—again a set of 37 lessons, six exercises each. Bonus Lessons, to accompany the video series, focus on drawing particular objects, such as holiday pictures, flowers, fire, people, and space.

The Bruce McIntyre drawing books are available from Learning at Home.

Hugh O'Neill and Associates
Big Yellow Drawing Book, $5 USA, $6.50 Canadians (U.S. funds only). Great book: buy 10 for Christmas and birthday presents.

And while we're concentrating on drawing as the foundation of all art, don't miss *The Big Yellow Drawing Book,* a product of the O'Neill clan. Dan O'Neill is a cartoonist of some repute in flower child circles. His *Odd Bodkins* comic strip gained quite a following in the sixties and seventies. His father Hugh (a genuine Ed.D.) helped by insisting that his wife Marian, an accomplished artist, and son Dan, the cartoonist, adhere to the known principles of learning. The end result of their labors is an extremely charming, simple introduction to drawing (in general) and cartooning (in particular) that has been proved 99 percent successful in teaching people of all ages to draw. You start by adding expressions, per the directions, to cartoon faces, and go on to practice six principles of perspective. A mere pittance gets you the book, which includes room for your practice exercises. Anyone four or five years old can tackle the beginning exercises. We got one for each member of our family. *The Big Yellow Drawing Book* makes a great stocking-stuffer (as long as you wear tights—the book is 8½ x 11").

NEW**
North Light Books
Perspective Without Pain, $39.80 for all four volumes. Shipping extra.

Four-volume series of 48-page workbooks designed to conquer your fears about perspective. Using it in drawings, that is! Workbook 1 covers the basics, workbook 2 gets into boxes and other cubic shapes, workbook 3 covers curves and indices, and workbook 4 puts it all together. Simple language, hands-on exercises, everyday terms.

NEW**
Vic Lockman
The Big Book of Cartooning, Volume 1, $10 postpaid.

A few years ago we got our hands on a copy of a little book called *Biblical Economics in Comics.* It explained free-market economics with engaging cartoons featuring little mice, rats, and cats, and their various struggles with the market system and encroaching bureaucracy (the dreaded Bureau-Rats). This book rapidly became our sons' favorite. Joseph in particular just about had the book memorized.

Came the time when I needed an illustrator for some children's books I had written. (The Old Wise

Tales™ series, published by Wolgemuth & Hyatt Publishers, in case you wanted to know.) For months nobody turned up. Then one day I was sent a cassette to review, and immediately recognized the style of the artist who has designed the package. It was Vic Lockman, the author of *Biblical Economics in Comics*. The second I realized he did illustrations for other people, and not just in his own books, I was on the phone to Wolgemuth & Hyatt begging them to try to get him to illustrate my books.

Vic, quite simply, is a great cartoonist. He's also a great teacher of cartooning. His first book on the subject, *The Big Book of Cartooning in Christian Perspective*, if faithfully studied and applied, will do your cartooning more good than a year at a pricey art school.

The book is intended for older children who have good control of their drawing hands. Vic assumes the reader is capable of putting good instructions into practice. Thus he provides more how-to-do-it examples than other writers of cartooning books, and less step-by-step instruction. He draws your attention to techniques rather than walking you through each one bit by bit. This allows him to pack his book with easily ten times more drawing instruction than other books on the subject. For example, he'll show you a drawing of a hose, with text saying, "Study bends," "Shadow holds hose to earth here," "Shadow lifts hose from earth here." You learn by copying the sample drawing according to these instructions.

The whole book is written from a professional cartoonist's viewpoint, and thus stresses essential doctrines of cartooning such as the need for *action* (figures should not pose woodenly) and how to draw a shoe

with character. Vic calls these "lines of action" and the "Breath of Life Method." Main topics include:

- Creating cartoon faces and figures
- Hands and feet
- Clothing: wrinkles, folds, and draping
- Animals
- Scenery
- Perspective
- Lettering like a real cartoonist
- Inking: tools and techniques

All is presented in that same zippy, non-threatening style that was such a hit with my children, lettered in cartoon style, and loaded with hundreds of fantastic, easy-to-copy sample cartoon illustrations.

Vic was kind enough to ask my advice about how to make this book more helpful, and so the finished version is spiral-bound with lots of exercise pages on which you can practice your new skills.

At the price, there's no reason why every fan of better drawing shouldn't get this book.

HOW-TO ART PROJECTS AND COURSES

Alpha Omega Publications
Art I, 1-year course, 10 LIFEPACs plus 2 (optional) answer keys and 1 (optional) test key $1.95 each LIFEPAC. Two resource items, Art-A-Color Plates ($5.95) and Construction Paper Packet ($1.95) are also required.

It is my policy never to endorse a product I haven't personally seen, and that is the only reason I am hesitant about piling on the superlatives for AOP's introductory art course for seventh-graders on up. First of all, the price is right. Secondly, the course hits *all* the bases: fine art, applied art, commercial art, and art appreciation. The course layout, which I have seen, maintains Alpha Omega's usual standards of logic and thoroughness, so each of these areas gets a real workout rather than a passing nod. Thirdly, and this is the part I like the best, the course is designed to provide *practical* art skills, giving the student the tools to use the artistic media (graphics, lettering, layout, cartooning, photography, and printmaking) as well as tools to analyze and improve his personal environment.

AOP says that the fine arts portion of the course can be personalized to fit the student's interests and opportunities.

Center for Applied Research in Education
About $10 for each book in series.

The 10 books in the Let's Discover art series for K-6 cover crayon, mobiles, paper, tempera, tissue, watercolor, puppets, papier maché, printing, and weaving with over 30 step-by-step activities for each. Excellent, easy-to-follow lessons cover *techniques,* moving from simple to advanced. Not just another "ideas" series. Exciting, open-ended project(s) for each technique. Each lesson step illustrated. *Very* suitable for home schooling.

EDC Publishing
Usborne Guide to Painting, Guide to Drawing, Guide to Technical Drawing, Guide to Lettering and Typography, $5.95 each. *The Usborne Young Cartoonist,* $6.95.

Inexpensive step-by-step guides to media and techniques. Full color, copiously illustrated. As with all Usborne books, the illustrations and layout teach as much or more than the text. This highly visual approach is ideal for visual subjects.

Drawing covers pencil, pen, charcoal, crayon, and pastels, as well as techniques of perspective, measuring and proportion, shading and texture, coloring, and just about anything else you'd like to know. Choosing supplies. Composition. Still life. Portraits. Figure drawing. Animals. Drawing from imagination. How to mount your drawings. How to fix mistakes. Plus an index! An amazing amount of information packed into 32 8½ x 11" pages.

Painting, in a similar format, covers oils, watercolors, gouache, and acrylics, plus basic information about painting preparation and supplies as well as techniques. Brushes. Easels. Cleaning materials. How to make your own painting surfaces. Cleanup. Composition, with or without viewfinders. Perspective, measurement, and proportion are just touched on; for detailed instructions in these areas you should consult the *Guide to Drawing.* Like *Drawing, Painting* also covers how to paint people, still life, outdoor scenes, painting from imagination, and how to frame and mount your art. A final section on abstract painting is a bonus. The entirely unnecessary picture on page thirteen of a young man painting a technically modest nude (arms and legs arranged to cover the essentials) may cause some to skip this otherwise fine book.

Finally, the *Usborne Young Cartoonist* is a sassy introduction to the art named. Lots of tips and techniques are crammed into less pages than you would expect. The boffo drawings are a bit too uncontrolled for my liking, themselves resembling kid art (perhaps intentionally). The second half of this book, "How to Draw Monsters and Other Creatures," speaks for itself.

UPDATED**
KidsArt
KidPrints, $9.95. Shipping extra.

Fine arts demystified, for kids everywhere. KidPrints, a special introductory unit, is designed to introduce you to the activities and methods of the regular KidsArt units. A complete three-month course in fine art printmaking, it contains simple activities with collage prints, eraser stamps, and monoprints. It also contains famous art study prints, an artist biography (Mary Cassatt), lesson plans, and teaching guide. All activities are presented with great respect for children. KidsArt provides the techniques and just enough open-ended project suggestions to launch your family into joyous artistic adventures.

Kim Solga, KidsArt director, really knows her stuff. Great tips in these art units, like how to keep stamp pad colors clean, how to make a sturdy portfolio for your kids' art. Graphically-pleasing layout reinforces the lessons. The monthly lesson plans are super-simple and really useful. We're looking forward to her projected KidsDraw and KidSculpt units, and hope many more will follow.

Learning at Home
Nourishing Creativity Through Art, $16.

Art experiences for your whole family. No lesson requires talent or previous experience. You will learn art terminology, art techniques, and to internalize and express your artistic feelings.

The primary author, Gwen Brennick, treats the reader, no matter how young, as an emerging professional entitled to professional tools and professional respect. Exercises begin with color play, movement of color and line, defining space, and clay sculpture. This level is suitable for the youngest artist. Level 2, for ages starting at six or seven, begin with creating secondary colors from the primaries and discovering colors as they occur in nature, and moves rapidly to using shapes in a composition (through printing, collage, and mosaic with "found" articles) and mobile-making, among other activities. Level 3 explores self-expression; Level 4, observation and expression; Level 5, working with nature (including geometrics in nature, which moves into abstract design); and Level 6 gets into perspective, portrait, and even pottery (clay sculpture).

Every lesson describes the concept covered, lists materials, and carefully leads you through the exercises.

More: appendices. The first appendix, The Language of Art, not only defines art terminology but explains how to "see" in an artistic way. Next, The Organizing Principles of Art, looks at movement, balance, rhythm, space, perspective, proportion, and art's universal qualities: completeness, appropriateness, and unity. Beyond this is another appendix with examples of possible results to the exercises in each unit.

As I said, these are *beginning* art experiences, created for people with little or no artistic background. If you've missed out on all the art your soul craves, or are looking for a place to start with your children, *Nourishing Creativity Through Art* looks excellent. Learning at Home also carries high-quality art supplies to go with this course—see writeup in chapter 3.

Motivational Art Training
Christian Art Manual, $25 plus $5 shipping and handling.

Here's a complete art curriculum for Christian kids. The *Manual* is truly Christian, as the exercises are designed to teach Christian truth by allowing the student to develop visual demonstrations of each concept. Example: Make a 3-D model to represent "me" as body, soul, and spirit. The art instruction itself is also excellent and covers most major areas of creativity: lettering, painting, modeling, etc. Each project has ideas for expansion, so the skill taught can be applied to other projects. Lists of easy-to-obtain materials are included.

The *Manual* is usable for all ages, including Mom and Dad, who are encouraged to have some artistic fun along with the kids. Projects can be self-instructional for older children, but younger ones will need some guidance.

Originally sold to Christian schools as a motivational tool to reward good behavior, the *Manual* now comes in a home version at the lower price listed above.

Optasia Fine Art Designs
Ten coloring postalettes for $5. Includes 10 of one design on a variety of paper stocks and colors, plus gold stickers.

The SCHOOL • MASTER • PIECES Guideline Series of cards takes coloring practice to its artistic limits. These very lovely cards come on a variety of colored, high-quality papers to encourage experimentation with various artistic tools and techniques. The publishers suggest that children use fine-line felt tip pens, pastels, wax pencils, and thick water colors (too much water wrinkles the paper).

It can be a great disappointment to a child to create a "masterpiece" on shoddy coloring book paper, which promptly tears or is otherwise destroyed. By using SCHOOL • MASTER • PIECES coloring cards, your youngster's best work can both really look good and be preserved. The cards make lovely gifts, too, thus solving the problem of what your child can do with excess artwork. I am also amazed at the price, which is less than you'd pay for many cheap mass-produced occasion cards.

SCHOOL • MASTER • PIECES crisp card stock is a treat for the fingertips, and the designs are a delight for the eyes. It's a way to both introduce your child to quality art and enable him to participate in creating at the same time.

Share-A-Care

Art with a Purpose: Art Pac for each level, $3.50 each book (two books per level). Teacher's Manual, 2 per level, $2 each, 4 levels in all (levels 0 through 3). Add 10% shipping ($2.50 minimum). Postage outside USA will be billed.

Simple, really sweet, step-by-step art courses for grades 1-10 that teach drawing, coloring, lettering, painting, and paper cutting. The art has a Mennonite flavor: simple dress, gentle little girls with braids, Christian messages.

Art with a Purpose comes in two-grade levels. Level 0, for grades 1 and 2, covers: simple drawing, including drawing with grids • tracing • craft projects • simple one-point perspective. Level 1, for grades 3 and 4, is considerably more advanced. It covers: • more complex drawing • tracing • crafts projects • simple perspective • balance (using stick figures). Level 2, for grades 5 and 6, includes: • drawing and shading • lettering • layout and design • Perspective I • drawing children in balance and proportion. Level 3, for grades 7 and 8, has: • Old English calligraphy • pen and ink sketching • layout and design • Perspective II • more advanced drawing exercises, again with fully-clothed child models. Level 3 book 2 is not available at time of this writing.

Each Art Pac has a corresponding Teacher's Manual which presents the lessons' goals and provides teaching guidelines.

Art with a Purpose was designed specifically to lighten the teacher's workload and to provide truly Christian art instruction. It succeeds at both. For these reasons, it may become the core art course of choice among Christian home schoolers.

Timberdoodle

Creating Line Design books, $4.75 each or $18/set of 4. Add 10% shipping ($4 minimum). Write for shipping costs outside continental U.S.

Learn pre-drafting skills through this series that trains a child's visual perception and memory. OK, that sounds pretty fancy. What are we talking about here? We're talking about the Creating Line Design series. You use a straightedge to connect numbers ranged along the sides of a box. Simple, right? Well, at first it is. In book 1, designed for kindergartners, you just connect numbers. This produces a variety of designs. Check yourself with the inset completed design to see if you did it right. In book 2, you have to connect pairs of letters as well as numbers in order to produce more complicated designs. Book 3 designs require you to lift your pencil occasionally while connecting dots, since the square now contains different shapes around which you must maneuver. In book 4 (intended for grades 7 through 9) the designs are very challenging, but even young children can complete them after finishing the first three books.

Making the designs is fun. You can color the finished product and display it. Some of the designs could be pasted on cardboard and made into puzzles. Whatever—the Creating Line Design series takes no teaching effort; kids like it; why not get it?

VIDEO ART LESSONS

NEW**
Art Video Library

Membership fee of $25 a year allows you to rent videos ($4/video for those priced $39.95 and under, $10/video for those priced at $40 or more, plus $6 shipping total for up to three videos at once). Rental fee applies to purchase price for videos priced at $29.95.

Now you can teach art (and I mean *real* art) at home without strain, even if you have never taken art lessons yourself. Art Video Library allows you to rent or purchase art instruction videos by a wide range of famous artists and art instructors. Art Video Library carries hundreds of titles, with something for everyone from rank beginners to advanced artists. *You do not have to join to purchase videos.*

I remember reading several years ago in *Growing Without Schooling* about a family whose daughter, age four or so, produced adult-quality art using acrylics. I now believe this is possible, because I have seen my own five-year-old do it. We bought a couple of Dolores Demeres art instruction videos from Art Video Library at $14.95 each, got everyone the recommended equipment from a local art supply store, and lo and behold, we could hardly tell the difference between the results from our five-year-old, seven-year-old, nine-year-old, and thirty-seven-year-old (otherwise known as Daddy)! The reason is that Mrs. Demeres tells you *how to paint,* whereas typical school art classes tell you to "express yourself" (whatever that is) without teaching you any techniques. She starts at the very beginning with advice about what materials to buy (paints, brushes, paper, palette, etc.) and explains everything step by step from there, while creating wondrous sample paintings before your dazzled eyes. I'm impressed!

Why art video? Well, consider what art lessons cost, and especially consider that *all* members of your family can take lessons as they are ready. The teacher will always be there and will never charge more for repeating the lesson!

I highly recommend the Demeres *Intro to Acrylics, Intro to Oil Painting,* or *Intro to Pastels* as introductory purchases if you want to prove this library's usefulness to yourself before joining. Each tape costs less than the membership fee, and is a wonderful introduction to the medium in question. If you're like me, you'll be hooked (we own all three!).

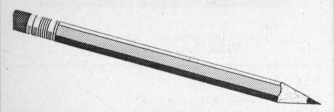

UPDATED**
Audio-Visual Drawing Program
California Easel TV Series (set of 37 2-hour VHS tapes), $16 each. Bonus TV lessons (set of 12), also $16 each. *Simple Simon Series* for kindergarten (6 lessons), $12 each or $50/set. *Drawing-Sesame Series* (6 lessons), $12 each or $60/set. *Home Learning Series* 1, 2, 3, 4, $12 each or $60/set of 6.

Large assortment of video art lessons originally presented on television. See writeup of Audio-Visual Drawing Program's drawing textbooks above.

NEW**
Flax Art & Design
Drawing and *Cartooning* videos, $29.50 each. Shipping extra.

Wanna learn basic drawing and cartooning with Bruce Blitz? Sure ya do! Who, you ask, is Bruce Blitz? Maybe if I get to see these videos I will find out. In the meantime, I can tell you that each video is actually a complete kit containing a 60-minute color videotape, a step-by-step instruction book, an 11 x 16" portfolio, and basic art supplies. Peering closely at the catalog picture I discern that the *Cartoons* video comes with a pencil, eraser, pen, and the marvelous Insta-Cartooner, a set of face and feature templates with which you can "create over one million faces instantly!"—although, unfortunately, not from different angles. The *Drawing Kit* includes 20 sheets of drawing paper, 12 color pencils, three sketch pencils, a kneaded eraser, and a sharpener. Not bad for the price (Flax's price is discounted).

NEW**
Legacy
Draw Squad videos, $19.95 each.

What's large, bouncy, dresses in orange, and wears pencils and markers all over its sleeves? Captain Mark Kistler of the Draw Squad, that's what! Capt. Mark is the energetic host of a brand-new video drawing program for kids, based on his popular in-person appearances at schools throughout the country.

Like other drawing programs, *Draw Squad* introduces perspective, foreshortening, shading, and all those other good things. Unlike the others, it features lots of pep talk ("Thumbs up for Pencil Power!"), animation, and crazy critters and structures of the type beloved by pre- (and post-) adolescents.

Capt. Mark has his own rocket ship connected to "Houston Control" in which he goes zooming about through the galaxies, meeting unusual critters like Pigasus. After landing somewhere or other (in front of a colorful and suitably weird background), Houston Control beams up his "launch pad" (a sketch pad, for you normal folks), and the lesson begins!

A typical drawing might feature, say, "The Escape of the Twinkies." You start by drawing a foreshortened box, then its flaps, then a bunch of little Twinkies peering over the edges. What's that! Oh, no! Fourth-graders have surrounded the box and are about to eat the dear little Twinkies! But fear not, gallant viewer, because with a few strokes of your pencil it's Super-Twinkie to the rescue! Next, you will draw Super-Twinkie's castle, complete with built-in cream vats and his own private skateboard ramp.

The series includes three videos. Video #1 is *The Escape of the Twinkies*. Video #2, *Pigasus Goes on a Diet*. Video #3, *Moonbot's Birthday Party*.

Our kids *love* this program. They played the tape over and over until they could all do all of the drawings, and I've noticed them drawing more ever since.

SOFTART

Art software will not teach you to do art. What it is, is tools of various usefulness. What it is not, is a miraculous invention that will make us all real artists.

We have probably a dozen computer art programs scattered around here. We also avidly read the reviews of new computer art programs. So we certainly are willing to try mixing art and computers. But the news is, so far computers are not too good at art.

"How can you say computers are not good at art? Don't they make all those neat graphics we see on TV?" That's right. Computer-aided art is for real. What it is not is fast and easy to control.

Consider what you go through to draw a tree by hand. You grab your pencil or pen, quickly sketch a trunk, some branches, suggest leaves, and that is that. On the computer, you first have to pick up your drawing tool on screen (choice of pen, brush, paint-can, whatever). You drag it to where you want it. Make a line or drop a circle. Size it. Let it go. Go pick up another tool. Drag it where you want it. Use it. Let it go. Pick another starting spot. Make another line. So far, you've just made the tree trunk.

Once you've made a computer drawing, the theory is that you can quickly manipulate it. But f irst you have to grab it, which can be difficult if you have lots of lines and shapes on top of each other, as is common in all but the simplest drawings. A break in the line of a drawing will cause your "fill" pattern (another computer benefit) to spread all over the place. Tweaking your drawing can take longer than making another by hand.

Computer art only really shines in technical applications, where measurements need to be exact and doing the work by hand can give draftsmen premature white hair. If your style is more á la Norman Rockwell or Van Gogh, or even Dr. Seuss, forget it.

It's true that since the last edition of this book, computer art has progressed somewhat. You can now both buy and produce PostScript art, which prints out as nice clean lines instead of blurry dots. On the Macintosh computer you can now do things in color that you previously couldn't do in black and white. Computer art software has become much more powerful, with dozens of new features. However, it takes forever to learn to use the power of the new generation of art software, and using it is *still* slow. For every line you draw, you have to select a beginning point, drag to your ending point, click, select a new beginning point, drag to a new ending point . . . not to mention time spent switching between the line tool, the polygon, the Bezier curve tool, and so on. It can still take you 10 minutes to crosshatch an area you could finish in 10 seconds by hand. Or, if you draw a line in the freehand mode, you can spend the time "saved" by clicking on and deleting unwanted endpoints that crept into your drawing.

What we really need are computer tools that let us draw on screen the same way we do in real life. Graphics tablets that you draw on with a special "pen" claim to approximate this, but have problems coordinating the on-screen cursor with the pen placement when you remove the pen from the tablet. In the meantime, serious computer art is prohibitively expensive for most of us.

The biggest disappointment of all is that there are no good popular computer art tutorials. Why doesn't someone invent a *Learn to Draw* program—perhaps based on Bruce McIntyre's *Drawing Textbook* or Dan O'Neill's *Big Yellow Drawing Book*?

Playing with computer art is lots of fun—don't get me wrong. My two-year-old loves to scribble on screen, and her older siblings like to fool with the special effects like airbrushing and design patterns. But this is no way to learn to draw, or to efficiently produce anything but straight geometric art. Not yet.

CHAPTER TWO

ART HISTORY AND APPRECIATION

The city of St. Louis, near which we live, is considering acquiring a work of art to adorn its new convention center.

Now, I know this is not earthshaking news. (Just as well. Although St. Louis is slated for a major earthquake sometime soon, we don't really *want* one!)

The dilemma the city fathers find themselves in, though, has a peculiarly modern twist.

The art commission appointed to recommend an artwork for purchase has selected one that the general public thinks ain't worth diddleysquat. It's one of these abstract things featuring large hunks of material in bright colors. Popular wisdom is that the whole thing is not only uninspiring to look at, but that it will probably fall and kill somebody if installed on the convention center wall.

"Why can't we have a nice mural or something?" laments one typical voice in the daily paper. Why not, indeed? Because the city fathers made the mistake of inviting the art elite to their party, and today the art elite has decided that only what is *new* is valuable. This means that Realism, Impressionism, Romanticism, Classicism, even Cubism and Dadaism are all out.

For an artist to impress his peers nowadays, he has to invent an entirely new user interface. Unhappily, the new user interfaces largely consist of silly kindergarten projects, like outlining Texas counties with cloth or painting oneself with mud and posing on a pedestal.

Bigger is better, too, following the Tilted Arc Theory. This holds that the true measure of an artwork's success is how many people can be forced to see it or walk around it while they would rather be doing something else. Rudeness is in, too, since the art should be making a "statement," and the statement should be "new," and what's new about love, beauty, faithfulness, and all that old stuff?

WHAT IS ART?

All this stems from a misunderstanding about the nature of art. Art is held to be something so ineffable, so undefinable that you simply have to accept anything produced by someone calling himself an artist as art. In theory, this means that bad handwriting, crumpled-up paper towels, and the crumbs on your kitchen floor all count as "art" if you have enough nerve to promote them as such.

I asked my husband Bill about this. "What do *you* think is the difference between real art and sham art?" I inquired.

"Well, for one thing," Bill mused, "real art ought to require some technical skill to produce. I mean, you shouldn't be able to show the art to a sixth-grader and have him whip up a facsimile copy."

"Yeah, that sounds reasonable," I responded. "I think one of the reasons so many people got upset at

Serrano's crucifix-in-urine stunt was not only that its message was insulting, but that any six-year-old could have done it. Normal people resent the government paying someone to hack around like that. I mean, blasphemy is bad enough, but having to subsidize *amateur* blasphemy is just plain insufferable."

"Sure. Art has to be more than having an idea, otherwise it's just graffiti. . . . Now what about someone like Jackson Pollock, the modernist who tried to simulate randomness in his paintings by techniques like splatting paint on the canvas from a plastic spoon? According to what you're saying, that wouldn't have been art, either."

"I'd say it was pre-drafting, like when a painter first sketches his subject. It's preparation for the real artwork. . . . Pollock eventually ended up inventing a whole line of equipment to try to simulate randomness in his studio. He failed—that's why he killed himself—but he at least was a successful technician and engineer. Anyway, Pollock's a borderline case. He was trying to eliminate the artist, or have the universe itself be the artist, whichever you will."

"So true art requires technical skill and/or the ability to use specialized tools," Bill summarized. "What about beauty and so on, the difference between good art and bad art, and between gracious art and despicable art?"

Here I had a thought. (It happens!) "Art can be despicable and still be art. If Serrano had produced a painting of Christ being showered with urine, it would have been despicable, but at least it would have been art."

REAL ART CAN BE APPALLING

"Right," Bill replied. "Remember that silver cross made of intertwined snakes that we saw at the science-fiction convention in Boston 14 years ago?"

I remembered, all right. Our non-Christian friend Ben had said, "Wow. What a great work of art. Let's kill the artist!" Now, Ben is about the least violent person in the world. He wasn't really planning on killing anyone. In his hyperbolic way Ben was saying that he admired the artist's technique, understood the artist's statement, followed it to its logical conclusion . . . and considered it appalling.

So. Art can be appalling or beautiful, but it has to at least be something better than the average untutored person can produce before it is worth calling "art" at all. Nor do we have to hug to our bosom every genuine work of art. The art critics may have their ideas of

what is wonderful, but we don't have to operate under their guidelines. If you happen to like beauty, humor, gracefulness, honesty, integrity, and so on, you have a perfect right to focus on works of art that contain these and reject those that don't.

Ben never shot the artist; neither did he buy the cross of snakes.

FORWARD TO THE PAST

What all this means is that children today and their parents, namely us, need more than ever to be exposed to the art of the past. If you're looking for beauty, truth, nobility, purity, or anything uplifting or basically honest, your chances of finding it are a lot better in the seventeenth century (or the seventh, or the seventh B.C.) than in the twentieth. Whatever their faults, artists of the past at least tried to deal with sublime themes. Throwing cultural temper tantrums was not "in" in the days of Fra Angelica, Michelangelo, Rembrandt, or even Winslow Homer. Technical expertise, an eye for beauty, and an ability to separate the significant from the trivial, was.

Art history, presented well, can speak to you in a way that huge slabs of plastic on the convention center wall never will. Learning from the past is the first step to producing something worthwhile in the present. And, unlike grim pilgrimages to the latest mind-numbing happening at the Museum of Trendy Art, it is *fun!*

So let's take a tour of the art of the past. Here are games, coloring books, prints, newsletters, time lines, and more, all to introduce you to great artists whose work will impress you and who we know you will enjoy.

ART APPRECIATION PROGRAMS AND PRINTS

Art Extension Press
Large (7 x 9 or 8 x 10) prints $1.50 each. Small (3 x 4) prints, $1.60 for packet of 10 or $14 for 100. Accompanying text, $8.50. Two hundred mini-prints (20 packs), $27.50. Add $3 shipping.

Learn art history and appreciation through a graded series of fine art prints. The text, *Learning More About Pictures,* includes background on each artistic school represented as well as a small version of each print for cross-reference with the actual print. All major schools of Western art are covered, from Primitive to Renaissance to Modern, including each country's distinctive contribution. This is an excellent concept, marred somewhat by poor lithography, especially apparent on the smaller prints.

NEW**
ClassicPlan
Set of 5, $34.50. Full semester (set of 15), $98.50. Full year (set of 30), $187.50. Available in Primary, Middle, or Upper set A-F. *Voyage of Life,* $29.95. *Trees,* $39.95. Binder, $12 each (very nice). Shipping: $3 per set of five, $5 per set of 15, $10 per set of 30. *Courier,* quarterly newsletter, free. Discounts on Plans for recognized home school groups or educational institutions.

ClassicPlan is a series of art prints and poems, some correlated with appropriate classical music cassettes. This is an "art immersion" program more than traditional art appreciation. Seldom have I seen such a lovely presentation of art. Lovers of the Charlotte Mason style of education will instantly recognize the idea behind giving children a carefully-chosen classic art print by a major artist, correlated with a famous poem whose subject is the same as the painting's.

Each ClassicPlan includes a lovely 11 x 14" full-color fine art print, classic poem, biographies of both the artist and the poet, and lots of follow-up stuff for those so inclined (discussion questions and suggested activities), all in a sturdy plastic envelope for safe storage. Music tapes and composer notes are now also correlated with the program. All comes in a protective plastic sleeve, and is available in sets of five, 15, or 30 prints. Over 100 ClassicPlans are available for each level: Primary, Middle, and Upper. Primary is for preschool through grade 3, Middle for grades 4-8, and Upper for high school level (grades 9-12).

The main difference between levels is in the increasing sophistication of the art subjects portrayed and the increasing literary challenge of the poetry selections.

Art periods covered are Renaissance, Baroque, Rococo, Neoclassicism, Romanticism, Realism, Impressionism, and 19th Century Traditional. A time line shows the artists, writers, and composers whose works are included in ClassicPlan—an impressive assortment.

ClassicPlan is experimenting with special packages. Two new ClassicPlan packages, as of this writing, are:

• *Voyage of Life.* This includes Thomas Cole's famous four allegorical paintings on childhood, youth, manhood, and old age, along with 10 compatible poems by Shakespeare, Blake, Kingsley, Markham, Keats, and Bryant, plus informative commentary. An introduction to philosophy from an artistic perspective. This is a truly beautiful set that can lead to some deep thinking. We have the prints framed under glass on our oldest son's bedroom wall.

• *Trees* is eight paintings, nine poems, and Beethoven's *Pastorale* symphony, plus a unit study on tree varieties. This is ClassicPlan's way of venturing into integrating art with science—an intriguing concept.

ClassicPlan is not an art history and appreciation curriculum as such. As Sally Jordan of ClassicPlan says, "Our purpose is to give children a cultural experience, not so much in the formal art and music appreciation tradition, but rather an integrated approach to the study of classic art, poetry, and music."

Eschewing the ugly and violent, the art and poetry selections hew to the standard of "Whatever is true, whatever is noble, whatever is right, whatever is pure, whatever is lovely, whatever is admirable . . ." (Philippians 4:8). Using ClassicPlan it won't take much of your time to expose your children to this very noble part of our cultural heritage, especially if you wisely skip most of the suggested activities and just enjoy the art.

NEW**
Cornerstone Curriculum Project
Adventures in Art, $50/year. Portfolio, $30. Add 10% shipping.

I am really impressed by this new four-year art history and appreciation program from Cornerstone Curriculum Project. WHAT YOU GET: Each year's offering includes 14 museum-quality full-color reproductions (up to 11 x 17" in size) of major artworks spanning the time frame from Byzantine art through the modernists, a parent overview, an art comparison sheet, and instructions on how to set up an art time line. You also get "a study sheet for each artist." This phrasing in the catalog might give you the impression that you are getting a sheet with historical background information about the artist. Actually you will receive a set of identical sheets, each having the same programmed series of observation exercises and activities and a space on the back for your child to fill in with his observations. For the historical interpretation, you have to wait for Year 3.

The program itself follows the five steps of observing single paintings, comparing paintings by the same artist, comparing paintings of different artists, developing an art history time line, and finally classifying paintings by schools of art. Children follow the first four steps in each year's curriculum, but only get into classifying by schools of art in Year 3.

Year 1 includes *Madonna and Child on a Curved Throne* (Byzantine), Cimbue's *The Crucifixion* , two paintings by Duccio, three by Rembrandt, three by Monet, three by Cezanne, and a still life by Picasso. One of the Rembrandt prints is an enormous 17 x 22½" print of his *Raising of the Cross,* suitable for display in your home and exclusively available through Cornerstone Curriculum Project. By the time you have finished all four years you will have also sampled Giotto, Van Eyck, Massaccio, da Vinci, Michelangelo, Dürer, Renoir, Pissarro, Degas, Van Gogh, Gauguin, Seurat, Kandinsky, Pollock, and Dali.

Two years of Adventures in Art are available at the time I am writing this. The last two years of the program are coming out in spring '91 and '92, respectively.

If you get this series you definitely should purchase the portfolio, unless you plan on framing the prints or otherwise providing a way to preserve them. It would be a shame to have these fine prints ripped up or wrinkled, as is all too likely to happen when such large prints are being handled by little hands.

Cornerstone Curriculum Project is serious that children should discover about art on their own, to the point of discouraging parents from telling children about the various schools of art. I understand their point, but all the same I do wish the program included more specific questions directed to the individual works and artists. The publishers should also consider making available books on each artist, for those who want to pursue a particular artist further. Art observation, after all, is supposed to generate interest in the artist. Museums understand this; when we went to the George Caleb Bingham exhibition at the St. Louis Art Museum, we were able to buy a book about Bingham with excellent reproductions of his paintings, as well as prints, postcards, and even buttons! Being able to satisfy your curiosity like this provides a wonderful feeling of closure. Even *without* these goodies, Adventures in Art is a wonderful program. With them, it would be phenomenal!

NEW★★
Modern Learning Press
See the Paintings book, $12.95. Set of prints for K-2, 3-4, or grade 5, $33 per graded set of 4 prints or $42 with *See the Paintings* book. Set of all prints (K-5) plus book, $99. Art print teaching units, $49 for 6-print units, $68 for 9-print units or $160 for 15-print units (the latter include a Change-a-Print frame). Teacher Reference Guide comes with each unit, or you can get the complete set of 22 guides for $39. Change-a-Print frame, $61. Discovering Art series: "Renaissance to Realism" or "Impressionism to 1980s," each 20 reproductions with textbook, each $198. Shipping 9%. Rush service, add $3.75.

For a serious art appreciation program, Modern Learning Press has come up with a *See the Paintings* program for introducing fine art into public schools. Their prints are more expensive than ClassicPlan's, but then they are more than four times as big. Where ClassicPlan's prints (at 11x14") are the right size for an oversized ring binder, the Modern Learning Press prints, each 22½ x 28½", are the right size for displaying on your walls. (Note: A few fine art prints on each wall are cheaper than wallpaper!) The museum-quality full-color reproduction allows you to see the artist's individual brush strokes, making them extremely useful when teaching art techniques. Other features: whereas ClassicPlan covers only "classic" art (including the Impressionists), Modern Learning Press has art from the Middle Ages to modern times.

Their new *See the Paintings* book has several sets of prints (for grades K-5) directly correlated with this book. I'd skip the whole first 30 pages and the last 20, which mostly talk about how to organize a complicated school art program involving volunteers, equipment, etc. The rest of the book is loaded with useful information and teaching units, covering such things as Art Vocabulary, types of paintings, styles of painting (e.g., cubism), elements of art (line, movement, light, etc.), an extensive resource list, and a very helpful Time-Line of World History and Art. Many more teaching units are available. Just a few from their extensive list: Family Life, America's Great Artists, and introductions to Famous Art and Modern Painting. These all come with teaching guides, or you can buy the entire set of 22 guides separately. Modern Learning Press also offer a unique Change-a-Print holder that you can use to both display and store up to twenty of their large prints at a time, in case you don't have enough wall space to display all your prints.

Parent-Child Press

Art appreciation program using art postcards. See review under "Art Postcards" below.

NEW**
Shorewood Reproductions
Full-color catalog of more than 800 art prints, $18 plus $3.50 shipping. *The Shorewood Collection Art Reference Guide*, $16.50. *Artists' Biographies for the Art Reference Guide*, $13.50. Both *Reference Guide* and *Artists' Biographies*, $25 when purchased together. Single prints, $12 to individuals, $6.50 to educators (home schoolers count as educators). Most art programs (those with 12 reproductions), $86 per program unmounted, $119 mounted. Add $2.25 per print for lamination. *American Artists: 1700 to the Present*, $170.50 unmounted, $239.50 mounted. *School Museum 50*, $325 unmounted, $462.50 mounted. *School Museum 100*, $650 unmounted, $925 mounted.

Modern Learning Press gets their art prints from Shorewood Reproductions, Inc. You can, too, if you are willing to pay $18 plus shipping for Shorewood's full-color catalog of over 800 art prints. These are printed on the same 65-pound quality paper stock used for the reproductions themselves, and listed by time period, e.g., Renaissance, Baroque, and Dutch Masters, Cubists. The chronological listing makes the catalog easy to use as a mini-tour of art history. Caution: This catalog contains a few absolutely inexcusable nudes, such as poor Marilyn Monroe's last sitting just before she killed herself. I wondered what public schools were doing buying pin-up *Playboy*-esque nudes for their students; Shorewood says these are not for sale to public schools, only to the trade. The simple solution here is for you to go through the catalog before the children see it and simply rip out the offending pages, thus rendering the catalog useful once again.

You can buy just one print or 100, or simply use the catalog as a mini art course in itself.

Other add-ons that make the catalog even more useful: *The Shorewood Collection Art Reference Guide* is three-hole punched to fit into the catalog binder and includes background information for most of Shorewood's art prints. *Artists' Biographies for the Art Refer-ence Guide* is another three-hole-punched book, with biographical sketches on artists whose works are carried by Shorewood.

Shorewood's free brochure lists more than 50 of their own art teaching units, each including 10-15 prints, a portfolio box, and a teacher's guide. Prints are mostly 22½ x 28½" and are available unmounted, mounted on heavy backing board, or laminated. Each teacher's guide includes a biography of each artist in the program, a critique of his work, suggested activities, and a bibliography in case you want to study the artists further. The guides do not assume you know anything about art at all. Each program is shipped in a portfolio carrying case.

One especially impressive set available from Shorewood is *American Artists: 1700 to the Present*. This set includes 25 reproductions. Other large sets: *School Museum 50* includes 50 reproductions. *School Museum 100* includes 100 reproductions. Buy either *School Museum* set and get a free copy of *The Shorewood Collection Art Reference Guide* and the *Artists' Biographies*.

Mention you are a home schooler when you buy from Shorewood to qualify for their hefty educator's discount.

ART APPRECIATION GAMES

Aristoplay
Artdeck, $25. *Main Street*, $12. *Good Old Houses*, $12.

First, *Artdeck*. Subtitled "The Game of Modern Masters," this beautiful card game is a mini-collection of 52 major works of modern art by 13 of the most famous artists. The game involves collecting "suits" of cards in a fashion similar to Rummy. All the aces, for example, are paintings by Joan Miro. The Artist Card for each suit gives pertinent facts about the artist, including a brief overview of his style and the titles of the works on the other cards. The cards are top quality. Shiny and colorful. No wonder art museums carry this game. Now, the $10,000 question: *Why only modern masters?* The same game format would work with medieval art, or Renaissance art, or traditional English art . . . This could be done by either enclosing a flyer offering additional card sets, or by producing "new" games with different cards but otherwise the same format. Would you be interested in this? I would!

Let me mention in passing that exposure to real art, even on this small scale, has sparked an interest in looking up the artists in our encyclopedia. One little thing leads to another.

Now, two games I have not seen but that look interesting. *Main Street,* billed as "a puzzle/game of historical commercial architecture," is on one level a puzzle for small children and on another a crazy-eight recognition game for older kids and adults. Each puzzle is cut into card-shaped pieces; put 'em together and you have a building. You get a fact sheet with historical and architectural info on styles from Federal to Art Deco-Moderne. *Good Old Houses* is more of the same, only residential properties instead of commercial ones. Each contains eight house puzzles, instructions for play on the possible four levels, and a fact sheet, all in a spiffy box.

You can also purchase a *Good Old Houses* cut-out and coloring book separately. This comes with 12 historical houses, some large to color (with factual text below) and some small to cut out and put together. Presto, your own unzoned neighborhood! Added benefit of these architectural resources: educational walks in the city.

UPDATED**
B&I Gallery Specialists
Gallery, $12.50 postpaid. *Background Notes,* $2.95/set postpaid.

Gallery: The Art Appreciation Game is an art card game played rather like Go Fish. The game comes with 40 full-color, 3½ x 5⅜" cards displaying four artworks from each of 10 famous artists—Corot, Copley, Cezanne, Cassatt, Cole, Degas, Renoir, Monet, Chardin, and Rembrandt. Each card has a small picture on it, along with a capsule description of the artist and a list of the paintings of that artist included in the game. Each 2 x 2¼" picture is a reproduction of originals found at the National Gallery of Art in Washington, D.C. Simple rules allow players to concentrate on the art, the artists, their country, their style, and the age in which each painted. Rules for young children are also now included in every game.

Each artist included in *Gallery* was chosen "for their classic style and value." The publishers of *Gallery* believe each artist they have included "was first in his area of influence for some reason." Chardin was first in presenting the common man and his interests. Corot was a pioneer in presenting landscapes realistically rather than romantically. Rembrandt was the greatest Dutch painter. Cole was America's first serious full-time landscape artist. Copley was the first American portrait painter to put backgrounds and other people into his scenes. Mary Cassatt was the First Lady of American Impressionism. And Degas, Renoir, Cezanne, and Monet, Impressionists all, were all pioneers in their way.

Now you can also get *Background Notes* to accompany *Gallery.* Each set includes two artists. The two sets now available are Degas/Monet and Cole/Copley. These include historical information about the artist, analyses of the paintings included in *Gallery,* and suggested activities and bibliographic references. Some of the paintings' details highlighted in the *Background Notes* are impossible to see on the cards, due to their small size. However, if the descriptions spark your interest, you can always buy a large-sized print of the painting from ClassicPlan or Shorewood Reproductions—and *Gallery* would have served its purpose!

NEW**
Flax Art & Design
Quartet, $16. Shipping extra.

Another art appreciation card game. In *Quartet* the object is to collect quartets of paintings. Thirteen famous artists, four different paintings by each of them, are included in this 52-card deck from the Tate Gallery. Picasso, Matisse, Dali, and Hockney are among the big names represented on these cards. Whether or not you choose to play the game described on the enclosed instructions, *Quartet* has obvious play value as a means of training children to recognize works by a given artist. Unhappily in this context, the featured reproductions include quite a few paintings of nudes, from Picasso's geometric distortions to Hockney's recognizable person about to take a shower. So call me a prude—I still don't think a four-year-old's first introduction to fine art ought to be bathroom scenes and naked women drawn in the carnal style of modern masters.

NEW**
Safari, Ltd.
Smithsonian American Art Rummy, Art Rummy, $4.95 each. *Smithsonian American Art Quiz,* $8.75.

Take your pick of the National Museum of American Art or the Metropolitan Museum of Art. Safari has a Rummy game for each. Each art Rummy game has 40 full-color 5½ x 4½" cards in an attractive acrylic box. Each card displays an artwork, the artist's name and lifespan, the name, size, and medium of the art, the date of its creation, and eight questions and answers. Artworks are grouped by category. Some sample Rummy categories from Smithsonian American Art Rummy are: abstract, folk art, landscape, portrait, and still life. Sample categories from Art Rummy's more eclectic collection: Japanese art, Egyptian art, Greek vases, medieval art, musical instruments, Western paintings. Lots of educational value in an inexpensive package.

Smithsonian American Art Quiz provides a number of open-ended questions for each of 40 artworks. I haven't seen this card game, so I can't tell you if any answers are provided or what I think of them. The sample questions I saw in the catalog weren't all that impressive—e.g., "What songs can you think of that sing about boots?"

ART HISTORY

EDC Publishing
Usborne Story of Painting, $5.95.

Colorful, copiously illustrated introduction to art through the ages. Includes information on how artists lived and materials they used, as well as introducing several important artists. Starts with cave painting, ends with modern art. Suggested for ages ten and up, but children of any age will enjoy looking at the pictures and listening to the text.

KONOS
Artists and Composers Timeline, $25. Timeline lines, $9.95. Add 10% shipping.

Time lines are one of the best ways to learn history. Now your child can get a real feel for art and music history, with the *Konos Artists and Composers Timeline.* You get five laminated blue sheets of figures to cut out and attach to a time line. Each painter holds a major work; each composer holds a major composition. Artists included range from Renaissance to modern, with most concentrated in between. A fun, hands-on way to study art history, and a natural taking-off point for study of individual artists and schools of art.

NEW**
Ladybird Books, Inc.
Each book, $2.95.

Get a quick introduction to nine major artists of the past with the Ladybird Great Artists series for children ages 10 and up. Each small hardback is fully illustrated. Book 1 introduces the Dutchmen Rubens, Rembrandt, and Vermeer. In book 2 meet the famous Italians Leonardo da Vinci, Michelangeo, and Raphael. Book 3 presents the French trio of Van Gogh, Gauguin, and Cezanne. Stories are well-written and give you a real feel for each artist's life and work. Unhappily, the series is going out of print when the current printing sells out, so write or call before you order.

NEW**
Milliken Publishing Company
Images series, $12.95 each book.

One of the most unusual art history resources I have found is Milliken's series of transparency/duplicating books by Sara Jenkins. Each includes striking full-color reproductions of original artworks, in transparency form. Designed for use by students in grades 7-12, each book provides detailed background information on the artist and art, along with lots of student exercises.

Images of Man, for example, includes Michelangelo's "Creation of Man" from the Sistine Chapel ceiling, Breugel's "Wedding Feast," Degas's "The Glass of Absinthe," Picasso's "Girl Before a Mirror," Trova's "Walking Man," Segal's "Cinema," Hans Holbein's portrait of Henry VIII, one example each of Roman and Greek sculpture (these share one transparency page), Piero della Francesca's portrait of the Duke of Urbino, an illumination of St. Matthew from the *Book of Kells* sharing the page with a head sculpture from Nigeria, Brouwer's "Fighting Card Players," Vermeer's "The Cook," and a Rembrandt self-portrait. The reproduction quality of the 8½ x 11" transparencies is excellent, putting most paper reproductions I have seen to shame, and so is the detailed historical information on the paintings and painters. The student response sheets are also excellent, bringing out both responses to the artist's technical skills and their philosophical outlook. Students are encouraged to both recognize and analyze the artists' philosophies—a major achievement, especially considering that so much "art appreciation" material never gets past the point of the student's emotional response to the art.

The author's own outlook is visibly relativistic. In the introduction she says, "Only through an awareness of the great range of ideas about man and their relationship within a cultural context can we perhaps gain perspective on our own concepts and values and understand that they too are relative." This is nonsense, of course: Hitler's regime produced art describing Jews as beasts and enemies of mankind, but I notice that no example of this art are included in the *Images of Man* series—and quite rightly so, because Hitler and his henchmen were *wrong.* Truth is not quite as relative as all that! However, with this caveat I must say I really enjoyed these books. Whatever else Sara Jenkins may be, she isn't superficial. You aren't likely to find as much useful information about a given painting and artist anywhere else for the price, and then there's those gorgeous transparencies as well!

The series includes *Images of Man, Images of Nature, Images of Fantasy, Images of Change Part I: Art and Society in Transition,* and *Images of Change Part 2: Art, Science, and Technology.*

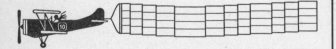

ART POSTCARDS

NEW★★
Learning at Home
Artpack, $8.75 plus $1.50 shipping.

A compact art appreciation course from the Museum of Fine Arts, Boston. You get five folders, each containing six 4½ x 6" full-color reproductions of famous paintings from the museum's collection. The reproductions are impressive; you can make out even fine details in the pictures. Topics include Portraits, Landscapes and Seascapes, Modern Art, Still Life, and Everyday Scenes. Right on each folder you will find information about the topic and questions and activities correlated to each painting, plus discovery activities designed to help you create your own artworks. The design of this kit and the depth of the activities and questions are likewise impressive, without being overbearing or tedious. You can pick *Artpack* up, toy with it for a while, and painlessly learn about composition, style, light and shade, texture, schools of art, and more, while learning to enjoy and recognize the work of famous artists. An inexpensive boost into the world of fine art. Recommended.

NEW★★
Museum of Fine Arts—Boston
Postcard book sets, $11.90 each (includes 64 postcards). Shipping extra.

The Boston museum has a fine selection of art postcard books. These are postcards featuring works by famous artists, preperfed and bound into a book. You don't have to use them as postcards—instead, you can use them as mini art appreciation lessons, as I do. The series includes American Watercolors, American Impressionists, French Impressionists, and Japanese Woodblock Prints (just gorgeous). These are all works from the Museum's own collection—take a look at them the next time you're in Red Sox Town!

NEW★★
Metropolitan Museum of Art
"Metropolitan" books, $16.95 each or all four for $60. Shipping extra.

The Met's catalog is heavier on the artsy jewelry and art books, with a good selection of do-it-yourself art, such as origami Christmas ornaments. You might like some of their prints and posters. How about a set of eight framable-sized Monet prints for $14.95, all color-corrected for accuracy? I can't stand Georgia O'Keefe, but they have her too, as well as Van Gogh, Degas, and other names familiar to us all. The "Metropolitan" book series, each with 95 full-color illustrations of Met artworks, covers Cats, Flowers, Children, and Zoo—an intriguing look at how different artists throughout history have handled the same subject.

Parent-Child Press
Mommy, It's a Renoir!, Child-Size Masterpieces, $10.95 each. Art postcard series for time lines: Men, Women, Musicians, Mothers with Children, Picasso, $12.25 each.

A terrific innovation in teaching art appreciation. *Mommy, It's a Renoir!* outlines a course of study based on Montessori principles and using art postcards. First, very young children practice matching identical postcards. They then try pairing two different paintings by the same artist and grouping four paintings by the same artist, eventually progressing to recognizing any studied artist's style in any context. Control cards teach the names of well-known artists and their famous paintings. The book does not include any of these cards, but does contain renditions of 71 works of art.

Child-Size Masterpieces is the growing series of art postcard books to be used with *Mommy, It's a Renoir!* You cut out the cards on the dotted lines and file them in pocket-folders. An extra, smaller card is included for each step for the cover of each folder. Volumes now available are • *CSM—Easy* (ages three and up) • *CSM—Intermediate* (ages four and up) • *CSM—Advanced* (ages five and up) • and *CSM—Famous Paintings* (ages six and up).

The first three volumes cover the first three steps (matching identical paintings, pairing companion paintings, and grouping four paintings by one artist) in increasing levels of difficulty. The fourth volume is for learning the names of artists. The fifth volume is for learning the names of famous paintings. You'll find a wide variety of artists in this series, from Renaissance to modern. The reproduction is excellent.

CHAPTER THREE

ART ACTIVITIES AND SUPPLIES

Remember the first time someone gave you a "Velvet Paint By Numbers" kit? You know, those inexpensive art projects sold in toy stores everywhere, especially around Christmas, that feature scenes of deer grazing by moonlight and other parent-pleasing pictures. Or maybe you got a mosaic kit, or a big box of crayons with its *very own crayon sharpener,* or a paint-with-water coloring book. Remember the rush of excitement and how you couldn't wait to start using your new art supplies?

Forget the Nintendo games. Forget the battery-powered race cars and animated dolls. If you want to *really* make a child happy, get your hands on these great sources for art activities and supplies.

ART ACTIVITIES

NEW★★
Basil Blackwell, Inc.
Family Art, $16.95.

An unusual book that presents "the ways in which families use images such as family portraits and photographs, objects like patchwork quilts and rugs, and rites and ceremonies—including holiday and birthday celebrations—to express and nourish their unique life as a group."

The philosophy of this book is that, by making artifacts together and sharing ceremonies, family art makes both the home and the world more homelike.

NEW★★
Bright Ring Publishing
Mudworks, $14.95. *Scribble Cookies,* $12.95. Shipping extra.

You have to kinda like a book subtitled "Creative Clay, Dough, and Modeling Experiences." At least you do if you're the kind of person who, like me, likes to breathe in the bouquet of a new box of crayons before passing it on to its rightful owner.

The name of the book with that compelling subtitle is *Mudworks,* a name you also have to kinda like. The author of *Mudworks,* Mary Ann F. Kohl, is to playdough as Michelangelo was to marble. Here, between two 11 x 8½" covers, are the secret recipes for playdough, plaster of paris, papier-mache, edible art, clay, bread dough art, and all those other gloppy goodies that the teachers of America have been hoarding all these years. In all you get over 125 modeling recipes and projects. Learn to make putty from toothpaste. Find out how to fossilize a sandcastle, so you can keep the thing around *forever.* Everything you ever wanted to know about adding strange things like vermiculite and glycerine to your innocent little crafts projects—

and what you can do with the resulting concoctions. Some taste good; others dry rock-hard in 24 hours (not in the kids' hair, you hope!). One page per recipe or project. Black and white line art hints at the possibilities of the finished item. Everyone who likes to squeeze the Charmin will hate herself if she passes up this book.

And there's more! Coming at you without warning from the same lady who perpetrated *Mudworks, Scribble Cookies* is a book of over 100 open-ended art activities. This is not your typical let's-make-a-torn-paper-collage book. Open *Scribble Cookies* at random and be amazed at author Mary Ann F. Kohl's ingenuity. Even if you've been teaching art for years I bet you never thought of letting your class roll small cars through thick tempera and then drive them around on paper to create designs. Ever try drawing with crayon while the paper you were drawing on was taped to tinfoil on a heated warming tray? Lots of clever, kid-pleasing ideas in the same format as *Mudworks*.

Scribble Cookies activities are separated into Paper, Chalk and Crayon, Paint, Printing, Sculpture and Ceramics, Crafts, and Recipes and Formulas. A very nice book, easy to use, uncluttered directions, *great* activities!

NEW★★
Covenant Home Curriculum
Art Masters, $29.95 or $19.95 if purchased with a full curriculum. See Volume 1 for description of Covenant Home Curriculum.

Here's something more stimulating than crayons and colored paper! The staff at Covenant Home Curriculum think that true art comes from God and that children can learn how to apply biblical thinking to art as well as to other areas, including how to create excellent artworks themselves.

Dale Dykema, Covenant's headmaster and the author of *Art Masters,* practices what he preaches. The layout and design of this series of teaching units is outstanding.

Each lushly illustrated unit is printed on a single 11 x 17" sheet of high-rag-content grey paper and folded in the middle to create a handy four-page booklet. Some units also have an extra sheet tucked in the middle. Text and pictures interweave to explain the concepts taught in the unit. Each unit has a glossary of new words related to the art topic studied and a brief "Plans and Projects" section. Units are:

- The Meaning of Art
- Rocks and Gems
- Birds and Animals
- Poetry in the Bible
- Patterns I (spirals and explosions)
- Patterns II (meanders, branching, vortex streets)
- Patterns III (bubbles, cracking)
- Ornamentation
- Architecture I (introduction)
- Architecture II (houses)
- Architecture III (churches)
- Calligraphy
- Trees

Each subject is approached from at least three ways: what the Bible says about the subject, how artists have handled it before, and techniques for applying it yourself. The Rocks and Gems unit, for example, gives a brief overview of how rocks and gems were used in Bible times and their symbolic meanings in Scripture (e.g., God's people are called "precious jewels" in 1 Corinthians 3:10-13). The unit then goes on to show the 10 most popular styles of gem cuts. Suggested activities include Bible look-ups, rock tumbling, rock identification, and observing gems at home and the jewelry shop, among other things.

The more I look at *Art Masters,* the more impressed I am with it. The unit on home architecture, for instance, explains the major periods and styles of American home design with more clarity and less words than I have ever seen before—plus you get a line drawing of each architectural style! The same clarity, biblical depth, and range of exercises is maintained throughout the series. Plus the entire series comes with a table of contents and bibliography for further study.

I would definitely recommend *Art Masters.*

NEW★★
Fearon Teacher Aids
Magic Mixtures, $7.95 postpaid. Canada, add 10% shipping.

"Creative fun for little ones." Recipes for 71 preschool-grade 3 concoctions: finger paints, fundoughs, molding mixes, clays, plasters, and more. Author Jean Stangl has a lovely outlook, approaching all these gooey goodies from a kid's-eye view. She waxes lyrical on behalf of mud pies:

> What ever happened to mud pies? Few of today's children have had the joy of experimenting with plain mud. Yet this is probably the oldest form of sculpturing and the first of all creative art mixtures. Don't let your students miss out on marvelous mud molding experiences.

Magic Mixtures makes even humble mud pies snappy, with ideas for making "mud dough" and crafting critters out of it, plus "mud dough variations" with sand or clay. She doesn't tell us to squish mud between our toes; that comes in the "Fun with Cornstarch" chapter, in which you'll find an activity named "Pedi-Squish."

Not quite as open-ended as *Mudworks* (see review above), *Magic Mixtures* is more teacher-oriented. The Fundoughs section, for example, suggests that you ask children to make specific geometric shapes or letters with rolled-out dough. Easy recipes, clear directions, all illustrated.

KidsArt News
$8/year (4 issues), 16 pages/issue.

Extremely helpful activity-based newsletter that really helps you teach art. You get: easy-to-follow activity pages (different topics each issue, like sculpture or photography) • nationwide artistic events • art teaching tips • interviews with artists, both home schoolers and pros • art product reviews • *and* a fine art print of a famous artwork in every issue. *KidsArt News* looks like it was produced on an Apple Macintosh™ computer, which means that if you like the way this book looks, you will probably like the clean, bold feel of *KidsArt News*.

NEW★★
Lovebug Press
Art on My Own, $8.48 postpaid.

Here's something unique—a book of open-ended art activities for children, printed on art-quality paper. Kids are supposed to draw, paint, glue string loops to paper, and do lots of other creative things right on the pages of this book. A sample activity page: "Here is the house of the April Fool. I made the door—you do the rest." The door is made with dotted lines down one side and across the top. Smaller text at the bottom of the page urges the child to "Cut on the - - - - - - fold and open the door."

Activities included in *Art on My Own* include exploring the quality of lines you can make with a pencil, line drawing, coloring, making rubbings, creative drawing (as in drawing a picture of the Man in the Moon's space dog), using watercolors and crayons, torn-paper collage, splatter painting, string drawings, and more. Activities are sufficiently open-ended to allow for lots of creativity, but directed enough to avoid frustration. The illustrations are a little "rough" so kids will feel comfortable, rather than threatened by a level of expertise they can't live up to. Text resembles neat hand-lettering, but is actually a printed typeface. Best use: A quickie activity book for energetic kids.

NEW★★
Motivational Art Training
Coloring Placemats, $9.75 postpaid. Includes set of 30 felt-tip marking pens.

I wouldn't normally bother to mention a set of doodle-art placemats in this section. You know, those intricate designs you color in with watercolor markers. Make placemats out of 'em by covering with contact paper or laminating. But I'm making an exception in this case, because (1) the publisher sent me a sample, and it's tacky to let your kids color them in without even writing the things up, and (2) this is doodle art with a difference.

Designed by William Ladwig, the author of the *Christian Art Manual* (see Chapter 1), these coloring placemats are subtitled, "Discovery—My Place in God's Creation." Each of the five scenes portrays children surrounded by a different subset of created objects: butterflies and insects, sea creatures, seashells, animals. The last scene is a view of the earth from amidst a host of hot-air balloons. Of course, non-Christians can color these in without any pious thoughts, but a Christian parent will have no trouble using these scenes to introduce meditations on the created world and our place in it as its gardeners and stewards.

Perhaps most impressive of all is the price, which not only includes the five 13 x 18" scenes printed on heavy paper stock, but a nice set of 30 fine-line watercolor markers. An ideal way to keep your five-and-ups happily occupied while teaching the older children.

NEW★★
Small Business Press
I Want to Paint a Zebra, But I Don't Know How, $14.95 plus $1.50 shipping.

First things first: *I Want to Paint a Zebra, But I Don't Know How* will not show you or your child how to paint a zebra. However, in author Elaine Heuer's own words, "It will help set up an environment that will leave the children free to create their own unique zebra, however they may see it."

Whenever I see that a Montessori teacher has written a book, I am pretty sure that it will be well-organized, proceed in a sensible step-by-step fashion, and cover the ground thoroughly. No surprises here: this is exactly what *I Want to Paint a Zebra* does. This basic-skills book shows children aged 3 to 8 how to cut, glue, make collages and prints, work with clay, and paint with tempera and watercolors. (Digression: Why do early-elementary and preschool teachers always stress watercolors, the hardest-to-use painting medium, when acrylics are ideal for little kids?)

When I said this book went step by step, I meant *step* by *step*. The first exercise in cutting with scissors includes teaching the child how to properly move his hand muscles in order to make a successful cut, as well as how to hold the scissors and paper. The parent or teacher is urged to use tagboard at first, as it is "the best weight paper for this activity—not too light or too heavy." The author obviously knows her stuff, including everything that can go wrong with each activity and how to guard against it.

I Want to Paint a Zebra has a nice, open format with many "how-to" illustrations. Don't let the book's apparent simplicity fool you, though. You are getting a method that has been tested for years in preschool, elementary, and Montessori classrooms. If you've never tried teaching basic art skills to a child before, you'll save yourself a lot of grief with this book. If you *have* tried teaching basic art skills before, you are perhaps even more likely to appreciate the 30 art activity "recipes" that make the whole thing so easy and so much more fun.

Warren Publishing House, Inc.
1•2•3 Art, $12.95. Add $3 shipping.

You've been tossing and turning at nights wondering what to do with your leftover deodorant bottles, crumpled paper, and wallpaper scraps, right? Your problem is solved. Warren Publishing House's *1•2•3 Art: Open-Ended Art Activities for Young Children* is possibly the biggest and best collection ever of wacky art activities using common household objects.

I've seen lots of art-with-simple-things books, but this one has special features. For one thing, the layout. All the "Painting With . . ." activities, like Painting With shaving cream or food coloring or ice or Q-Tips and so on, are all in the same section. Ditto for the

• Painting On . . . • Gluing • Glue Substitutes (can you see peanut butter as a glue substitute?) • Printing With . . . • Prints of . . . • Modeling With . . . • Marking With . . . • Tearing or Cutting • Lacing • and Miscellaneous Art. A Seasonal Index directs you to activities appropriate to that season and its holidays (e.g., forget painting on snow in June). Every page lists materials needed, preparation required, hints, and variations on the activity, plus there is a cute cartoon of a bear doing the activity. These activities are suggestions submitted by teachers from all around the country, and represent true creative thinking. Gonna get us some squeeze bottles, spray bottles, and tongue depressors and paint us up a storm.

STANDARD ART SUPPLIES

ABC School Supply
Chasselle, Inc.
Hoover Brothers
Lakeshore Curriculum Material Center

These school supply houses all have a wide selection of arts and crafts materials at very attractive prices. I like the Lakeshore catalog best, although they all are good, because Lakeshore offers some crazy items the others don't: wiggly eyes for freaky collages and a device that makes clay into stringy "spaghetti" suitable for providing a clay model with hair, for instance. All the catalogs sell glitter, paints, pens, markers, clay, glue, and dozens of varieties of art paper: everything a young artist needs.

Dick Blick
Catalog, $3.

Blick has a complete selection of art, craft, and related materials for all ages and skill levels. Blick's special emphasis is on fine and graphic arts: many supplies geared to the working artist. You name the art medium or craft, from spinning to sign-making, from oil painting to light tables, they've got it. No serious artist, young or old, should miss this catalog. Worth the $3.

Pearl Paint

"World's Largest Art & Graphic Discount Center." Everything for the serious artist, all at discount. The no-nonsense newsprint catalog includes heavy-duty

equipment like airbrushes, compressors, and easels as well as the usual artistic media (pencils, paper, gouache, oils, brushes, canvas, etc.). Items are listed by category (e.g., Oil Colors) and manufacturer (e.g., Grumbacher). Little or no description of items is offered; it's up to you to know what you want. Less than 2 percent of Pearl's stock is mentioned in the catalog, so if you don't see it, ask.

Toys to Grow On

If you're looking for fancy art supplies for elementary-age kids, this is the place. Every glitzy art material your little heart could desire—stickers, puff paints, colored paper in rolls, foil, doilies, collage kits, fabric kits—this just scratches the surface! Great birthday presents. Ask for the special Art Supplies catalog.

ART SUPPLY KIT FOR HOME SCHOOLERS

NEW**
Learning at Home
Art supply kit, $47. Pentel watercolors, set of 12 5cc tubes, $6.25. Pentel color pens, set of 12 for $8, set of 18 for $12.

About a year and a half ago we decided we were going to get *really serious* about teaching art to our children. This meant making a list, checking it twice, and heading off to the art store where the prices aren't nice. There we were bedazzled by rows and rows of gorgeous art supplies: papers, paints, brushes, ink, carving tools . . . By the time we staggered back home, the family bank account was down $200. We haven't used all that stuff we bought, either.

This true-life story illustrates why Learning at Home decided to develop their art supply kit. Based on the suggestions of Gwen Brennick, author of their *Nourishing Creativity through Art* teaching guide, it includes the basic supplies you need to do the activities in her guide or to stock your own home art cupboard. I've seen this set, and can assure you that it includes only top-quality materials. You get:

- Three .25 ounce tubes of watercolor paint: cadmium yellow, ultramarine blue, and cadmium red

- A size 6 bamboo watercolor paint brush. (For the uninitiated, this brush has a BIG barrel and a decent-sized pointed tip—perfect for little kids or anyone who has trouble using those tacky little brushes in the paint sets down at the supermarket.)

- Gorgeous art tissue paper—five sheets each of canary yellow, medium blue, and national red

- A spiral-bound pad of 11 x 15" Strathmore watercolor paper—12 sheets

- A spiral-bound pad of 11 x 14" Strathmore drawing paper—100 sheets

- One charcoal pencil, size B

- One box of 12 semi-hard pastels

- One compass with a spare lead (can be used for inking, too)

- One set of three square beeswax crayons in primary colors

- Three containers of Speedball printing ink: red, yellow, blue

- One hard brayer (the gizmo you use to press down your print when making linoleum block prints)

Items on this list can be purchased a la carte, or you can get the whole set for about $10 less. And you won't have to drive to the art supply store!

Not included in the art supply kit, but also available from Learning at Home, are a lovely set of Pentel watercolors and two sets of Pentel color pens. The color pen sets come in a snazzy snap-shut carrying case. It's not the biggest selection of art supplies I've ever seen, but it's certainly well-designed for the needs of the average home-schooling family.

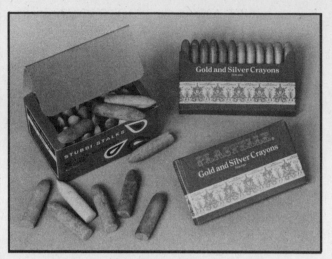

HARD-TO-FIND AND UNUSUAL ART SUPPLIES

DIDAX, Inc.

Rubber stamps, crayons, and other fun stuff for kids. Small art selection, but nice. DIDAX also sells all sorts of manipulative learning devices for other subjects, especially math and phonics. If you like the hands-on approach to learning, you'll drool over this colorful catalog

NEW★★
Flax Art & Design
Wooden models, $27 for 16", $59 for 20", choice of male or female. Full-sized plastic model, $888, comes with an interchangeable chest to make it either male or female. Hardwood hands, $67 each, choice of male or female, right or left.

Every artist needs a model, right? But brother Dave or sister Janie might not feel like sitting still for two hours or so while you doodle around on your sketch pad. Here's a sufficiently wacky solution for this common problem: wooden models. I mean *really* wooden models, not human models with emotionless expressions.

Flax's The Perfect Model series of wooden manikins are hand carved and fully articulated. This means you can move their joints around in all directions. Get the model into the pose you want, and it can't decide to scratch itself or walk away from you. The smaller models are reasonably affordable and are held up by a wire sticking out of a wooden stand. The big six-foot guy, who hardly anyone reading this needs, is made out of space-age light gray plastic. He, too, comes with a base. (Why gray plastic? Because it's supposed to photograph well.)

Realism in these figures does not extend to facial features or fingers and toes, so that's where Flax's "attractive hardwood hands with light oil finish" come in. Hands are hard for many of us to draw, but not when you can simply pose the fingers of your very own hardwood hand and bend the hand at the wrist, as you can with these fully-articulated models. The catalog says the hands are "ideal for display, sketching, or as a unique gift," but I'd say price puts these out of range of all but serious artists. A pity, as they are such a useful drawing aid. As for the "unique gift" idea, those grotesque wiggling hands advertised (heaven knows why) in card decks aimed at business execs have reduced the uniqueness of such a gift—unless the giftee is an artist, in which case he might appreciate you giving him a hand.

NEW**
FLAX Art & Design
Sculpey, about $6-$7/pound, quantity discounts. Friendly Plastic, about $20-$30/pound. Set of iridescent acrylics, about $15. Van Gogh paints, about $90 for the oils and $185 for the watercolors.

This really neat graphic arts and art supply catalog has a host of unusual art supplies I have not seen elsewhere.

Sculpey modeling compound, according to the catalog, "will not shrink and can be used over armatures of wire." The stuff stays pliable until baked, and all you have to do to harden it permanently is bake it at 300 for 15-20 minutes. You can paint the finished product with acrylics, drill it, carve it, and so on. Comes in white, colored, brilliant, metallic, and super. Super Sculpey is shatter-proof and chip-proof. About $6-$7 per pound, discounts for quantity purchases.

I have seen Friendly Plastic, the next neat item, advertised elsewhere, but can't remember where, so I might as well write it up here and tell you to get it from FLAX. This non-toxic, biodegradable modeling material becomes moldable in warm water. You shape it with your hands. After it cools, it holds its shape permanently, unless you decide to warm it up again! Comes in one-pound screw-top jars, each containing about 100-115 thin sheets of either regular, fluores-

cent, or metallic colors (your choice). Flax offers a fairly hefty discount off retail on this product.

You probably already know about Fimo, the next modeling compound I'm about to describe. Flax has a very good discount price on this easy-to-use material. Mix the colors, harden it in the kitchen oven, carve it, file it, cut it, paint it. Once you've done all that, the end result is supposed to be watertight and washable. Comes in blocks with cryptic German comments written all over the packaging. Available in regular colors (for normal people) and glow-in-the-dark Night Glow (the suggested use in the Flax catalog is a mobile of the solar system).

En passant, let me mention that if you're into iridescent colors, Flax also carries "luminous acrylic paints" in a set of six two-ounce tubes of silver, red, blue, yellow, red gold, and gold. If they look at all like the catalog picture, these are super colors, and Flax swears that "when combined with other colors they lend an electric quality to the hue of the color." Other unusual paints: a set of "the actual paints of Van Gogh and Vermeer," as produced by the folks at Old Holland Oil Color Works (est. 1664). Available in a set of 10 40-ml. oil tubes or a set of 40 six-ml. water color tubes. Also great deals on bristle brush sets, easels, brush carriers, markers, colored pens and pencils, airbrushes and accessories, and other necessities. These are top-quality, technologically-advanced items, not dusty leftovers that have been clogging up the shelves in some warehouse. In fact, if I had only one word to describe the Flax catalog, it would be "high-tech." Just about every item in it looks like it deserves to win a design award, and some of them have! One example: the Pocket-Sized Painting Studio, a super-compact container shaped like a Swiss army knife. Inside you find 10 watercolor blocks, a mixing palette, a sketch pencil, three mini-brushes, a water container, and an eraser. These swing out from the parent container, again like a Swiss army knife. The whole sleek, black thing is only one inch wide, 4½ inches long, and about two inches high.

Other art supply catalogs are two inches thick and list every art accessory known to man. Flax seems to settle for just carrying the best and prettiest of everything. At least it seems that way in the categories with which I am familiar.

Maybe it's just the way the catalog presents the items that makes them stand out so much. I dunno. Anyway, it can't hurt that the people trying to sell you graphic arts supplies know a thing or two about catalog design and layout themselves!

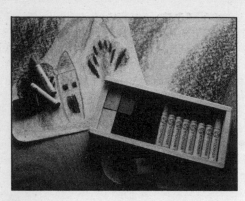

HearthSong

Superb quality art and craft supplies, small but well-chosen selection, not cheap. Hearth Song emphasizes natural fabrics and materials, e.g., their wool-stuffed dolls. Modeling beeswax, non-toxic paints and crayons.

UPDATED**
KidsArt
My Bag kits, $9.95 each. Bellerophon kit books, $2.95 to $3.50 each. Powdered tempera paint, $4.35 for one pound of regular color, $8.65/one pound metallic gold or silver. Block printing kit, $19.95. Many more items available. Shipping extra.

Creative art activities and materials abound in KidsArt's "All Time Great Art Products" catalog. KidsArt offers a full selection of teaching manuals, including the *Mommy, It's a Renoir* series, the classic *Art for Children* by Herberholz, *Scribble Cookies, Teaching Drawing from Art,* and *The Big Yellow Drawing Book.* You'll find activity books and kits for all grade levels, such as the My Bag kits. These are handy burlap storage bags full of all the materials needed to create puppets and clothespin dolls. Older children enjoy Bellerophon's Cut Out and Put Together kit books, which enable them to create scale models of castles, trains, and famous American airplanes. KidsArt also carries selected art materials: hard-to-find items such as powdered tempera paint, Speedball's block printing kit, and colorful sets of pastel chalk and Prismacolor pencils. All materials are non-toxic, child-safe, and 100% money-back satisfaction guaranteed.

The KidsArt philosophy is to carefully teach the techniques of art, from drawing to sculpture to photography, then turn kids loose to experiment and create on their own, with open-ended assignments and lots of fun and success. Good stuff; you'll like it.

Sycamore Tree
Multicolor erasable crayons, 15 for $1.75. Plasti-Tak $1.95. O'Glue $1.49. Fimo modeling set $10.95. Lots more. Shipping extra.

Sycamore Tree, along with their thousands of curriculum resources for all subjects, offers a good-sized selection of some of the most progressive art supplies.

Multicolor erasable plastic crayons are non-toxic, washable, non-smearing, melt-resistant, beautiful, and *erasable.* That is, almost completely erasable. Some colors are more persistent than others. Still, at last young artists can more or less erase those erratic marks that wandered outside the lines.

Plasti-Tak looks and feels like putty, but it comes off walls and papers. Use it to tack that priceless artwork up without marring surfaces.

O'Glue is a long transparent squeezable tube of glue with a neat applicator. Works on just about anything. Non-toxic, non-flammable, water soluble. No mess!

Imported from West Germany, the Fimo Modeling Set contains eight colors of special Fimo material, a work pad, lacquer, and a modeling tool. Fimo is a brilliantly colored, nontoxic, odorless modeling compound you can harden in your oven. Used by some professional sculptors.

This only touches the surface of the hundred or more art books, supplies, and projects Sycamore Tree carries. Watercolors, brushes, Bible coloring books and models (build your own Tabernacle!), paint-with-water, Funthinkers,™ scissors, coloring markers, lots more.

HOW TO STORE YOUR CHILD'S FINISHED ART

NEW**
Warren Publishing House, Inc.
Displaying Children's Art, send $1 for shipping and handling.

Every parent has this problem. Samantha has created an absolutely *gorgeous* masterpiece. With pride beaming in her eyes, she brings it you. "Oh, that's beautiful, darling!" you say. Then you're stuck. What to do with it?

Traditional solutions include sticking the art on your refrigerator door (gets messy *very* quickly), scotch-taping it to the wall (leaves little dribs of tape and glue everywhere), and even throwing it out once everyone has seen it. Not very satisfying.

Warren Publishing House has the answer to this early-childhood dilemma. Their free 16-page booklet, *Displaying Children's Art,* is loaded with 32 ways to attractively display at-risk artworks. Suggestions range from permanent adult-artist-style displays (attaching the artwork to a piece of posterboard, along with a photo of the child and a personal description) to temporary (display strips made out of corkboard from which you hang art with push pins). You get a lot for your $1 shipping here, even suggestions of how to *use* children's artwork rather than merely displaying it (wrapping paper or patchwork quilts, anyone?). Each idea was contributed by a subscriber to the *Totline* early-childhood newsletter, and the contributor is prominently honored. *Totline* has smart contributors. These are really good ideas! As usual with Warren Publishing House, each idea is presented with a drawing and nice big type explaining how to do it.

You really *need* this booklet. It can bring harmony out of chaos and smiles to your children's faces.

CHAPTER FOUR

CRAFTS ACTIVITIES AND SUPPLIES

I deally, there should be no great distinction between arts and crafts. After all, every art is a craft, and there's no such thing as a true artist who lacks craftsmanship. (See the introduction for Chapter 2!)

However, historically the "fine arts" of drawing, painting, and sculpture have been separated from "crafts" such as woodworking and weaving. This is because kings and nobles patronized the fine arts, while fabric arts and so on were the province of the housewife and peasant. Every woman spun, wove, sewed, and knitted; every man knew how to use a knife to carve wood or make a whistle for his son. Under those circumstances, it was hard to make a living producing crafts for their sake as art. You—and everyone else—could make a beautiful quilt, but it would be put on the bed, not on the wall.

Today the situation is reversed. You can buy oil paintings for a relative pittance at the mall, but a beautiful quilt is expensive, hard to find, and more likely to end up on the wall than on the bed. Girls today don't know how to sew or knit or crochet, let alone how to tat or make lace. The average American boy can't make a wooden whistle that works or a kite that flies. This is not because gender-free education has triumphed; today's boys can't knit and today's girls can't make whistles, either.

Let's do something about this, already!

Here is a fine potpourri of how-to crafts programs and supplies for all sorts of crafts. You won't find the typical crafts catalogs and magazines here, because (1) I'm sticking with projects and instructions for beginners and (2) I'm not convinced that anyone *really* wants a latch-hook rug featuring Santa Claus and his twelve tiny reindeer. Nothing wipes out enthusiasm for crafts faster than an elaborate, time-consuming project that isn't even beautiful when it is finished, so this list sticks to the quick, fun, and inexpensive, plus sources of materials for your own creative inventions.

CRAFTS ACTIVITIES

NEW**
Dale Seymour Publications
Little Fingers: Creative Ideas for the Young at Art, $7.95.

Here's a neat, inexpensive crafts program for children in preschool through grade 3. Arranged by months of the school year, the seasonal emphasis is interspersed with teacher hints on techniques such as scissors use, printing, painting, paper sculpture, and use of line and texture. Each month has activities appropriate to that month. For example, in September you will find leaf rubbings. October has Halloween and harvest themes. November features Thanksgiving.

December has a secular Christmas theme (Rudolph and Santa rather than Jesus). January concentrates on snow. In February it's Valentine's Day and patriotism. March is a potpourri of circus, spring, and St. Patrick's Day. April features secular Easter activities. May looks at spring. June has an animals emphasis.

Some sample activities from among the 115 included:

• Giant Texture Puzzle. Teacher draws a puzzle outline with magic marker and cuts it out. Students each take a piece and color it in with a different arrangement of shapes and lines. The object is to practice ways of simulating texture in drawings and paintings.

• Clown collage made with craft sticks, fabric scraps, and other materials.

• Blot-print Valentine made with white and red tempera paint. Student will discover that they mix to make pink!

• Stuffed Christmas ornament made with paper, fiberfill, and decorations.

I really like the layout of this oversized book. Each activity starts with a list of materials and a drawing of the finished craft. Directions are easy to follow. Recipes and teaching tips are included where needed. Some activities are open-ended, some are project-oriented, leaving room for both experimentation and practice with techniques. The scope of activities is quite broad, and none take very long to do.

NEW**
Dale Seymour Publications
The Special Artist's Handbook: Art Activities and Adaptive Aids for Handicapped Students, $18.95.

This oversized quality paperback is an absolutely wonderful resource for anyone who wants to introduce special-needs students to basic crafts techniques and activities. See the complete review in Chapter 27.

GENERAL CRAFTS SUPPLIES

NEW**
Betterway Publications
The Crafts Supply Sourcebook, $14.95.

This is the *Big Book* of crafts supplies. More than 2600 listings, plus photos and line drawings, telling you where to get supplies for every kind of craft. The book is a combined and updated version of author Margaret A. Boyd's two previous resource volumes, *Catalog Sources for Creative People* and *The Sew & Save Sourcebook*.

The Crafts Supply Sourcebook has two major sections. General Arts, Crafts, and Hobbies are covered in one section, while Needlecrafts, Sewing, and Fiber Arts are covered in the other. Each listing includes the supplier's name and address, catalog and ordering information, and a description of the products and/or services offered. The author also includes lots of crafts tips.

Sounds good, doesn't it? All the above info was cribbed straight from the publisher's catalog description, and I guess it must be true, since *The Crafts Supply Sourcebook* is a Book-of-the-Month Club selection. Never got my hands on a review sample, though I tried, but this book sounds good enough that I'm including it here nonetheless.

S & S Arts & Crafts

Now here's my favorite crafts supply catalog! This large catalog of all kinds of arts and crafts projects, many sold in classroom-sized packs, has got most of what you're looking for, all in one place. In bulk, these projects cost almost nothing apiece. Tons of neat stuff unavailable elsewhere. Golden Foil projects make fancy pictures for 22¢ and up. Mobiles. Kaleidoscopes (make your own). Wind wheels. Philippine Wind Chimes. Rhinestone studding sets. Japanese Fish Kites. Southwestern Indian Sand Painting (enough supplies for 50 projects, $18.88). Plastic Weaving Baskets. Color-n-Throw Boomerangs. Rainbow Tops. Clothespin art, a page of projects and supplies. Craftsticks in bulk ($2.15/1,000), with projects and accessories. Pop-It Beads, $4.35/one pound bag (approximately 800). Mosaic Tiles at low prices—all kinds (I *loved* making mosaics as a child). Paper projects. Leather projects. Copper and metal tooling. Paper and posterboard supplies and projects. Wood projects ($10.55 for one of those fancy wooden trains in kit form). Holiday crafts.

Beadcraft with fusible beads. Classroom art supplies (scissors, glue, etc.).

PAPER CRAFTS

NEW**
Dale Seymour Publications
Geometric Playthings, $8.95.

Want a really neat crafts project that increases spatial thinking skills and provides a foretaste of advanced geometry? How about a bunch of those projects? Then here's a book for you! In the line made famous by the TV show *Star Trek*, "It's like nothing I've ever seen before!" WHAT YOU GET: An oversized (9¾ x 12½) book with eight double-page spreads of unusual objects to color, cut, and fold. You start from the centerfold (three attractive Moebius strips) and work your way out. By the time you're done, you will have constructed deltahedra, hexaflexagons, and polyhedra of all sorts. If you don't know what these are, don't worry—you will by the time you finish these enjoyable projects! Each geometric object is decorated to the hilt with attractive designs that you can color in, for added crafts value. The price is also right. I've seen glitzy catalogs for yuppies offering make-it-yourself geometric playthings for considerably more than Dale Seymour is asking.

Dover Publications
Publishers of over 3,000 paperbacks in all fields of interest, including many specially suited for home study and instruction. Most priced between $2 and $5.

Tons of economical art and craft books. Paper models—cut and assemble the Emerald City or a Western Frontier Town, among others. Unique coloring book series (human anatomy: favorite birds: American Revolution uniforms: Bible stories: make your own calendar . . .). Also books on origami, books about art, books on "how to" almost anything.

NEW**
EDC Publishing
Know-How series, $5.95 per book. Make This Model series, $7.95 per book. Add 15% shipping.

The Know-How series from EDC Publishing is the niftiest hands-on resource I have seen in ages. Unlike so many how-to-do-it books, kids actually *want* to try those experiments, make those puppets, put together

those action games, and so on. The series includes Jokes and Tricks, Detection, Experiments, Fishing, Action Games (like tabletop hockey—games to put together and play), Action Toys (toys and machines to make), Paper Fun, Puppets, Batteries and Magnets, Print and Paint, Spycraft, and Flying Models. You might also like to try the Make This Model series, which includes an English town, a cathedral, a castle, and a village of preprinted light cardboard that you simply cut out and glue together.

NEW**
Teacher Created Materials
Graph Art series, $5.95 each. *Paper Plate & Cup Art, Paper Sculpture*, $5.95 each. *Box Art Projects, Container Art Projects, Milk Carton Art Projects, Paper Bag Art Projects, Paper Plate Art Projects*, $4.95 each. Shipping extra.

Graph Art is something new (at least to me). You start with a sheet of blank graph paper. (You'll need to photocopy lots of these sheets; a sample sheet is provided in the back of each book.) Then you follow directions such as,

1) Color 11B
2) Color 4B, 1 B/G, 1G, 5B

Translation: Color 11 squares in one row blue. On the next row, color the first four squares blue, the next square half-blue and half-green (separating the colors on the diagonal), the next square green, and the last five squares blue. The directions continue on, and eventually you end up with a jack-o-lantern. That's Mystery Picture #1 from the *Graph Paper Art* book. The book comes with complete directions for 22 pieces of graph art and an answer key showing how each completed project should look. This largish series from TCM includes *Graph Paper Art, Holiday Graph Art, Patriotic Graph Art, Simple Graph Art*, and *Challenging Graph Art*. Develops spatial skills, listening skills, direction-following skills, hand-eye coordination, etc., etc.

Moving right along, we come to TCM's series of "found art" books. The series includes books with ideas for making something out of boxes, containers, milk cartons, paper bags, and paper plates. Some of the ideas are more clever than others; quite a few projects in the *Box Art* book consisted of simply gluing a puppet outline onto a box. You need access to a photocopy machine to really get the most out of these books.

NEW**
Fearon Teacher Aids
PaperCrafts series, $7.95 each. Other paper crafts books, $4.95 to $8.95 each.

PaperCraft series members are inexpensive books designed for home art and craft projects. *Papercrafts* is correlated to K-5 children's literature and includes *Folk Tale PaperCrafts, Fables and Tales PaperCrafts,* and *Mother Goose PaperCrafts.* Each book contains instructions for making puppets, masks, paper sculptures, and other 3-D art projects. Since book pages are printed on both sides, you will need to copy the patterns by eye onto paper of your own unless you have access to a photocopy machine.

The *Fables and Tales* book is especially useful for lingering over the character-building lessons in such classic fables as The Tortoise and the Hare. Some magical elements appear in the *Folk Tale* book. *Mother Goose* is just that: paper crafts for a selection of favorite children's rhymes. The introduction to all three books suggests that children staple each of the coloring pages (one is provided per rhyme or tale), followed by a sheet of lined writing paper, together in a book. Children can then either copy the rhyme, summarize the story, or perform some other writing activity correlated with the craft.

The resulting paper crafts are really cute, and when made with different colors of paper look quite professional.

NEW**
Fearon Teacher Aids
Paper Menagerie, $4.95.

Construction paper cut-outs with three-dimensional features. Add brads to make them movable. Patterns and directions for 25 animals. Basic materials needed: construction paper, something with which to draw or color on it, brass fasteners, scissors, glue, and stapler.

Paper Menagerie is divided into three sections: Mobile Menagerie, Stand-Alone Creatures, and Paper Roll Animals (the latter made with bathroom tissue rolls). The mobile characters are put together with brass fasteners, so heads and limbs can wiggle. Stand-along creatures can sit on the table.

Like other reproducible books designed for schools, *Paper Menagerie* has patterns on both sides of each page. This means you will need to copy the patterns by eye onto the construction paper.

NEW**
Flax Art & Design
Set of four barkwood papers, $20. 100-page blank book, $22. 250-page blank book, $27. Shipping extra.

I have no idea what you would ever use it for, but this is such an unusual resource that I just have to mention it. See, you have these Otami Indians. For hundreds of years they have occupied themselves hand-pounding the bark of downed fig and mulberry trees. "Why?" you ask. To produce hand-made heavy paper of, as the Flax catalog says, "most unusual texture." The catalog also says the resulting 16 x 24" sheets are "wonderful for numerous uses," but unhappily fails to specify exactly *what* those uses might be. Obviously not as scribble paper for Junior. How about as outer covering for a blank book? Good idea—so Flax also offers two different 6 x 9" blank books, each covered in buckskin barkpaper and containing 80-pound superfine archival paper.

The basic set of four bark papers comes in ivory and buckskin (these look like you might be able to write on them) and cinnamon and marble (in the catalog picture these look too dark for writing on). What I really want to know is what the *Otamis* use this paper for . . .

Peccl Publications
Color Words, $9.95 plus $1 shipping.

What do you do when it's been raining for two solid weeks and the kids are about to eat the living room drapes from sheer frustration? I smile sweetly and say, "Go get Mary Pecci's *Color Words* book." Now you know that you don't need one hundred pages of assignments to teach those little color words—red, orange, yellow, and so on—so what are all those pages about? Aha! Good question! What we have here is the niftiest bunch of primary crafts assignments that I have ever seen. All you need are scissors, crayons, glue, and a brad or two and you can: Build a (paper) log cabin! Make an Easter egg which opens up to hatch a chick! Make Thanksgiving napkin rings featuring a Pilgrim girl and boy! Put together a 3-D circus parade! The activities are seasonal, which is great for emphasizing holidays, and the results are so charming that I have our boys glue them onto cardboard to make them last longer.

NEW
Teacher Created Materials
Grocery Bag Art, $5.95 each pattern book. Shipping extra.

This is so unique I just had to put it in. Picture this: A large brown grocery bag. You cut a hole in the front and two slits up the sides. You then turn to one of TCM's *Grocery Bag Art* books, find a pattern you like, copy it onto several sheets of paper, color it in, cut it out, glue it onto the grocery bag—and bingo! instant costumes for your kids. The series includes grocery-bag patterns for circus, farm, career, and holidays. (Note to parents: TCM expects you to copy the patterns on a photocopy machine. If you don't have easy access to one, just copy them quickly by hand onto a piece of paper. The patterns are so simple this won't take long.)

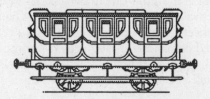

SCISSORS STORIES

Warren Publishing House, Inc.
"Cut & Tell" Scissor Stories, $6.95 each (Fall, Winter, Spring). Shipping extra.

Three seasonal collections of scissor stories, with eight stories each. You've never heard of scissor stories? All right, I'll tell you about scissor stories. What they are, is a paper plate. You take the plate. You begin to cut the plate as you tell the story. At each stage of the story, the plate turns into a different prop. For example: In "The Spirit of Christmas," one paper plate becomes first two mice, next two pieces of cheese, and then the rest of the plate becomes a fancy candle. Or how about the Chanukah basket that becomes a dreidl that becomes a menorah? No kidding! Jean Warren, the author, stayed up nights thinking of these crazy scissor stunts. Full directions and stories are included.

Jean Warren has produced *"Cut & Tell" Scissor Stories* for Fall, Winter, and Spring. In theory, you, the adult, perform these to an admiring group of children at a daycare center. In practice, you, the adult, can try your luck at home and possibly flub the story, but it won't matter, because your kids will be ready and able to take over and show you how it ought to be done. With a little help from you in figuring out the directions, *"Cut & Tell" Scissor Stories* could be the ultimate cut-paste-'n-color kids' books.

MAKE A MASK

Educational Insights
Make-A-Mask Kit, $9.95. Extra gauze, $4.95. Add 10% shipping.

You want something unusual? This is unusual, all right! Educational Insight's Make-A-Mask Kit includes one face form, one roll Plastergauze, six colors of tempera, paintbrush, and 16-page full-color instruction guide with some project suggestions. Add a little yarn, feathers, or fake fur and you've got . . . something. One model mask project strongly resembles Miss Piggy, another a horrible monster. Kid-pleasing for sure (but skip the monsters!).

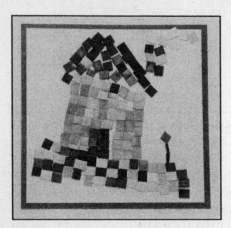

MOSAICS

NEW**
HearthSong
Mosaic chips, $7.95 for a bag of about 1,600. Shipping extra.

I absolutely loved making mosaics as a child. Unfortunately, real ceramic mosaic chips are relatively expensive, and the finished piece is *heavy*. So I was delighted to see HearthSong offering something new—wood mosaic chips! These colorful ⅜" squares are easy to glue on paper or cardboard, and provide much of the pleasure of mosaic for a fraction of the effort and expense.

HearthSong also sells Stockmar block crayons, stick crayons, candle decorating wax (plus candles to stick the decorations on), modeling beeswax, and watercolor paints—plus Chunki Chalks (great for sidewalk artists!), cakes of beeswax plasticine, and giant colored pencils. Lots of beautiful and colorful fun for your child!

S & S Arts & Crafts

Traditional ceramic mosaic chips. Choice of styles. Mosaic kits also available.

TRASH ART

NEW**
Fearon Teacher Aids
Trash Artists Workshop, $8.95.

Trash Artists Workshop is a mind-blower! Enter a universe in which newspapers metamorphose into modeling compound; boxes become boomerangs; old clothes become a rag person; styrofoam chips live as sailing ships. Over 50 trash art projects, plus tales of legendary trash art and trash artists. Loving attention is paid to recycling paper, plastics, and cloth into works of art, but odds and ends like pencil stubs are not forgotten. Would you believe egg grenades? (Relax: it's just egg shells filled with confetti.) Resource list and Trash Artist's Guide to Trash (what industry throws away what). If you want to save money with art, this is the place to start.

WAXWORK

NEW**
Learning at Home
Modeling beeswax, set of 8 sheets, $7.75. Decorating wax, set of 15 sheets, $7.75. Shipping extra.

It doesn't stick to the rug, your fingers, or the wall. It never dries out, yet holds its shape. Nice smell, and it's practically good to eat (a consideration with small children who like to eat their crafts supplies)! What is it? Modeling beeswax! Here's one source for the stuff. It comes in colored sheets. You warm it up in your hands, then use it for modeling. I have never had much success in getting pieces to stick together. Apparently I am not the only one with this problem, as Learning at Home recommends that you "pull shapes from the wax, keeping the wax as a whole, unbroken piece." Aside from this one drawback, it's neat stuff!

Also available is decorating wax. This comes in thinner sheets, designed to be cut out for decorations and placed on candles, Easter eggs (I recommend hard-boiling the eggs first!), and anywhere else that they'll stick. Jewel-like colors, lots of fun!

WEAVING

UPDATED**
Harrisville Designs
Twenty-four-inch loom, $159; 36-inch loom, $168; 48-inch loom $176. Lap looms: Size A, $19.50, with accessories $29.95; size B, $24.95, with accessories, $36.95. Starter Kit, $27.50. "Software" weaving projects, $13.95 each. Shipping extra.

Our children have always been fascinated with weaving. One of son Ted's first independent purchases was a potholder weaving kit. But potholders rather limit the scope of one's imagination, and a real loom is exorbitantly expensive and space-wasting. Not to mention the way the kids would fight over it.

Our kids have all woven serious projects, all at once, on the same loom. How did this happen? The Friendly Loom™ from Harrisville Designs. You get a pegged frame that you can adjust up and down, depending on how long you want your finished piece. This rests on a floor stand. You set up the loom quickly by running cotton warp back and forth over the pegs, then select whatever you want to weave through it and weave! Patterns and materials can be as wild or wooly as you wish: feathers, cloth or rag strips, grass bundles, plants, seaweed, twigs, vines, leather or fur strips, plastic bread bags, rolled or twisted paper bags, bead strings, bias tape, ribbons, ric rac, or even yarn! The accompanying booklet tells you how to set up and weave, and gives ideas for patterns. And because the Friendly Loom is so wide, several children can work side by side on individual projects.

The Friendly Loom comes in three sizes and a new lap version. The larger looms each have adjustable sides. You loosen or tighten a knob to adjust the height of your weaving space. Each fits flat along a wall when not in use. The lap looms come in a 12 x 16" size (size A) and the larger 14½ x 18½" size B. Each is available with an optional accessory package that includes one ounce of cotton warp yarn, two ounces of wool weft yarn (two colors), a plastic needle, wooden shed stick, and 6" wooden stick shuttle. This lap model is definitely preferable for home use, and I'd advise you to buy it with the accessories included. It's cheaper to buy one for each child than to get the floor model, and the lap model is much more portable, easier to store, and prevents sibling rivalry!

New from this company: "Software" weaving projects designed to fit on the lap looms. Each "software" kits includes complete instructions, plus enough 100 percent virgin wool yarn and any other materials necessary to complete the project. So far, two kits are available. Design #10 is a wallhanging with a sheep woven into the picture. Design #20 is a purse.

Harrisville Designs also sells the supplies you will need to get started weaving on the bigger models in the form of a Starter Kit. The kit contains four wooden maple shed sticks, four wooden maple stick shuttles, four brightly colored balls of thick 100 percent wool yarn (different colors), and one 440-yard cone of cotton warp. I wish they sold yarn separately, since when you run out, you're forced to search for thick weaving yarn locally, and it is not always easy to find. (Hint: try S & S Crafts.) Otherwise, recommended.

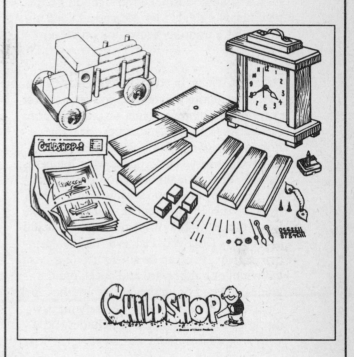

WOODWORKING

NEW**
Childshop
Basic Plans, $2.50 each. Discovery Plans, $3.50 each. Hardware packages, from $4 to $10, most items. Complete kits, from around $10 to $15, most items. Shipping extra.

Childshop woodworking kits are designed to help you bond with your kids. "Build strong bonds with your children through simple woodcraft experiences," reads the copy above Childshop's logo. It's true, too; each of Childshop's three-dozen-plus woodworking projects can be built by children ages five and up with only a small amount of assistance from an adult. These projects are safe for children and can be built using only normal hand tools.

Childshop kits and plans are beautifully produced with quality materials. Our children have put several of them together, and I feel confident in saying that you will feel proud to give these to your children or young friends and relatives.

Childshop projects come in four flavors:

(1) Basic Plans. These include a list of materials and tools needed, drawings showing how the parts go together, and step-by-step directions. Easy to follow, illustrated throughout. Each plan fits on a single 11 x 25" sheet folded in thirds. Nice printing: brown ink on cream paper.

(2) Discovery Plans. In addition to the Basic Plan, now stapled into the middle, you get an outer cover of heavy brown paper on which is printed safety suggestions and educational questions and answers. Example: The Logging Truck Discovery Plan explains what lumber is, its uses, the two main classes of lumber, examples of softwood and hardwood trees, how trees are turned into lumber, and how lumber was cut in early colonial America. Also included in every Discovery Plan is a "Build a Memory" activity. This can be a field trip (e.g., visit a sawmill or lumberyard and check out the grades of wood or lumber) or game (the Clock Discovery Guide suggests you use your new clock for a timed game). Most Guides end with an apt Bible quote.

(3) Hardware packages. These include a plan and all the hardware you need for a project, packed in a poly bag. You supply the wood.

(4) Complete kit. A plan, all the hardware you need for the job, and pre-cut, ¾" thick, solid pine or basswood parts, all packed neatly in a heavy-duty poly bag. The wood feels chunky and nice in your hand; the package begs, "Make me!" Irresistible.

Finishing materials, such as wood glue, kid-sized sandpaper, varnish, stain, acrylics, and brushes, are also available from Childshop. These are all specially chosen for their kid-friendly features, such as non-toxicity, washableness, and ease of use.

More about those Discovery Guides. Again, the emphasis is on fun and bonding with your kids, not on heavy-duty education. The included questions and "Build a Memory" section are enough to kick off a unit study, but you could just as easily settle for learning a little bit by going through them once together. This is a plus in my book, because who needs extra guilt?

Kits available so far are: book rack (discover about books and education), hanging planter (plants), wall sconce (heat and light), recipe box (health and nutrition), pet bed (caring for pets), clock (time), toolbox (tools), bird feeder (birds), bug box (insects), sailboat (air and wind), sports car (cars), jeep (jeeps), caboose, box car, flat car, coal car, train engine (trains), entire train, pickup truck (trucks), logging truck (lumber), biplane (airplanes), helicopter (helicopters), wagon, tractor (tractors), doll cradle (dolls), doll highchair, wren house, step stool, what-not shelf, musical bank, napkin holder, paper towel holder, fruit tray, letter holder, candle sconce, and mug rack. As you can see, not all kits come with Discovery Guides. The clock and musical bank come with electronic movements.

S & S Arts & Crafts

As I mentioned above, S & S Arts & Crafts has a fairly decent selection of woodworking projects. Nothing terribly fancy or gorgeous, but rock-bottom prices.

Toad's Tools

Basic tool set, $174.95. Sample individual prices: $5.40 for 3 screwdrivers, $15 for a 10-ounce hammer. Shipping extra.

Kid-sized but serious tools for young woodworkers and carpenters. Prices are "reasonable"—see above. This is not your typical made-in-Taiwan tinware.

The Toad's Tools basic set includes everything a young carpenter could ever need except power tools. All items are available separately. All items, except normal replacement parts like saw blades, carry an unconditional lifetime replacement guarantee.

OTHER CRAFTS

NEW★★
Fearon Teacher Aids
Writing Crafts Workshop, Nature Crafts Workshop, and *Native American Crafts Workshop,* $8.95 each.

Writing Crafts Workshop is not about how to write. It's about crafts surrounding writing. Thus, the first chapter shows how to make a Victorian lap desk, a quill pen, berry ink, and a personal seal, among other things. Chapter 2, "The Book Bindery," explains marbleizing (including how to make your own marbling comb), how to fold or stitch a book, how to make a hornbook, and lots more. Chapter 3 has all kinds of printing crafts, from an old-style playbill to a rolling pin press. The "Secret Writing" chapter has Spartan scytales (yeah, that's a real word), secret ink, a cipher slide, and more. Plus a "Writing for Fun" chapter that shows kids how to put together an adventure board game, make phototoons, make a treasure map, and more. At the back of the book you'll find fancy alphabets, monograms, and little artistic items used by printers (devices and dingbats, as they're called in the trade). This is a book for preteens through adult, but not for little kids. Each activity comes with historical and cultural information about the particular craft. Thus Chapter 2 has a history of writing and bookmaking along with illustrative activities, and Chapter 4 tells the tale of great moments in secret writing. A terrific book for unit studies.

Nature Crafts Workshop and *Native American Crafts Workshop,* two other titles in this series that don't fit into neat categories, are reviewed in Volume 3. Briefly, *Nature Crafts* is crafts with natural objects plus nature observation projects. *Native American Crafts* revives authentic Indian crafts. More than a little eco-religious preaching in the latter.

PART II

MUSIC

CHAPTER FIVE

MUSIC READING FOR THE REST OF US

Learning to read music is like learning to read English. Not altogether easy. And the way you are taught to read music makes a real difference in how (or if) you learn.

I find that the resources available for learning to read music break down into these categories:

- Activity-oriented materials for young children. Teaching kids to read music this way can be rather exhausting for the parents, but is a blast for the kids.

- Sobersides adult programs. These lay it out like so: "This is a treble clef. (See illustration.)"

Just as with phonics instruction, a skilled teacher doesn't really need a course, manipulatives, or activities. However, since lots of us parents don't really understand how to read music ourselves, you may find that it's worth investing in the goodies.

If you're determined to skip the process of learning to read music, your choices narrow down to playing everything entirely by ear or getting songbooks written in note-and-chord notation. Davidsons Music has lots of these kinds of materials. If, however, you want to sing along with everyone else on Sunday morning or play tunes out of a regular songbook, here's how.

MUSIC READING FOR KIDS

Christian Education Music Publishers, Inc.
K workbook $3.95, grades 1-4 $4.95, teacher's guide $3. Shipping $3 extra per order for workbooks only (USA and Canada). Sample set includes all above for $29.95 postpaid. You need *all* workbooks for the complete program. Sample set with corresponding cassette tapes, $79.95 postpaid. Corresponding cassette tape for each workbook, $9.95 each. Songbook, $4.95, corresponding tape $7.95. Shipping extra on these items. Other musical items available. Free phone consultation on music instruction or any other "musical" questions you may have regarding home school music training.

The *Your Musical Friends* workbook series is a music reading program for K-4. Each musical symbol is carried by a cartoon animal. Quacker Treble Clef, for example, has a body made of the treble clef, a tail like a bass clef, and quarter notes for feet! There's Crescendo Whale and Forte Lion and Sixteenth Note Bird and Ritard Turtle—29 animals in all.

The kindergarten book introduces the characters in the form of a coloring book. The first grade book, *Fun with Your Musical Friends,* gets into the two staffs and notes and rests. The second grade book, *Enjoying Music with Your Musical Friends,* looks at line and space note values and the loud and soft signs. The third grade book, *Learning More with Your Musical Friends,* includes sharps, flats, tempo, repeats, and accents. Finally, the fourth grade book, *Reading Music with Your Musical Friends,* covers the last details of dotted notes and so on, and launches into actual sight reading.

Each book begins with a review of the previous book. The exercises and stories are fun and colorful and *very* Christian. An example: a fill-in-the-blanks-with-the-note-name exercise in the fourth grade book about how Isaac Watts' mother had to spank him for continuing to drive her crazy by always speaking in rhyme gives Isaac's reply: "Mother, do some pity take. I will no more verses make!"

The instructor needs no musical background.

Because the publisher strives to keep costs low and therefore uses medium-grade paper, the art is muddy, but that is my only quibble.

New: cassette tapes to accompany each workbook. The Musical Friends animal characters lead your child through each workbook. Each character has his own voice and personality, as well as a Scripture verse representative of his or her musical function. A song tape called *Your Musical Friends Songs, Plus More!* (with corresponding songbook) is also available.

If your children want to know what all those funny little squiggles in the hymnbook mean, this is the easiest-to-use series around.

NEW**
Elijah Company
Keyboard Capers, $17.95. Manipulatives set to accompany *Keyboard Capers,* $35. Both, $49.95. Shipping extra.

Keyboard Capers, a terrific music-reading program for kids, consists of 100 easy activities for parents and teachers of children age three and up. It covers everything: learning the letters A-G forward and backward • staff and clefs • locating keys on the keyboard • rhythm • intervals • notes • music words and signs (e.g., pianissimo) • ear training • and major scales.

I *like* this book! Author Rebecca Doyle Lennon has managed to come up with 100 easy activities "for parents and teachers of Suzuki piano students age 3 and up" that actually teach kids (whether Suzuki-ized or not) to read music *without any struggle!* Sample activity: practice rhythm using the pink (half-note), purple (whole note), and blue (dotted half-note) cards.

This is the easiest, most fun music-reading course I've seen.

The program relies heavily on manipulatives, for which patterns are included. If you decide to manufacture the manipulatives yourself, no supplies more complicated than Magic Markers, index cards, posterboard, scissors, and tape are needed. Or you can buy a beautiful set of colorful, laminated manipulatives for *Keyboard Capers.* It takes quite a while to make the manipulatives from scratch, so I'd suggest buying the prefabbed set if you're strapped for time.

Praise Hymn
God Made Music Student Book, each grade, $4.98 retail/$2.98 wholesale. Teacher's Manual, each grade, $9.98/$5.98, except Kindermusic Teacher's Manual, which is $14.98/$8.98. Student Songbook, each grade, $4.98/$2.98. *Sing-A-Long Cassette,* each grade, $9.98/$5.98. Home schoolers who prepay are eligible for wholesale rates. Add $2 shipping.

Christian music-reading instruction. Praise Hymn's bag of tricks includes:

• The *God Made Music* series (K-7), with accompanying Teacher's Manuals for K-6 (the grade 7 book can be studied alone or with an instructor). For K-2, the instructor may have only a limited musical background; for grades 3-7, the instructor needs to understand basic music concepts. This is a much more complete musical program than *Your Musical Friends,* covering band instrument recognition, songs to be learned by heart, classical music introduction (with the recommended selections available on correlated records and cassettes), music styles, Old and New Testament music, and lots more. Of course, this also requires a deeper commitment on the part of both parent and child.

• *We Sing Music* songbooks and cassettes are a collection of American heritage and fun songs to be used with *God Made Music* or alone. This is a completely different series than the *Wee Sing* series from Price/Stern/Sloan, in spite of the similar format and name.

• *Music Invaders* , designed for junior highs (but usable by motivated elementary-age home schoolers), is 24 twenty-minute lessons designed to teach vocal music reading with a "space invaders" theme. It was designed for junior high choirs. You will need the accompanying Teacher's Manual.

• The *Hymnplayer* series teaches how to play hymns (surprise!) on the piano. The series has three books for each section: Beginning Hymnplayer, Primary Hymnplayer, Intermediate Hymnplayer, and Advanced Hymnplayer.

• And for those of us who get behind the idea of a home school marching band, the *Christian School Band Method* series has children learning to play hymns and gospel songs while they learn to play their: flutes, clarinets, alto saxes, trumpets, trombones, and basses.

• Plus correlated filmstrips, classical records and cassettes, felt board and music symbols, and an Instruments Picture Poster.

MUSIC READING FOR ADULTS

NEW★★
Davidsons Music
How to Read Music, $7.95. Shipping extra.

Davidsons Music has been around for years and years. It is a publisher of simply-produced how-to-play music books, all written by music teacher Madonna Woods, and generally aimed at nice middle-aged or older Christian people who have "always wanted to learn to play the piano or organ someday," or who want to upgrade their music-playing skills.
How to Read Music is Davidson's book that "reduces music reading to its simplest form." From the catalog description:

> You learn to read treble clef and professional secrets on how to remember your notes. You're shown a short cut to learning bass clef notes. Rhythm is explained in an easy to understand way. You learn time values of notes and how to tell how many beats the different notes get. Time signatures are explained and you are shown how to count.

The various key signatures also are explained, showing you how to tell what sharps and flats to use. . . . Everything clearly illustrated.

I got a copy of this 8 ½ x 11" booklet and can tell you that the catalog description is right-on. Madonna Woods is a truly excellent teacher. Everything is presented step by step with lots of explanation and encouragement. You feel like you are taking personal music lessons with an unhurried, traditional teacher. She not only explains how to read music, starting with the clefs and the notes, but tells you how to maximize your learning—what new concepts you should study and restudy, for example. I surely wish *my* music theory teacher had urged me to take the time to be perfect at locating the individual notes, like Madonna Woods does, before pressing on to more complicated things. Recommended.

Jeffrey Norton
Learning to Read Music, 80-minute cassette and booklet, $14.95. Shipping extra.

A self-instructional course. *Learning to Read Music* covers all the basics in only an hour and a half. Pitch. Duration. Rhythm. Note heads. Rests. Dotted notes. Clefs. Sharps and flats. Key signatures. Naturals. Repeats. Other musical symbols and terms. The little booklet *shows* what the cassette *describes,* plus providing some reinforcement exercises. A total beginner would want to listen through several times; a rusty adult wanting to brush up might only need to go through this once. Any wide-awake and motivated person, no matter how young, could pick up a lot of musical notation through this inexpensive course.

MUSIC-READING GAMES

NEW★★
Harlan Enterprises
Games, $2.99 each. Buy four and get one free.

Harlan Enterprises publishes a vast array of simple match-the-cards drill games. Their *Music Fun* matches notes on the treble and bass clefs to their names—a simple application at a basic price. For a more detailed description of how these games work, see the Supplemental & Drill chapter.

NEW**
Rhythm Band, Inc.
Galaxy Games vary in price from $9 to $12.25. Complete set of 13 games, $124. *Fun with Music Symbols*, $7.95. *Pulse*, $12.50. *Music Bingo*, $13.50.

Rhythm Band is the place for music-reading games! Let's see how well I can distill down for you the four pages of their catalog devoted to these items.

First, Galaxy Games. Each game has the same packaging. You get a laminated game sheet, playing pieces, and answer sheet, all in a mailing tube. We tried the *Rhythm Review* game and found it to be a simple, useful review of note values. You roll dice to move along a path. Land on a note or rest and say its name. If you can't, you go back to your previous position. First to arrive at "Fine" wins! Only gripe: I wonder why the game drilled us on eighth- and quarter-note rests, but not on whole or half-note rests.

Games in this series are not all played the same way. I can tell from looking at the catalog that some are strategy games or card games while others are follow-the-path games like *Rhythm Review*. Some are for beginners, others are for advanced students. Other games in the set include:

- *Blast Off*. A two-person card game that teaches treble clef, bass clef, note and rest values, three types of chords, and notes of major triads.

- *Stu Stegasurus* for second- and third-graders teaches note values and other musical signs. Dinosaur theme.

- *Treble Trek*. Move along a path designed like a giant treble clef while practicing treble clef notes, dynamic markings, and note values.

- *"Bass" Ball*. Lines and spaces of bass clef. Cards for this game are "written in baseball language," whatever that means.

- *Soccer Saga* is another move-along-the-path game. Note values and I, IV, and V chords in the keys of C, F, and G.

- *Mixed-Up Metronome*. Musical tempo markings.

- *Satellite Sentinel*. Major and minor key signatures in the circle of fifths.

- *Advanced Blast Off*. Major and minor key signatures, musical terms, alto, bass, and treble clefs.

- *Music Match*. Recognize note combos that add up to a measure of music. Four different time signatures.

- *Rhythm Rummy*. Special 54-card deck of plastic-coated playing cards bearing note values. Large playing board marked off in several time signatures. Form complete measures from chance assortments of note values. For advanced students and adults. *Rhythm Rummy Limited* is a simplified version not requiring a game board. The limited version is not included in the set price.

- *Meter Maze*. Relationships of note and rest values.

- *Instrument Music Match*. Classify instruments as string, woodwind, brass, or percussion. Strategy game.

Fun with Music Symbols is an entirely different type of game invented by the wife of Rhythm Band's founder, Mrs. Laura Bergin. Hang up the white foamy fabric sheet on the wall. On it is printed a target; on the target are printed 16 note values, rests, and other musical symbols. Heave a velcro ball at the target. Call out the name of the musical symbol it hits and get five points. Any number can play. Lots of fun, inexpensive.

Pulse and *Music Bingo* are both bingo games. Pulse is the "rhythm bingo game." Apparently a leader claps or counts out a pattern, which students try to find on their bingo cards. For two to eight players or teams. *Music Bingo* more prosaically drills names, descriptions, and uses or music symbols. For two to 36 players.

MUSIC-TEACHING ACCESSORIES

Rainfall, Inc.
Piano Play-Book, $12.99.

Really cute way to introduce single-note keyboard playing. Rainfall's *Piano Play-Book* combines a color-coded electronic keyboard that really plays with a hard-bound book of 11 best-loved Bible songs. Each song is laid out with both traditional music notation and color codes, so even a three-year-old could play the tunes, if so inclined. Happy pictures and words to every tune round this out. Batteries are replaceable and the book is surprisingly tough. A real bargain at the price.

NEW**
Rhythm Band
Velcro double staff board, $125. Accessories for board, $35. Easel, $49.50, is adjustable for either floor or table-top use. Giant staff paper, $3.75 for a 25-page pad. "Re-Markable" music writing board, $5.50.

You ain't never seen nuttin' like this before . . . Sunday school teachers, children's choir leaders, and music teachers everywhere, take note. Here is your ultimate teaching aid: a three-foot-wide and foot-and-a-half-high cloth board with aluminum frame. On this board you can stick Velcro musical symbols. Included with the board are 16 quarter notes, 20 bar lines (bar lines divide measures in a composition), 25 ledger lines (these are the lines used above or below the musical staff), two grand staff lines, two treble clef signs, two bass clef signs, one keyboard window, 24 disc-notes (red, yellow, and blue), and a two-compartment storage bin. If that's not enough, you can get a separate accessories set including 10 each of sharps and flats, five naturals, eight meter numerals, four breath marks, six ties, one fermatta, and a five-section storage bin. Rhythm Band will also sell you the easel on which to prop this marvelous teaching device, if needed.

If this is a bit rich for your blood, Rhythm Band has giant 11 x 17" pads pre-ruled with two staffs on each page. If the pad isn't flashy enough, how about the "Re-Markable" music writing board, an 11 x 14" Grand Staff board suitable for use with erasable markers or wipe-off crayons?

Rhythm Band also has an extensive series of music flashcards. These are being revamped as I write to you. The new sets will be made of plastic for added durability. Rhythm Band will also be adding a line of "Music-touch" flashcards with the name of each music symbol in Braille.

Rhythm Band also has old-fashioned chalk-holding staff liners, metronomes of both the key-wound and electronic persuasions, pitchpipes, and all those other widgets without which music teachers cannot function. One-stop shopping.

NEW**
TREND enterprises, Inc.
All bulletin board sets, $5.99 each, come with free Discovery Guide. Require 4 x 6' bulletin board.

Teach music reading from your bulletin board with TREND's colorful *Discover Music* bulletin-board kit. The six visual aids include:

• "Musical Alphabet," showing the letters of the scales on both clefs

• "Rhythm," in which a kindly tiger explains the notes and rests

• "Written Music Tells" explains how written music is used to convey pitch, time value, rhythm, and expression

• "Time Signatures"

• "Musical Symbols & Words"

• A visual explaining the difference between the bass and treble clefs.

Plus you get a "Discover Music" caption and a Discovery Guide. The latter contains background information on all aspects of written music, nine simple educational activities, and a reproducible matching exercise to test your students' knowledge of musical terminology.

MUSIC SOFTWARE

The following excellent programs are written up in detail in the Educational Software Buyer's Guide in Volume 3, where you'll also find the names and addresses of their publishers. I simply mention them here in case you don't have Volume 3, so you can track them down on your own in computer magazines or at the local software store, or get them from the *Coda* catalog (see below).

For the Apple family:
• EduSoft's *Magic Piano*
• Great Wave Software's *KidsTime II*
• Wenger Corporation's *Music Class*

For the Macintosh:
• Ars Nova's *Practica Musica*
• CTM Development, Inc.'s *Listen*
• Electronic Arts *Deluxe Music Construction Set*
• Great Wave Software's *KidsTime* and *Concert-Ware+*

For IBM and compatibles:
• University of Delaware's *GuidoMusic Learning System*

Wenger Corporation/Music Learning Division
Coda catalog, $4. Worth it.

Don't waste your time wandering all over the woods looking for music software, MIDI interfaces, books, and accessories. The gorgeous Coda catalog from Wenger has it all. Really. For Apple II family, Commodore 64 and 128, Macintoshes of all sorts, IBM PC (and PCjr, XT, AT, and compatibles), Atari 8-Bit and ST, and Amiga. Did we forget anyone? I don't think so.

What you see is more than you expect to get. The catalog is a work of art. Printed on highest quality paper, illumined like a cross between a medieval manuscript and an Art Nouveau clip-art book. Colorful. Beautiful. Thorough product descriptions. Every bit of music software I review, plus about a thousand music items I don't review, is in this catalog. Really.

CHAPTER SIX

MUSIC COURSES FOR JUST ABOUT EVERY INSTRUMENT

Some of us have suffered at the hands of piano teachers. As a result, we cast a jaded eye on the prospect of teaching or learning music at home, or anywhere else.

Fear not! This chapter is mostly free from the musical exercises Miss Grump tried to force your sweaty fingers through. Yes, some music teachers still make scale exercises and theory the meat of their diet, but they are fewer and farther between.

Let me explain that I'm not down on playing scales or learning music theory. Scales and finger exercises are good for developing agility, and music theory provides one sort of framework for the art. It's just that people take music lessons to learn to play an instrument, not to learn *about* playing an instrument. I myself quit taking piano lessons when my teacher refused to let me attempt Tchaikovsky's *Nutcracker Suite*, condemning me instead to more weary months of Bartok piano exercises. I liked Tchaikovsky; I was familiar with the music—unlike Bartok's, which always sounded to my youthful ears like a mistake. So why didn't my teacher let me try it?

That question propels us into a hot debate among music teachers. Do people learn music best by proceeding step by cautious step and not being allowed to try advanced pieces until they have been taught how to play them? Another issue: Is it a good idea to concentrate on learning pieces you have never heard? One

more question: Is it best to learn theory before, during, or after having mastered elementary playing techniques?

It is a good idea to become familiar with how a particular piece sounds before trying to play it yourself. Listening to music builds up your "data" on which your musical knowledge will be based. It would also be a good idea to mess about on the instrument before settling down to serious learning. Playing provides tactile data—you discover what movement makes what sound. Sight reading, a highly refined skill, would follow playing by ear in this view. You'd want to get a "feel" for the instrument and for music in general before attempting to delve into the complexities of music notation and theory.

Part (not all) of the musical approach outlined above is the famous Suzuki method. Shinichi Suzuki, a Japanese man, developed a method of music instruction that begins by exposing the student to lots of good music—in fact, the very pieces he will learn to play. Once he has become thoroughly familiar with these pieces, he is allowed to begin lessons. Music theory is only introduced after the student has already been playing for some time.

Mr. Suzuki has some other ideas as well. Children's parents are present for all lessons, and are encouraged to learn along with the children. Students also spend some time in group lessons and recitals, where they get to hear musicians of various ages and skill levels play. This gives them a taste of what they can look forward to accomplishing, as well as getting them used to playing before a friendly audience. All is ideally done in a spirit of helping and comradeship. Using this method, very young children have demonstrated amazing musicianship.

True, Suzuki follows the "mastery learning" approach of forbidding children to tackle anything new until the old is thoroughly learned. And controversy swirls about the questions of how much and if and when parents should make children practice, an issue over which Suzuki teachers have split. But access to an instrument of the right size; a wide mental library of good music; the support of other musicians and the encouragement of one's family; putting off academic studies until the student can see the need for them—these old-fashioned ideas, so well proven in the lives of musicians like Mozart and Bach, are again gaining ground.

Another big name in music instruction is Zoltan Kodaly, a Hungarian man. Kodaly was vitally interested in singing as the best introduction to music of all kinds. As Laszlo Eosze relates in *Zoltan Kodaly: His Life and Work* (Crescendo Publishing Company, 1962),

> "That the teaching of music is best begun with singing," he writes, "that it is through singing, and before ever touching an instrument, that the child should learn to read music, are recognized as truths by a good many people . . . Mechanical training in instrumental playing, without corresponding theoretical education; music-making with the fingers instead of the soul; the omission of any thorough musical grounding; and neglect of solfeggio—these are the direct causes of the present decadence of singing and of the increasing number of second-rate professional musicians . . ."

Kodaly's great desire was to revive solfeggio, the art of being able to recognize notes and intervals by ear in any key and sing them. We are familiar with this as Do-Re-Mi-Fa-Sol-La-Ti-Do style singing. In this way, the student would be able to pick up a score of music, once trained in sight reading, and hear it in his head. He would also be able to translate music into staff notation, and duplicate it by ear in his instrument.

Kodaly was also a champion of Early Childhood Music Education. He deplored the use of the piano in teaching songs and choral music as a (possibly untuned) crutch that prevented children from appreciating pure, virginal melody. Kodaly was active in encouraging music societies and choral singing, writing a number of volumes of choral exercises for young people. He also worked on popularizing the pentatonic scale, in an attempt to revive a national Hungarian musical consciousness.

Suzuki has been popularized for the family music market much more than Kodaly. This can perhaps be attributed to Suzuki's firm insistence that parents spend time with their children during music lessons and practice. In today's society, this is one of the few excuses for family togetherness left for upscale parents! *Any* educational method which brings parents and children together unleashes dynamic possibilities far beyond the lessons' content.

Take Suzuki's stress on exposing the student to lots of good music and a supportive atmosphere. Mix in Kodaly's singing and solfeggio training. Add the common-sense idea that music is for *playing* and *enjoying,* not for showing off. What do you get? The family that plays together . . .

Who ever said learning to play music was just for kids, anyway? If you want to be a concert star, perhaps it helps to start practicing two hours a day at the age of four. But if you want to *play,* the time to start is now!

In this chapter, you will find basic and advanced courses of musical instruction for different kinds of instruments. Check out the instrument that interests you, and see the many innovative music-learning approaches available today, from music video to

BASIC MUSIC THEORY

NEW**
American Institute of Music
Preliminary Rudiments Course, Grade I Rudiments, Grade II Rudiments, $95 each. One-time registration fee for new students, $14.95. Grade III and IV History, $149.95 each. Grade V History (Mahler through Modern Music), $54.95. Textbook, *The Enjoyment of Music, fifth edition* used for all history courses, $32.95. Grades III and IV Harmony are each $152.95, or $85 for individual halves of these courses. Grade IV Counterpoint is $152.95 plus $8.95 for the workbook. Piano Pedagogy Level I, $239.95 plus $23.95 for textbook. Individual lesson units available for the Rudiments and Harmony courses.

AIM is the U.S. branch of the Tritone Music Group, a private music school based in Toronto, Canada that since 1977 has been providing correspondence courses for students preparing to take the written exams of the major Canadian conservatories. Complete courses range in price from $75 to $239.95, which includes any needed supplementary work. This is a good deal compared to other correspondence schools which charge by the lesson, often costing a lot more.

AIM is accredited by the National Home Study Council, and its Target Learning courses qualify for college credit in America. These include Rudiments courses (beginning to advanced music theory), two levels of Harmony, one of Counterpoint, and several of Music History. Plus, AIM offers a "Piano Pedagogy" course for aspiring piano teachers. Please keep in mind that the grade levels are *Conservatory* grade levels, not elementary school grade levels!

These are *correspondence courses,* not just home study courses, so you send in your homework to be corrected and returned to you. AIM lets you work at your own pace, with no deadlines for work completion. If you don't "get" a particular lesson, you will receive additional explanations and supplementary exercises at no charge. Partial refunds are available until the point where you have completed more than half of any course—with a 100% refund if you cancel within five days of receiving your course.

When enrolling, you are asked to fill out a placement quiz, to make sure you are starting at the right level. This is very helpful. You also receive detailed descriptions of each course that includes a complete course outline—also helpful.

I must say that the courses look absolutely fascinating. Keep in mind that these are designed for mature learners—high school and adult—not for young children. Also, the Piano Pedagogy course has several segments promoting the unbiblical "behaviorism" theory of learning. (If you wonder why behaviorism is unbiblical, read Ruth Beechick's *Biblical Psychology of Learning* or my own *Schoolproof!*) Aside from these caveats, what you get (as far as I can tell without actually taking a course) is thorough, easy-to-follow instruction in subjects that many people have found difficult to study on their own, and that you would have to travel long distances (in many cases) to take at a good on-site school.

NEW**
Homespun Tapes
Understanding the Language of Music, tapes 1 and 2, $12.95 each. $65 for the entire 6-tape set. Shipping extra.

Wanna know musical lingo? Wanna know why marches are written in major keys, never in minor?

Wanna stop getting confused about sharps and flats, chords and rhythm? Then perhaps concert pianist *cum* composer Daniel Abrams can help.

Homespun's complete *Understanding the Language of Music* series tackles both music theory and music history. The music history part I have written up separately under the heading, appropriately enough, of Music History. Here's the dope on the music theory part.

WHAT YOU GET: Two audio cassettes, 60 minutes each. Tape 1 is basics of music theory. This is really basic: major and minor scales, intervals, key signatures, sharps/flats/naturals, chords and progressions, and arpeggios. Why major keys sound happy and minor keys sound sad. Lots of discussion of whole and half steps. Better keep the handout in front of you, or this will get confusing. Tape 2 is how music is put together. The place of the I, IV, and V chords in blues, rock, and classical. Seventh chords. Dominant chords. Inversions. Rhythm. Time signatures. Syncopation. Dynamics (playing loudly or softly) and interpretation (subtleties of timing). Plus a history of orchestra instruments.

This introduction to music consciousness is certainly user-friendly. Not terribly time-consuming or expensive, either. Wish Homespun provided more written matter to accompany it, though; the few pages of definitions are not really enough to help a novice become comfortable with all the new terminology.

MUSICIANSHIP

NEW**
Davidsons Music
Cassette/booklet courses, most $12.95 plus shipping.

Musicianship cassette/booklet courses for fairly novice pianists and organists. Some titles available: *How to Play Fills and Runs, How to Play Intros and End-*

ings, *Improvising in Chord Accompaniments.* Plus Madonna Woods' largish selection of courses on playing keyboard instruments by ear. These are all very unpretentious—photocopy quality—but have more solid meat per page, presented more simply, than I have seen anywhere else. Look into it!

NEW**
Homespun Tapes
All audio tapes come with tablature or music booklets. 60-minute single tapes, $14.95. 90-minute single tapes, $19.95. Three-tape series, $37.50. Six-tape series, $69.95. Video cassettes, $49.95. Shipping extra.

Homespun, as befits a company started by professional musicians, has a number of courses stressing practical musicianship. Note first the excellent series on ear training. Matt Glaser does the honors, and I can't think of a better introduction to real musicianship for anyone mature enough to do the exercises. In other words, most five-year-olds won't dig it, but Mozart would have. Consider also *The Homespun Songwriter's Workshop,* a little six-cassette-tape number featuring tips of the trade from notable songwriters Pat Alger, Fred Koller, Steve Gillette, Eric Kaz, and John D. Loudermilk. This set takes you from the moment of inspiration (and how to hurry it along) to putting together a finished demo. Plus Daniel Abrams's cassette and booklet on practice techniques for all musicians and Matt Glaser's three-tape series on developing your musical skills. Lots more: see the other Homespun Tapes listings in this chapter.

PIANO

NEW**
Davidsons Music
Most courses are $10.95 for the book or cassette or $12.95 and up for the full course (both book and cassette). *Play Gospel Songs by Ear,* $20.95 for each full course (specify piano or organ), or $10.95 per course for either book or cassette. *How to Play Gospel Music,* same prices. *Fills and Runs by Ear,* $14.95 for cassette and book. Shipping extra.

Large newsprint catalog loaded with learn-to-play courses. Keyboard instruments are most strongly represented here. Most courses are by Madonna Woods, a lady who has pioneered her own method for learning to play by ear.

Some notable courses in this catalog:

• *Play Gospel Songs by Ear,* a two-course program that teaches you to play the melody line in the right hand and accompany yourself with chords in the left hand. Courses are available for either piano or organ. Uses note names instead of music notation, for the benefit of those who neither know nor want to know how to read standard music. Really good instructional method tells you how to find the right starting notes for the song in the key of C, learn additional keys, add chording, and dress up your playing with some easy tricks. That was all in Course One; Course Two goes on to more advanced stuff. The cassette follows the book's general format but adds additional explanations, and of course it has the musical examples played out for you. All you need to learn to play by ear is to be able to hum a tune!

• *How to Play Gospel Music* starts with a mini how-to-read-music course. Its 20 lessons, designed for both organ and piano, take you all the way through chording, filling out your right hand with 3rds and 6ths, runs, "evangelistic" playing techniques such as cross hands, walking basses, and intros and endings. It uses standard music notation. This is the best-looking Davidsons Music book I have seen, with a glossy cover and professionally-printed pages.

• If that sounded a little tame, Madonna also offers a new course, *Fills and Run by Ear,* that explains how to add walking bass line, alternative basses, chord runs, cross hands playing, right hand fills, grace notes, and different rhythms. Other advanced material includes *Learn Chords for Piano, Organ, and Electronic Keyboard, How to Play Intros and Endings, How to Accompany,* and lots more.

• Several books of *Playing in Church by Ear,* simple arrangements of popular gospel songs written with note and chord names. *Playing in Church* is the same material in standard musical notation. Each also has instructions about music and playing to improve your church piano or organ playing. Also courses on Southern Gospel style playing and evangelistic style piano.

• *Easy Adult Piano* is a three-part method that includes keyboard stickers with note names, chord charts, quizzes, and explanations of eighth, sixteenth, and dotted notes and many musical terms.

• *Home Music Lessons* shows how to set up a music-teaching business from your home. Detailed.

Songbooks include both Christian and pop music. Also available: Electronic keyboard courses. Piano courses for children from different publishers. Chord guitar courses. Learning Unlimited guitar series. Mel Bay Modern Method courses. The "Fun With" series for over two dozen different instruments that is supposed to give you a taste of each.

Intermediate and advanced courses are also available, as is a large selection of easy songbooks in both play-by-ear and standard notations.

Holt Associates

John Holt was not only a major voice in the home school movement, but also an amateur musician. Unlike many others, he believed that it's *Never Too Late* to begin learning music, and he published his musical biography under that title. Holt Associates sells the book, which contains valuable insights on the subject of music instruction from the viewpoint of an empirical thinker. Holt Associates, although primarily the publisher of *Growing Without Schooling* and a vendor of materials for alternative education, also carries a select line of music counter-culture: books like *How to Learn the Piano Despite Years of Lessons* and *Mrs. Stewart's Piano Method.* The latter encourages beginners to roam

over the entire keyboard by applying solfeggio principles to instrument playing. Here's a different view of music: music for the people instead of music for the snobs.

NEW**
Homespun Tapes
Put Your Hands on the Piano and Play!, $69.95. *Play Your Favorite Piano Classics,* $69.95. Other audio tape sets, also $69.95. Videotapes, $49.95 each. Shipping extra.

For total beginners, concert pianist Daniel Abrams has produced a six-tape series that takes you step by step from finding what's what on the keyboard to playing slow blues, diminished chords, and unusual rhythms. *Put Your Hands on the Piano and Play!* includes "beautiful" (as opposed to rowdy) piano pieces in all styles, from classical to pop and blues. You start off slowly with major and minor scales. Plan on working through each tape several times to capture all the information.

Once you've progressed beyond the greenhorn stage, you can add to your piano technique while learning to play pieces by the great classical composers. *Play Your Favorite Piano Classics* includes music scores by Haydn, Bach, Beethoven, Dvorak and others in a spiral-bound book tucked into the cassette album. Daniel Abrams talks you through each piece on the included audio tapes, pointing out potential trouble spots and giving hints to make your playing more exciting. He also plays each selection, so you can hear what it sounds like. If you're really feeling brave, you can play along with the tape, since pieces are separated into left and right channels.

Homespun also has rock and jazz piano courses, plus New Orleans and ragtime piano courses. These are available in audio or video versions. I admit that I've flubbed around with David Cohen's *Beginning Blues Piano* audio tape, and found I could actually follow it. (Whether I *want* to play blues is another question—reviewers have to take what they're given!)

Jeffrey Norton
Key to the Keys: Volume 1 (one cassette and instruction book), $15.95; Volume 2 (two cassettes and instruction book), $21.95. Both volumes, $35. Shipping extra.

Key to the Keys is a self-taught piano method that begins with chords and gets you playing before you learn to read notes. You start with short familiar melodies and advance to more complex songs and musical compositions. So says the brochure.

VIOLIN FAMILY

Ability Development

"The Suzuki Place." Violin books, music, strings, cassettes, and accessories. Ability Development stocks an outstanding array of books about music, including of course all of Suzuki's books and many books about the Suzuki method. I found about a hundred dollars' worth of books I wanted just by glancing through their catalog.

To make your shopping easier, Ability Development has prepared several "Book Packs" for Suzuki beginners. These include essential books for understanding Suzuki.

Ability Development has Suzuki series for violin, viola, cello, and flute, plus all necessary accessories.

If you're serious about music, this is a catalog not to miss.

NEW★★
Homespun Tapes
All audio tapes come with tablature or music booklets. 60-minute single tapes, $14.95. 90-minute single tapes, $19.95. Three-tape series, $37.50. Six-tape series, $69.95. Video cassettes, $49.95. Shipping extra.

Violins mutate into fiddles when you're looking at Homespun's music courses. Audio series include *Bluegrass and Country Fiddle,* taught by Kenny Kosek; *Texas and Swing Fiddle Styles,* taught by Matt Glaser; *Irish Fiddle,* with Kevin Burke; *Learn the Real Cajun Fiddle,* with Michael Doucet; and *Improvising Violin,* which has nothing to do with classical violin, by Julie Lynn Liebermann. Homespun fiddle videos are *Learning Bluegrass Fiddle* from Kenny Kosek and *Contest Fiddling, Championship Style* by Mark O'Connor. More new titles all the time; send for latest newsprint catalog.

Shar Products

Shar sells the Children's Music Series by Evelyn Bedient Avsharian. This contains workbooks and games for teaching music reading by several innovative methods, plus fun and easy songs. Example: the *Mississippi Hot Dog Lonely Hamburger Band* is said to include "exciting pieces on A alone, E alone, and both strings. Duets and rounds in two basic Twinkle rhythms." Clever of them to make playing one string exciting.

Shar's listing of sheet music for string players and records and cassettes of string music is as complete as you can reasonably expect. Plus a large selection of hard-to-find video-cassettes of great string players and teachers, writers, artists, opera, and ballet. You will probably want to send for this no-frills catalog.

Summy-Birchard, Inc.

Suzuki™ Method International, a division of Summy-Birchard, Inc., is the sole publisher of the Suzuki method for the world outside Japan. They distribute the core music books and recordings for the Suzuki Piano School, Violin School, Viola School, Cello School, Flute School, and Harp School. In addition they carry supplementary material (both music and texts) for the Suzuki Method. Your local music dealer can order direct from Summy-Birchard, Inc.

Summy-Birchard Music, another division of Summy-Birchard, Inc., carries other educational music methods/texts (e.g., Frances Clark® Piano Method).

GUITAR FOR KIDS

Alexandria House
Learning to Play the Guitar for Jesus, complete course $14.95 (item #SA0101).

This is a *wonderful* course! You start by learning how to tune your guitar and end up after 13 lessons knowing the primary chords in six keys (the keys of C, G, D, A, E, and F), plus learning simple music theory and several accompaniment styles.

Based entirely on familiar Christian songs, *Learning to Play the Guitar for Jesus* is ministry-oriented as well as educationally excellent. The instructions and diagrams couldn't be clearer. Every lesson goes step by step. Hints and suggestions are highlighted in separate boxes.

Even the packaging of this course couldn't be nicer. You get a specially-designed three-color ring binder containing your lessons and a cassette practice tape. This binder is designed to stand upright when set on a desk or table—no music stand needed!

NEW**
Chroma Corporation
Learning Kit, $19.95. Book Two and cassette, $14.95. Chroma Coded nylon guitar strings, $6.95. Chroma custom acoustic guitar, $89.95. Chroma custom electric guitar, $99.95. Shipping extra.

This is revolutionary. The Chroma guitar-learning system just about eliminates the high dropout rate of kids just learning to play guitar. Eighty-five percent of beginners drop the guitar within the first three months. With Chroma, 92 percent are still playing by the end of the first year.

Invented by Howard Roberts, the man *Guitar Player* magazine has called "the most listened-to guitarist of this century," the Chroma approach uses an innovative system of color-coded frets and strings *and* a method based on teaching children to play melodies *before* they learn chords. Why? Because, as studies at the University of Southern California have shown, children up to the ages of approximately 10 to 12 years old simply aren't able to handle the sounds of three or four notes at once. However, using Chroma, public school classes have put on concerts of four-part Bach concertos.

If you already have a steel-string guitar, you need the Chroma Learning Kit. This includes *Chroma Learning Book One*, the *Play and Sing Along* booklet, finger/fret tabs, coded string labels to stick over the nut of your guitar, and an audio training cassette. Book 1's 12 lessons introduce the basics of melody and rhythm, plus a few ultra-simple chords, while teaching the student how to play familiar songs. The *Play and Sing Along* booklet has lyrics and chords for all those songs.

If you already have a classical (nylon-string style) guitar, you'll need the color-coded nylon guitar strings.

If you don't have a guitar, Howard Roberts has designed two one-size-fits-all guitars especially engineered for ease of learning for all ages. The electric guitar can be plugged right into your home stereo system for extra oomph. The sound's OK, and the price is definitely right. Both guitars come with a free Learning Kit and color-coded strings.

And if you're wondering why you've never heard of Howard Roberts before this—it's because they don't normally highlight the name of the musicians who lay down the sound tracks for movies, motion pictures, and TV, or who do background for singers like Elvis Presley, Ray Charles, and Frank Sinatra. Howard has performed on literally thousands of recordings that you hear every day, as well as recording nearly two dozen LPs under his own name, authoring several method books for adults, designing guitars for Gibson, and co-founding the Guitar Institute of Technology (now Musicians Institute).

Howard tells me that the Chroma system will eventually take a child straight from his first tentative strums through the most advanced techniques. Two books are now available, with more to follow. (I'm looking at a rough draft of one of these, *Exploring the Fingerboard,* as I write this.) Write for the latest brochure.

NEW**
Davidsons Music

Source for several books and videos on children's guitar that I haven't seen elsewhere. I didn't have time to review them, but the rest of Davidsons' selection is excellent, so why not check these out?

NEW**
Homespun Tapes
Kids' Guitar, $39.95. 90-minute video. Adult music lesson videos, $49.95 each. Shipping extra.

Marcy Marxer, a well-known performer of children's music, teaches this hour-and-a-half video course of guitar basics for kids. *Kids' Guitar* follows the traditional method of starting with tuning and easy chords, and proceeds to simple children's songs. Marcy is cheerful and easy to follow. She also is well aware of the usual pitfalls of early guitar learning, and helps you avoid them. Good competent guitar lessons—nothing glitzy or unexpected. Course comes with booklet of song chords and lyrics.

Homespun also has a wide assortment of video lessons for adults taught by well-known artists. We're talking the likes of Dr. John, John Sebastian, and Amos Garrett. Instruments covered are acoustic and electric guitar (from basic to advanced), dobro, fiddle, bass, banjo, keyboards, mandolin, autoharp, dulcimer, and flutes of the Andes. These are all recorded on good-quality tape, unlike the cheap stuff some other companies use. This not only helps save your VCR from getting chewed up, but enables you to actually hear the music without strain.

Homespun Tapes, both audio and visual, have an cheerful energy and affability that makes learning from them really fun. You know you're being taught by real musicians who enjoy their work, not by time-serving "educators" who think music is good for you. The tapes are supremely non-threatening. Homespun's teaching musicians typically wear something comfortable, and the set itself often is a room in Homespun founder Happy Traum's house. It's like stepping out to the front porch and asking Artie Traum, who happens to be sitting there, "Hey, how about showing us some of your cool chord progressions?"

FRETTED/FOLK INSTRUMENTS

Homespun Tapes
All audio tapes come with tablature or music booklets. 60-minute single tapes, $14.95. 90-minute single tapes, $19.95. Three-tape series, $37.50. Six-tape series, $69.95. Video cassettes, $49.95. Shipping extra.

If I told you how much I like Homespun Tapes, you'd think I was exaggerating. So let's stick to bare facts. Here is a company run by professional musicians that sells music instruction tapes produced by themselves and other professional musicians. Styles covered are folk, blues, rock, bluegrass, country, and jazz. The instruction is mellow and familiar and you can rerun

the tape any time you want. Along with the tapes come printed matter giving the music scores and perhaps some explanatory notes. It's like having a private lesson with one of the best musicians in the country, and you can repeat the lesson as many times as you like!

Who teaches the courses? Here's some examples: Livingston Taylor on "Hit Guitar Styles," Amos Garrett (several series, including "Electric Guitar"), and Lorraine Lee on "Appalachian Dulcimer." These are top musicians, folks, and you couldn't get a private lesson of this quality if you signed up and waited for a year, let alone one that costs less than $7.

In all, there are 66 different series as of this writing, most consisting of more than one tape. Aspiring musicians will find Homespun a feast.

Mandolin Brothers, Ltd.

Instruction books for every fretted instrument you can think of: dulcimer, fiddle, cello, acoustic bass, violin, mandolin, autoharp, banjo, guitar, and bass guitar. Large selection. Not to mention the huge selection of instruments, accessories, and songbooks mentioned in the next section.

NEW**
Rhythm Band, Inc.
Songbooks, $3 each. *Happy Strumming*, $3. *Complete Method for ChromAharP*, $9.95.

A word about the "autoharp" and the "ChromAharP." These are the same type of instrument, but manufactured by different companies. "Autoharp" is a brand name of the Oscar Schmidt company, while "ChromAharP" is a brand name of Rhythm Band, Inc. People tend to use the word "autoharp" for all the instruments in this category, mainly because Oscar Schmidt was the first large manufacturer, just as we tend to call all nose tissue "Kleenex" and all photocopies "xeroxes." Whatever. Both these instruments are chorded zithers—more on them in the Music Instruments chapter.

Rhythm Band has lots of music books with familiar songs in chord notation for your budding autoharpist/chromaharpist. We enjoy their *Favorite Hymns, Hymns of Faith, and Gospel Favorites* books. For instructions in how to play the instrument, your best bet is to start off with Dr. Howard Doolin's *Happy Strumming* and then go on to *Complete Method for ChromAharP*, a much larger book that starts with chord changes and simple strums but goes on to reveal many advanced techniques, e.g., banjo style picking and broken arpeggio strums. The latter is a Mel Bay production, and if you know anything about the huge Mel Bay series of how-to-play books, you'll realize that when Mel Bay mentions ChromAharP by name in the title of one of their books, this is a *popular* instrument.

WIND INSTRUMENTS

EDC Publishing
First Book of the Recorder, $6.95.

This Early Music book is 64 oversized, colorful pages. Friendly little colored Blob People give you a pile of information about music in general and how to play the recorder in particular.

NEW**
Loucks Music, Inc.
The Recorder Factory, book $3.95, book plus recorder $8.95. Add $3 shipping.

This is the best beginning recorder method I have seen. *The Recorder Factory* uses a step-by-step approach and lots of visual aids to teach well-known Christian songs, hymns, and choruses plus a few familiar folk tunes. Very easy to use. Covers the C scale plus F sharp, B flat, and high D. Book plus recorder is the least expensive introduction to actually playing music you are likely to find.

BAND INSTRUMENTS

NEW**
Loucks Music, Inc.
Jubilant Sound Band Method, levels 1 and 2. Instructor's guide/score, $14.95 each level. All instruments, $3.95 each level, except percussion, which is $4.95 each level. Add $3 shipping.

Band method for Christians. Tunes learned are familiar folk melodies and Christian songs, hymns, and choruses. King David appears here and there in these books, quoting Scripture and encouraging students to be diligent and pious. This leads to some humorous anachronisms, as when King David, who died almost 1000 years before the birth of Christ, talks about "our" heritage of Black American music.

Loucks Music has band method for C flute, B-flat clarinet and bass clarinet, E-flat alto sax and baritone sax, B-flat trumpet and cornet, French horn in F, trombone, baritone, bass and tuba, and percussion (SD/BD/mallets). The approach is melody-based; students are supposed to first sing the songs, then play them. This is easy enough, since all the tunes and lyrics are familiar.

Are these self-teaching books? No, they are not. But if you are already in a band, or taking lessons for a band instrument, they can be used for supplementary practice.

Also available: Sacred band music; sacred music for brass ensembles, woodwind ensembles, and string ensembles; and sacred instrumental solos.

Praise Hymn
Christian School Band Method: Flute, Clarinet, Trumpet, Trombone, $3.98 retail/$2.48 wholesale; Saxophone, Bass, $4.98/$2.98; Band Director, $14.98/$8.98. *Music Invaders*: Student Book $4.98/$2.98; Teacher's Manual, $9.98/$5.98. *Hymnplayer* series, each book $4.98/$2.98. Home school parents may receive the wholesale discount if order paid in advance. Add $2 shipping.

For those of us who get behind the idea of a home school marching band, the *Christian School Band Method* series has children learning to play hymns and gospel songs while they learn to play their: flutes, clarinets, alto saxes, trumpets, trombones, and basses.

Music Invaders, designed for junior high choir students (but usable by motivated elementary-age home schoolers), is 24 20-minute lessons designed to teach vocal music reading with a "space invaders" theme. You will need the accompanying Teacher's Manual.

The *Hymnplayer* series teaches how to play hymns (surprise!) on the piano. The series has three books for each section: Beginning Hymnplayer, Primary Hymnplayer, Intermediate Hymnplayer, and Advanced Hymnplayer.

VOICE AND UNUSUAL INSTRUMENTS

NEW★★
Homespun Tapes

All audio tapes come with tablature or music booklets. 60-minute single tapes, $14.95. 90-minute single tapes, $19.95. Three-tape series, $37.50. Six-tape series, $69.95. Video cassettes, $49.95. Shipping extra.

Homespun Tapes, besides its essential series on guitar, harmonica, bass, banjo, fiddle, autoharp, and piano, has a potpourri of courses on unusual instruments and techniques. We finally moved out of a two-family building with very near neighbors, and I bought the *Learn to Yodel* two-cassette series. It's a great way to call the kids (or the hogs!) home. More singing courses:

Singing for Tin Ears video is supposed to break down your inhibitions and help you sing in tune. *Learn to Sing Harmony* with our old friends Cathy Fink and Marcy Marxer, plus Robin and Linda Williams, has parts recorded on separate tracks for your practicing pleasure. You can get a pennywhistle (not for a penny, unhappily) to go with the *Irish Pennywhistle* three-tape set. Folksy types can latch on to a selection of Dulcimer courses, and weird ones can tackle something called "Dawg Mandolin." Homespun's new *How to Play Flutes of the Andes* video not only shows you how to play the pan pipes (*zampona*) and the *kena,* but as an option allows you to purchase both these instruments along with the video for a total price of $95. Optional accompanying workbook is $10.95 plus postage. More weird stuff added all the time; write for latest brochure.

CHAPTER SEVEN

MUSIC HISTORY AND APPRECIATION

I dig . . . Irish folk music, and I love to hear the steel bands play.
I think Haydn is the grooviest guy going down today.
And when the madrigal singing
Just sets my eardrums ringing
It's like a new beginning today (hey, hey).
(With all due apologies to Peter, Paul, and Mary)

In this complex world in which we live, sometimes we find ourselves at the health club. There I am always amazed to find that music comes in just one flavor—hard sex rock 'n roll. Except at Yuletide, when the strains of "Rudolph, the Red-Nosed Reindeer" waft through the hallowed halls of sweat, nothing surges out of the stereo system at my neighborhood Mademoiselle club except Madonna doing her usual impersonation of a sex-starved eight-year-old.

The underpaid teenagers who run this establishment are oblivious to any other musical possibilities. For them, the dial stops at KSHE, our local raunch 'n roll station whose mascot is a pig in dark sunglasses and whose programming exactly matches the personality of this mascot. Great lyrics like,

I wanna buy you
I wanna buy you
I wanna buy you
(grunt, grunt)

When Peter, Paul, and Mary sang, "I dig . . rock and roll music," it was clear that what they wanted to dig was a grave in which to bury the beast, or at least its most hoggish offspring.

Good idea, guys. Here's the shovel.

LEARNING ABOUT THE GREAT COMPOSERS

No, we're not going to learn about Prince or Frank Zappa or other modern decomposers. We come not to praise sleazers, but to bury them. Or, more properly, to ignore them altogether in favor of something better.

For anyone raised on modern music (any variety), the great music of the past has to become an acquired taste. It's like yogurt: the first time you try it, it tastes strange. I'm not going to pretend that I liked this kind of music the first time I heard it, or even the tenth time. It's too big, too important, too *intelligent*. You can't reduce it to one pat phrase and a mindless grunt-grunt, mere background for your self-actualizing in the foreground. You have to sip, savor, and digest this kind of music before becoming really comfortable with it, and anyone who pretends otherwise doesn't understand it at all.

So you don't have to try to pretend to me that you are familiar with all the musical greats from Bach to

Stravinsky, and I won't pretend to you that most of these names used to mean anything to me, either. Most of us were raised, at best, on the Tijuana Brass and Bob Dylan, not on Vivaldi's *concerto grossi*. Some of you are exceptions, I know; you are the kind of people who go to the opera and actually know what all that Italian warbling means. But for the rest of us, here are some fun resources that can fill in the holes in our backgrounds.

GAMES

NEW**
Aristoplay
The Game of Great Composers, $25.

Want to learn to match a composer to his period, the places he worked, and his major works? Want to learn something about European geography while you're doing it? *The Game of Great Composers* is an ambitious attempt to do all this for 32 of the Western world's greatest composers.

WHAT YOU GET: Game board, 32 Composer Cards, six Period Cards, 67 Travel Cards (includes three wild cards), 67 Works Cards (includes four wild cards), cassette tape with keyboard selections, playing tokens, dice, Great Composers Booklet, and instructions. Each Period Card has a brief summary of one of the six historical musical periods: Medieval, Renaissance, Baroque, Classical, Romantic, and Modern. Each Composer Card is a biographical sketch of one of the great composers, plus an abstract portrait of the composer apparently done with markers. Each Travel Card tells

you about some trip a composer took and his musical period, e.g.,

> Romantic
> Go to LEIPZIG with ROBERT SCHUMANN to study law before returning to study music with his future father-in-law.

Works Cards also are headed with a musical period, but focus on a composer's work. Example:

> Baroque
> You are the lucky student chosen to be soloist in the first performance of VIVALDI's "Violin Concerto in A Minor" from the collection called *L'Estro armonico* (Musical Fancy).

The instructions are clear as pea soup. Our children gave up after reading them! When Mom and Dad came to the rescue, things improved, but only slightly. It still took me another 20 minutes of struggling to figure the instructions out. To save you time when *you* get the game, this is how I understand *Great Composers* is to be played:

(1) You are trying to collect Composer Cards and (depending on the number of players) 0-2 Period Cards.

(2) To do this, you move about the map of Europe in the center of the game board. On the map is a network of lines connecting various symbol dots together. Some of these dots appear at cities (names are on the map) where great composers worked or visited. You move from dot to dot collecting Works and Travel Cards.

(3) As you recall, each of these cards has the name of a musical period at its top. Whenever you collect three cards from the same period, you can trade them in for a Composer Card. The first person to collect a composer from a given period gets that Period Card as well. You then lay down the cards you traded facedown next to the composer's picture on the outside of the game board.

(4) If you land on a Public Information symbol, you may pick up any card that has been placed by a composer's picture, unless it is the last card left there. That one can't be removed.

(5) If you land on a Works symbol, you pick up a Works Card from the deck, read it aloud, and keep it.

(6) If you land on a Travel symbol, you pick up a Travel Card and read it aloud. If you want to keep it, you have to travel to the city named on the card. If you don't want to do this, stick it back at the bottom of the deck.

(7) If you land on a spot already occupied by another player, you can ask him for a Travel or Works Card of a particular period. If he has one of that period, he has to give it to you. If he doesn't, tough luck.

(8) You find out how far you can move by rolling the dice. You can move any number up to the total number rolled. Doubles means you get an extra turn.

All clear so far? Then you doubtless have fathomed that the educational worth of this game comes from (1) reading the information on the cards aloud, and (2) learning to locate major cities on the map game board. For further educational value, the Composers Booklet includes realistic pictures of each composer, additional information about him and his works, and a few questions and answers about the composer. For even more educational value, listen to the narrated cassette. This includes examples from keyboard works of half of the composers featured in the game, plus some musical extracts from other composers not mentioned, all played on authentic period instruments.

Now, the bottom line. I like this game. Its only problem is the murky instructions, which as I have simplified them here, need not be a problem for you. (Aristoplay tells me that better instructions will be included in the next printing.) It doesn't make the fatal mistake of requiring you to listen to or identify cassette selections—that sort of thing is a royal pain in the middle of trying to play a game. The cassette, being just for enrichment, is appreciated. Composers are viewed in both their historical and geographical context: a nice touch. The connections between composers are also highlighted—e.g., Schubert's hero-worship of Beethoven. A fun, relatively painless way to get the family involved in figuring out who did what when and where.

NEW**
Rhythm Band, Inc.
Play the Composers, $6.95.

Nice, simple little game helps familiarize you with major composers and their four most famous works. You get a deck of 52 jelly-proof playing cards, each featuring a picture of a composer, his birth and death dates, and the names of four major works by that composer. Two rules cards explain the game. *Play the Composers* is played like "Go Fish"; you try to collect sets of four cards featuring one composer. Learning comes naturally as you ask, for instance, "Do you have the 'Moonlight Sonata' by Beethoven?" Composers featured are Beethoven, Mozart, Wagner, Handel, Bach, Schumann, Copland, Tchaikovsky, Debussy, Haydn, Brahms, Chopin, and Grieg.

WORDS AND MUSIC

Cornerstone Curriculum Project
Year 1, $55. Years 2-4, $50 each. Add 10% shipping.

Here's something perfectly delightful for music fans. Cornerstone Curriculum Project's Music & Moments with the Masters series is a four-year music curriculum. Year 1 features J.S. Bach, Handel, Haydn, and Mozart. Year 2 has Beethoven, Schubert, Berlioz, and Mendelssohn. Year 3 it's Schumann, Chopin, Verdi, and Grieg. Year 4 you get Wagner, Brahms, Tchaikovsky, and Dvorak. For each musician you get one professionally-narrated cassette tape that tells the story of the man's life interspersed with excerpts from pieces he composed during the period being narrated.

You also get a second tape of the master's "Greatest Hits." Each year, then, has eight tapes in all. *The Gift of Music: Great Composers and Their Influence* (Crossway Books) also now accompanies this series.

CCP is using cassettes published by Allegro and CBS Records. The quality is superb, and they have great kid-appeal.

NEW★★
Homespun Tapes
Understanding the Language of Music, tapes 3-6, $12.95 each. $65 for the entire 6-tape set. Shipping extra.

Concert pianist and composer Daniel Abrams takes you through the history of music and the development of important musical forms, such as the symphony and sonata, in the last four tapes of his six-tape audio-cassette series. Tape 3, "The History of Music," explores the evolution of the orchestra, how worldview influences music, and the major musical periods from early to modern. Tape 4 is an in-depth look at the Baroque period. Tape 5 covers the classical period, while tape 6 takes us from the sonata through twentieth-century music. Little-known facts about the musicians and their times spice up the tapes. Mr. Abrams illustrates his occasionally witty and usually insightful comments by playing numerous illustrative pieces on piano, organ, and harpsichord. Low-key teaching style, easy to listen to.

If you get the whole set, it comes with two additional cassettes on music theory and construction, a lovely cassette album, and a thin, spiral-bound book. The latter illustrates and defines for you the notes of the keyboard, shows the instrument groups that developed into the symphony orchestra, outlines the form of a classical sonata, defines musical symbols (notes, rhythm, tempo), and gives a list of suggested listening.

Laissez-Faire Books
Music: Theory, History, and Performance (12 cassettes), $129.50 plus $2.50 postage or $3.50 UPS.

Twelve-part series of lectures of Allan and Joan Mitchell Blumenthal, delivered in 1974 under the auspices of Ayn Rand. Set includes: • The Nature of Music • The Birth of Western Music • The Beginning of the Modern Era • The Pace Accelerates (late Baroque and Rococo) • Consolidation (classical period) • The Climax of Musical Development (Romanticism seen as the climax) • Romanticism Explored • The Later Romantics (nationalist composers, post-romantics, Impressionism) • Music as the Reflection of a Culture (with particular reference to the parallel disintegration of Western music and culture) • The Identification of Composers Through Style • The Role of the Performing Artist • Landmarks (recorded performances of great artists from Caruso through Segovia and Horowitz), • The Role of the Conductor • and Greatness in Music (a comparison of great and not-so-great music, an outline of the listener's role). This series, reflecting the pragmatist, libertarian viewpoint of Rand and her followers, is available exclusively from Laissez-Faire Books.

NEW★★
M-L International Marketing, Inc.
Basic Library of the World's Greatest Music, regularly $240, home schooler's discount price of $175.

Here is a truly remarkable new music program. *The Basic Library of the World's Greatest Music* from M-L International Marketing is not only a 24-cassette collection of the greatest classic compositions, bound in two very attractive albums. At the special $175 discount price for home schoolers (down from the $240 it retails for elsewhere) this program would be a great buy for the excellent music alone. Figure it out for yourself—that's only about $7.29 per cassette! But this is not only a music collection. It's "A Musical Learning System." You get a 300-plus page manual containing (are you ready?):

• The Library contents listed in the order the composers will be studied in the manual.

• Ways to fit the program into a variety of educational settings

• Timetable charts for the Baroque, Classic, Romantic, and Modern periods showing the chief styles, chief vocal forms and instrumental forms, great composers of the period, and what was happening in literature, philosophy, architecture, the other arts, and general history of each period. This section is introduced with an ultrasimplified time-table showing all four periods at a glance—ideally suited for introducing the young child to music history.

• The heart of the manual: 31 chapters on the composers and their music. Each chapter begins with an outline portrait of the composer and a brief outline of his life, followed by a more in-depth biography. Next comes a brief overview of the composer's works contained in the *Basic Library*. This is followed by listening activities and related activities, such as making up a story to go with the music, a short list of questions to ask the student about the composer's life and the musical selections, a word search, and a cross-word puzzle.

• A very helpful Music Glossary.

• Answers to the questions in the chapters.

Sounds easy to use, doesn't it? You can pick it up when you have time, work through a composer, and put it down until you again feel the energy to tackle musical studies. In the meantime, you simply play the cassettes you have studied or are about to study until they are second nature to the children.

The only other program that even comes close to this is Cornerstone Curriculum Project's *Music and Moments with the Masters.*

You might want to supplement *Basic Library* with Betty Carlson and Jane Stuart Smith's *A Gift of Music: Great Composers and Their Influence* (Crossway Books: $12.95 for the new edition) which gives more nitty-gritty details of the composers' lives and shows how their relationship to Christ, or rebellion from Christianity, affected their music. This book is included in the Cornerstone Curriculum Project program.

NEW**
Rhythm Band, Inc.
Music Maps of the Masters, $7.95. *More Music Maps of the Masters,* $6.95.

If you've ever wondered how to teach kids to follow along and notice the different themes and instruments in a classical piece, wonder no longer. Pam Enrich has invented something called "Music Maps." Each map outlines a famous musical piece in a totally weird way. Bach's *Brandenburg Concerto #3, First Movement,* for example, takes the form of a curly wig around Bach's head. If you look closely at the wig, you see that the darker curls correspond to the recurring three-note motif which distinguishes this composition. Start at Bach's left shoulder and follow the spiraling curls all the way to the end of the piece. Mussorgsky's *Pictures at an Exhibition* is presented as a map passing by churches and other buildings, crossing and recross-

ing a river, and ending up at the Great Gate of Kiev. Each sight along the way represents a part of the composition. Look for "fast-moving strings" while crossing the river, while at the churches the style is hushed and hymn-like.

This innovative, visual style of representing music is repeated for all 12 pieces in the original *Music Maps of the Masters,* and for 10 pieces in *More Music Maps of the Masters.* Instructions on the back of each map explain exactly how to use the map to follow—and remember—a composition. You'll also find the recording from which the map was drawn, and its source. Most recordings come from the Bowmar Orchestral Library and Holt, Rinehart and Winston's Exploring Music series. (Many can also be found in the M-L Marketing *Basic Library,* described above.)

The twelve composers in *Music Maps* are Bach, Beethoven, Chopin, Gabrieli, Gould, Grieg, Handel, Haydn, Ives, Kodaly, Mussorgsky, and Sousa. The ten in *More Music Maps* are Armstrong, Copland, Gounod, Grieg, Haydn, Mendelssohn, Rossini, Strauss, Tchaikovsky, and Vivaldi.

NEW**
Vision Video
The Joy of Bach, $39.95.

Normally I would not review a video that concentrated on just one composer. Bach, however, was no common composer, and *The Joy of Bach* is no ordinary video. Hosted by British actor Brian Blessed, this lavishly-produced program intersperses historical reenactments from Bach's life and modern renditions of his music by everything from the Trinidad and Tobago Steel Band to the Brooklyn Boys Chorus. Switched-on Bach? Brass Bach? Bach drifting over the Paris rooftops . . . swinging in the shopping mall . . . tinkling in an upper-class salon . . . Bach is everywhere in our world today, and this video does its best to follow him everywhere. A fine gift for musicians, educational for everyone else.

HISTORY

NEW**
American Institute of Music
Preliminary Rudiments Course, Grade I Rudiments, Grade II Rudiments, $95 each. One-time registration fee for new students, $14.95. Grade III and IV History, $149.95 each. Grade V History (Mahler through Modern Music), $54.95. Textbook, *The Enjoyment of Music, fifth edition* used for all history courses, $32.95.

Here's probably the heaviest-duty music history courses you would want to take at home. As mentioned in the previous chapter, since 1977 AIM has been providing correspondence courses for students preparing to take the written exams of the major Canadian conservatories. AIM is accredited by the National Home Study Council, and its Target Learning courses qualify for college credit in America.

Grade III and IV History each include loaned audio cassettes, study notes, and homework questions. Grade III covers music forms (e.g., art songs, symphonies, chorales, opera). Grade IV goes chronologically from Ancient World and Music in Christian Europe (lesson 1) through Classical Symphonies (lesson 25). Each lesson involves listening to musical selections from the loaned tapes. Please keep in mind that the grade levels are *Conservatory* grade levels, not elementary school grade levels!

When enrolling, you are asked to fill out a placement quiz, to make sure you are starting at the right level. This is very helpful. You also receive detailed descriptions of each course that includes a complete course outline—also helpful.

AIM courses are designed for mature learners—high school and adult—not for young children. These are *correspondence courses,* not just home study courses, so you send in your homework to be corrected and returned to you. AIM lets you work at

your own pace, with no deadlines for work completion. If you don't "get" a particular lesson, you will receive additional explanations and supplementary exercises at no charge. Partial refunds are available until the point where you have completed more than half of any course—with a 100% refund if you cancel within five days of receiving your course.

EDC Publishing
The Story of Music, $5.95. Add 15% shipping.

Starting with Music in the Ancient World and proceeding to the different kinds of music around the world, this lively, colorful book covers music history from the Middle Ages to the present, including opera and a look at the orchestra. Musical techniques, instruments, and great composers are all introduced.

Like all the other Usborne books, the illustrations and quality of information are both fascinating and exceptional. You won't find a simpler, more fascinating introduction to music history anywhere.

Konos
Artists and Composers Timeline, $25. Time line lines, $9.95. Add 15% shipping.

Time lines are one of the best ways to learn history. Now your child can get a real feel for art and music history, with the *Konos Artists and Composers Timeline.* You get five laminated blue sheets of figures to cut out and attach to a time line. Each painter holds a major work; each composer holds a major composition. Artists and musicians included range from Renaissance to modern, with most concentrated in between. A fun, hands-on way to study art history, and a natural taking-off point for study of individual musicians and schools of music.

NEW**
Ladybird Books, Inc.
Each book, $2.95.

Small traditionally-illustrated hardback books for preteens and up, or for advanced younger readers. Series includes *Musical Instruments, The Story of Music, Ballet, Great Composers I* (Bach, Mozart, and Beethoven), *Great Composers II* (Handel, Haydn, Schubert), and *The Story of the Theatre.* Engaging text presents lots of information. This series is supposed to go out of print when the remaining stock sells out, so get yours while you can.

LEARNING ABOUT THE INSTRUMENTS

Aristoplay
Music Maestro, $25.

As a game, I personally haven't found Music Maestro to be all that thrilling, but it is a good overview of musical instruments and their functions and sounds. You get an audio cassette with the sounds of over twenty instruments, a game board, several decks of cards, and rules to play five games of increasing difficulty. Instruments included are classical 'n medieval, bluegrass, rock, and jazz. We have decided the medieval is our favorite period, and our favorite instrument is the one that sounds like a giant kazoo (now is that the rebec?).

Players not only identify individual instruments, but learn to place them in the correct ensembles and the correct period. Even little kids can play the simplest games—which, as I said, are not that exciting. Part of the problem is that the same instrument always plays the same song on the cassette, thus making it possible to identify instruments by the tunes on the tape without really knowing which instrument makes which sound.

As a teaching tool, Music Maestro is worth the money.

ESP
Worksheets, $5/set. *The Orchestra, $80. What's Music All About?, $80.* Each of the latter is 24 15-minute lessons on 12 cassettes plus 24 spirit masters.

ESP, a public school supplier, has a line of spirit master worksheet exercises that cover such things as Introducing the Treble Clef; Music Signs; Music Notation; and so on. More ambitious are their two twelve-cassette-plus-spirit-master workbook sets, *The Orchestra* and *What's Music All About.*

The Orchestra covers: • What Is an Orchestra? • The Symphony Orchestra • History of the Symphony Orchestra • Players in a Symphony Orchestra • The Conductor • Music Played by a Symphony Orchestra • Who Supports the Symphony Orchestra? [Good question!] • Instrumental Families of the Symphony Orchestra • The String Family • The Woodwind Family • The Brass Family • The Percussion Family • The Concert Hall • Enjoying a Concert • Other Kinds of Orchestras • Dance Orchestras and Jazz Bands • Bands • Small Orchestral Groups • Pop & Rock Groups • Accompanying Orchestras • Unusual Orchestras • Unusual Instruments in the Orchestra • How You Can Join an Orchestra • Future of the Orchestra in America.

What's Music All About? covers: • Origin of Music • Early Musical Instruments • Basic Music Notation • Musical Notation Drill • Major and Minor Scales • The Chromatic Scale and Others • What Is a Melody? • Characteristics of Melody • What is Rhythm? • Characteristics of Rhythm • What Is Harmony? • Characteristics of Harmony • Forms Used in Music • Common Terms • Identify Instruments—Visually • Identify Instruments—Audibly • Vocal Skills • Famous Composers • Classical Music • Music of the Opera • The World of Marches • Jazz • Music from Other Lands • Modern or Popular Music.

NEW**
Random House
Music volume of Eyewitness Books, series, $12.95.

Like the other volumes in the Eyewitness Books series, *Music* features a fantastic layout with hundreds of gorgeous full-color pictures and classic black-and-white engravings. The highly visual format lends itself to the topic of "how instruments work" and "types of musical instruments." Accompanying text provides background information; instrument features are pointed out with arrows and explanatory text. A typical double-page spread is a three-ring circus with maybe a dozen pictures, historical information, and lots of high-interest comments on unusual instrument features, with a few classic engravings of people using the instrument mixed in. Covered are: Seeing sound (sound waves from different instruments), wind tunnels, pipes and flutes, vibrating reeds, long-lasting hybrids (e.g., the saxophone), bag instruments, piped music, beginning of brass, blazing brass, curly horns and big tubas, background of stringed instruments, early and unusual strings, the violin family, making a violin, harps and lyres, from pears to fishes (odd-shaped lutes), from gourd to board (zithers), Indian strings, creating a guitar, background of keyboard instruments, the upright piano, background of percussion instruments, rhythm instruments and rituals, a modern drum setup, other percussion instruments, instruments that clang and crash, how an electric guitar works, rock guitars (a brief history), and digital music, plus an index. Even the title page is beautiful and educational, featuring strange instruments from around the world. A gorgeous coffee-table book at one-fifth the price of a coffee-table book, and it'll teach you about musical instruments into the bargain!

NEW**
Rhythm Band, Inc.
André Previn Guide to Music Kit, $149.95. Topic books, $7 each. Set of 24 wall charts, $29.95. Activity book, package of 10, $40. Quiz books, package of 10, $25. Activity and quiz books only available in packages of 10.

The people who put this kit together say that its purpose is "to challenge 9–13 year olds to find out how musical instruments work and a little about the music played on them." Wrong on two counts. First, no way should this kit be limited to such a narrow age range. As a 34-year-old, I found it fascinating. All our children did too, from ages five on up. Second, you learn more than "a little" about the music.

The reason the kit is described in such understated terms is, I am convinced, because its makers, not knowing about home schooling or afterschooling, had in mind to sell it to public schools only. And we all know what priority the public schools put on music instruction. What's the first part of the school budget to be cut when the money supply tightens up? How many hours do schools devote to music training? Good guessing. Add this to the rigid public-school schedule ("Children will learn about music instruments in the second semester of eighth grade, weeks four and five") and we discover why pre-teens are the only group considered likely to use this program.

A pity, because what we have here is a terrific guide to all significant musical instruments and musical forms, presented by a man particularly qualified to do the job. André Previn is famous both as a composer and a conductor, and his career spans the gamut of classical, jazz, and film music. He also (O rare talent!) knows how to communicate what he knows.

Inside the heavy box in which the kit comes you will find four cassettes narrated by André Previn, eight topic books, 24 wallcharts, 24 copies of the activity book, 24 copies of the quiz book, and a teacher's copy of the quiz book with answers. Seven of the topic books cover a type of instrument: one book each for strings, woodwinds, brass, percussion, piano, voice, and electronic and mechanical. The eighth deals with the often-neglected subjects of composing, arranging, and recording.

I didn't expect all that much from the topic books. Sheer naked text was about all I had in mind. So imagine how flabbergasted I was to discover these books match the caliber of Usborne books or Eyewitness books! Just about every instrument known to man is covered in those books, along with fascinating facts about how they work, how they originated, and how they are used. Charts, graphs, photos, and line drawings interweave with carefully-crafted text on each page. Everything is designed for maximum visual impact and memorability. Lots of color throughout.

If the kit were nothing but these topic books, it would already be the best introduction to music via the study of instruments that I have ever seen. But now add to this the four cassettes, whose eight sides each correspond to a topic book. Here's where André Previn's experience really shines. Brilliantly-chosen musical excerpts illustrate the distinguishing features of each instrument and instrument family. He locates a Brahms concerto that shows off the cello's two "voices"—one high and the other low. He presents us with the same Bach piece played once by plucking the notes and once by bowing, in order to illustrate the different sounds of these two techniques. Similar approach to each musical family shows off each instrument's capabilities and foibles. You hear how instruments are used in jazz, classical, pop, and modern styles. (No rock 'n roll, though!) Anyone who has an ear to hear can't help learning how to recognize the different instruments *and* what each is mainly useful for.

Add to this, now, the 24 colorful wall charts. Each highlights an instrument or two, showing where it is placed in the orchestra, detailing its parts, showing how the player holds it, and other useful information, all most attractively presented in full color.

On top of this is the quiz booklet, which tests students on the concepts taught in the topic books, and a teacher's quiz booklet that has the answers. (You get 24 copies of the student's quiz booklet—public school influence, again.)

Add to this the activity book (24 copies of the same book). Here we go far, far beyond anything I have ever seen on the subject of music-making, as students are shown how to construct their own instruments. The teacher's guide expresses the hope that students will actually be given the class time to do this, but an underlying hopeless tone makes it clear that in most cases, they will not. At home you will have the chance to pursue all the activities, which are indeed impressive. Cookbook instructions for science experiments with sound are combined with couldn't-be-simpler step-by-step instructions on instrument construction. Your child will have the chance to make the following types of instruments: strings, woodwinds of the whistle and reed varieties, brass instruments (made from garden hose!), percussion, and mechanical, plus fascinating sound experiments with voice and electronics.

André Previn's Guide to Music is truly the antidote to musical illiteracy. Put this one high on your wish list.

NEW**
TREND enterprises, Inc.
All bulletin board sets, $5.99 each, come with free Discovery Guide. Require 4 x 6' bulletin board.

TREND's *Musical Instruments* bulletin-board kit includes detailed, realistic illustrations of 24 instruments grouped in five families: brass, string, woodwind, percussion, and keyboard. You also get a set of 15 basic music symbols, proportionately sized to the kit's music staff. The included Discovery Guide has basic background informations about each instrument and family, including suggested recordings that feature each instrument, plus simple music-appreciation activities and a match-the-instrument-to-its-name reproducible activity sheet. For visual learners, it's the cleanest, simplest introduction to musical families I've seen.

FOLK MUSIC OF OTHER TIMES AND PLACES

NEW**
Audio-Forum
Each LP or cassette, $10.98 postpaid. Minimum order is two titles.

Audio-Forum's brochure, "Ethnic Music from Around the World," lists a vast collection of ethnic music both by region and by instrument or musical format. Hundreds of recordings are available. For more info, see the writeup in the Worldview chapter of Volume 3.

Price/Stern/Sloan
Wee Sing book/cassette sets, $8.95 each. Wee Sing video, $21.95 (VHS or Beta). Wee Color Wee Sing coloring book/cassette/marker sets, $6.95. All prices postpaid.

Music history includes the history of children's music. Wee Sing authors Pam Beall and Susan Nipp performed the formidable task of collecting the best classic children's music, arranging it into sensible order, and producing it with panache. The Wee Sing line now includes the original *Wee Sing, Wee Sing and Play, Wee Sing Silly Songs, We Sing Around the Campfire* (this includes a section of campfire gospel songs), *Wee Sing Nursery Rhymes and Lullabies* (a story motif holds the songs together), and their latest production, *Wee Sing Bible Songs.* Each cassette comes with an illustrated songbook containing all the songs on cassette, plus some extra. The presentation is so varied and excellent and the price so right that these are the best-selling children's cassettes today.

New from Price/Stern/Sloan Publishers, the *Wee Color Wee Sing* series trades the songbook for a coloring book with pictures illustrating the songs and markers to color the pictures. The cassettes in this series provide music and instructions for creative activities including in the coloring book. Also, the new *Wee Sing Together* video includes 21 songs from the series embedded in a fantasy plot about a little girl's birthday party.

MUSIC EVALUATION

Playing or listening to music is one thing. Answering the question, "Is this music any good or not?" goes one level deeper.

Many parents today have a feeling down in our guts that contemporary bump 'n thump music isn't the most wonderful medium ever invented for the entertainment of our children. Going no farther than the lyrics of typical rock artists of the slam, glam, metal, thrash, death, punk, and other breeds, parents with traditional values can easily make a case for consigning these works to the dustbin. When these parents are Christians, though, things become much more difficult. For lo and behold, we now have *Christian* thrash 'n trash artists; *Christian* torch singers; *Christian* bands with frizzed-out hairdos, alienated expressions, and vocal styles that sound like tormented bats out of Hell.

The rationale for all this avid copying of the world is that musical style is just a matter of personal taste;

all styles are morally neutral; and since kids today like these styles, in order to reach them where they are, Christians need to adapt the user interface of the secular rock market. With better lyrics, of course!

Here are two ministries with different approaches to the vexed question of music evaluation.

NEW★★
Advanced Training Institute of America
Striving for Excellence, $15.00.

Striving for Excellence is subtitled "How to Evaluate Music: A Course for Leaders." Leaving aside the flattery implied in the title, here is a serious attempt to define the components of any kind of music and apply Biblical principles to them, in order to determine if the music in question is edifying and godly or something to pitch in the dumpster as quickly as possible.

Straight up now I'm going to tell you that Ron and Inge Cannon, the presenters of this seminar, do not see any redeeming qualities in rock music, "Christian" or not. However, their presentation is not a mere knee-jerk response to the horrendous lyrics and lifestyle of modern rock 'n roll. Introduced are basic definitions and principles of melody, harmony, rhythm, dynamics, form, text, and performance. The sections on text and performance are particularly hard on Christian pop artists, as just about every popularizing tactic their industry has taken is questioned, analyzed, and roundly condemned. The booklet closes with a brief summary of culture, from classical Greece up until now, showing how the cultural pendulum swings back and forth between intellectual and emotional emphases. Throughout, the seminar stresses the need for balance in all things, from balanced melodic line through a proper balance of musical appeal to the intellect and emotions.

WHAT YOU GET: An attractive cassette binder with two cassettes and an equally attractive booklet. The tapes follow the booklet, but also include musical excerpts to illustrate the principles taught in the booklet, plus some additional material. The booklet has numerous illustrations, musical scores, charts, graphs, quotes, and other aids to help your understanding. You can learn quite a bit about music theory and history as you proceed through this mini-course.

Striving for Excellence is certainly thought-provoking. You certainly can find some answers here, whether or not you will agree with them. The seminar's approach is also far simpler than evaluating the entire

rock music scene group by group. Just junk it all—*none* of it belongs in a believer's life or in Sunday morning worship!

This focus on "sacred song" leaves a number of important questions unanswered, though. Such as: What is the place of "everyday" music in the Christian life? Must all songs be hymns, or is there a place for work songs, love songs, car songs, humorous songs, and so on? I asked about this, and was told, "The Cannons do endorse well-written classical music," which still leaves some of these questions unanswered. It would have been helpful if the Cannons had provided more examples of music they consider OK. Practically every example of OK music given on the tape was hymns sung by choirs; the exceptions were some classical orchestrations and one vocal solo. I would also have appreciated more emphasis on *personal* music-making, since after all the Bible commands us many times to "play skillfully" and "make melody." Talking to Inge Cannon about this, I found she agrees that Christians have, in her own words, a "primary responsibility" to not just be passive consumers of other people's music. She expressed an interest in adding some material on that subject to their verbal presentations, and possibly even to a sequel of *Striving for Excellence.* I'll be looking forward to it!

NEW★★
Al Menconi Ministries
Heavy Metal Madness, $2.95 plus $2 shipping. *Media Update,* $12/6 issues, $15 Canada and foreign. Back issue, $1.50. *Everything You Need to Know About Rock Music* videos, $19.95 secular music, $19.95 Christian music, $34.95 for both. Curriculum guide for video series, 99¢ or $19.95 for one guide and unlimited permission to duplicate.

Taking the opposite viewpoint, Christian evangelist Al Menconi believes that rock is not evil in and of itself and that Christian rock can be "an effective tool for a young person to strengthen his walk with God, to focus on things above, and to identify with Jesus Christ." *Media Update,* the attractive, well-written, bi-monthly magazine of Al Menconi Ministries, spotlights what's happening on both the Christian music and secular rock scene, including blow-by-blow descriptions of what the various groups are up to and reviews of the latest contemporary Christian music. The ministry also publishes special reports from time to time. The first special report, *Heavy Metal Madness,* provides biblical evaluations of the most popular metal groups (every single secular group flunks), with some insightful glimpses into the theology and psychology informing this type of music. A list of Christian metal groups and recommended resources rounds the booklet out.

Al's video seminar *Everything You Need to Know About Rock Music* presents his "How's it affecting your spiritual faith and joy?" approach to analyzing all forms of music. Al is not entirely subjective: he unearths secular rock's "Do whatever feels good" message and shows what this means in religious terms and why secular artists are so obsessed with sex, drugs, and death. Some clips of both secular and Christian music illustrate his points. The set includes two videos, one with two sessions on secular music and the other with two sessions on Christian music. One free curriculum guide is included.

As I've told Al myself, I can't buy into the plugged-in scene, whether the music you're listening to all day long is secular or Christian. Kids need to learn to use their brains for something besides processing other people's music. He could also use firmer guidelines for determining what stuff is out of bounds just by its style. Demonic wailing and hoarse screaming aren't "true, noble, right, pure, lovely, and admirable" no matter how you slice it. The man's knowledge of the whole teen music scene is vast, though, and if you need to find out what's happening there, here's the place.

CHAPTER EIGHT

MUSICAL INSTRUMENTS AND SUPPLIES

I *When* should your child start learning to play an instrument? And *Which* instrument should he learn to play? Let me share with you what a reader (Colleen Story) shared with me.

The Right Instrument for Your Child, by Atarah Ben-Tovim and Douglas Boyd (Quill imprint of William Morrow, Inc., 1985), a $12.95 paperback, is a must for anyone considering starting a child on a musical instrument. The authors did 10 years of research and concluded choosing the wrong instrument was the most common factor in musical failure—not lack of "musicality" or music potential. The second most common factor was starting at the wrong time—too early. They felt their research indicated that, for 95 percent of children, the best time to begin an instrument is between eight to eleven years old. The book is designed to help you determine, through questionnaires and profiles of musicians who like specific instruments, which instrument(s) are best suited to your child's temperament, physical characteristics, and readiness. The one instrument suggested for six to eight year olds is the recorder . . .

Thanks, Colleen. I suspected as much. In spite of all the frantic rush to get nurslings involved with a musical instrument, *spiritual* readiness (the ability to persevere and the desire to create a work of art) still seems a logical prerequisite to serious musical instruction.

Play around with music all you like; expose your children to great music and let them fool with instruments, by all means. But if you want to nurture a life-long love of music, you might be better off telling your youngsters to wait until they've shown they're mature enough to make good use of official music lessons.

EASIEST INSTRUMENTS FOR CHILDREN AND BEGINNERS

NEW**
HearthSong
Children's Lyre, $88. Diatonic Lyre, $135. *Pentatonic Songs*, $5.75. *Clump-A-Dump and Snickle-Snack,* $5. Shipping extra.

Possibly the simplest instrument for little kids, and one that *never* sounds unpleasant, is the Auris Children's Lyre imported from Sweden by HearthSong. The lyre is very pretty—made of maple hardwood and carved gracefully with a "Y"-shaped cutout. The reason it always sounds good is that the seven strings are meant to be tuned pentatonically. The pentatonic scale simply can't sound bad, since all the five notes in each scale harmonize with each other.

You should know that this is not a loud instrument—good news for mothers, bad news only if your child expects every instrument to put out the decibels of hot-wired guitars. We found the tones *very* soft. For more sound, use finger picks.

My son Joseph immediately commandeered the Children's Lyre, toting it all over the house. Joseph is our poetic son, and this is just the instrument for a daydreaming child. You don't need to sweat and strain to make music with it. The music is rather otherworldly and peaceful—great accompaniment for deep thinkers!

Expect to tune the Children's Lyre more frequently at first, until the strings get settled in. Included are instructions on how to tune it, how to play, and how to change the strings. You also get a tuning wrench and order sheet for replacement strings.

You might wonder what your child will be able to play on this lyre once he or she stops noodling around just improvising. Anticipating this question, Hearth-Song carries two books of pentatonic songs used in Waldorf schools. *Pentatonic Songs* includes Advent songs ("Come, oh Christ child, do Thy part/Thy creche awaits Thee here"), Psalm 150, and other Christian songs, along with some famous children's poetry (e.g., "Don't Care" and "Mr. Nobody") and some songs by the compiler. Fair amount of emphasis on dwarves, knights, and Archangel Michael, in keeping with Waldorf founder Rudolf Steiner's Germanic cultural roots. *Clump-A-Dump and Snickle-Snack* is another collection of songs used in Waldorf kindergartens. Archangel Michael is joined by Mary, Joseph, St. Nicholas, and a collection of lullabies and nature songs. The dwarves also make an appearance.

If you absolutely can't live without the ability to produce normal Western music, HearthSong also has a diatonic lyre from the same maker. It looks similar, but has 12 strings spanning the C major scale, plus two tones above and two tones below—e.g., from A to E. It also costs quite a bit more—another factor to consider while making your decision.

NEW**
Homespun Tapes
Making and Playing Homemade Instruments, $29.95 plus $3.50 shipping.

Kids can make their own simple instruments with the easy-to-follow instructions on Homespun's *Making and Playing Homemade Instruments* video. Make two models of homemade banjo; finger castanets from pop-bottle tops; a washtub bass; a mouth bow; and other simple instruments that really work! Directions are easy to follow, materials are mostly stuff you have lying around the house. (You may need to pick up a few inexpensive items during your next trip to the hardware store.) Video hosts Marcy Marxer and Cathy Fink evidently enjoy making these instruments, and so will your kids. Recommended.

Also available from Homespun: kid-sized guitars to accompany Marcy's *Kid's Guitar* video. Check catalog for latest prices.

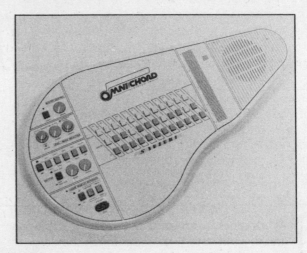

NEW**
Rhythm Band, Inc.
Omnichord System Two, $275. AC adapter, $9.50. Plastic modular carrying case, $39.50. Foot switch, $19.95. Stereo headphones, $9.50. *Omnichord Spoken Here*, $19.95.

The Omnichord System Two may be the ultimate beginner's instrument. Unlike other electronic instruments, you need no keyboard skills to play it. Instead, you get a 12 x 3 panel of chord buttons. The top row is major chords; the middle row is minor; and the third row is seventh. By pressing various combinations of major, minor, and seventh, you can make all seven possible variations on one chord, including major seventh, minor seventh, augmented, and diminished. All together you will be able to produce 84 different chord combinations right off the buttons. This means you can play *any* song written in chord notation, not just some that limit themselves to a few chords. Along with this you get 10 different rhythm patterns and an automatic bass line.

Playing the Omnichord is simplicity itself. First you set the volume levels and decide whether or not you want a background beat. You have a choice of 10 built-in beats, from dance and march rhythms through country and rock. Next, you press a chord button and run a finger across the amazing SonicStrings touchplate strum bar. Strumming this bar is supposed to simulate the sound of strumming a guitar. The actual effect is more light and tinkly, like a harp. By dancing your fingers around on the strum bar, or strumming backward or in circles, you can make all sorts of different sounds.

What you can't do is play individual notes. For this you have to enter "playback" mode and use the chord buttons as your chromatic keyboard. This mode only allows you to play one note at a time. I wasn't too excited about this feature, since the loud single melody notes overpower the much fancier background sound, making the Omnichord sound like a four-year-old plinking out a tune in time with an orchestra. Look upon the single-note mode mainly as a specialty feature for personal enjoyment—you will mainly want the Omnichord for its major use as an awesomely accessible accompaniment instrument. (The sound is too bland for solos, but just right for background accompaniment.)

As someone whose finger dexterity is short of breathtaking, I found I could immediately accompany songs at any speed with the Omnichord. This is a real breakthrough for non-musicians, who until now needed years of practice to work up to normal playing speed. The Omnichord is also easy for kids to play—the only requirement is that they be able to read the chord letters. I mean, how hard is it to press a button and run your finger along a bar?

The instruction manual explains everything that you can't figure out by yourself by noodling around with the Omnichord for five minutes. You can also get an AC adapter (do it!), a plastic carrying case, stereo headphones, and a foot switch that lets you leverage your Omnichord's ability to handle a pre-recorded chord, bass, and drum background while you play a melody line and strum the SonicStrings. Since Omnichord comes in a very sturdy styrofoam box, you really only need the carrying case if you plan on lugging your Omnichord to Sunday school or other public performances. You can also get a book, *Omnichord Spoken Here,* with over 200 hit songs, mostly rock songs and tunes from musicals. This really is just a regular songbook, with very little about it uniquely directed to the Omnichord. If your needs run more to hymns and folk songs than to pop, Rhythm Band's large selection of songbooks for autoharp will work just as well.

"Omnichord is so versatile, it's like playing strings, keyboards, bass, and drums all at the same time," says Rhythm Band's catalog. I'd say, "Amen," to that, as long as you remember that the keyboard feature only works one-note-at-a-time, as mentioned above. The output sound is really nice, and can be plugged into an amp, stereo, or P.A. system for those who need to accompany large-group singing.

Omnichord is an instrument any kid can play, and it isn't too childish for adults. If you want an easy-play accompaniment instrument, but don't want to take a lot of time learning to play, and you can afford an Omnichord, go for it!

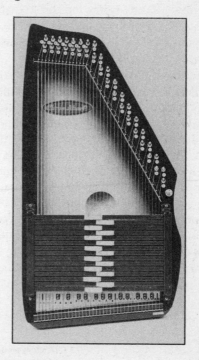

NEW**
Rhythm Band, Inc.
ChromAharP models range from $115 (the 15-chord model) to $275 (the "Jewel" model). Recommended 21-string model, $139. Economy carrying case, $19.50. Deluxe carrying case, $34.50. Songbooks, $3 each. *Happy Strumming,* $3. *Complete Method for ChormAharP,* $9.95.

Oscar Schmidt Company invented the word "autoharp" to describe the chorded zither. Today everyone knows how easy it is to play the autoharp. Even the name "autoharp" means "self-playing harp." You press down a chord key and strum the strings. Pretty easy, right?

Rhythm Band has a fine selection of chorded zithers ranging from a very inexpensive 15-chord model to a deluxe model with interchangeable chord brackets.

Let's look at these one by one.

We tried the 15-chord ChromAharP, which is Rhythm Band's most popular model, and found some drawbacks. First, lots of songs you will want to play use chords not found on this model: A, B7, A-flat, B-flat-7, Cm, and Em. Check out your favorite songbooks and see how often these chords are used—it may make a difference in whether you want a 15-chord model or a 21-chord. (The 21-chord model includes all those chords, plus every chord on the 15-chorder.) Also, on the 15-chord model pressing the chord bar down tightly is beyond the strength of our under-eights. Rhythm Band stresses that the 21-chord model responds to "the lightest touch"—this should be another factor in your decision.

Rhythm Band has two other special-purpose models. Their PortAharP™ is a 15-chord ChromAharP built right into a carrying case. Engineered to eliminate cross-hand strumming, the PortAharP is designed especially for on-the-go music teachers and others who need an extremely portable instrument. The "Jewel" ChromAharP is a special chorded zither which lets you switch chord bars in and out. Just press a release button on both sides of each chord bar bracket to change it out. Each bracket holds eight chord bars, so in effect you are buying four eight-chord autoharps. Brackets are set up to play in two major keys, and each uses the same chord pattern, making song transposing easy. The "Jewel" comes with a free deluxe carrying case.

Each ChromAharP model comes with a tuning handle and picks.

Older children can get a very nice sound out of any of these instruments with very little effort. The only skill required is the ability to read chords and remember which chord key is where. Of course, if you like to get fancy, you can do much more impressive stuff than this on a ChromAharP.

Rhythm Band has lots of music books with familiar songs in chord notation for your budding Chromaharpist. See reviews in previous chapter.

I personally would suggest that if you want a ChromAharP, you start right off with a 21-chorder. The only reason for preferring a 15-chorder is its lower price, but the price difference is not that substantial. All those extra chords really come in handy, and the lighter touch is a definite benefit. Your harp is not likely to rust in a corner, either, since anyone can pick one up and play it right away, so it makes sense to get the more-advanced model rather than being forced to trade up to it later.

INSTRUMENT SOURCES

NEW**
Andy's Front Hall

A reader wrote saying that this was a good source for folk instruments, how-to books, advice on appropriate instruments, and folk music for children. I sent for the catalog, and now have mixed feelings.

What we have here is a good source for a huge variety of folk instruments, all the how-to-play books and videos your little heart could desire, tons of songbooks of folk music, and a number of great sourcebooks for those who are interested in looking farther into folk music and instruments. I refer to *Musical Instruments of the World* ($22.95), an illustrated encyclopedia with over 4,000 drawings; *Making Folk Instruments in Wood* ($12.95), with detailed instructions for making 51 different folk instruments; *The Folk Music Sourcebook* ($16.95); and so on. They also carry what seems like thousands of recordings, and here's where my doubts start creeping in. For reasons known only to themselves, most Christian musicians do not work as folk artists, and thus the field is increasingly left to those of the leftist/Green/slasher/unleavened persuasions.

The people who run Andy's Front Hall are musicians first, but are not nearly skeptical enough of eco-religion (you know, Mama Earth the Living Planet) and other new age stuff. I say "they are musicians first" because they do want the albums on these topics that they carry to measure up musically, and take to task the feeble efforts of some new age bandwagoners who feel that simply warbling with political sensitivity should be enough to validate a recording. E.g., in a positive writeup for *Living Planet* you read, "There are many folks who try to deal with these issues who come off preaching to us or whose songs simply aren't very musically memorable." How true. I immediately thought of *Peace Is the World Smiling*. On the other hand, what can you say about this description they wrote of a Steeleye Span album:

> Raise the flags! Release the doves! Fire the cannons! Hang out the infidels! Ritually disembowel yet another kitchen boy! . . . which is to say that in honor of their 20th anniversary, we have an album of all-new, mostly traditional material from Steeleye Span. This album is a wonderfully upbeat [sic] album containing all the key themes which have made this band so popular for so long, namely, love, death, fear, murder, treachery, thievery, the plague . . . you know them all by now. Those of you who view The Seventh Seal as a comedy will certainly go for "Shaking of the Sheets" and for those of you who are big slasher-ballad fans, there are "The Cruel Mother" and "Two Butchers" (nice guys are always finished first).

Educational, isn't it? I feel I learned a lot about Front Hall customers just from that one writeup. "Give me misery or give me death." They at least must not feel that anyone would be *offended* by disemboweled kitchen boys—just good, clean, post-Christian fun.

Now let's be fair here. You'll also find quite a few country dance books and tunes, Christmas albums, some spirituals, etc. Most of the catalog is instruments and how-to-play books and songbooks, too. But do you want to pay the price of being grossed out by rave reviews of "slasher ballads"? My overactive imagination shudders at the thought of what "The Cruel Mother" could be about.

NEW★★
Crane's Select Educational Materials
Catalog $1, refundable on first purchase. Banjo kit, $39.95. Renaissance Harp kit, $165 (add $30 for optional spruce soundboard). Dulcimer kits from $29.95 to $169. Mandolin kit, $46.95. Harpsichord kit, $895. Completed harpsichord, $3500. Instrument books and accessories also available. Shipping extra.

David and Marilyn Crane, a home-schooling couple, have for several years published a catalog loaded with really neat, somewhat offbeat resources to supplement your home education program. Their fairly large line of instrument kits covers everything from the folky dulcimer to the baroque harpsichord. Kits' construction time varies, from 6–10 hours for the musician's and church dulcimers to 200 hours for the harpsichord. Woodworking ability required likewise varies. The simplest dulcimer kits are also the simplest to construct, with predrilled holes even. You have to drill your own holes for the banjo and hourglass dulcimer, and you need to do a careful job on the fretting, stringing, and general woodworking required for the mandolin. The harpsichord project you'd better not tackle unless you really love to work with your hands, as this can easily stretch into a half-year part-time project—but what a fantastic project for a mechanically-inclined teenager!

NEW★★
Homespun Tapes

Fretted and folk instruments: hammer and Appalachian dulcimers, autoharps, harmonicas, kid-sized guitars, and accessories. Plus pan pipes and some other unusual ethnic instruments. Founder Happy Traum tells me that one of their most successful items is the Marantz home-study tape recorder, a "very-well made" cassette deck that switches to half-speed (exactly one octave lower) for figuring out and playing instrumental passages from records, tapes, and so on.

The Instrument Workshop

If you'd like to make your own old-fashioned keyboard instrument, this company is the source. You have to buy their catalogs of tools, parts and plans, replacement parts and accessories, kits, and plan sources. They also have a *List of Recordings of Historical Keyboard Instruments* that has about 150 listings of pre-1850 instruments with artist, record title and content, record company, and record number.

Lark in the Morning

Purveyor of rare and unusual instruments, as well as instruments and books for ethnic and folk music. Everything from bagpipes, bodhrans, mandolins and dulcimers to crumhorns, sackbuts, double-bell euphoniums and all points in between. Also instructional video.

I didn't even know there was such a thing as a Hungarian bagpipe; but Lark in the Morning has it! Also all kinds of Eastern instruments, South American music-makers, kits for everything from guitars and tabors to Renaissance lutes and an incredibly low-priced spinet harpsichord. "The best possible Musical Saw . . . the Sandvik Stradivarius." Pages and pages of one-of-a-kind items, too.

Mandolin Brothers, Ltd.

If you're a music-lover, don't you dare send for this catalog unless you have at least several hundred dollars in hand. Mandolin Brothers specializes in new and vintage guitars, mandolins, and banjos, and the selection will knock your eyeballs out. The brothers are recognized authorities on vintage fretted instruments, and they offer goodies in their catalog such as a 1946 Martin D-28 Herringbone. "We don't know one player who wouldn't like to own this guitar," the brothers say. Too true. The lovely creation goes for $4975. Another Martin D-28 made in 1960 was advertised as "You be the judge—we can ship this guitar to you, on approval. $1800."

If, like me, you can't play in this league, Mandolin Brothers carries an outstanding assortment of fretted instruments for small-timers. Plus every fretted instrument accessory known to man, songbooks for dulcimer, fiddle, cello, acoustic bass, violin, mandolin, autoharp, and banjo. Plus instruction books in all the above plus guitar and bass guitar.

Music for Little People

It's a pretty catalog, very successful, and as new age as it can be. World peace and save-the-whales. Unusual instruments are carried in this catalog not just for their beauty and tone, but apparently to supply odd ritual uses. Whatever the motivation, you can find items here that just aren't available at the corner music store. Some examples: pan pipes are $19. Kallisti Marimba, $109. Irish Bohdran Drum, $98. Ukelele, $25.50. Gianinni Little Guitar, $79.95. Flute, $14.95. Mbira (African Thumb Piano), $21.50. Japanese Shakuhachi flute, $75. Lots more. All items chosen for beauty of appearance and tone.

Rhythm Band

If you've got kids, and the kids like music, and you're willing that they should, you'll really like this catalog. Rhythm Band is one of those entrepreneurial success stories that public school economics courses keep forgetting to mention. Started with two employees and a borrowed $6,000, Rhythm Band has grown to be one of the largest conglomerates in the music industry, employing over 3,000 people. The reason for this outstanding success will become obvious the minute you open RB's catalog. It's something for everybody, at prices anyone can afford, and covering 99 percent of the field of kids' music.

Rhythm Band has pages and pages of instruments for sale. You can get rhythm band sets (but of course!), in sizes for small families and for large institutions. Low-priced folk instruments from many countries. Beginning instruments for young players. Fun instruments even a baby can fool around with (you've probably noticed these in the posher baby catalogs). High-tech instruments. Chromaharps. Pianicas. Metronomes. Orff instruments. Bells.

Rhythm Band also has instructional materials: pitchpipes, staff liners, musical notation flash cards, and books on music instruction. More, they sell educational games for teaching music concepts. The catalog has several pages of these, enough to make any music teacher lose control of her pocketbook. There's a page of Hap Palmer records and a page about Andre Previn's *Guide to Music*. Plus supplementary items like full-color prints of orchestra instruments and composers.

Rhythm Band's prices are outstanding. You can get an Aulos Soprano Recorder for only $2.95 (school price: suggested retail is $5.50). We have one of these and it's no Cracker Jacks job. No wonder schools, with their strapped music budgets, patronize Rhythm Band so freely.

The catalog is full-color and easy to use. Many school suppliers sell Rhythm Band instruments, but if you have a music-lovin' kid, why not go to the source?

Shar Products

Shar is really two companies in one. On one level, they're a heavy-duty supplier of violins, cellos, basses and all the paraphernalia that professional players of the same require. On the other level, they're a big-time Suzuki supplier, with a comprehensive listing of books about Suzuki, Suzuki recordings, and instrument outfits for little players. For more information, see the Music Instruction section above.

SHEET MUSIC

Ability Development
Dover Publications
Homespun Tapes
Mandolin Brothers
Shar Products
Summy-Birchard, Inc.

These are all sources for a wide variety of sheet music. Ability Development and Shar carry classical and Suzuki sheet music. Mandolin Brothers has mostly folk and pop sheet music for fretted instruments, Homespun has folk plus jazz and rock, and Dover carries over 150 classic and pop music scores, at possibly the lowest prices in music publishing today.

NEW★★
Davidsons Music

Huge selection of popular and easy-play music in both standard music notation and melody note/chord format. Lots of hymns and gospel songs; equal amount of pop and country. "Fake" books, more.

Warren Publishing House, Inc.
Piggyback Songs series, $7.95 each. Add $2 shipping.

Sheet music for every child. No notes to read, no tunes to forget. What you get are new songs to sing to familiar old tunes. Example: (to the tune of Farmer in the Dell)

Christmas time is near.
Christmas time is near.
Merry Christmas everyone.
Christmas time is near.

It's time to trim the tree.
It's time to trim the tree.
Merry Christmas everyone.
It's time to trim the tree.

Each song has chord names above it (F, C, C7, and so on), so you can play along with an autoharp, guitar, or other chorded instrument.

The series so far includes: *Piggyback Songs, More Piggyback Songs, Piggyback Songs for Infants and Toddlers, Piggyback Songs in Praise of God,* and *Piggyback Songs in Praise of Jesus.* Each book is organized into categories of songs (e.g., *More Piggyback Songs* includes Songs About Winter, About Spring, About Summer, About Fall, About School, About Me, About Animals, and Just For Fun). All books are a large 8½ x 11" and contain between 64 and 96 pages.

LANGUAGES

ZUT, ALORS!
L'ANGLAIS, C'EST
DIFFICILE!

CHAPTER NINE

FOREIGN LANGUAGES FOR YOUNGSTERS

Why learn a foreign language? Here are some reasons: a desire to broaden your mind through exposure to another culture, the need to communicate with non-English speakers in your business, or just the fun of cracking a strange code. In years past, the man or woman who didn't know at least one language other than English was considered only half-educated. Even today it still is true that those who know several languages have an edge on those who do not.

Why learn a foreign language? Here's an economic reason: it can land you a job. I was amazed, during a visit to New York City, to see the many newspaper ads begging for executives who were fluent in German. It also doesn't take a genius to see that we could use a few good men in the computer field who speak Japanese, or that an importer of African artifacts might want to know Swahili. And knowing the languages in which English has its roots—namely French, German, and to a lesser degree Latin—increases your command of our own native tongue. One of the most famous classic texts on preaching recommends that ministers study French and German for this very reason.

Learning another language sharpens not only your speech, but your thinking. Habits of analysis and organization are increased by the study of the patterns that make up any language.

You've now heard most of the arguments that foreign language teachers dredge up in order to convince someone (*anyone!*) to please enroll in their classes. These really are good arguments. The only reason more students don't act on them is that you can get just as many credits for Basket Weaving I as for Advanced French I and learning a language is, frankly, harder than learning to weave a basket.

You, however, are made of sterner stuff than the average basket-weaver. For you, the question is not so much, "Ought I to learn another language?" or "Should my children learn another language?" as "How do I go about it?"

ESCAPING THE TYPICAL TEXTBOOK TRAP

I am well qualified to speak on the subject of foreign languages, having had 10 years of French instruction, two years of German, and one year of intensive Russian. All these classroom courses, none of which resulted in actual fluency, have burned into my soul several basic truths about how not to learn a foreign language.

The first thing you must watch out for is the Typical Language Textbook. It comes in all sizes and colors but only one flavor: boring. You can recognize the Typical Language Textbook by the endless drills and list-less dialogues that make up 99 percent of the book. The writers of these books have got it into their heads that you do not want to *speak* the language: rather, you want to *read* it. Furthermore, the stories you want to read all have sentences like, "Jean rode his bicyclette to the store. Marie rode her bicyclette to the store. See Rex catch the ball. Run, Spot, run." This Dick-and-Jane approach to foreign languages not only leaves you gaping with boredom, it also leaves you fluency-free, as no normal Frenchman or Italian or Bulgarian talks like that.

Another trap to watch out for is the Cute Language Textbook. This is the Dick-and-Jane-Go-To-The-Disco version. We still get Dick and Jane, or maybe, Jean and Marie, but now our young friends are doing "contemporary" things. Unless you really just want to read teenybopper magazines in the target language, this approach won't get you much of anywhere either. Furthermore, in their anxiety to be "with it," publishers tend to overstress the negative aspects of youth culture abroad. Life in France isn't an eternal no-adults-allowed camping trip, like some books make it out to be, any more than it is here in the good old U.S.A.

The last all-too-common trap is the language course that consists of phrases you're supposed to memorize. My first year of junior high French was larded with dialogues *sans* grammatical explanation, and my classmates unanimously agreed that it was a waste of time. Some adult self-study courses for tourists do this also. Naked phrases go into short-term memory, which they quickly evacuate on the slightest encouragement. Pattern drills, on the other hand, whether or not they incorporate overt grammar, lock the language into place.

THE BASIC TOOLS OF FLUENCY

Obviously, the best way to learn another language is the way that already has worked for you once.

You know English: how did you learn it?

First, people talked to you a lot. Your mother grabbed your chubby little foot and said, "Foot. Foot." Or perhaps she said, "My ittle baby has a cutesy itty-bitty footsie," in which case it took a while longer to catch on to what she was talking about. In any case, you heard the word "foot" a lot in many different contexts ("Yike! I hurt my foot!" "Stick your foot in the shoe.") until finally you made the connection. This was the intake, or data-gathering, stage.

Then one day you tried to say, "Foot." If you were really successful it came out sounding like "Foo." If you weren't so successful, it might have been "Doof" or "Voob." Why did you try to say "Foot?" It wasn't because you needed to pass a test! No, you needed someone to do something and do it *right then*. Perhaps your foot hurt or you wanted to put on your shoes. If your father or mother caught on to what you were trying to say, you all were happy. If not, you tried again. "Boof? Foob?" Sooner or later you made a noise that was close enough, and everyone was ecstatic! "Our baby is talking!" Take note of this: they did *not* try to make you feel like a fool for your mispronunciations. Instead, they encouraged you. If they didn't do this, it's a fairly sure thing that you were slow in learning to talk.

You also developed a pattern of asking for data in a certain way, and your parents responded predictably. "What dat?" "That's the saltshaker, Johnny. Saltshaker. Saltshaker. No, don't grab it, dear." You also became accustomed to the rhythms and patterns of English through hearing thousands of simple sentences. "Give Mommy the spoon." "Lift up your arms." "Swallow the nice medicine." You heard additional thousands of sentences not addressed to you, that you were under no pressure to translate but were curious to understand. "Little Johnny spat out all his medicine all over his shirt this morning, and I had to feed it to him four times before I got any down him."

So kids learn to talk by seeing and feeling objects and asking other people to do things for them and doing the things that other people ask them to do and hearing sentences that nobody even wants them to understand. But how do we ask kids to learn foreign languages in school? Too often it's by filling out workbook pages. They only get to hear the language spoken an hour or so a week in Language Lab, and even if the classroom teacher is a native speaker of the language, he or she only has the students for another few hours.

If you or your children really want to learn to *speak* (not just read) another language, at the minimum you will need:

- Cassettes or records of the spoken language. (Video is great!)
- Transcripts of the above, so you can make some sense out of it.

- Translations of the above, so you don't get stuck forever wondering what *izquierda* or *wiederkommen* means.
- Plus a reasonable framework for the language's patterns, which may or may not need to resemble a conventional grammar.

If you only have a few hours a week to learn a language, it makes sense to spend as much of the time listening to it as possible. At home you can listen to a cassette again and again until you have it memorized from sheer repetition. More and more publishers are adding songs to their material, making use of the musical part of the brain to help you retain your lessons. One publisher that I know of uses pictures in all his courses to help you associate the spoken word with a visual image. With the advent of the VCR, we are just beginning to see courses developed featuring sound-sight association. Computers can take you even farther, with interactive oral language drill. These are all steps forward in foreign language instruction.

Let me tell you what's missing. We need someone to import the actual coloring books and preschool workbooks that little kids use in France, Spain, and other places. If our kids read the same early readers, sing the same preschool songs, and use the same preschool materials as kids from other countries, they will not only pick up the foreign language much faster, but be acclimated to the country's customs. Then if they ever have a chance to visit the foreign country or speak with a visitor from that country, they will fit in much more easily.

I don't know of one course that does it all—gives you extensive hearing practice, action practice, sight-sound association, pattern drills, and authentic target-country materials. Still, you can learn quite a bit from some of the select programs following.

LANGUAGE COURSES FOR VERY YOUNG CHILDREN

AMR Educational Systems
Spanish for Children. Reviewed in manuscript form. $12.95.

It's Spanish á la kindergarten! AMR has produced a "fun time coloring book" with activities for children ages three through nine. Accompanied by a Spanish audiocassette containing stories, games, and songs, the coloring book stars engaging characters like Senorita

Tortuga (Miss Turtle) and Senor Conejo (a savvy rabbit). Each page (some in full color) features classic non-threatening activities: dot-to-dot, coloring, mazes, etc. Pictures are labeled in Spanish and English. Covered are colors, numbers, days of the week, and other simple vocabulary. To be added to this series: French, German, and Italian.

Audio-Forum
Springboard to French, German, or Spanish: $19.95 each set. Shipping extra.

A play-oriented introduction to the target language for very young children (preschool-early grades) based on the Total Physical Response method. Children learn by acting out commands given by the teacher ("*Levante los brazos, uno, dos. Tome la banana. Corte la banana en dos pedazos.*"— i.e., "Lift your arms, one, two. Take the banana. Cut the banana in two pieces.") Activities include songs, coloring, cutting with scissors, and games. Content includes basic body movements (standing, sitting, walking, running, etc.), parts of the body, colors, counting from one to fifteen, clothes and dressing, members of the family, eating, playing, and everyday activities.

Like the other language materials for very young children reviewed in this section, each *Springboard to . . . language* course follows an identical format, making the transition to additional languages easy.

Neither teacher nor student need previous foreign language experience. Pronunciation is handled on the two included cassettes. Each command is repeated in the target language, then in English, then again in the target language. You then get a few seconds to act out the command. Once you have done this, the section is repeated in the target language only, with time to act out every command.

Every foreign phrase or sentence in the 40-page booklet is translated into English. The booklet also includes cutout shapes for the games.

NEW★★
Audio-Forum
Storybridges, $19.95 each set plus shipping.

The *Storybridges* program is a fun and easy way to introduce the kids to a few words in a foreign language. In *Storybridges to Spanish for Children*, narrator Veronica Foster tells classic stories (e.g., "The Shoemaker and the Elves"), slipping in Spanish phrases as she goes. Daughters Sadie and Sydney repeat the Spanish, providing an example for your children. Story context makes the Spanish meanings clear: there is no English translation either on the cassette or provided in booklet form. After the story ends, Mrs. Foster quizzes you gently to find out whether you know some of the words and phrases used in the story.

Storybridges to German for Children is more of the same, only this time a native-born German lady, Annemarie Arnold, says the German phrases.

You get three cassettes, each with one story on each side, for a total of six stories in all. Stories are "Goldilocks and the Three Bears" (a version in which Goldilocks apologizes and makes friends with Baby Bear), "Little Red Riding Hood," "The Turtle's Music," "The Nightingale," "The Shoemaker and the Elves," and "Peter and the Wolf."

I was sorry to find the Lord's name occasionally used in vain on the German tape. I've mentioned this concern to Audio-Forum, and they might revise these sections of the tapes.

Storybridges are "bridges" to foreign language instruction, not demanding language courses. They are a non-threatening way to (1) get young children used to the concept of a foreign language, (2) present them with an example of a proper accent, and (3) help them pick up a few words and phrases, while they (4) are enjoying listening to the tapes entirely on their own.

If you want a comprehensive language course, you are better off with one of the others reviewed in this section. None of the others, however, will enable your child to learn entirely without supervision.

Christian Character Concepts
Conversational Spanish I, $17 postpaid.

Sing, play a board game, make paper-bag puppets, and flip flash cards with Christian Character Concepts' new Spanish I and II programs for young Christian children. The songs are really cute (if anything, *too* cute!) and the activities are fun. The lessons don't include very much vocabulary, and some of the speakers have a Texas accent, but the music is professional and kids will like it. (Shucks, *I* wander around the house singing the songs!)

NEW★★
Optimalearning Language Land
French for Tots, $19.95 plus $3 shipping. *Spanish for Tots* and *English for Tots*, TBA.

I am impressed! Here is a foreign-language minicourse for children ages 2½ and up that really works with almost no effort on your part. You get two cassettes (one with just the songs plus some supplementary vocabulary at the end, to play throughout the day for reinforcement, and one with both lesson vocabulary and songs), and an activity book with parental guide. Dialogs are spoken, and songs are sung by fluent French speakers. The woman has a beautiful voice, and the original music is very sweet and pleasant.

This program is based on the OptimaLearning educational method. They ask you to use a special symbol associated with the study of French, a special place where you have the lessons, and a little "alerting technique" ritual to announce that the lesson is coming. This sounds a bit new-ageish, but actually is just a way of shedding the day-to-day environment and entering into a proper frame of mind for study. Memorization is *not* stressed. Rather, it is considered important to expose the young child to the rhythms and intonations of the foreign language, before he begins to lose his ability to reproduce these sounds. Exactly what those sounds *are* is explained quite well in a special Pronunciation Guide in the activity book. Each lesson also includes phonetic pronunciation as well as English translation for each phrase, right under the phrase where it does the most good.

You are supposed to go through the lesson with the child, perhaps explaining what it all means, and then he can play the song tape as often as he likes during the day until he memorizes it without any effort. This, of course, would accomplish little if the songs did not aid building vocabulary and expression. For this purpose, the course is set up very well. Each lesson introduces one set of vocabulary, as follows:

LESSON NUMBER	LESSON NAME	LESSON CONTENT
1	Bonjour	Greetings, what's your name, my name is . . .
2	Clown	Face parts
3	Le Chat	Animal names, what is this?
4	Le Fête des Canards	More animals, how do they sound?
5	Flic Floc	Water, rain, frog
6	Polichinelle	Body parts, directions
7	Papillon	Where do you live, friends
8	Au Marché	Counting, fruits, vegetables, shopping
9	Bon Appétit	I'm hungry, meal time
10	Bonne Nuit	Bedtime, good night greetings

Supplementary vocabulary is found on the second side of each tape. Vocabulary words are read "with special intonations to affect receptivity" against a background of Baroque music.

You don't need to know French to use this very cuddly, motivational program. For its purpose—presenting French to tots—it's about as simple as you can get.

NEW**
Timberdoodle
Berlitz Jr., $17.95 each for French and Spanish ($2 off retail). Add $4 shipping for orders up to $40.

This cute 'n cuddly set is the first kid-oriented introduction to foreign languages from the mighty foreign-language educational company, Berlitz. It includes a 64-page full-color hardcover book and a 60-minute audiocassette. The book is super quality, with charming illustrations and large print. A school-age teddy bear and his family (two parents and a little brother and sister) are the main characters. Teddy introduces himself and his family and some common toys. He then invites you to his school, where you learn the colors, the numbers, the alphabet, and the days of the week. Playtime in the park is followed by a visit to a circus. Along the way you pick up some basic vocabulary (you know, words like *chocolate ice cream* and *monkey*) and sentence expressions.

You will have to be there with your young child while he goes through the program the first few times, to help him understand what the phrases mean. Here's how it works: Each page of the book has a few illustrated phrases or words, plus English translation. The cassette follows the book, but its review sections are *not* in the book, although they use only words found in the storyline. To avoid confusion, help your child understand that when the (somewhat intrusive) teacher on the cassette says it's time to review, the following part will not be in the book. Each phrase on the cassette is pronounced slowly (for the French) by native speakers, with a nice long pause after it so you can repeat it. Music and special effects are dotted throughout, to add to the fun. There is no special teacher's guide—this program was designed for parents to share with their children without any special preparation or strain. Success depends on the child learning what the phrases *mean*, which as I said requires going through the cassette and book with him several times. One good idea might be to go through one section a week, repeating it each day until your child understands it. After that, he can simply listen to the cassette on his own, or (once he learns to read) read the book again and again on his own.

ACTIVITY-BASED PROGRAMS

The following programs are designed to give you a "taste" of a language. They are not meant as serious, comprehensive language instruction. Each includes a certain amount of activities. Age range: five to ten.

NEW**
Audio-Forum
Phrase-a-Day French, Phrase-a-Day Spanish, $19.95 each plus shipping.

Just as we were going to press Audio-Forum sent me copies of their two new *Phrase-a-Day* programs for young children. Intended for children ages 5-11, each features two audiocassettes and an attractive activity/coloring book.

Here's how it works. First, you listen to the five speakers introduce the program. Then you turn to page 1 of the coloring book. There you'll find four pictures showing children engaged in everyday activities. Each picture has one or more phrases under it, with English translation in smaller type. Look at the pictures and phrases while following along on the cassette. On the next page are two more pictures and a large, empty panel. Under the empty panel are some questions referring back to the activities illustrated in the illustrated panels for that unit. The questions for the first winter unit are,

What's the weather like in the wintertime?
What do you wear to go out?
Do you ever lose anything?

These refer back to the panels showing a girl looking out at the snow, getting dressed for the outdoors, and losing her glove.

You are supposed to echo the speakers on the cassettes, color in the pictures, and perhaps even draw a picture in the empty panel.

Each unit consists of this same two-page format and ends with a sound cue: a ringing bell for the French tape, a few musical notes for the Spanish tape. At this point you may either rewind the tape and replay the unit or go on to the next unit.

The program has a seasonal theme. You start off with winter, then proceed to spring, summer, and fall. If you try to learn just one phrase a day, as the program suggests, and use it as often as you can that day, you will finish the entire program in about a year. By that time you will be counting in the language, know the names of all the colors and seasons, and have a vocabulary for playing and cooking and setting the table, for sickness and weather, for grooming and school, for directions, for playing with a baby, and lots more.

All these phrases are introduced in story vignettes. Some of the vocabulary is introduced in a structured fashion—for example, listing off the colors of the rainbow. Most is introduced via dialogs. Since English translation is provided, you will be able to follow along. Conversation is mostly at a comfortable pace, except for the little girl on the Spanish tapes, whose words gallop out like rodeo horses!

The coloring books for French and Spanish are exactly the same, except that the phrases are in (respectively) French and Spanish. That's the way to go, since once your children have used the version for one language, they will already be familiar with the approach.

I hope soon we will see *Phrase-a-Day* programs for German and other languages.

I like this approach. Don't plan on using it for basic language instruction—for that, the simple method of introducing nouns first, verbs second, and phrases last works better. But once your child has had his first French or Spanish lessons, and knows a few of the words in the book, the *Phrase-a-Day* program is one way to move him from words to sentences.

NEW★★
Gallopade Publishing Group
French for Kids, Spanish for Kids, $14.95 paper each, $19.95 hardcover each. Add 10% shipping ($2.50 minimum).

Like Carol Marsh's book *Of All the Gaul: Latin for Kids,* reviewed in Chapter 11, her two books for French and Spanish are brash, easy to read, and easy to do. *"False Paw": French for Kids* teaches numbers, colors, school words, animal names, family names, tableware names, clothes names, common phrases, and some cultural notes. Phonetic pronunciations are included next to the French words, so you will see that *noir* is pronounced "nwarh."

"Uh, oh, Amigo!" Spanish for Kids is more of the same, minus the pronunciation notes. Find out about Spanish names, numbers, colors, household objects, clothing, and some Spanish cultural trivia. Clever definitions abound. See if you can figure this one out: "*Blanco* as snow." What color is *blanco*? How about "the *amarillo* rose of Texas"? See how easy this is?

Don't think these are foreign-language courses. Every other resource in this section will teach you more vocabulary and grammar. These are really *introductions*, to get kids comfortable with the idea of learning a foreign language.

UPDATED**
Hear An' Tell
Cassettes, $7.95 each. Flash Cards, $4.95 each. Game Boards, $6.95 each. Teaching manual $4.50. Little Lamb wooly puppet, $9.95. Illustrated storybooks, $3.95 each.

A new idea in foreign language study based on the Suzuki approach, Hear An' Tell believes that children can and will learn the basics of a new language long before they learn to read or are ready for formal language study. Author Patricia Al-Attas believes "words must be embedded with caring and feeling" when teaching children a new language. In other words, dull vocabulary lists do not have the appeal of stories. This approach fits with the new emphasis on "learning in context" in language-teaching circles.

Hear An' Tell Adventures are based on a series of well-known stories: "Goldilocks;" "Simon, James, and John;" "Little Lamb;" "Noah's Ark;" and a nonmagical version of "Cinderella." All these stories are available in English/Spanish; "Cinderella" also comes in English/French. "Goldilocks" has the simplest vocabulary, lots of contrasting and comparing, the numbers 1-3, and simple adjectives. "Little Lamb" teaches body parts and action verbs, among other things. "Cinderella" teaches the numbers 1-12, clothing, more body parts, and items found in a house. "Noah" has weather words, animal names, and words used in ark construction.

Hear An' Tell's cassette story tapes have the story in the target language translated phrase by phrase. The teacher's manual suggests pantomiming the story with hand motions while you listen and adding props to illustrate the words. The correlated flash cards illustrate words from each story, with the picture and English on one side and the foreign words on the other. The game boards come in sets of four (Picture Tic Tac Toe, Four Word Ho, Tengo, and Lotto). Up to four children may play at once. Workbooks and storybooks are available for each tape. You can even get a fluffy lamb puppet to accompany the "Little Lamb" story!

The new expanded teacher's manuals have activities for children of different ages. Parents don't need to know the language to use these materials.

Since the last edition, Hear An' Tell has come out with several new items, including a story text for "Cinderella" in Spanish and French and a phonetic Spanish coloring book (*The ABC's of Spanish*) based on Bible words. Send an SASE for the latest developments from this energetic new company.

NEW**
Optimalearning Language Land
French for Tots, $19.95 plus $3 shipping. *Spanish for Tots* and *English for Tots*, TBA.

In my opinion, *French for Tots* is actually superior for an introductory minicourse for children in this age group as well. What works for tots works just as well for elementary-age children.

NEW**
Teach Me Tapes, Inc.
Teach Me . . . series: book and cassette, $11.95 each language; book only, $5.95 each language, Teacher's Guide, $5.95 each language. Teach Me More . . . series: book and cassette, $13.95 each language; book only, $6.95 each language.

Cartoon characters Marie and Peter are your hosts for this series of foreign language programs. Favorite songs and basic vocabulary are introduced via a 20-page coloring book with written text and a cassette with songs performed by native children accompanied by professional musicians. English translations are included (thanks, guys!). The songs are a mix of classic children's songs and more "pop"-style modern songs. No rock.

The Teach Me series now includes *Teach Me French, Teach Me Spanish, Teach Me German, Teach Me Japanese, Teach Me More French, and Teach Me More German*. The author has wisely used the same format for all languages, so children can go from one to the other with a feeling of comfort and familiarity.

You really are better off thinking of these as "culture introductions" than as foreign-language-learning courses. The spoken vocabulary is not introduced step-by-step or simplified, but rather serves to introduce the songs. The songs are not "learning" songs per se, but regular songs that children might sing just for fun. *Old McDonald Had a Farm* and *Day-O* were not written to introduce vocabulary, after all! These programs are best suited to parents who who don't want to spend any time systematically teaching and just want to expose the kids to a foreign language through coloring-book exercises and songs.

REAL LANGUAGE COURSES FOR CHILDREN (AND ADULTS!)

Here is your more-or-less traditional language instruction, simplified for children. The goal is to really learn to speak the target language, not just to get acquainted with it. Adults who don't mind having a bit of fun can use these courses, too!

NEW★★
Calvert School

French course tuition, $110, $35/additional child. Advisory Service, $65/child. Free domestic parcel post shipping or foreign regular surface mail. Air parcel post to U.S. address with zip code, $3.50/course. Foreign air mail, $6-$12/course. Parcel air lift to APO addresses only, $1/course.

After years of development and testing, both in their Day School and with a select group of homeschooling families, the famous Calvert School of Baltimore, Maryland now offers a beginning French course, consisting of five audiocassette tapes, a student workbook, a parent instruction manual, and all necessary supplies.

The course covers basic vocabulary and grammar in Calvert's famous step-by-step fashion. No confusion, no difficulties.

Besides the lesson manual, you get a written tape script, so even parents who know no French at all can follow along with the cassette tapes. You also get a full set of answers to the daily lesson questions.

Students learn a basic oral and written vocabulary including colors, seasons, weather, months of the year, time, common objects, the names of family members, animal names, and more. They also get lots of practice in using their new French words, since lessons include both ample opportunity for oral conversation and practice in following written and oral instructions. Kids also learn basic grammar. French is also made fun with kid-pleasing exercises, songs, and games, all found in the student workbook.

Calvert recommends Beginning French for students in grades 4 and up, but will also accept younger students in the French course if they have strong reading and writing skills. You do not need to enroll in Calvert to take the French course. The Advisory Teaching option is available for this course.

For more information on the entire K-8 program offered by Calvert, see the Curriculum Buyers' Guide in Volume 1.

NEW★★
Carden Educational Foundation

French for the Young Child, $6.10. Manual, $9.55. Cassette, $9. *French Songs for the Younger Children* (lyrics only), $3.60. *French for the Elementary School*, $5.65. Manual, $9. Cassette, $13. *Le Français pour les Élèves Americains*, $5.65. Manual, $10.10. Cassettes, $24. Many other items available. Basic Carden Course, 15 hours of onsite instruction to groups of 10 or more, $120/person attending.

The Carden Educational Foundation provides training and textbooks to scores of private Carden schools around the country. These are based on the philosophy of its founder, Miss Mae Carden, a Christian woman of great energy and spirit. Like good private schools of the days gone by, Carden schools offer French courses. For preschool, it's *French for the Young Child*. Grades kindergarten and 1 study *French for the Elementary School*, while grades 2-5 have *Le Français pour les Élèves Americains*. Starting in grade 6, French literature and serious grammar study is introduced.

Although I have not yet had the chance to see these materials, if they are at all like the other Carden materials you will find serious study for children presented in a way that challenges and respects them.

The brochure you will receive from the Carden Educational Foundation states that materials may only be purchased by those who have received Carden training. The people at Carden do recognize, however, that some of us live in remote areas or have trouble getting together 10 like-minded people for 15 hours of training; so you can write for a waiver of this condition. Indicate you are a home schooler and the circumstances that prevent you from attending a Carden Basic Course.

Carden materials were all designed for classroom use, meaning that the teacher's manuals are not the simplest books to zip through. If you can't attend Carden Basic Training, you will be well-advised to obtain the teacher instruction cassettes for subjects and grades you want to teach, as these will greatly enhance your ability to get the most out of Carden materials.

For more information, see the writeup for Carden Educational Foundation in the Curriculum Buyers' Guide of Volume 1.

International Linguistics Corporation
Courses in English, Spanish, French, German, Chinese (new!), and Russian. Set of five cassettes plus book, $42. Extra books, $9.50 each. Four levels available for each language. The set for Book 2 contains 6 cassettes and is $48. Intermediate series in English and German only, another 4 books plus cassettes, same prices. Shipping extra.

My heart still belongs to "The Learnables" from International Linguistics Corp. This is the first complete language program designed especially for very young children. They now offer English, Spanish, French, German, Chinese *and* Russian. You learn to count to ten on the tape, then look at pictures (numbered 1-10), hear the sentences illustrated in the picture, and learn the language. It works, too! I know, because our children (studying the French) are making up whole new sentences inspired by the lessons—crazy stuff, like *"La grosse pomme mange la maison,"* accompanied by the sounds an apple might make while eating a house.

Unlike other programs, which stress repeated sentences, grammar, and drill, International Linguistics teaches language through word-picture association. Cassettes accompany picture books; each sentence or phrase goes with a picture. This results in "natural" learning the way a baby learns. No written words are in the text, either English or in the other language. International Linguistics is insistent that you must learn through sounds only. It is possible to get a transcript of the tapes, but International Linguistics does not sell translations. This is an unnecessary hindrance, and the only feature to which I object.

Pictures are in amusing but understandable cartoon style. The stories are clever. Our sons love the sequence with the baby throwing eggs at the window and the harried mother rushing about looking for a paper towel to wipe up the mess. Every language uses the same picture book, so subsequent languages can build on the first one learned.

Book 1 has 1,000 sentences, as does Book 2. Stories begin in Book 2, and you are introduced to prepositions and pronouns. Book 3 has more complex stories and gets into verb tenses. Book 4 has complex sentences. The Beginner Series of all four books contains a total of 3,000 basic words and grammatical constructions. The Intermediate series, available only in English and German, teaches 1,500 words and advanced grammatical structures.

When you buy a whole series (Beginner or Intermediate), International Linguistics throws in a vinyl cassette case. You can buy a little at a time and easily branch out into new languages.

I recommend that you buy a separate picture book for each learner (they are not expensive), as otherwise squabbles develop over who gets to hold the book. We found that mealtimes are a good time to turn on the cassette player and learn a little French, and you might try it too, if you don't mind getting the pages greasy!

NEW**
Speedy Spanish
Elementary Spanish Book, $10.95. Set of 5 tapes, $30. Written for third-grade level, but has been used successfully by children in grades 1-12 and adults.

If you're looking for glitz, tinsel, professional mood music backgrounds, and a va-va-voom brochure, you came to the wrong place. But if all you want is to give your children (and maybe yourself) an inexpensive, simple, excellent elementary Spanish course with Biblical content, here is something that may interest you!

The Bechtel family, who have home schooled and who attend many West Coast conventions as Christian Light representatives, have put together a really fine course here. I'm not talking about the graphics; all you get is basic typewriter-and-photocopy quality in the manual. I'm not talking about the accompanying cassettes, either; these are strictly bare-bones here's-the-words-in-English-and-Spanish. But the 36 lessons of *Speedy Spanish* have what it takes to teach you over 500 vocabulary words, many basic phrases, basic grammar, Spanish Bible songs, and Spanish Bible verses.

With the cassettes, *Speedy Spanish* is self-teaching and self-correcting. You get a total of 30 lessons plus 5 review lessons. Each lesson introduces about a dozen new words and is planned to take one school week. On Monday, you look at the words and practice with the tape. On Tuesday, you read sentences in English and practice them in Spanish with the tape. On Wednesday, you do a matching exercise. First you color and cut out the vocabulary cards for the week. These are printed on the same paper as the rest of the manual, so you will want to laminate them, or at least cover them with clear contact paper, to make them last longer. You now try to match the columns of English words to the Spanish words in the next column, using the tape to correct your work. Thursday is Memory Day. Now it's time to memorize your Spanish Bible verse and song for this week. On Friday you review and play "Quiz-nish," matching your vocabulary cards to the game chart included for that lesson. After five lessons, the review lesson gives you a chance to master the extra vocabulary words you have been picking up in your Bible verses and songs.

A follow-up course, *Speedy Spanish II,* will be introduced in the summer or fall of 1990. The price will be about the same as that of *Speedy Spanish I.*

The Bechtels' Spanish background includes three years of Spanish study, one year teaching three third-grade Spanish classes, three adopted children from Guatemala, and a son who is a missionary in Guatemala. As far as this non-Spanish speaker can tell, the accent on the tapes certainly sounded authentic. And the price is quite inexpensive for a program that will really get you started on this language.

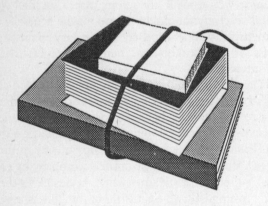

FOREIGN LANGUAGE BOOKS AND WORD BOOKS

NEW★★
EDC Publishing, Inc.
  The First Hundred Words, $7.95. *The First Thousand Words,* $10.95. *The Word Detective,* $10.95. *Round the World,* $10.95. *Beginner's Dictionary* (French, German, or Spanish), $8.95 each. Add 10% shipping.

EDC Publishing strikes again! *The First Hundred Words* and *The First Thousand Words* are now available in a slew more languages. *The First Hundred Words* now comes in French, German, and Spanish. *The First Thousand Words* is available in (are you ready?) French,

German, Spanish, Italian, Russian, and Hebrew. *Round the World* comes in French and Spanish so far, and even *The Word Detective* is also available in French and German. All books also come in English.

These are foreign language vocabulary books for young children with a consistent user interface. Each book has the same pictures on each page as the others in the series, making it at least theoretically possible to add on new languages with little effort. Each page illustrates an environment (the kitchen, a street corner . . .) full of labeled objects. Even the margins contain more labeled pictures. (Those familiar with Richard Scarry's word books will recognize this format.) In the back of each book is a foreign language/English dictionary.

On every page of *The First Thousand Words* a little yellow duck is hiding. Finding this duck fascinates my children—more than learning the target words, to be frank.

Round the World carries on where *The First Thousand Words* left off. More vocabulary, more colorful amusing illustrations by the same illustrator.

Since the format for each hardbound book is identical from language to language, if your child can follow the book for one language he can easily pick up the written rudiments of another. Pronunciation guides in the back help a little, but you will want to either know the studied language yourself or get some cassette materials. In either case, these adorably-illustrated picture-word books are a great first exposure to a foreign language.

For follow-up vocabulary development for the 11-and-up crowd, the new Usborne *Beginner's Dictionary* in French, German, or Spanish is just wonderful. These fully-illustrated , full-color, witty picture dictionaries group vocabulary words together in context or by word type. Thus the numbers are all on one page, with a picture of a man holding many balloons, and body parts (no genitals) and things you do with your body are all shown on another two-page spread. Each noun, action, or phrase is clearly labeled in both English and the target language. The English-target language word list in the back of the perfect-bound book also gives a rough pronunciation for each word. (Too bad the pronunciations weren't alongside the words in the book itself; this would have made it a lot more useful for use by parents and students who are not fluent speakers of the target language.) You could easily use these dictionaries as the heart of a vocabulary-development course, after running the kids through some simple introduction to the language. This is also a really quick way for adults who once took, but never used, the language to brush up on our vocabulary—and learn some new words, too!

NEW★★
Gerard Hamon, Inc.
Tintin books, $8.95 each. *Babar* books, $9.95 each. Larousse des Tout-Petits, $13.95 each for *Les Noms, Les Verbes,* and *Les Adjectifs. Mon Premier Vocabulaire* (Larousse), $12.50. *Le Larousse des Enfants,* $29.95 hardcover. Many other French children's books, from $4.95 to $7.95. When writing for the price list, specify that you want children's materials in French.

Source for hundreds of children's books published *en France.* The Tintin series (22 books) and Babar series (17 books) would be appropriate for children who have already studied French long enough to have a good basic reading vocabulary. Other books, such as *Madeleine,* might be usable if your child has memorized *Madeleine* in English (as mine have). You or your child do have to know the language to use these books. Less background is needed with the Larousse vocabulary books for French children.

The benefits of using actual books used by French children outweigh the difficulties of struggling with the extra vocabulary found in these non-vocabulary-controlled books, in my opinion. Books that kids read because they *want* to read them are always better tools than textbooks. Wanting to find out what Tintin meant provides motivation to learn new vocabulary, as well as opportunity to use existing vocabulary in a meaningful way. And then, there *are* a few vocabulary-controlled books, e.g. *Une Paire d'Amis,* otherwise known as *Frog and Toad Are Friends.*

NEW★★
Ladybird Books, Inc.
Each book, $3.50.

Ladybird's Ready to Learn series of basic books for preschool children has been translated into French. Now available are *Apprenons L'Heure* (a book about telling time), *Les Nombres* (numbers), *Les Formes* (shapes), *Les Couleurs* (colors), and *Grand et Petit* (sizes). Each book has vibrant illustrations in bright colors and is ideally suited for presenting its early-learning vocabulary. It's easy to figure out which word means what, even if you know no French at all. The hitch comes when trying to teach your children with these books. Non-French-speakers then have the choice of (a) reading aloud in an accent you know is wrong, or (b) settling for teaching children to read the words without being able to pronounce them.

If you can speak the language, these books provide a charming way to share early education, French-style, with the kids.

Also available are 26 classic fairy tales in French, including "*Boucle d'Or et les trois ours,*" "*Le vilain petit canard,*" "*Hansel et Grete,*" "*Les trois petits cochons,*" "*Blanche Neige et les sept nains,*" and "*L'apprenti sorcier.*" Being translated, these are, respectively, "Goldilocks and the Three Bears," "The Ugly Duckling," "Hansel and Gretel," "The Three Little Pigs," "Snow White and the Seven Dwarves," and "The Sorcerer's Apprentice."

New: By October 1990 Ladybird hopes to have brought out around 20 children's Spanish titles, similar to the French ones listed above. A great way to practice elementary French or Spanish vocabulary!

CHAPTER TEN

FOREIGN LANGUAGES FOR TEENS & ADULTS

Don't use this chapter until you first go back and check out the foreign language programs for children. Especially if you have had trouble with a foreign language before, you may find that the super-simple approach of children's language instruction is just the thing to break your learning block. And some of those programs, like International Linguistics and Speedy Spanish, might rightly be said to cross all age boundaries. The only reason you will find them in the children's chapter, and not here, is for reasons of space. They really belong in both places.

So, what makes the courses listed in this chapter different from the children's courses? Generally you'll find an emphasis on business or travel. Learning is more workbooky. Often the course revolves around sample dialogs. Several native speakers have a simulated conversation, with pauses inserted for you to repeat the sentences or phrases. These courses also often include a fair amount of written work: translating, reading in the target language, grammar exercises, and so on. The user is expected to know common grammatical terms, and to be willing to learn more.

For your convenience I have separated the foreign-language courses in this chapter into self-study courses, high-school courses, Christian courses, and business courses. "Self-study" means the course was designed to be used by an individual studying on his own. Most adult readers should look at these first. The high-school courses are just that—programs used in junior high and high school. I have tried to concentrate on programs that cross over well to home instruction. These generally are more comprehensive than the self-study courses, and will be of most interest to home schoolers, although people with children enrolled in a school that does not offer these languages might also find them useful. Christian courses make a point of teaching Bible verses and "witnessing" vocabulary in the target language. Business courses specialize in both business vocabulary and explaining how to cut deals in a foreign country without making any awful social blunders. Plus foreign language games, widgets, and software. Dig in!

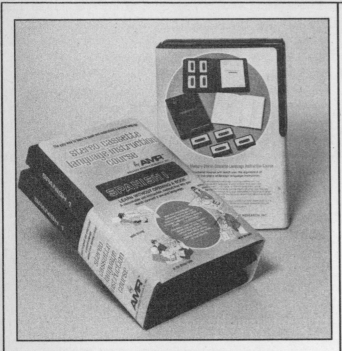

SELF-STUDY LANGUAGE COURSES

AMR Educational Systems

French, German, Italian, Latin American Spanish: same format for all (2 album sets, 5 cassettes/album). Level I, $110. Level II, $130 (Italian not available). Individual albums (4 cassettes plus extra vocabulary cassette): $55 (Spanish, German, French, Italian Level 1) or $65 (Advanced levels, and Japanese and Chinese). Single cassette and manual, $12.50. *Strictly Vocabulary*, Levels I and II, $49.50 each. *Practical Spanish*, $79.50. Also available: Medical and Law Spanish. Japanese and Mandarin Chinese, $135.

What kind of foreign language courses would two Wheaton college professors design? Believe it or not, the profs don't want you to hit the books. In fact, AMR lets you learn the language right off the cassettes. Courses are recorded in stereo, with the foreign language and the English translation on separate levels. Thus you can fade out one or the other, and test yourself. This method, unique to AMR, is protected by a U.S. Patent.

All Western languages follow the same format (your choice of French, German, Italian, and Latin American Spanish). You hear a short, useful dialog with very soft mood music in the background. Each sentence has the English translation. Next, individual words and phrases are repeated with their translations. Finally, the dialog is repeated without translation, so you can try pronouncing the phrases and see if you

understand it. Each dialog introduces new grammar; for example, the "I" form of the verb might be used for the first time.

After several dialogs, AMR has a short section on how to expand your speaking power by adding extra vocabulary words and phrases to what you have already learned. This section also includes very simple explanations of some essential grammatical features.

AMR uses native speakers, both male and female, carefully chosen from different regions of the target country so you get a cross-section of the different regional accents.

AMR's accompanying manual contains a complete transcript of every cassette, plus informative cultural notes.

AMR's approach would be suitable for anyone except young children. They, not seeing the need for learning the language, would be bored by the adult dialogs. For the traveler, AMR is excellent. Not only do you learn the essential vocabulary for coping with life overseas, but AMR includes cultural notes in its accompanying manual. These notes are obviously written by someone who has been there and who understands that Americans need to know if French hotel rooms have a bathroom (most do not: in fact, you're lucky to have a bathroom on your floor) and other vital facts.

Japanese and Mandarin Chinese are available in Level I only, and are different from the others in that they have been adapted to include significant features of Chinese and Japanese culture. Each course teaches a phonetic form of the language using the English alphabet. The Japanese and Chinese written characters are also provided as they correspond to each dialog.

Each course contains eight one-hour stereo cassettes, a manual with cultural notes and the transcript of the recordings, and a dictionary listing words used, all bound in two very impressive gold-stamped vinyl-leather cases.

AMR also has *Practical Spanish* courses for medical workers, policemen, and firemen. These are less expensive than the foreign language courses, probably because nobody had to fly overseas and locate native speakers. You get six high-quality C-60 cassettes and all the other gear included in the regular language courses.

Also from AMR: a *Strictly Vocabulary* series using its patented Bilingual Stereo Self-Test method. This series, available in all the languages mentioned above, is arranged in topics and supplements the Level 1 and Level 2 programs. The price is quite reasonable for a memory and pronunciation tool covering about 2,000 words. Those using a standard language text might want to consider getting AMR's *Strictly Vocabulary* program to help them with pronunciation. In this way you could create a total language program for around $60. (It will, of course, be more work than if you got the total AMR language course.) Contents: four cassettes, dictionary of words used, and vinyl-leather case.

AMR's program is among the best for those who want to learn a foreign language with reasonable fluency, but do not plan on permanently moving to the country in question. It is not boring, the recordings are excellent, and you can test your progress as you go.

Audio-Forum
Individual courses all have different prices. Prices range from about $100 to over $200 for FSI courses. Languages: Many Spanish courses, including Business, Medical, Spanish for Policemen and Firemen, Spanish for Health Professionals, and Household Spanish for Home Managers, plus FSI Spanish (several levels). FSI French, plus Basic Haitian Creole and several dialog series. German. Italian. Modern Hebrew. Arabic (several dialects). Chinese (several dialects). Portuguese. Japanese. Polish. Russian. Modern and Classical Greek. Classical Latin. Scandinavian languages. Eastern European languages. Turkish. Urdu. Thai. Vietnamese. Khmer (Cambodian). Trade languages of Africa. Survival English. Living Language® Videos: French, German, Spanish, $34.95 each; In all, 191 courses in 56 languages. Less expensive courses available.

Audio-Forum does not develop their own courses. As they say, "We have drawn on the expertise of our academic advisory board to help us identify and locate the most effective courses in use anywhere in the United States or abroad. We then obtained the rights to offer these by mail throughout the English-speaking world."

Most Audio-Forum courses are duplicates of the Foreign Service Institute courses used to train U.S. diplomats and overseas personnel. These are the full-length, in-depth courses. Unlike others' language programs, Audio-Forum FSI courses do not all follow the same basic format. They do, however, offer a wider variety of languages than anyone else, including Arabic, Cantonese, Hungarian, Hebrew, and Vietnamese, to name just a few. If you want to dig down to your family's "roots" and learn the language of your non-English ancestors, Audio-Forum probably has it.

How does it work? Repetition, repetition, repetition . . . FSI students normally memorize the dialogs,

and one can understand why, since you hear the same one over and over and over. I was surprised to hear the street French of the French I series: *Juizreux* or some such mangled remnant for *Je suis hereux*. That may be the way they talk in France, but it puts a stumbling-block before beginners to not hear extremely distinct pronunciation. We don't mumble at babies, after all!

FSI courses come with culture notes and big, fat textbooks. Make no mistake about it, FSI is the heavy artillery of language instruction.

The Living Language® video courses from Crown Publishers are also offered by Audio-Forum. These consist of real-life tourist situations—hotel, airport, restaurant, store. A friendly emcee explains what's happening in between the adventures of our totally-fluent tourist couple. Phrases and words are introduced at conversational speed, then repeated slowly with English subtitles. The emcee then shows how to use the sentence structures you just used to create more new sentences. You're learning to speak, not to read, since the target language never appears on screen. A booklet with additional vocabulary and dialog transcripts would add a lot to this program.

Berlitz Publications
One-hour course, $9.95: Arabic, Chinese, Dutch, Finnish, French, German, Greek, Hebrew, Italian, Danish, Japanese, Norwegian, Portuguese, Russian, Serbo-Croatian, Spanish (Castillian and Latin American), and Swedish. Basic Home Study Cassette Course, $59.95: French, German, Italian, Spanish. Comprehensive Cassette course, $140: same 4 languages. Berlitz also has travel guides and phrase books for almost everywhere—get these at bookstores.

Berlitz is now, according to itself, "the world's leading publisher of books for travellers . . . plus Cassettes and Self-teaching courses." Berlitz, as you may recall, started as a you-attend-the-classes language school. The company has wisely decided to put together inexpensive courses using the Berlitz method. These are aimed mostly at the tourist market.

The bottom of the line is Berlitz's one-hour cassette course. You get basic phrases spoken in four voices and a little booklet with the text of the recordings, plus translation. I don't think much of these phrase-books as a serious learning tool. If all you want is a taste of the language, that's all you'll get.

The Berlitz Cassette Course looks more promising. You get a 90-minute "zero" or beginner's cassette with ten basic lessons in four voices. These are not just random phrases, but follow a grammatical plan. This is followed by two more 60-minute cassettes. You also get two illustrated books with the text of all lessons plus helpful notes, a rotating verb finder, a Berlitz phrase book, and a pocket dictionary.

The Berlitz Comprehensive Cassette Course includes all the above, plus two more C-60 cassettes and four more illustrated manuals.

I believe in "baby-talk"—slow, exaggerated pronunciation—for beginners, and Berlitz apparently does not. The Spanish cassette I heard didn't quite race along at Puerto Rican speed, but was pretty brisk nonetheless.

Conversa-Phone Institute, Inc.
Round-the-world courses, $9.98: Indonesian, Serbo-Croatian, Chinese (Mandarin and Cantonese), Hindi, Arabic, Czech, Ukranian, Eastern European and Scandinavian language courses, Turkish, Malay, Irish Gaelic, Korean, Yiddish, Thai, Afrikaans, and Tagalog, plus all the standard European and Asian languages. Modern Method courses, $19.98: French, German, Italian, Spanish, Portuguese, Swedish, Russian, Modern Greek, Mandarin Chinese, Advanced Spanish. Many courses available on cassette. New Compact Disc courses in French and Spanish, $29.95 each. Also English for Foreigners series, $19.98: 20 courses, including European, Asian, and Scandinavian languages plus Arabic and Greek. $2 shipping for the first course, 50¢ additionals.

Let me skip quickly over Conversa-Phone's Round-the-World courses. These are one record plus text. I'm skipping over these little courses because I am anxious to extol the Modern Method courses. These come boxed, with your choice of four LP records or two C-60 cassettes, plus a 100-lesson illustrated instruction manual. In my estimation, as one who has suffered under many language teachers, these courses are the cheapest, most effective means of brushing up a previously-studied language around. You not only get the recorded text plus translation—all companies provide this—but a number of lists and

simplified grammar lessons, plus pictures of hundreds of subjects. The text is even witty in spots, and since the text goes beyond the cassettes you are not limited in your learning to what can be said in two hours of recording time. The whole course comes conveniently boxed.

To this line Conversa-Phone has just added the first spoken word language compact disc courses. These include two compact discs and a fully illustrated instruction manual. Presently available in French and Spanish, the compact disc quality should make it easier to pick up on the nuances of correct pronunciation.

ESP

ESP has the very cheapest language instruction around. For eight dollars you can get a cassette with 60 minutes of instruction, plus a student workbook and tests. I have not tried one, but for a low-risk taste of another language it sounds reasonable. Available in Beginning, Intermediate, and Tourist Spanish and Tourist French.

NEW**
Penton Overseas, Inc.
How to Learn a Foreign Language, $14.95. The VocabuLearn series, $14.95 each. VocabuLearn/ce software, $59.95 per course. Add $3 shipping per order.

How to Learn a Foreign Language is a three-hour audiocassette program with accompanying informative booklet. Written by a man who learned 16 languages in the foreign service, its mission is to help first-time language students, and those who have failed at languages in the past, learn the tips and techniques necessary to master another language.

Learning foreign languages is different than other disciplines in that you can't just tack on the knowledge to what you already know. To become fluent, you must learn to *think* in the target language, literally replacing your normal thought patterns while you're talking, reading, or writing in that language. *How to Learn a Foreign Language* explains how to do this, as well as concepts like how to discover the roots of words, the way to master proper pronunciation, how to pick up grammar skills, and lots more. The book has received rave reviews from the experts.

VocabuLearn, also from Penton Overseas, is a popular vocabulary-development program available in 16 languages. These are *not* standalone programs. Think of them as "audio flash cards." Each VocabuLearn course includes two 90-minute audiocassettes and a word list containing over 1500 words and expressions used on the cassettes. The words are not in any particular order, except that nouns, verbs, and other parts of speech are presented separately. Here's how it works. On one side of the tape, an American voice says a word in English, followed by a pause long enough for you to vocalize the word in the target language, if you know it. Then a native speaker of the target language says the word nice and slowly in that language. Halfway through the tape, the process is reversed. The target language word or phrase comes first, followed by a pause, then by the word in English. This "reversible" feature means non-English speakers of the target language can also use these tapes to learn or improve their English. The word lists are different for both sides of the tape, by the way, to allow more vocabulary on the tapes.

VocabuLearn courses come in three levels. Level I is basic skills—simplest words and phrases. Level II includes more words and expressions. Level III includes more complex and sophisticated vocabulary. The tapes are supercrisp, thanks to Dolby Stereo, and the packaging is nice.

Levels I and II are available in Arabic, Armenian, Mandarin Chinese, Danish, French, German, Hebrew, Italian, Japanese, Korean, Polish, Portuguese (South American), Russian, Spanish, Swedish, and a special French/Spanish course. Level III is now available for French, German, Italian, Japanese, Russian, and Spanish.

Foreign language teachers, libraries, and bookstores seem quite fond of this system, judging by how the courses sell. Remember, this is more of a *testing* device than a teaching program. What's the difference? Typical teaching programs group the words together that go together, like emotions, parts of the body, days of the week, and months of the year. These words *are* taught on the first VocabuLearn tape, but they show up in no particular order and spaced widely apart. This deliberate randomness is designed, like the deliberate highway curves in the middle of flat prairie country, to "wake you up." You are forced to associate words *only* with their meanings, not with the surrounding words. This can have its advantages over systems that associate lists of words. Consider how many of us still have to run through the entire ABC song to find which letter comes before V! VocabuLearn, in contrast, forces you to *think* about which word means what. Its publishers claim this results in significantly quicker vocabulary learning.

VocabuLearn's big selling point is that "it is the first audio language system that concentrates on simple vocabulary and helpful expressions." In other words, *no grammar studies*. As the authors correctly point out, grammar is what foreign-language students fear. Grammar is just a way of arranging your speech in orderly patterns, which we all picked up by osmosis at the ages of 3–5 after we learned a basic vocabulary in our native tongue. In languages like Hebrew where the word roots are heavily changed when you change tenses and cases, you are not going to be able to escape grammar study of some sort. However, any such study will be a lot easier if you already have a basic vocabulary to begin with.

VocabuLearn/ce, a computer enhanced version of VocabuLearn for both IBM-PC and Macintosh users, is also now available in both levels I and II for Spanish, French, Italian, German, Japanese, Russian, and Hebrew. Each level comes with the same cassettes and booklet as regular VocabuLearn courses, but also has computer disks that allow you to drill yourself on the written words using your computer. For more info, see the review in the Educational Software Buyer's Guide in Volume 3.

SyberVision
$245 apiece for Spanish, French, German, and Modern Hebrew. $229 each for Modern Greek and Russian.

SyberVision, a purveyor of sports, exercise, and self-improvement videos, has a winner in their Speak, Read, and Think foreign language series. Based on Dr. Paul Pimsleur's language learning techniques, SyberVision courses feature anticipation, recall, and the use of basic sentences as a model for creating new sentences—just like *Artes Latinae*, reviewed in chapter 11.

First, you hear a dialog in foreign speech. It sounds like gibberish! Were you foolish to buy this course? Don't despair. Help is on its way. The cassette instructor breaks down the sentences into words and the words into syllables. You are asked to repeat these words and syllables. Then, using what you have learned, you are asked questions in the target language. The correct response is then given, so you can see if you answered correctly. The course also repeats previous matter at scientifically-determined intervals to reinforce your memory. By this means, you actually learn to think in the target language.

The SyberVision courses are not cheap. But if you can't pass the built-in test at the end of the course at the 1+ level—that required for the diplomatic corps—you can return the course for a complete refund.

NEW**
Visual Education Association
Think Language series, $14.95 each level. Specify records or cassettes. Levels available: Spanish I and II, French I and II, German I and II, English I (for foreign students and remedial). Shipping extra—they bill you.

For older children or adults, the Best Inexpensive Language Program award goes to Visual Education's Think French/German/Spanish series. Each language comes in two levels, each corresponding to a year of high-school language instruction or a semester of college. You get a set of white Concept Cards flash cards with cartoons illustrating the sentences, phrases, or words introduced on the card, a set of correlated green Structural Pattern or Usage cards giving grammar principles and drill, a cassette with both male and female native speakers of the language repeating an hour's worth of phrases from the Concept Cards, and an accompanying booklet with all the vocabulary translated alphabetically into English, plus study tips and an outline of the lessons, all neatly packed in a sturdy box for just *$14.95 per level!*

Each of the Think languages has its own unique program design. The Spanish cards are different from the German cards, etc. Maria and Juan, our friends in Spanish Level I, start right in dancing, but Käte and Erich, from German Level I, are more interested in studying. Make of this what you will!

The Think series starts right in with complete but simple sentences, so for young children you are better off with the more expensive but slower-paced Learnables (mentioned in the previous chapter). Otherwise, anyone with a basic grasp of English grammar and sentence structure can, thanks to the illustrations and patterned approach, learn to *think* in the target language, as opposed to merely mentally translating words from one language to another. (Hint: If you are unacquainted with the target language try looking through the cards first, translating words you can't figure out from the cartoons, before studying with the cassette.)

HIGH SCHOOL STUDY TEXTS

NEW**
A Beka Books
Spanish I text, $17.95. Teacher's guide, $20. Pronunciation/Scripture cassette, $8.95. Vocabulary manual, $10.40. Teacher's edition of manual, $12.40. Vocabulary tape, $8.95. Spanish II text, $18.95; teacher's guide, $20. Vocabulary manual for II, $11.40; teacher's edition, $13.40. Test booklet for either I or II: student, $3.45; teacher, $7.40. Songbook, $4.95. Add 10% shipping, minimum $2.75.

Por todo el mundo and *Mas que vencedores* are the titles of two Spanish texts for Christian students. Strong emphasis on witnessing for Christ includes Bible memory verse for every week, practice lessons from the life of Christ, and a missionary motif. Lots of grammar drill and practice exercises. Separate vocabulary-building program. Vocabulary and Pronunciation/Scripture cassettes coordinate with the texts. Plus a songbook with Christian praise songs in Spanish.

Spanish I and II are also available as video courses through A Beka Video School. See Curriculum Buyers' Guide in Volume 1.

A Beka hopes to expand their foreign-language courses. Look for French I and II, coming soon.

Alpha Omega Publications
$19.50 for complete set of 10 LIFEPACs. Spanish Instruction and Testing Tapes (set of 3 per LIFEPAC), $10 per set, $100 for all 30 tapes. Shipping 10%.

Alpha Omega Publications has LIFEPAC worktexts for both Spanish and New Testament Greek, one full year of each. The Spanish course comes with a set of three cassette tapes, two for practice and one for testing. Along with the dialogs and grammar, each LIFEPAC in the series of 10 Spanish worktexts has sections on Cultural Activities, The World of Music, and a What Does the Bible Say? translation exercise.

NEW**
Bob Jones University Press
Grundstufe I and *II*, *Mittelstufe I*, $8.45 each. Cassettes, $52.45/set.

While A Beka concentrates on Spanish and French, Bob Jones University Press, another Christian publisher, offers German. Their *Praktisches Deutsch* three-year high-school program uses the "total immersion" approach. Each of the student texts has nothing, *nichts,* but German in its pages. Translation is avoided; rather, teens are expected to build vocabulary through "association, description (in German), and illustration." BJU is trying to get you *thinking* in the language, as well as reading it, writing it, and speaking it.

What are your chances of teaching this course at home? Slim, unless you already know German. You can't lean on a teacher's edition, because there isn't any. Instead, BJU provides sets of cassette tapes for language practice: six in year 1, seven in year 2.

Student lessons, as in other Bob Jones material, cover a wide range of topics: German history, art, literature, daily life, travel, amusement, songs, politics, and, of course, religion. Students learn German Bible verses, and the program has an evangelistic bent.

You have to be careful with this total immersion stuff. They tried it in my seventh-grade French class, and everyone in my class agreed that we didn't understand what we were supposed to be learning. Memorizing dialogs is fine as long as they *are* explained. BJU, to their credit, does expect the teacher to clear up confusion and explain what the students can't figure out for themselves.

NEW**
EMC Publishing
Some sample prices: *Spanish for Business,* Beginning or Intermediate versions, textbook $9.95 each version, teacher's guide $3 each version, complete kit with three cassettes, textbook, and teacher's guide $55 each version. Mystery readers $2.50 on up. *Passport to Germany* kit, $128. *Passeport pour la France,* $8.95. *Lander und Sitten,* $195 (3 cassettes and teacher's resource guide). *In Europe,* $8.95.

At the very last minute I ran across this colorful catalog of foreign language materials for public and private high schools. Languages included are Spanish, German, Italian, French, Russian, Portuguese, and Greek. EMC has foreign-language drill and practice for the Apple II family software in all these languages except Greek, and Easy Readers for every language except Portuguese and Greek.

For most languages, EMC offers BBC learning kits or adaptations. Its BBC Spanish series, *España Viva,* digs into the culture and everyday life of Spain. (Accompanying videocassettes for these and other BBC programs from EMC are available from Films Incorporated.) *España Viva* now has a new intermediate program, *Paso Doble,* as well. Lots of easy-read mystery thrillers in different languages.

The *Spanish for Business* series (not the same as Audio-Forum's) follows the trials and tribulations of the Comercial Hispana, a fictional Spanish import/export firm with connections in Latin America, with a "striking variety of unconventional exercises." Two levels, not terribly expensive for a business language course.

These are just a few of the Spanish materials. I wouldn't have space to list all materials for the other languages either. Each has one or more beginning programs and cultural introductions, except Portuguese and Greek. Taking those for granted, let's look at some of EMC's more interesting products.

Passport to Germany is for those with filmstrip projectors. It includes five filmstrips, five cassettes, and a teacher's guide with reproducible activity worksheets, and is intended to present a realistic experience of traveling in the target country.

Passeport pour la France is a textbook with "vivid, full-color photographs and illustrations," "unconventional learning activities," and "a wealth of information not generally found in French textbooks."

Buongiorno Italia! is a BBC program for beginners that features conversations and interviews with Italians filmed and recorded in Italy.

Lander und Sitten sounds absolutely fabulous, but unfortunately is too expensive for me to check out for you. This is a three-video visit to Germany, Austria, and Switzerland, narrated in both German and English. It hits all the historical (and tourist!) hot spots: the Black Forest, the Bavarian Alps, the Rhine, Frankfurt, Munich, Salzburg, Innsbruck, Vienna, Lausanne, Zurich, and more.

EMC's Russian line-up includes an adapted BBC series (textbook, workbook, study guide, cassettes, teacher's guide) with optional accompanying video series; *Let's Practice Russian* software for the Apple; and seven Russian Easy Readers (three at level A, two each at levels B and C).

In Europe introduces you to everyday life, traditions, and cultures of modern Europe. Lots of drawings, photos, and maps. Can be used "before, during, and after a trip to Europe." Sounds like fun!

NEW**
Longman Publishing Group
France-Français, Italia-Italiano, Deutsch-Deutschland, $13.16 each. *Le Phénomene du Langage,* $11.96 student text, $5.96 teacher's guide/answer key.

Longman is now a subsidiary of Addison-Wesley, a major player in the public-school textbook market. Longman recently purchased Independent School Press, a major prep-school text publisher. Between these two connections, you now get 20 pages of foreign-language textbooks, workbooks, activity books, and so on for French, Spanish, German, and Italian.

Now, I couldn't possibly work through every single one of these dozens of books and still be serious about ever finishing my book. So I settled for checking out books with unique features that looked doable at home.

Le Phénomene du Langage was my first discovery. This discovery-oriented text takes a different approach to language instruction; children are taught *how to study* a foreign language (in this case, French). The heart of *Le Phénomene* is its analytical exercises. Students are led through a series of questions to formulate the rules governing French grammar and sentence construction. Along with this are regular written and oral exercises, pronunciation practice, vocabulary lists, cultural notes, and some whimsical little narratives featuring the like of Françoise the Ant. Even more: "Latin Links" show the connections between Latin and French—especially valuable for those who have already used the corresponding Latin book, *The Phenomenon of Language.* The course is designed to take about 10-12 weeks when taught daily for a half-hour or so.

Another intriguing idea are the three FLEX courses, *France-Français, Italia-Italiano,* and *Deutsch-Deutschland.* FLEX stands for Foreign Language Exploratory Course. The idea is to present more than one foreign language in a year, so students can shop around and get used to the structures of several languages. Recognizing that many students will not continue with foreign language learning, but that many will one day be tourists, the vocabulary and language is chosen to be useful when the student visits the target country. These courses are *very* simple and effective and will not take much teaching time. Both are written by Australians, by the way!

Neither program has an accompanying cassette, so unless you already know how to pronounce these languages, you will need to either purchase one of Longman's cassette-based programs or try tuning in France on the shortwave radio.

Other neat-looking stuff I didn't have time to personally investigate: *Radio France* is authentic French radio recordings (to hear) and actual French newspaper articles (to read). *French Talk* is a cassette-based program to beef up your listening and reading comprehension. Two *French Fun Books* are loaded with games, puzzles, and riddles using basic French vocabulary (directions in English). Similar resources available in other languages.

NEW**
North Dakota State Department of Public Instruction/Division of Independent Study
$27/semester course, North Dakota residents. $47/semester course, nonresidents. Books and supplies extra (about $13-$40 for most courses). $5 handling fee on all course registrations. Video supplements, about $10 total per videotape. Example: $180 for Russian I (36 lessons on 18 tapes). Current video selection includes Russian I and II, Spanish I-IV, and French I and II. All tapes 60-minute VHS. You may preview a one-part video for each course free if returned within 30 days.

North Dakota Department of Independent Study (DIS) offers *six* languages: Latin, German, Spanish, French, Norwegian, and Russian (these courses include cassettes). Some of these now have optional video supplements, and the Spanish course even has a (slightly) interactive computer supplement.

DIS courses are rather easy, as far as the assignments go. If you can understand the texts and syllabi you can breeze right along. These are correspondence courses, so you'll have a real live instructor to interact with. Wrap your lessons in the provided wrappers, stick on the postage, and send them in every so often.

DIS videos are simply taped lectures. The Russian teacher says the words, but does not act out the sentences. Thus, you get part of the educational benefit of a video (hearing a foreign language), but not all (no connection of words to images).

Most screens in DIS's new computer-assisted Spanish course are just text from the course curriculum, although in some you can click on, say, days of the week and hear them pronounced in Spanish. You move back and forth between the Spanish teaching video and the computer.

You can get credit for these courses through your local public high school. See the expanded review of the North Dakota State curriculum in the Curriculum Buyers' Guide in Volume 1 for details.

FOREIGN LANGUAGES FOR CHRISTIANS

A Beka Books
Bob Jones University Press

See writeups under "High School Courses" above.

American Bible Society

When I was a child I read a novel whose main character learned new languages by studying a Bible in the target language. This method could work well if you (1) know the Bible very well and (2) only want to read the new language, or (3) also have cassettes to help you with pronunciation. If you're a Christian and want to talk about Jesus in a foreign country, it wouldn't hurt to have some Scripture memorized in that language.

American Bible Society has the Bible in many languages. Avoid the "classical" translations that correspond to our King James Version; nobody overseas understands these any better than we understand Elizabethan English today.

ABS's free *Scripture Resources in Many Languages* catalog lists Scripture publications in the forty most popular languages, about half of the languages they normally have available. Many Scriptures can be specially ordered even if they are in a language ABS does not normally offer for sale.

All ABS materials are inexpensive.

NEW**
Hosanna
Single Gospel of Mark cassette, $3, or $6 for two-cassette languages. Gospel of Mark in 12 different languages, $28.80.

Reader Donna Young tipped me off to Hosanna. This ministry-minded company sells Bible audiocassettes in many languages. Originally Hosanna intended its Bible cassettes for use with native speakers of each language, but as Donna pointed out, this is a way to introduce our children to a foreign language as well.

Since buying an entire New Testament on tape can be fairly expensive ($20–$32 per language), Hosanna is very sweetly offering you the option to purchase just the Gospel of Mark in any given language, or a set of Mark in 12 different languages for those who want to taste a lot of different languages.

Of course, those who want to witness in any of these languages will be grateful for the chance to learn the Scriptures in these languages. This is also a wonderful way to learn a language, once you have a basic grasp of the grammar and some of the vocabulary. I have heard of several people who learned foreign languages through studying foreign language Scriptures.

Hosanna offers the entire New Testament in the following languages: Arabic (Van Dyke translation), Cantonese (Union version), French (Louis Second version), German (Martin Luther version), Haitian (Alliance Biblique Universelle translation), Hindi (Lockman Foundation), Italian (Reiveduta/Luzzi version), Kiswahili (Kenya Bible Society), Korean (Hankul version), Malagasy (Malagasy Bible Society), Mandarin (Union version), O'Othham (Wycliffe Bible Translators), Portuguese (Almeida Versao Atualizada—can't be shipped to Brazil), Spanish (New International Version, or Reina Valera), Tagalog (common version), Taiwanese (Union version), Telugu (Pakistan Bible Society), Tewa (Wycliffe), Urudu (Revised Version), English (King James Version or NIV). Gospel of Mark is available in (note that starred languages require two tapes): Arabic, Cantonese, Farsi (Persian), French, *German, *Haitian Creole, *Hindi, *Italian, *Japanese, Korean, Mandarin, *Portuguese, Romanian, *Swedish, *Tagalog, Telugu, *Thai, and Urdu.

NEW**
Logos Language Institute
Introductory Study set, $13. In-Depth Studies, $17 each level. Languages available for introductory study: Spanish, Portuguese, French, Italian, Creole (Haiti), German, Dutch, Modern Greek, Modern Hebrew, Swahili, Tagalog, Mandarin Chinese, Taiwanese Chinese, Japanese, Korean, Vietnamese, Farsi, Indonesian, Arabic, Cambodian, Ibo, and Russian. Add 10% shipping.

Logos Language Institute is unique in offering a wide range of language programs geared to enabling the student to *witness* in the target language. They also have a wonderfully inexpensive pricing format. An Introductory Study set for any of their dozens of languages covers about 200 expressions, about half "everyday" and the other half a special spiritual-biblical vocabulary useful for witnessing, plus ten evangelistic Scripture passages in the target language. You get a study notebook and cassette. In-Depth Studies are available in Spanish and Portuguese—five levels of Spanish and two levels of Portuguese. These continue the heavy emphasis on evangelistic vocabulary while adding a lot of well-thought-out formal language instruction—about a month's worth or two per level, by my calculations.

While the Introductory Study Packet emphasizes memorizing phrases, the In-Depth Studies follow more traditional language-learning methods. The folks at Logos urge you to consider purchasing Spanish In-Depth Level One along with the Introductory Spanish course, as they complement each other.

Believe it or not, the Introductory Study packets do give enough material and pronunciation help to get you actually started witnessing in the target language—including a complete gospel presentation, phrases useful for sharing your testimony and inviting a hearer to your church, and so on. They also include a lot of valuable spiritual instruction on how to study with a Christian attitude. I see no reason why you couldn't use this program with older elementary-aged children, provided they have good study habits and really want to learn. And of course it works well with teens and adults. If you love Jesus, you'll really like this program!

NEW★★
Speedy Spanish
Elementary Spanish Book, $10.95. Set of 5 tapes, $30. Written for third-grade level, but has been used successfully by children in grades 1-12 and adults.

This Spanish course for third-graders and up also caters to Christians, with a special emphasis on Bible verses and witnessing vocabulary. See writeup in previous chapter.

FOREIGN LANGUAGES FOR BUSINESS

NEW★★
Audio-Forum
French for Business, Spanish for Business, $175 each. *Fast-Track Japanese, Mandarin*, $115 each. *Executive Japanese*, three volumes, $45 each. Shipping extra.

Beginners, beware: doing business in a foreign country is more than your high-school French or Spanish teacher prepared you for. Business lingo is a foreign language of its own, with its own peculiar expressions. So Audio-Forum now offers two courses for near-beginners entitled *French for Business* and *Spanish for Business*. Both courses cover similar ground, so I'll just describe the French course for you.

WHAT YOU GET: Eight 45-minute cassettes, a binder, and a 137-page text with the dialogs and exercises, plus explanations of the grammar and other features where needed. The course assumes some prior knowledge of the target language, but not very much. Thus lesson one in the French user's guide runs you through practicing the French "r." Each lesson includes several dialogs relevant to some aspect of business travel, "fluidity in speaking" exercises, pattern drills in which you insert different words into prechosen phrases, and listening comprehension exercises.

The whole course is built on the concept of learning by hearing and saying, rather than by memorizing grammar. You listen to and repeat an expression again and again, substituting different words into it. Example (practicing *je voudrais,* which means *I would like to*):

> Je voudrais trouver un taxi.
> Je voudrais encaisser un travellers cheque.
> Je voudrais acheter un journal.

Fluency in speaking is achieved by pronunciation exercises that drill difficult sounds and "backward build-up exercises" (the "fluidity in speaking" exercises I mentioned above). These latter help you learn to repeat dialog expressions smoothly by feeding them to you in gradually bigger chunks. If, for example, you wanted to say in French, "I would like a room overlooking the park," the speaker on the tape would ask you to say, "overlooking the park . . . a room overlooking the park . . . I would like a room overlooking the park."

Where feasible, vocabulary is introduced in units. For example, you learn the numbers together, the colors together, and the days of the week together. You then immediately use this new vocabulary in patterned sentences.

Topics included in the course are:

• Business travel (going through customs, renting a car, cashing a check, asking directions)

• At the hotel (checking in, requesting a quiet room with full bath, wake-up calls, having your clothes cleaned)

• Phone calls (telephone expressions, leaving a message, dealing with a bad connection)

• A visit to a subsidiary (job titles, company sites)

• Good and bad times (a merger, good market conditions, automation, unions, cost problems, lagging profits, relocation)

• Marketing and advertising (market studies, buying trends, advertising)

• Making contacts at a trade show (registering, meeting people, learning about new products, asking for information)

• Negotiating a deal (talking about credit, reductions, terms of payment)

• Importing and exporting (packing, shipping, insurance, and documents)

• Dining out (drinks, lunch, a gourmet dinner, social conversation)

Appendix 1 includes invaluable information on how to cut deals in France, plus expressions for emergencies. Appendix 2 explains the etiquette, layout, and meaning of French business letters, with several photocopied examples of such letters. Appendix 3 lists abbreviations and their meanings, while Appendix 4 is a handy review of basic French grammar. There also are English/French and French/English glossaries covering all the vocabulary used in the course.

French for Business and *Spanish for Business* are extremely well-laid-out courses that are definitely worth the money if you plan on doing business in a country where either of these languages are spoken.

Also available from Audio-Forum, but not personally seen by me: *Fast-Track Japanese* is "a streamlined

introductory course designed for the businessman or traveler who wishes to acquire more knowledge and practice in using the language than provided in brief programs." Program has an emphasis on business situations as well as everyday travel situations. Six cassettes, 367-page text. *Fast-Track Mandarin* was developed by the same professor and covers the same . ground. *Executive Japanese*, unlike the Fast-Track programs, was designed exclusively for business purposes. This program starts at the beginner's level and takes you through "all the language fundamentals required for doing business or living in Japan." Each volume includes dialogs, pronunciation key, terms and definitions, and business information and comes with two cassettes and a 160-page or longer text.

NEW**
Penton Overseas, Inc.
Going International, $14.95. *Customs & Manners* series, $14.95 each. Add $3 shipping per order.

Going International: How to Make Friends and Deal Effectively in the Global Marketplace is a two-cassette series, plus booklet, designed to teach you how to operate overseas without coming off like a clod. How to conduct business meetings and transactions in foreign countries. How to work with foreign banks. The differences among European countries. Asian business customs. Dynamics of the new Europe. Etc. Includes a country-by-country guide to our 30 leading trade partners overseas.

Also available from the same publisher: *European Customs & Manners*, *Latin American Customs & Manners*, and *Asian Customs & Manners*.

DICTIONARIES, READERS, FLASH CARDS, &C.

American Map Corporation
Lilliput Dictionary, $1.75: English/Danish, Dutch, French, German, Italian, Latin, Portuguese, Spanish, or Turkish. Also Danish, Dutch, French, German, Italian, Modern Greek, Portuguese, Spanish, and Turkish/English. *Pocket Dictionary*, $6.95: French, German, Classical Greek, Classical Hebrew, Latin, Portuguese, Russian, and Spanish. *Polish Pocket Dictionary*, $8.95. Other helps available.

Words, words, words in these dictionaries from the matchbox-sized *Lilliput* with 10,000 entries to standard and college dictionaries. The most useful dictionary for most purposes is the pocket-size. It's 3¾ x 6" with between 33,000 and 58,000 entries.

NEW★★
Audio-Forum
The Languages of the World, $15.95. *Foreign Languages and Your Career*, $7.95. Shipping extra.

All I've seen of these two books are the catalog descriptions, but those look fascinating.

The Languages of the World is a reference book that gives you a taste of nearly 200 languages. Each language is described (the catalog says the descriptions are "fascinating"), and you get a sample text in that language, with translation. Find out where more than 500 languages are spoken in the cross-referenced index.

Foreign Languages and Your Career is the third edition of a book that tells you how to make some moola if you know how to *parler, sprechen, hablamar, lego, gavaritsiya,* or so on. Sounds good! As long as it doesn't involve translating German for international bankers in the deeps of New York City, that is!

Caedmon Tapes

Caedmon has recordings of literature in several languages. The Caedmon catalog is immense and you're bound to find something you want in it, whether in English or not.

NEW★★
EMC Publishing
Easy Readers, $5.95 each. Mystery readers $2.50 on up.

Easy Readers series, available in Spanish, French, German, Russian, Italian, Portuguese, and Greek, are classics originally written in those languages, condensed and simplified for easy reading. Reading levels are marked as A, B, C, or D. A-level books contain a 600-word vocabulary (about what you can expect after a semester of high school or a year of junior-high study). B-level is 1,200 words; C-level, 1,800 words; D-level, 2,500 words. EMC also has hi-lo mystery thrillers in some languages.

Hammond
Qu'est-ce Que C'est? $22.95.

Hammond has come out with something that every French enthusiast will want: a visual dictionary! Thousands of pictures and photos show familiar objects, with all the parts labeled in both the target language and English. Now you won't have to stumble around wondering what the French word for "wheel" or "shin" is anymore. It's called *Qu'est-ce que C'est*, which is French for "What's What?," the name of the original English visual dictionary. *Qu'est-ce Que C'est?* looks like a fine addition to a French course.

Jeffrey Norton Publishers

The company that owns Audio-Forum also has a wide line of spoken-word cassettes, including literature in other languages. You can get stories in Chinese, songs from Israel, an Italian interview with Federico Fellini, or Alexander Solzhenitsyn reading *One Day in the Life of Ivan Denisovich* in Russian. J-N also has the complete New Testament on cassette in Spanish, French, Arabic, Hindi, Mandarin, Italian, Portuguese, English, Urdu, German, and Korean. Plus classical Greek and Latin works (see the Classical Languages chapters).

Visual Education Association
Vocabulary Flashcards, $6.95/language. *Compact Facts*: Conversation, Grammar, Verbs—$3.95 each in English, French, German, Russian, and Spanish. Shipping extra.

Vis Ed is your premier source for flash cards. *Vocabulary Flashcards* are 600 to 1,000 small cards plus study guide with index: available also in classical languages. *Compact Facts* are prime ideas, rules, and grammatical formulas in plain speech on 60 pocket-sized cards.

FOREIGN LANGUAGE GAMES

NEW★★
Audio-Forum
Polyglot, $29.95 plus shipping.

Polyglot is a six-language board game for two to six players. The game board portrays the "legendary" tower of Babel—their word, not mine! You try to get to the top of the tower, following one of three paths, the beginning, intermediate, or advanced. The path you choose determines the level of difficulty at which you will be playing.

Polyglot comes with more than 1,800 words on 302 Word Cards, 150 commonly-used phrases on 50 Phrase Cards, six pawns, and one die. Each Word Card has six words in English on one side and on the other side the same words translated into French, German, Spanish, Italian, and Yiddish, along with phonetic pronunciation. Phrase Cards are set up similarly, with three English phrases on one side and on the other side the same phrases translated in the above languages. As you move around the game board, you will land on spaces that require you to translate and pronounce a word or spell a word and/or translate a phrase. Penalty spaces and challenge spaces add excitement.

Players choose which language and degree of difficulty each will play at. You can decide, for example, that all players will use French but play at different degrees of difficulty, or that each player will use a different language at the intermediate level.

Polyglot can be a learning tool as well as a chance to show off your foreign language knowledge. By selecting only a few of the Word Cards and playing the game with them again and again, you can become familiar with those words. Using this method, you gradually increase the number of cards in play until you know them all.

FOREIGN LANGUAGE WIDGETS

NEW★★
Audio-Forum
Transidioma 5-Language Dictionary, $15.95. *Linguatour*, $12.50. Shipping extra.

Here are two versions of the same unusual phrase dictionary. *Linguatour* is an English/target-language word-phrase dictionary whose pages are waterproof plastic 1¼ x 6" cards punched on a ring. Fan out the cards and read the one you want underneath the magnifying-glass cover. Available in English/Spanish, English/French, English/Italian, and English/German. *Transidioma* is the five-language version of *Linguatour*. Selected words and phrase are cross-referenced in English, Spanish, French, German, and Italian.

NEW★★
BDA&M,
Hexaglot, $169.

This might win my "widget-of-the-year" award, if I ever get to try one and it's as good as it sounds. Hexaglot is a hand-held electronic translator with a 40,000 word vocabulary in each of six major western languages: English, French, Italian, German, Spanish, and Portuguese. You enter the word or phrase (50 built-in phrases) from any of these languages on the built-in alphabetic touchpad. (The touchpad is in A-Z order rather than keyboard order—for the benefit of non-typists, I presume.) Hexaglot then pops the translation up on its LCD screen. Did you type in a word with a number of different meanings? Then Hexaglot will provide an ultra-short definition and translation of each of them. Bonuses: Program in up to six different currency exchange rates and then use the numeric keypad to instantly find out how many francs (for example) $5 is worth. Plus play Hangman or scrambled words, for those times when your plane is two hours late. A teeny-tiny device (only 5½ x 3"), Hexaglot is easy to pack . . . and easy to lose. Don't let little kids play with it unless you plan on combing the house daily to find where they stashed it this time.

For foreign language study, Hexaglot would be too slow as an electronic flash card. After all, you have to type in an entire word to find its translation. Where I can see it being most useful is as a substitute for endless dictionary searches while reading foreign literature or working on your homework. When Louis XIV says *L'état, c'est moi* and you have forgotten what *état* means, just type it in and keep on reading.

NEW★★
Crane's Select Educational Materials
Spanish Flipper, $5.95. Add $2 shipping.

"Flippers" are easy-to-use references with 25 3½ x 5½" cards printed on both sides and enclosed in see-through sleeves overlapping each other. Each card has its topic printed on the bottom part that always shows. The whole thing is less than a quarter of an inch thick, and can be snapped into a 3-ring binder.

The Spanish Grammar Flipper has as much grammatical info in it as you will find in most Spanish 1 and 2 textbooks. Topics are in alphabetical order, starting with "Adjectives: Demonstrative" and ending with "Verbs: *Ser* and *Estar*," for 49 topics in all. A really handy, inexpensive reference guide, especially for someone who once studied Spanish and is now trying to brush up on the language.

NEW**
DAK Industries Incorporated
"PLL Digital Shortwave Breakthrough" (order #5534), $49.90 plus $4 shipping.

"I took three years of French in school, but I never get to use it, so I've forgotten it all." This fate need not happen to you if you have a shortwave radio. Shortwave radio signals, unlike your basic AM and FM signals, can travel clear to the other side of the world. That's because they "bounce" off the earth's atmosphere, off the ground, off the atmosphere, and so on, until you pick them up in your shortwave radio. This process is a bit erratic, depending on the weather conditions around the world, so you can't always be sure of tuning in the exact country you want—but you'll always be able to hear *something*.

One major use of shortwave radio is to hear the news from other countries that broadcast in English. Another use is to keep your foreign accents and languages current. For French, listen to our friends in Quebec . . . or Paris! For Spanish, pick up Radio Madrid . . . or the folks down in Honduras! This can be especially valuable if you are studying one of the less-popular foreign languages. Also, you will pick up on what's happening in that culture as a "freebie."

I'm mentioning DAK's deal here, although it may not be current at the time you read this, because DAK generally has some good shortwave radio deal going.

This particular offer is the best I've seen in several years of perusing DAK's catalog. It's a PLL (phase lock loop) radio. This means digital tuning instead of analog. Digital means a digital LCD display with the exact station number, and a *very* compact package ($4\frac{1}{2}$ x $7\frac{1}{4}$ x $1\frac{1}{2}$"). Plus this battery-powered radio has an automatic timer that turns it on whenever you like, if you have a favorite broadcast you don't want to miss. It also comes with a shortwave handbook that lists the frequencies and broadcast times of radio stations around the world, an external antenna jack, the capacity to preset up to 20 stations, and AM and FM bands.

FOREIGN LANGUAGE SOFTWARE

Most foreign-language software is still in its babyhood. It'll let you talk to it, but it's not too good at talking intelligibly to you. Mainly it's on-screen tutorials (if that) plus type-it-in drill-and-practice. Example: EMC's complete line of *Let's Practice* software for the Apple II family, with three lessons in each language—French, German, Russian, Italian, Spanish, and Portuguese. Exceptions: Penton Overseas' *VocabuLearn/ce* series relies on audiocassettes for your "hearing" practice, but allows you dozens of ways to drill yourself on the written words. HyperGlot Software's terrific lineup of interactive software for both the Macintosh and the IBM family has native speakers translated into digitized sound, plus interactive instructions, plus all that great grammar and vocabulary drill you love so much. Great interface, too. Read all about them in the Educational Software Buyers' Guide in Volume 3.

CHAPTER ELEVEN

CLASSICAL LANGUAGES FOR YOUNGSTERS

Where is that schoolboy? Lead me to him! You know, the fellow who first chanted

"Latin's a dead language
As dead as it can be
It killed the ancient Romans
And now it's killing me."

That poor boy obviously never had viewed the fabulous list of resources you are about to see. If he had, he wouldn't have been complaining!

Many of us have hang-ups about tackling the classical languages. We picture them as stuffy and difficult. PBS is to blame here: all those high-toned announcers from the BBC snorting up their noses at us and dropping Latin *bon mots* like monarchs used to scatter gold coins before the peasants. You get the impression that Latin and the other classical languages are for aristocrats and scholars, and that anyone who turns first to the sports page or funnies is automatically disqualified from learning them. Absurd! Or, as Julius Caesar used to say, *Absurdum!* Compared to other languages, both Latin and Greek are laughably simple. Old Testament Hebrew is a bit trickier, because of the verb structure, but still quite learnable.

Now, let me share a secret: learning these languages is *fun!* You and your children can learn them together, or you can learn alone and teach them later.

Your vocabulary will grow by leaps and bounds. Good books will make more sense, as you will be able to pick up the literary allusions and decipher the classical quotes. TV fluff will seem less filling when compared to the treasures of the past. Who knows? You or your children might even start writing *new* classics!

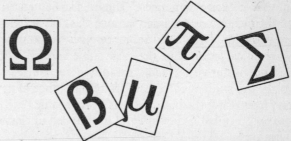

LEARNING THE DREADED GREEK AND HEBREW ALPHABETS

Piece of cake. Just get the Lauri crepe rubber Hebrew letter puzzles from Timberdoodle (they're really inexpensive). Also check out the Hebrew bingo and alphabet cards from EKS Publishing. For Greek, you could invest about $7 in Walter Jerry Clark's *How to Use New Testament Greek Study Aids* or, for deeper study, blow $10 (retail price) on Jim Found's *Basic Greek in 30 Minutes a Day.* Both of the latter are available for less from Great Christian Books and possibly also from Christian Book Distributors. Now, where did I put that catalog?

LATIN FOR KIDS

Bolchazy-Carducci Publishers
Student Text, Level I, Book 1 (Units 1-15), $17; Book 2 (Units 16-30), $24. Unit Test Booklet, $10. Graded Reader, $11. Reference Notebook, $7. Teacher's Manual (covers both books in Level I), Teacher's Graded Reader, Guide to Unit Tests, $11 each. Set of 15 coordinated drill cassettes (units 1-30), $13.50 each. Set of 5 *Artes Latinæ* filmstrips, $12.50 each. Set of 5 *Roma Antiqua* filmstrips, $12.50 each. Level II materials also available at similar prices.

Looking for the best Latin course for youngsters? Waldo Sweet's *Artes Latinæ* course wins here, hands down. This programmed language Latin course is so easy to follow, our seven-year-old uses it by himself.

The course begins with a series of cassette lessons correlated with the attractive programmed text. These teach the student how to use the course. *Artes Latinæ* then proceeds to teach Latin pronunciation and a number of "Basic Sentences." These Basic Sentences are famous quotations from famous classical writers and the Bible. Each Basic Sentence gives the student a grammatical form—like the basic subject-verb-object sentence *Vestus virum reddit*. By adding vocabulary words, the student can create an infinite range of new sentences using the basic models. At the same time he is exposed to Latin thought and introduced to classical literature.

Graded readers correlated with the student text contain proverbs, poems, and other readings, plus Latin question-and-answer exercises. The Reference Notebooks give your learner a place to record what he is learning. These are not bare sheets of paper. The page for Principal Parts of Verbs, for example, has places for students to write out the first conjugation of a number of listed verbs. Unit tests and teacher's guides for those tests let you know right away how your learner is doing. The drill cassettes provide painless practice in Latin pronunciation, and make it unnecessary for the parent or teacher to know Latin before embarking on the course. Teacher's manuals ex-

plain the whole program and provide extra activities. Plus you can get two sets of filmstrips, one on the Basic Sentences and the other on Roman culture, and even Latin buttons featuring the Basic Sentences.

NEW**
Gallopade Publishing Group
Latin for Kids, $14.95 paper, $19.95 hardcover. Add 10% shipping ($2.50 minimum).

Of All the Gaul: Latin for Kids is such an intriguing title I just had to send away for a copy. What arrived was a 31-page, spiral-bound, desktop-published book with an off-the-wall style. Carol Marsh, the prolific author of this and scores of other educational books for kids, provides reasons for learning Latin and a taste of the language in a super-easy-read format. She talks directly to the child reading the book, egging him on with questions, hints, and multiple-choices. Example: "HI-HO, HI-HO - it's off to *laboro* we go." Figured that one out? How about these choices for the definition of *prohibeo*:

a) You are all for hibs
b) Something you put in pizza
c) Stop, prevent

Not too tough, huh? You couldn't call this a Latin course, since the words taught are more-or-less at random, but I'd have to say this is probably the least-threatening introduction to Latin I have seen.

NEW**
Longman Publishing Group
Student activity books, $4.98 each. New hardcover edition includes both books, price TBA. Teacher's guides, $23.16 each. Cassette, $20.28. Cue cards, $36. These are school prices. If materials are to be shipped to a non-school location, multiply prices by ⅓.

First Latin is a program for children in grades 4-7 that can be used as a FLEX program (foreign language exploratory course) or spread out however you choose as a first basic Latin course. *First Latin's* special charm is that it is designed to be taught by people who may not necessarily know any Latin at all. Since this is 99 percent of average American parents, read on.

First Latin's teacher's guide and pronunciation cassette explain everything you need to know to use this program, assuming you are familiar with the terminology of basic English grammar. All Latin expressions are translated, and you are led step by step through every lesson. If you can manage to read one lesson ahead of your learners, you can teach this course.

Students first listen and speak, then they read the Latin and write it in their activity book. The program starts with oral question/answer dialogs and songs, and follows up with readings in the activity books. Grammar emerges in the Language Discovery sections.

The complete program includes two student activity books, two teacher's guides, one audiocassette, and Picture Cue Cards. The latter are large cards with outline drawings on the front and Latin questions, with English translations, on the back. You point to the card and ask the questions. Say you ask in Latin, "Who is he?" while pointing at the card with a picture of a Roman boy. The student, having done the lesson, is supposed to answer in Latin, "He is Lucius." You use the cassette and cards with both books.

First Latin is designed as a self-contained introduction to all second-language study, and therefore is not as comprehensive in its coverage of Latin forms and grammars as a regular Latin I course. Its other goal, of improving students' English vocabulary, is reached through studying Latin roots and their English derivatives. A third goal is acquainting children with the pagan Roman culture, which could at times be pretty raw. Lesson 1, for example, jumps right in with the story of Romulus, the mythical founder of Rome, murdering his brother Remus and the story of Mucius Scaevola burning his hand off to impress the barbarians. Part 1 of Book 1 ends with a visit to a temple and learning about the gods and goddesses of Rome and Greece. You'll also find a bit of liberal preachifying about lifestyles, brave girls rescuing helpless boys, and so on, mixed in with a lot of helpful cultural notes about everyday Roman life.

Tons of supplementary material is included: songs, activities, games, competitions, greeting cards, toga-making, ideas for writing a Roman soap opera, and so on. Never a dull moment with this program.

LATIN READERS

Bolchazy-Carducci Publishers
Latin Easy Readers, $11 each.

The publishers of *Artes Latinæ* also carry a huge line of classical texts in the original languages. You know, get-down stuff like Euclid, Plutarch, Cicero, Ovid. For those not quite ready for the Big Time, here

come the Easy Readers! The first, exotically titled *Elementary Latin Translation Book,* introduces students to Roman history and Greek mythology. The second, a Latin translation of Vergil's *Æneid* by none other than *Artes Latinæ* developer Waldo Sweet, substitutes an easy Latin paraphrase for the usual student notes in English. Lots of other readers are available.

NEW**
Longman Publishing Group
The Romans Speak for Themselves, Book 1 and 2, $6.96 each book. Teacher's handbook, $5.96. *Ecce Aeneas,* $7.56. *Longman Latin Readers,* $8.97 each. Teacher's handbook, $12. *Ritchie's Fabulae Faciles,* $9.96. *Lively Latin,* $5.96. Lots more. These are school prices. If materials are to be shipped to a non-school location, multiply prices by ⅓.

You want to read Latin? You've got it! First, *The Romans Speak for Themselves.* These are short readings adapted from genuine Roman authors and correlated to Longman's *Ecce Romani* program, described above.

Ritchie's Fabulae Faciles is a first Latin reader in which "100 passages of connected narrative retell the myths of Perseus, Hercules, the Argonauts, and Ulysses in readable style." Lots of notes and 100 English to Latin translation exercises. *Lively Latin* is a graded reader for slightly more advanced students.

Ecce Aeneas is selections from Virgil's *Aeneid.* *Longman Latin Readers* are for third-, fourth-, and fifth-year Latin students in high school (is there still such a thing nowadays?) and intermediate Latin courses in college. This series of five books has selections from a series of famous pagan Roman authors, such as Cicero and

Ovid. Accompanying teacher's handbook gives background, notes, bibliography, and (this is the important part!) translations of the Latin text in the readers. Many more readers available.

CLASSICAL MAGAZINES FOR KIDS

Pompellana

Memberships: Student, $3.50 (mailed to home address); Adult, $10; Contributing, $15. Classroom orders, mailed to the teacher at a school address, 6 (minimum) to 50, $3.25, less for larger quantities. Australia, add $15. Canada, add $2. Sweden, add $10. Other countries, write and ask.

Cross *Teen World* with *People*, translate it into Latin, and what do you have? Good heavens, it's *Pompeiiana*! Simple Latin stories highlighting current sports, music, and media idols, Top Ten rock titles in Latin, games, riddles, puzzles, word searches, student articles, self-test quizzes, and a bunch of other "relevant" stuff. Also info directly relating to classical studies. About 10,000 subscribers.

LATIN & GREEK BUTTONS

Bolchazy-Carducci Publishers

Buttons catalog, $2.

I know you've been waiting to hear about those buttons. Picture your junior egghead proudly sporting a button that declares *Veritas Vos Liberabit* ("The Truth shall Set You Free") or some pithy Greek aphorism. Each of these buttons costs only $1. Unfortunately, you have to order at least $15 worth. How about handing them out as rewards? Covering a T-shirt with buttons and pretending it's armor-plated? Giving them as Christmas presents to your favorite librarians? *Verbum sapienti satis*.

HEBREW FOR KIDS

EKS Publishing

Giant Hebrew Alphabet Chart set (4 charts), $9.95. *Handy Hebrew Alphabet*, single alphabet $1. *3-Way Aleph-Bet Lotto*, $7.95. *Sounds of Hebrew Bingo*, $11.95. *Hebrew Grammar Poster Set* (10 posters), $18.95. *Sounds of Hebrew Flashcards*, $5.95. *Verb Flash Charts*, $5.95.

EKS is the place for all sorts of Hebrew study aids and games.

The *Hebrew Alphabet Chart* set of four classroom-sized posters covers the shape, sounds, and English-letter names of Hebrew letters and vowels, and three ways Hebrew is written: printed, block, and handwriting. The *Handy Hebrew Alphabet* is the same information scaled down to one three-hole-punched card designed to fit in a ring binder.

3-Way Aleph-Bet Lotto is a matching game that teaches recognition of the print, block, and script alphabets. It includes six heavy cardboard playing boards and three sets of 36 cards (one each for print, block, and script). Each set has a differently colored background. The game can be played solitaire or with up to six participants.

Sounds of Hebrew Bingo takes 104 of the most frequently used letter-vowel combinations and can be played with up to 12 people. The Bingo caller needs to know Hebrew pronunciation. Flash cards are included to teach how the combinations look. These are also sold separately as *Sounds of Hebrew Flashcards*.

The *Hebrew Grammar Poster Set* of classroom-sized charts printed on heavy card stock has Hebrew roots in brilliant magenta while the endings and vowel patterns that change are printed in black. English translations appear below each example. *Hebrew Verbs Charts for Beginners* is a set of 20 sturdy cards. Ten each show a complete verb pattern, and 10 have blank charts for student practice.

CHAPTER TWELVE

CLASSICAL LANGUAGES FOR TEENS & ADULTS

"People who live in a small town know more than an outline of its history; they are themselves woven into the textures of its life. They know whom to respect, whom to despise—and why. They understand the code, they get the jokes. To be familiar with the classics is to be on that same sort of small-town footing with the civilization we have inherited."

—Thomas Fleming

Is the main reason why Latin and classical studies are not standard fare for elementary schoolchildren that there are no Latin questions on the Iowa Test of Basic Skills? That would be a pity, because studying Latin has been shown to actually increase those test scores!

Chronicles editor Thomas Fleming, in his excellent report "The Roots of American Culture: Reforming the Curriculum," points out,

> Studies done in several major American cities reveal an astonishing record of success for Latin programs. What is particularly striking about these experiments is the fact that most of them have been conducted in inner-city schools with a high proportion of disadvantaged and minority students. The best experimental program has been conducted in Philadelphia, where between 1967 and 1976 Latin enrollment in the public schools rose from 490 to 14,000. In 1971 the Philadelphia schools conducted a study in which fifth graders were given fifteen to twenty minutes of Latin a day. The Latin students were matched with a control group selected for both ability and background. At the end of the year, the Latin students were found to be one year ahead of the control group on the vocabulary section of the Iowa Test of Basic Skills. In a similar experiment conducted in Washington, D.C., a randomly-selected group of poor students took part in daily Latin instruction. These were students who had been rejected for other foreign language training, because of their below-grade level reading skills. At the end of the year, it was discovered that these students had come "'from behind to achieve above average achievement in vocabulary and total reading." The most impressive aspect to the Washington experiments was the comparison with students given another foreign language. In one study, sixth graders were given Latin instruction for only eight months and succeeded in climbing "'from the lowest level of reading ability to the highest level for the grade, equalling the achievement of pupils who had studied French or Spanish for 38 months."

> Similar results were reported in Indianapolis, Boston, and Worcester, Massachusetts . . .

In one case in Colorado, with which I am familiar, a young Spanish teacher was told by her principal that she was going to have to teach Latin. Being a good sport, she gave it a try. The good results she witnessed made her a convert. She proved to be so successful a teacher that in five years Latin enrollments increased from one section to five. This year she sent her best students on a five-year scholarship to Harvard . . .

So, no problem, you just sign your kid up for one of those neat Latin programs at your nearby public school, right? Not so fast . . .

Despite these successes, Latin is not growing as rapidly as ought to be predicted. The program in Washington has been scaled down, and it was only public outcry that prevented a massive budget cut in Philadelphia. Rudolph Masciantonio, who directed the Philadelphia program, comments ruefully that "Decision-makers sometimes tend to ignore the research data . . . for budgetary, political, or other reasons."

Ah, yes. Here come those "decision-makers" again. Let's put them on hold for a minute while we consider Mr. Fleming's synopsis of classical education:

Under the old dispensation, most of what a student learned beyond the three R's were the Bible and the Greek and Latin Classics. Some higher math was taught, and a student might dabble in one or another of the sciences, but what we now call the humanities was at the center. I say what we now call the humanities, because the term has come to be used so broadly that it includes everything that isn't *science*. It once meant nothing more (nor less) than the languages and literatures of ancient Greece and Rome. It was supremely interdisciplinary, since it included the teaching of grammatical theory, several genres of literature, philosophy, and history. What is more, it relied heavily on comparing two quite dissimilar civilizations. Above all, the long winnowing-out process—a matter of some two millennia—ensured that students were typically exposed to nothing less than the most splendid achievements of the human mind. Finally the old humanities was a central core of learning that could be taken for granted in anyone who had stayed in school to the age of sixteen.

Just makes you drool, doesn't it? Imagine, education with elegance! Now here's where to find it.

LATIN FOR TEENS AND ADULTS

NEW**
American Map Corporation
Lilliput Dictionary, $1.75: English/Latin. *Pocket Dictionary*, $6.95 Latin.

Dictionaries in several sizes, from the matchbox-sized *Lilliput* with 10,000 entries to standard and college dictionaries. The most useful dictionary for most purposes is the pocket-size. It's 3¾ x 6" with between 33,000 and 58,000 entries.

AMSCO

AMSCO has Latin texts, workbooks, and dictionaries. Unlike other publishers, AMSCO has third-year texts for all its languages, and even a fourth-year text for Latin. Texts are inexpensive and sample copies may be obtained by writing on school letterhead.

UPDATED**
Bolchazy-Carducci Publishers
Pronunciation and Reading of Classical Latin, $24.95. *Selections from . . .* tape series, $29.95 each. Latin Stories, $10. Add $3 shipping per item.

The *Artes Latinae* program reviewed in the previous chapter actually was developed for teen students. Don't rule it out just because it is so much easier to use than regular teen-and-adult Latin courses!

Or, if you want to know whether Caesar said "Vainy veedy veeky" or "Wainy weedy weechy,"*Pronunciation and Reading* guide to classical Latin comes with two cassettes and a booklet with demonstration texts and practical exercises. You'll find out how to pronounce the vowels, consonants, and diphthongs of classical Latin, how and why Latin is accented, and how to read Latin poetry by integrating its natural word accents with a rhythm based on the number of syllables in a line.

Other Latin readings available on cassettes from Bolchazy-Carducci: selections from Cicero, Virgil, and a combined set of selections from Catullus and Horace, all read in classical Latin style by Robert P. Sonkowsky. Each of these three programs includes, besides its two cassettes, an accompanying booklet with the complete Latin text and a facing English translation. This is fascinating stuff, too, let me tell you. The whole world would watch C-Span if our modern Senators had one-tenth of Cicero's oratorical gifts! You haven't seen negative campaigning until you've experienced Cicero's oration against Catiline.

Bolchazy-Carducci also has a tremendous line of Latin and Greek texts, readers, and supporting material. They are also the only source I could find for medieval and Renaissance Latin, the form of Latin recommended for study by Dorothy Sayers, author of "The Lost Tools of Learning" and many famous literary works, fictional and otherwise.

Let's mention just one reader useful for teen students: *Latin Stories*. This little book is designed to accompany Wheelock's *Latin: An Introductory Course Based on Ancient Authors*. The first 18 of the 28 Latin stories are tales from classical mythology. The last 20 are adaptations of passages from famous Latin authors. The book has vocabulary lists with each story, plus a list of the grammar required to read the story and a capsule description of the story theme in English. Interesting reading!

Cambridge University Press
Unit I, $8.95. Unit IIA, $4.95. Units I and IIA Language Info, $1.95 each. *Short Latin Stories*, $4.95. Also available: units IIIA-B (pupil's book, workbooks, teacher's book, language info), IVA-B (pupil's book, teacher's book).

This Latin course is the same used at English prep schools, revised for North American students. In Unit I, you meet the family of Lucius Caecilius Iucundus, a merchant living in (of all places) Pompeii. As you progress through the 12 stages of Unit I, you learn about Roman civilization (through English text, illustrated with graphics). You also study Latin grammar and vocabulary. Lots of humor and interesting cultural sidelights.

In Unit IIA, we are following the adventures of a Roman official in Britain.

Each unit has an accompanying Language Information booklet. This includes more language information and exercises, and also the invaluable Latin-English dictionary of words used in the unit. The units themselves feature high-interest stories (some illustrated).

Short Latin Stories, a separate reader correlated with the Cambridge Press series, is really fun! Starting with easier stories, and progressing to the more difficult, *Short Latin Stories* offers a mix of fables, history, myths, and humor, all selected for entertainment value.

This excellent series is designed for middle grades and up, although I see no reason why motivated, intelligent preteens couldn't use it.

UPDATED**
Longman Publishing Group
Preparatory Latin, Book I and II, $14.24 each. Answer keys, $5 each book. These are school prices. If materials are to be shipped to a non-school location, multiply prices by ⅓.

Here is Longman's Latin text for junior-high students. Bright elementary pupils could use it too, in my estimation, which is a giant step towards providing Latin for suckling infants: my fond dream.

Preparatory Latin was intended to help young preppies prepare for that inevitable moment when they are flung into a sea of Latin translation. As is so often true, in striving to make a text usable by younger students the authors have produced a book that makes their subject accessible to all, not just the young.

Prep Latin is not merely simplified explanations. It incorporates a variety of teaching methods: "the Traditional, the Aural-Oral, the Linguistic, to name a few." Technical terms are not introduced until absolutely necessary. Grammatical elements show up one at a time before being pinned into a framework. Drill consists of 30 brief sentences per lesson that include the elements being drilled. Also, you get the romance of Pauline the Ant called, you guessed it, *Pericula Paulinæ* or *The Perils of Pauline*, complete with cliffhangers.

UPDATED**
Longman Publishing Group
Phenomenon of Language, $10.95 for text, $5.96 for teacher's manual/answer key, $8 for tests, $5.96 for test answer key. These are school prices. If materials are to be shipped to a non-school location, multiply prices by ⅓.

What do you get when you cross Latin with an introductory course in linguistics? It sounds awful, like pasta with barbecue sauce, but really it's good enough to deserve a separate review of its own. It's *The Phenomenon of Language*, a sprightly text that uses Latin as a vehicle for giving students a method for learning all languages quickly and efficiently. Besides the charming Roman-style cartoons and clever activities, the student spends a lot of time discovering how languages work. The exercises are designed according to the Platonic method: students are gently led to draw the correct conclusions on their own.

I cannot overemphasize the usefulness of a text like this. Competence in handling language is really competence in thinking, and as Dorothy Sayers says the student who masters these processes will reduce by at least 50 percent the amount of effort it takes him to learn future subjects.

NEW**
Longman Publishing Group

Ecce Romani student books 1-5, $6.24 each. Old hardcover version: Volume I is combined student books 1-3, $19.98. Volume II is combined student books 4 and 5, $19.98. New hardcover version: Volume I is combined student books 1 and 2, $17.94. Volume II is combined student books 3 and 4, $17.94. Student language activity books 1-5, $3.96 each. Teacher language activity books 1-5, $6.96 each. Teacher handbooks 1-5, $8.94 each. Tests 1-4, $21.96 each. Cassette, $15.96. *The Romans Speak* Book I and II, $6.96 each. *The Romans Speak* teacher's handbook, $5.96. These are school prices. If materials are to be shipped to a non-school location, multiply prices by ⅓.

Ecce Romani is a reading-based (as opposed to listening-based or programmed-learning) Latin program with a heavy emphasis on Roman culture. Through all five levels students follow the adventures of an A.D. 80 Roman family with two teenage children.

Roman culture is introduced through the novel device of letting the Romans speak for themselves. Starting as early as book 2, authentic bits of Latin from Roman times are inserted in the form of graffiti, inscriptions, and fragments of ancient Latin verse. If this is not enough, two separate books, *The Romans Speak for Themselves*, are correlated with the series. Book I of *The Romans Speak for Themselves* has 14 short readings adapted from real live (make that "dead") Latin authors. Book II has eight readings. Readings from such diverse passages as Augustine's famous description of a youth catching "gladiator fever" and Petronius's humorous description of an unexpected bath at Trimalchio's are correlated with the cultural emphases in books 1-4 of *Ecce Romani*.

Each of the five levels has a student book, student's language activity book, teacher's language activity book, teacher's handbook, and test booklet with cumulative reviews. Book 1 is *Meeting the Family*, followed by *Rome at Last, Home and School, Pastimes and*

Ceremonies, and *Public Life and Private Lives.* Colorful covers, black-and-white illustrations throughout. Other *Ecce Romani* features:

• Macrons (long marks) and standard English punctuation in the Latin text, so you won't be struggling with pronunciation and phrases.

• Traditional verb conjugation tables and other language helps.

• Both Latin-to-English and English-to-Latin exercises.

• Dictation drills.

• Spiral structure. Material taught at one level is reviewed at the next levels.

• A cassette that allows your students to hear Latin as a spoken language, and tests.

• Starting in book 2, you'll find *sententiae.* These are famous Latin sayings, such as Julius Caesar's *Veni, vidi, vici* ("I came, I saw, I conquered"). The teacher's handbook gives ideas for how to incorporate the *sententiae* into your Latin instruction. Shades of *Artes Latinae!*

Besides all this, each *Ecce Romani* student book includes reading selections, vocabulary and grammar information, exercises, activities, and notes, plus English-language culture sections about life in ancient Rome, Word Study units, and Latin verse. The correlated 48-page Language Activity Books are packed with enrichment activities and drills, such as word mazes, puzzles, as well as traditional Latin translation exercises. The Teacher's Language Activity Books are exactly the same as the student's books, with answers to the exercises. (I suggest you get the teacher's books if you buy the student books—you'll save *hours* of correction time, or your student can even correct his own work!)

The *Ecce Romani* teacher's handbooks explain the program and walk you through each lesson. These are written for professional educators, so plan on taking a while to digest the information presented. No difficulties with the student's materials—you'll be whizzing through these in no time. A nice program. I like it.

If all you want is a taste of Latin, try Longman's *Phenomenon of Language* instead. Home schoolers and teachers looking for a "real" Latin course, though, may well be interested in *Ecce Romani*.

CLASSICAL AND BIBLICAL GREEK

Alpha Omega Publications
$19.50 for complete set of 10 LIFEPACS. Greek Manual, $3.95. *Textus Receptus* (Greek New Testament), $12.95. *Greek/English Lexicon*, $24.95.

AOP has LIFEPAC worktexts for one full year of New Testament Greek. New Testament Greek covers the essentials of grammar, with plentiful exercises for translating both Greek to English and English to Greek.

NEW**
American Map Corporation
Lilliput Dictionary, $1.75: English/Classical Greek. *Pocket Dictionary*, $6.95 Greek.

Need a Greek dictionary? You've got it! The matchbox-sized *Lilliput* has 10,000 entries. The most useful dictionary for most purposes is the pocket-size. It's 3¾ x 6" with between 33,000 and 58,000 entries. These are resources for Classical Greek, not Biblical (*koiné*) Greek. Remember, you can also get Biblical Greek dictionaries and other study aids from Great Christian Books.

Bethany House
Basic Greek in 30 Minutes a Day, $9.95.

Subtitled *New Testament Greek for Laymen*, *Basic Greek in 30 Minutes a Day* is a book for people who don't need to be Greek scholars, but do want to study the New Testament in the original. After completing it, you will • feel at home with the Greek alphabet • pronounce Greek words fluently • know the meanings of hundreds of New Testament words • understand theological terms that came from Greek • see connections between Bible words that are not obvious in English translations • be able to use Greek dictionaries and other valuable reference tools, and • understand the basic principles of Greek grammar.

How is this possible in 30 minutes a day? Author Jim Found uses cognates (words that resemble English words of similar meaning), introduces Scripture quotes very early on, and avoids long-winded grammatical explanations and convoluted terminology. The book is laid out like a junior high school workbook and is about as easy to use. Designed for Real People, not scholars who dote on tiny print and footnotes, *Basic Greek in 30 Minutes a Day* can either be used as a stand-alone introduction to Greek study through reference aids, or the gateway to serious Greek study.

UPDATED**
Bolchazy-Carducci Publishers
Pronunciation and Reading of Ancient Greek, second edition, $24.95. *Selections . . .* tape series, $29.95 each. Add $3 shipping per item.

As I mentioned above in reference to Bolchazy-Carducci's classical Latin *Pronunciation and Reading* guide, the ancient Greek program also comes with a booklet and two cassettes. Explains how to pronounce the vowels, consonants, and pitch accents of ancient Greek. Booklet has demonstration texts and practical exercises, and presents a method of reading Greek poetry that integrates the pitch accents with the rhythm.

Bolchazy-Carducci has several classic Greek selections on audiocassette, all read by Stephen C. Daitz, the same man whose voice is on the tapes of *Pronunciation and Reading*. Choices include *A Recital of Ancient Greek Poetry* (four cassettes), Aristophanes' *Birds*, Euripides' *Hekabe*, *Selections from the Greek Orators*, and *Plato's Portrait of Socrates*. Each of these three programs includes, besides its two cassettes, an accompanying booklet with the complete Greek text and a facing English translation.

Christian Book Distributors
Great Christian Books

These discounters both offer a huge selection of all kinds of Biblical Greek one-book courses and study aids, including many only sold in seminary bookstores. Most of these are aimed at seminary students and pastors (e.g., educated adults)—not suitable for teaching young children. Also huge selection of theological works and current Christian books.

NEW**
Leonardo Press
Greek Roots and Their Modern English Spellings, $18.95 plus $2 shipping.

Unusual dictionary contains more than 500 modern English roots with their original Greek meanings. Each root is shown with all its forms, but not, unhappily, all the meanings of the forms. Learned notes explain any special cases or discrepancies. An appendix lists the roots with just their meanings.

Author Raymond Laurita contends that modern English spelling is not the aimless hodge-podge modern educators make it out to be, but a rigorously regular system based on root forms from three major sources: Greek, Latin, and Old-Middle English. He says that confusion comes in when the syllable is made the basic unit of spelling, rather than the word root with its prefixes and suffixes. In time he hopes to produce one book each on Latin roots and Old-Middle English roots to accompany his first *Greek Roots* volume.

So what's the use of a book like this? Having been brought up by a father whose idea of fun mealtime conversation was to point out the Latin and Greek roots of words, and subsequently getting an 800 on the verbal SAT at the age of 15, I can see some use in this sort of study—especially for word lovers, who will find it a treasure trove. Like a mule, it may not look like much, but you sure can do a heap of plowing with it.

Loyola University Press
A Reading Course in Homeric Greek: Student Text, Book I and II, $14.95 each; Flash cards, Book I and II, $3/set; Teacher's Manual and Key, $14.95.

A colorful revision of the original program introduced over 30 years ago. *A Reading Course in Homeric*

Greek helps students quickly tackle selected undoctored passages from Homer's *Odyssey*. Contains "stimulating essays on aspects of Greek art and culture which highlight humanistic values and increase literary appreciation." Includes a special supplement, "Transition to Attic Greek," to help the student read more recent versions of Greek, whether classical or *koiné*.

Moody Correspondence School

Correspondence courses in Biblical Greek. Inexpensive, designed for success. Plus, of course, Moody's famous large selection of Bible study courses, Hebrew study, and so on.

BIBLICAL AND PRAYERBOOK
HEBREW COURSES

NEW**
American Map Corporation
Lilliput Dictionary, $1.75: English/Classical Hebrew. *Pocket Dictionary*, $6.95 Hebrew.

Need a Hebrew dictionary? Here it is! And don't forget, you can also get Biblical Hebrew dictionaries, concordances, and other study aids from Great Christian Books.

NEW★★
EKS Publishing

The Beginner's Dictionary of Prayerbook Hebrew, $12.95. *Teach Yourself to Read Hebrew*: 5 cassettes and book, $29.95; book only, $8.95. *Prayerbook Hebrew the Easy Way*, $15.95; Teacher's Guide, $6.95. *The First Hebrew Primer for Adults*, softbound $18.95. *Tall Tales Told and Retold in Biblical Hebrew*, $9.95; Teacher's Guide $4.95. *Giant Hebrew Alphabet Chart* set (4 charts), $9.95. *Handy Hebrew Alphabet*, single alphabet $1. *3-Way Aleph-Bet Lotto*, $8.95. *Sounds of Hebrew Bingo*, $12.95. *Hebrew Grammar Poster Set* (10 posters), $18.95. *Sounds of Hebrew Flashcards*, $6.95. *Verb Flash Charts*, $5.95. Add 10% shipping. HI, AK, and non-USA orders, add 15% shipping.

One-stop shopping for all kinds of great Hebrew language gear. *Teach Yourself to Read Hebrew* is a pronunciation/letter recognition guide using Sephardic pronunciation. It does not teach translation skills, just how to make the proper Hebrew sounds associated with the words. Each cassette tape has one lesson per side. You would be smart to get the cassettes. *Prayerbook Hebrew the Easy Way* is designed for those who can already read the Hebrew words in the prayerbook but don't understand their meaning. The 21 chapters provide a simplified introduction to grammar, oral reviews, and lists of new vocabulary, and each ends with a prayerbook selection. The Teacher's Guide provides answers to the exercises and teaching tips. *The First Hebrew Primer for Adults* is a complete course of 33 lessons requiring no previous language experience. You get some heavy-duty grammar here—all seven regular conjugations and three of the most common variations on same. Exceptions are presented in the same chapters as the basic rules, making for completeness but somewhat impeding easy learning. No separate teacher's guide is necessary, since exercise answers are in the back of the back. You will have much more success with this course if you first study through *Teach Yourself to Read Hebrew*. *Tall Tales Told and Retold in Biblical Hebrew*, designed to accompany *The First Hebrew Primer for Adults*, expands and supplements the *Primer* with familiar fairy tales translated into the style and vocabulary of Biblical Hebrew. This you gotta see, right?

The remainder of EKS's line is study aids and games.

The *Hebrew Alphabet Chart* set of four classroom-sized posters covers the shape, sounds, and English-letter names of Hebrew letters and vowels, and three ways Hebrew is written: printed, block, and handwriting. The *Handy Hebrew Alphabet* is the same information scaled down to one three-hole-punched card designed to fit in a ring binder.

3-Way Aleph-Bet Lotto is a matching game that teaches recognition of the print, block, and script alphabets. It includes six heavy cardboard playing boards and three sets of 36 cards (one each for print, block, and script). Each set has a differently colored background. The game can be played solitaire or with up to six participants.

Sounds of Hebrew Bingo takes 104 of the most frequently used letter-vowel combinations and can be played with up to 12 people. The Bingo caller needs to know Hebrew pronunciation. Flash cards are included to teach how the combinations look. These are also sold separately as *Sounds of Hebrew Flashcards*.

The *Hebrew Grammar Poster Set* of classroom-sized charts printed on heavy card stock has Hebrew roots in brilliant magenta while the endings and vowel patterns that change are printed in black. English translations appear below each example. *Hebrew Verbs Charts for Beginners* is a set of 20 sturdy cards. Ten each show a complete verb pattern, and 10 have blank charts for student practice.

New from EKS Publishing: *The Beginner's Dictionary of Prayerbook Hebrew*, a very attractive, easy-to-use, large-format book. Unlike all other prayerbook Hebrew dictionaries, here words are listed in the same grammatical forms as they appear in the prayerbook. This is wonderful for those who struggle to remember the Hebrew roots, which often are so different from the words made from those roots. For ease of use, the dictionary contains only words encountered more than 50 times in the prayerbook. A pronunciation guide for every word is appended after the dictionary. At the bottom of each page are simple instructions for finding the words you want (e.g., disregard beginning *vav*). Truly a wonderful resource for beginners!

Great Christian Books

Biblical Hebrew Step by Step: Volume 1 book $13.95/$9.95, cassette and book key each $7.95/$6.52; Volume 2 book $13.95/$9.95, cassette and book key each $7.95/$6.52. *Biblia Hebraica Stuttgartensia*, $25.95/$24.65, larger edition $35.95/$33.95. *The New Englishman's Hebrew/Aramaic Concordance to the Old Testament*, $39.95/$23.75. Discount prices for members are listed second. Shipping extra.

GCB has literally dozens of Hebrew courses and study aids, including interlinear Bibles, concordances, lexicons, study charts, grammars, and so on. Let me just mention a few of these that we have found most helpful.

Menahem Mansoor's *Biblical Hebrew Step by Step*, a usable introductory Hebrew course for adults, has just been improved with the addition of cassettes. You still might find the introductory how-to-pronounce-Hebrew sections tough sledding—try EKS instead for this. Once into the actual lessons, though, the course proceeds briskly. A typical lesson begins with vocabulary words separated into nouns, adjectives, and so on, followed by grammar notes, study hints, and well-designed exercises. I marvel that I ever attempted this course without an answer key; you will be smarter!

The *Biblia Hebraica Stuttgartensia* is the standard Hebrew Old Testament used worldwide. Thanks to excellent printing and quality paper, you can actually read the type, including all point marks. The *New Englishman's Concordance* (available in both Hebrew and Greek) helps you find all Biblical references of a given word in the original language. Each word is coded to *Strong's Exhaustive Concordance* and several other major language references.

Moody Correspondence School

Beginning Biblical Hebrew courses for Christians. Write for brochure.

MAGAZINES FOR CLASSICAL SCHOLARS

Ares Publishers
The Ancient World, 4 issues/year, $10. Single copies $2.50.

"An up-to-date current-research library for the student of Antiquity." They said it! Reports on what's new in ancient history. Some past issue themes: Alexander the Great (the Great One got four issues!), Ancient Games and Athletics, Corruption in Ancient Greek and Roman Politics, Hellenistic Warfare, and Where Was the Cretan Labyrinth?

Ladislaus J. Bolchazy, of Bolchazy-Carducci Publishers, is one of the editors.

NEW**
Charles Coyle
Roman Coins and Culture, $27.50 U.S. and Canada (4 issues), $45 all other countries (foreign students, $38).

Here's something unusual I ran across in the Bolchazy-Carducci catalog. Charles Coyle has started a different kind of classical journal whose integration point is Roman coinage. *Roman Coins and Culture* will cover the ancient authors, archaeology, art, and architecture, all with a tie-in with numismatics, the study of coins. Why coins? Because:

- "Ancient texts all lack one feature: illustrations. Roman coinage provides over 10,000 images of a political, historical, artistic, or architectural nature."

- "Works of art have survived in a haphazard fashion. Coinage supplies a continuous and systematic record of statuary and many other forms of art."

- "Surviving records, particularly those of the third and fifth century A.D., are fragmentary, of uneven quality, and occasionally contradictory. Coinage again forms a continuous testimony that appends, amends, or ever supersedes the written tradition."

This sounds like classical studies as a Unit Study freak might do them. Intriguing! And then, there's Mr. Coyle's offer of a *free Roman coin* ("at least 1400 years old") to any new subscriber. I am tempted, I really am.

UPDATED**
Classical Bulletin
Four issues/year, $20 U.S. Single copy, $5 U.S.

I know that a member of the Great Unwashed such as myself is not supposed to get absorbed in reading a classical journal. ("Unwashed," in this case, refers to missing out on the cleansing ablutions of Latin study when I was yet a *puella,* which has been the case with most of my generation.) I was even thinking of leaving the "Magazines for Classical Scholars" section out of this edition because, "Who reads this stuff, anyway?"

Then I picked up my sample issue of *Classical Bulletin.* Staggering under the burden of the title, "Detecting the Real Sherlock Holmes: A Stylometric Comparison of Doyle and Meyer," was an article investigating whether a clever literary forgery really could be detected by computer—the new field of "stylometrics." In this case, the forger lost. Absorbing reading! Flipping through the pages, I found writer after writer piquing my curiosity about Herodotus, Homer, Aristotle, and (I would not have believed it could be done) Kafka. Happily, most contributors do not assume their readers are fully versed in every jot and tittle of the literary works or history they describe, so a halfway-educated person such as myself can follow most of it.

I'm not saying that you should necessarily rush out and subscribe to *Classical Bulletin*. If, however, you are a home schooler who has decided to use the Classical style of education, you will find this journal stimulates a lot of unexpected studying!

University of Calgary Press
Echos du Monde Classique/Classical Views, 3 issues/year. Subscriptions: individual $12, institution $20. Single copy $7 plus $1.50 shipping (Canada), $3 (outside). Outside Canada prices are in U.S. dollars.

Articles and reviews on classical history, literature, archaeology, and culture. The classical community is invited to share in the ongoing scholarly discussions, which include the how's and why's of teaching and learning the classics. *Echos du Monde Classique/Classical Views* also has up-to-date archaeological progress reports on sites excavated by Canadian archaeologists. A taste of what *Echos du Monde Classique/Classical Views* has recently offered: Helen Saradi-Mendelovici on the demise of the ancient city; E. L. Harrison on the tragedy of Dido; Beert Verstraete on the literary-critical study of Roman poetry; archaeological reports on Canadian projects at Mytilene and elsewhere.

OTHER CLASSICAL HELPS

American Classical League
Membership includes *The Classical Outlook*: $27 U.S.A, $25 Canadian and foreign. U.S. funds by international money order only.

Whatever remnants of Oxonian thinking still survive in the American graves of academe find their home at the American Classical League. ACL offers its members *The Classical Outlook* magazine, teaching tips and materials, info on new products, the National Junior Classical League (is it open to home schoolers?), national Latin and Greek exams, teacher and student scholarships, fraternal support, and an annual Institute. The latter mainly concentrates on pedagogical issues, with only a frigid nod to the usual feminist/special issues hype that has overcome most school programs. Lest the attenders be overcome by their mental exertions, the Institute program includes such things as picnics, riverboat rides, sing-alongs, social hours, and tours.

Visual Education Association
Biblical Hebrew, Latin, Biblical Greek, and Classical Greek vocabulary flash cards, $6.95 each set. Add $1.50 postage (U.S.) or $3.50 (outside the U.S.) for first set.

Bill's constant seminary companion was a box of Vis-Ed vocabulary flash cards. Each set contains approximately 1000 cards, 1½ x 3½" in size, plus a very useful study guide with index. For example, the Biblical Hebrew study guide shows words in frequency of occurrence and by grammatical categories. Each card has the target language word on the front and both its English meaning and pertinent grammatical info on the back. Recommended if you're seriously studying any of these languages.

CLASSICAL LANGUAGE SOFTWARE

Yes, Virginia, you can practice ancient languages on high-tech computers. Three packages here: Centaur Systems' *Latin Vocabulary Drill*, Davka Corporation's line of Hebrew software, and University of Delaware's Office of Computer-Based Instruction's *Latin Skills* series. See the Educational Software Buyer's Guide in Volume 3 for details.

CHAPTER THIRTEEN

SIGN LANGUAGE

What United States language group today has nearly as many people as the entire country of Canada, but is hardly ever noticed when it comes to "foreign" language instruction? Since this is the Sign Language chapter, you probably guessed I was talking about the deaf. You're right!

In the old days, deaf people were encouraged to forget signing and concentrate on lip-reading and learning to speak. This was supposed to help them fit in better with the mainstream population. Today, educators realize that lip-reading is far harder than signing. So the "mixed" approach is stressed, with some lip-reading and a lot of signing.

For the non-deaf, signing is not only a neat language to teach the children, but a way of including a large proportion of our fellows in our everyday lives.

One outstanding feature of Sign Language is that it is the same in every culture. Deaf people around the world all speak this language, and non-deaf people can often understand at least part of it right away. The symbol for *baby*, for example, is to cradle an imaginary baby and rock your arms.

With so many deaf people all around us, and with Sign Language's usefulness as a universally-understood language, I really don't see why every child in this country isn't taught Sign Language. Don't test us on this yet, but in the next year or so we Prides intend to all learn at least the basics of this fascinating language.

With such an enthusiastic introduction, I'm embarrassed to have so few resources to offer in this chapter. However, at least they are *good* ones! You have a choice of "survival" signing for everyday situations, two in-depth courses to help you really start communicating, or flash cards with the signed numbers and letters. And I will be delighted to hear from any of you who have more or better sources of Sign Language materials to recommend.

NEW**
Audio-Forum
Say It by Signing video, $34.95. VHS or Beta: specify. Shipping extra.

Say It by Signing is a 60-minute video course with subtitles in English. Dramatized lessons include greetings, introductions, time expressions, transportation, eating out, shopping, sports, and recreation. Dialog-based "survival" approach.

NEW★★
Putnam Publishing Group
Signing Made Easy, $10.95 (U.S.), $15.50 (Canadian).
Perigee Visual Dictionary of Signing, $9.95. *Pocket Dictionary of Signing*, $4.95. Add $1.50 shipping.

Rod R. Butterworth and Mickey Flodin, authors of the *Perigee Visual Dictionary of Signing* and *Pocket Dictionary of Signing*, have produced a thorough step-by-step guide to learning sign language, complete with drills and practice exercises. The book introduces the history of signing and gives tips for easier signing. It shows and explains the basic hand shapes and inflections (word endings such as *-ment* or *-ly*), numbers, and the manual alphabet.

The authors stress that you must take the time to learn the manual alphabet first, and they include fingerspelling exercises in every chapter. Chapters cover family and social life, work and careers, food, travel and holidays, sports and recreation, seasons/time/weather, emotions, money and shopping, health and emergencies, religion, and animals and nature.

Each chapter starts with a "Practice Learning Signs" section, with fully-illustrated signs for complete English sentences. Each sign is also explained in detail at the bottom of the page. Then comes a "Practice Giving Signs" section, where you are asked to translate from English into signs, fingerspelling practice (this increases in difficulty as you go through the book), and a "Practice Receiving Signs" section where you translate from the signs into English. A variety of other exercises are also provided: matching, multiple choice, fill in the blanks, vocabulary review, and so on. An index helps you locate any of the 3,500 signs used in the course.

English sentence order is used, as the authors feel that this option is growing in popularity, and in any case it's easier for a hearing person to learn the signs without struggling with strange grammar as well.

The text is very wholesome, and its "Religion" chapter would actually be useful to Christians. I was told that author Mickey Flodin, who studied at Baptist Bible College, is a home schooler; author Rod Butterworth is an ordained minister.

The large format design is very easy to use, and the whole course looks excellent.

By the same authors, the *Perigee Visual Dictionary of Signing* provides a quick way to translate over 1,200 signs of American Sign Language, and the *Pocket Dictionary of Signing* has 450 signing entries with accompanying directions and illustrations.

NEW★★
Timberdoodle
Sign Language for Everyone: video plus book, $45; book only, $14.50. Finger Alphabet Cards, $5.50. Signed Number Cards, $5.25. Shipping extra.

Sign Language for Everyone is a course taught by Cathy Rice, who with her husband Bill has for almost 40 years run the Bill Rice Ranch, Inc. in Murfreesboro, Tennessee, a year-round camp and publishing ministry for deaf and hearing young people and a center for teaching others Sign Language. The Bill Rice Ranch is the world's largest missionary work to the deaf. This Christian ministry started as a result of the Rices' experience with their own deaf daughter, whose hearing was destroyed at the age of 18 months during a bout of spinal meningitis. During the years, more than 800 churches have established Sign Language ministries as a direct result of the Ranch work.

Cathy Rice's vast experience as a mother, teacher, and interpreter to the deaf shines through in this series. I have not seen the video myself, but Deb Deffinbaugh of Timberdoodle tells me that Cathy has an unpolished, natural manner on tape, showing and explaining the signs. The book, which I have seen, is impressive. Hardbound with a glossy cover, it starts off with a brief education about deafness and Sign Language. Next you learn the hand positions for the signed alphabet. The next seven lessons are illustrations of related signs, with Cathy's unique memory aids to help you remember the signs. She starts with the basic sign for *man*, for example, and shows you how this can be transformed into *father, grandfather, father-in-law, brother, son, husband, nephew,* and *uncle*. The series concludes with lessons on how to interpret spoken words into signs, how to remember signs, and other technical details.

Unlike the Putnam course reviewed above, this one stresses the unique grammatical structure of American Sign Language.

For a low-key introduction to signing, Finger Alphabet Cards are oversized (8½ x 11") cards illustrating (surprise!) how to spell the sign alphabet with your fingers. Signed Number Cards are more of the same—20 sturdy oversized cards illustrating how to sign the numbers 1 to 20.

CHAPTER FOURTEEN

ENGLISH AS A SECOND LANGUAGE

English is a second language for all of us. The first language, somewhat more primitive, consisted of gurgles, shrieks, giggles, and other emotional inflections. This universal language, which includes every sound made by people around the world, gradually diminished until we had forgotten the nasal and trilled "r"s, the guttural German "ch," the lemon-kissing French "u," and all their cousins. The sounds we were left with eventually turned into the sounds of our region, formed into English words.

People from other countries and cultures also went through this process, but they forgot different sounds. The English ones. Like our hissing "s." (Did you know that in some cultures English is known as the "snake language" because of our "s"es?) And our funny "r" that sounds like a dog growling. And our almost unpronounceable (to the Orientals) "l." English is just loaded with shibboleths like these (and if you don't know what a shibboleth is, look up Judges 12:6!)

Then there's the little matter of English grammar and spelling. I thank God (seriously!) that I grew up learning English naturally and never had to struggle with it as a second language. What a horror English is, with all its irregularities, strange and complicated grammatical constructions, and phonograms like *ough* (as in *cough, through, dough,* and *enough*). I still remember the time Bill's very intelligent Chinese-born colleague spent 15 minutes explaining to him all the secrets of her great "cookie duff"! Not that I would have done any better in her place, I am sure.

So let's salute all those brave souls who are willing to tackle English as a second language . . . and here are some resources that can lend a helping hand.

NEW**
Audio-Forum
Ingles en Tres Meses, $115 Volume 1, $145 each Volumes 2 and 3. *Survival English,* Cassettes and book around $30-$40. Book alone, $7.50-$9. *Living Language,* $23.95 each course except Chinese which is $19.95 (no dictionary). *Ingles Para Emergencias,* $15.95. BBC audio courses, about $50 each. BBC video courses, $250 each. Speechphone courses, $39.50 each. Shipping extra.

Audio-Forum has a vast array of ESL helps, as you can see from the list above! Let me briefly capsulize these programs.

Ingles en Tres Meses is a programmed basic English course. All instructions and drills are recorded with Spanish translation. Volume 1 is for total beginners. Volume 2 is for brushing up and refining your English. Volume 3 is for those who can speak in English but "lack the native *feel* for it." This last volume concentrates on idioms and idiomatic expressions.

The *Survival English* series consists of three or four cassettes with accompanying phrasebook of vocabulary necessary for everyday living in the USA. Language groups served are: Khmer, Hmong, Cuban Spanish, Cantonese, Lao, and Vietnamese.

The *Living Language* courses, distributed by Audio-Forum and published by Crown Publishers, Inc., are brief two-cassette courses with a two-way dictionary/phrase book and conversations manual. Covers rudiments only. Language groups served are native speakers of French, German, Italian, Spanish, and Chinese.

Ingles Para Emergencias is all the English you hope you will never need to use. Discover basic questions and answers useful when chatting with the telephone operator, fire department, ambulance service, medical attendants, and police.

The British Broadcasting Corporation, or BBC, has both audio and video courses for English as a second language. The basic audio courses are available only in bilingual editions. *Let's Speak English* comes in Arabic, Chinese, German, and Indonesian. *Calling All Beginners* is in Arabic, Chinese, French, Greek, German, Italian, Portuguese, and Spanish. Intermediate versions are English-only and specialize in areas such as business, international trading, technology, travel, international meetings, medical practice, and aviation. The BBC video ESL courses are all for businesspeople, and come only in intermediate and advanced levels.

For those who know English up in their heads but have trouble making it sound like English when they say it, there's the Speechphone audiocassette series. This three-course program helps overcome the problems of incorrect stress and faulty rhythmic patterns, enabling those listening to the speaker to make sense of what is being said. A worthy mission, as those of us who have suffered in college under the ministrations of foreign teaching assistants will testify.

This list is itself only a subset of what Audio-Forum offers. Write for their free ESL catalog.

NEW**
EDC Publishing

Children's Wordfinder, Round the World, The First Thousand Words, The Word Detective, $10.95 each. *The First Hundred Words*, $7.95. Shipping extra.

Here are some terrific teaching aids for English as a second language!

The *Children's Wordfinder* is a colorful picture dictionary with 3,000 words of high interest to preteens. When I say "picture dictionary," I mean in this case that you get a pile of labeled pictures, not a pile of text with occasional pictures thrown in. You can easily use this to build vocabulary with a child who can read English sounds. And since it also comes in French and German, children whose native language is either of these could simply compare the English version with their native-language version even if they can't read. For ages seven and up.

The First Hundred Words is mostly large illustrations with labeled items from each illustration around the edges. Simple words like *apple* and *fork* are introduced. Also available in French, German, and Spanish. For children 18 months old and up.

The First Thousand Words is a more-advanced version of the same. Detailed, amusing illustrations in full color depict everyday scenes, while items shown in each picture appear, with their names, in a frame around the edge of each page. Available in English, French, German, Spanish, Italian, Russian, and Hebrew.

The *Round the World* series could be called "The Second Thousand Words." This takes up where the *First Thousand Words* series leaves off. More of a travel theme in this book, which comes in English, French, and Spanish versions.

The Word Detective is just as good at introducing basic English to non-English speakers as it is at introducing English grammar to the rest of us. Available in English, French, and German. See complete writeup in the Grammar chapter of Volume 2.

NEW**
International Linguistics, Inc.

The Learnables, full set, $155. Book 1 plus 5 cassettes in binder, $42. Book 2 plus 6 cassettes in binder, $48. Book 3 plus 5 cassettes in binder, $42. Book 4 plus 5 cassettes in binder, $42. Intermediate English, full set $150; books 5-8 plus their accompanying cassettes, $42 per book/cassette combo. Specify English version. Each Verb book plus cassette, $19. Set of three books and three cassettes, $55. Additional books, $7 each. Language Through Pictures, complete set of 8 books, $36.95. Individual books: *Prepositions* and *Plurals and Possessives*, $3.95 each; all others, $4.95 each. *All About Language* series, most book/cassette combos from $19 to $29 each, full set $185. Shipping extra.

I have already written up the excellent picture-based language program, the Learnables, in Chapter 9. Suffice it to say that the Learnables are also available in English, for use in teaching English as a second language. Each book has 1,000 sentences, each correlated with a picture. In all, the course teaches 1,500 basic words and elementary constructions.

For the critical skills of using English verbs properly, Harris Winitz, the author of the Learnables, has created a *Using Verbs* series of books and cassettes, with one volume each for verbs of walking, eating, and placement. On the left side of each page are 12 numbered pictures, correlated with 12 sentences on the right side of the page. The accompanying audiocassette for each book affords the student the opportunity to improve his pronunciation and reading.

Also by Harris Winitz, the *Language through Pictures* series includes one illustrated book each for prepositions, plurals and possessives, questions, negatives, conjunctions, articles, pronouns, and verbs. This series does not come with cassettes, and is intended for all ages from the youngest beginners on up. Over 2,500 illustrations in the complete eight-book series.

All About Language, a collaboration between Douglas Moore and Harris Winitz, is for late-beginning and early-intermediate language learners. Students should understand the vocabulary and sentence structure of books 1 and 2 of the Learnables before tackling this program. Each book in the program teaches a "lexical field." What's a lexical field, you ask? It's "a group of words that reflect a common core of meaning." In other words, a bunch of words related to a single topic. The series includes the following book/cassette combinations: Business I and II, Entertainment (Movies), Family, Houses & Buildings, Post Office, School, Telephone, Transportation, and Weather. Some sets come with two cassettes. These books have the same format as the other picture/text books from International Linguistics. Great for kids or adults.

NEW**
International Linguistics, Inc.
Student Kits, $8-$10 each. Shipping extra.

Total physical response (TPR) is the foreign-language-learning equivalent of learning by doing. You tell the child what to do in the foreign language, and if he does it correctly, you both know he understands. You can also model what you want him to do. Endless possibilities, and a rather similar approach to the way we learned English as kids.

International Linguistics offers peel 'n stick kits, each with 10 TPR lessons. Kits include the town, the airport, the home, the farm, the gas station, the kitchen, the playground, the hospital, the classroom, the supermarket, and the beach. Each is in full color and is available in your choice of French, German, Spanish, or English. (For ESL instruction, you get the English kit.)

Now, the moral of the story: if it works for teaching foreign languages to English-speaking kids, it should work the other way as well. Since the heart of these kits are the peel 'n stick figures, and since you already know their names in English, why not use them to teach English? As I said, endless possibilities.

NEW**
Penton Overseas, Inc.
The VocabuLearn series, $14.95 each course. Add $3 shipping per order.

The popular VocabuLearn series from Penton Overseas is a vocabulary-development program available in 16 languages. Each language course is "reversible," meaning it can be used by English-speakers to learn the target language, or by speakers of the target language to learn English. Each VocabuLearn course includes two 90-minute audiocassettes and a word list containing over 1500 words and expressions used on the cassettes. The words are not in any particular order, except that nouns, verbs, and other parts of speech are presented separately. Here's how it works. On one side of the tape, an American voice says a word in English, followed by a pause long enough for you to vocalize the word in the target language, if you know it. Then a native speaker of the target language says the word nice and slowly in that language. Midway through the tape the process is reversed. The word lists are different for both sides of the tape, to allow more vocabulary on the tapes.

VocabuLearn courses come in three levels. Level I is basic skills—simplest words and phrases. Level II includes more words and expressions. Level III includes more complex and sophisticated vocabulary.

The tapes are supercrisp, thanks to Dolby Stereo, and the packaging is nice.

Levels I and II are available in Arabic, Armenian, Mandarin Chinese, Danish, French, German, Hebrew, Italian, Japanese, Korean, Polish, Portuguese (S.A.), Russian, Spanish, Swedish, and a special French/Spanish course. Level III is now available for French, German, Italian, Japanese, Russian, and Spanish.

VocabuLearn/ce, a computer enhanced version of VocabuLearn for both IBM-PC and Macintosh users, is also now available in both levels I and II for Spanish, French, Italian, German, Japanese, Russian, and Hebrew. Each level comes with the same cassettes and booklet as regular VocabuLearn courses, but also has computer disks that allow you to drill yourself on the written words using your computer. For more info, see the review in the Educational Software Buyer's Guide in Volume 3.

NEW**
Visual Education Association
Vocabulary flash cards, $6.95/set of 1,000 cards. Shipping extra.

Everyone knows you can't really study English without flash cards. Here they are, boxed in sets of 1,000 cards. Vis Ed has two English Vocabulary sets. Together they comprise the 2,000 words most frequently seen in SAT tests. Words plus their pronunciation are on the front of the cards, definitions are on backs. Accompanying booklets include alphabetical indexes of words and study hints, plus some instruction on synonyms, antonyms, prefixes, suffixes, roots, and so on. The *English Scientific and Technical Vocabulary* set is just what you'd think—1,000 words boxed and numbered in alphabetical order, cross-referenced in the index by the discipline in which they occur.

PART IV

EDUCATIONAL VIDEO AND OTHER MEDIA

CHAPTER FIFTEEN

USES & ABUSES OF VIDEO LEARNING

Video learning—the greatest thing since computers. Right? Well, just as computers aren't the electronic messiah, neither are videos necessarily the salvation of Western education.

Video learning does have its good points, though. Let's look at them first:

- Price. Although educational videos *seem* expensive, when you consider what it would cost you to attend a similar course in person, including transportation time, video is usually a better deal. When you also consider that everyone in your family can view the course as many times as he wants, whereas in person you'd have to pay tuition for every student, video becomes a bargain! And some are even *free* (see the next chapter for details).

- Flexibility. If you like to learn to paint with watercolors at 10 P.M., you can do it. Video learning fits into any odd niches of your schedule.

- Time-saving. We often watch educational videos together at mealtimes, thus taking no time at all out of our workday. In fact, I watched every single video I reviewed for all four volumes of *The Big Book of Home Learning* at mealtimes!

- Effectiveness. Research has shown that we remember more of what we see than of what we only hear. Video lets us both hear and see at the same time. If the educational video asks us to perform an action as well, such as painting along with an art video, than the amount of retention climbs drastically.

- Instant replay. If you don't get it the first time, just rewind and watch again.

- Freeze frame or slow motion (if your player has these features) allow you to focus in on the details of an art lesson or a juggling move. This is not possible when you're attending a course in person.

- Like computer simulations, video can take you places that are too dangerous or expensive to visit on your own. Like Iran, or an erupting Hawaiian volcano, or the New York subway system.

- Togetherness. Your whole family, or any subset of it, can watch and learn at once.

Video can be used to teach just about anything. I've even found a video that shows some of the special virtues of educational video! See below.

NEW★★
Aylmer Press
Video and Learning video, $29.95 postpaid.

In the mid-1400s, Johannes Gutenberg invented a practical way of producing and using movable type. With Gutenberg's printing press, books became mass media for the first time. Now in 1990, Steve Kokette asks the question, "Are we living in the 'Gutenberg Age' of video?" He answers this question with a video pastiche of interviews with children who share their experiences with educational video.

Video and Learning is designed to make viewers aware of the possibilities of educational video. Mr. Kokette envisions a future where popping in a video will be as natural a way of learning a new skill as cracking a book or taking a seminar is today.

Don't expect glitz and glamour. This is not a Hollywood production, but a philosophical statement. One point the producer is trying to make is that video can be for Everyman, and in tune with this philosophy he hasn't indulged in fancy animation and technological wizardry. You get simple interviews, simply filmed, not big-screen staging and lighting.

Video and Learning is most useful as a fund-raising tool for those struggling to put together video libraries for their libraries, schools, and home-school groups. Aylmer Press allows non-profit groups to show the videos to groups, and even to take donations to cover its cost, two generous practices most producers forbid. The video is also close-captioned for the benefit of the deaf.

DARK SECRETS OF THE ELECTRONIC AGE

That was the good side of educational video.

Now, welcome to the Dark Side.

The Dark Side is not educational video per se, but the simple act of watching flickering images on an electronic screen. Video comes closer than anything seen yet to constituting an alternative reality (although new total-sensation media are on the way which will let you *feel* as well as see and hear). You can live in another world that is totally constructed for you by other people, unlike the world of books or recordings, where you do most of the constructing inside your own head. Now, is this new world "true, noble, right, pure, lovely, and admirable"?

Be aware that the video world has considerable advantages over the real one. The refresh rate of the screen flickers just on the edge of consciousness, exerting a subtle hypnotic effect that has been well-documented by researchers. This is an unavoidable part of the technology itself. In addition, due to the passive body position most of us assume while watching, the emotions aroused by video images have nowhere to go, creating bodily disharmony, which in turn adds to the disorientation. Sitting for hours in a darkened room, another inevitable part of video-watching, has also been shown to increase both passivity and depression. Kids, especially, tend to lose control of themselves after long tube sessions, becoming noticeably cranky and/or hyperactive. (Note: To spark up a passive kid, or slow down a hyperactive, try unplugging the tube. It works!)

Neither books nor spoken-word cassettes have anywhere near the grip of video, although rock music seems to run a close second. In this case, the "eyes" have it. The Bible says, "Death and Destruction are never satisfied, and neither are the eyes of man" (Proverbs 27:20), and as so often happens, this statement is literally true. No matter how many hours you may have sat in front of the flickering screen yesterday, it doesn't make you feel "full" and satisfied to watch less today. You are likely to feel just the opposite. The less satisfying your past viewing has been, the more likely it is that you will feel compelled to watch even more. In other words, watching video can be a form of unintentional surrender . . . but to what?

So I would warn you against becoming overdependent on the video medium, even educational video. We want our kids to be active learners, not passive types who will accept anything anyone who calls himself an authority tells them. We also don't want them to be couch potatoes or hypers! So our family picks times when we are already sitting (mealtime) to watch educational videos, or picks videos that require us to work along with them, such as exercise or art videos. We also do not dim the room lights excessively when watching, and don't encourage the habit of watching videos as a substitute for genuine creative activity. When the meal is over, we stop the video at that point and pick it up at another meal. (This exercise is a great help in preventing video addiction!) The player is in our kitchen, so there's no chance of kids sneaking off to a bedroom and watching it without our knowledge for hours. And, of course, we do not knowingly purchase or rent questionable videos of any sort. Those we have any concerns about (e.g., a war history video), Bill and I watch first before showing to the kids.

With these safeguards in place, educational video has definitely brought a new richness to our lives. Educational video is not really what I'm warning you against, although even education can be carried to extremes! Few of us will ever become obsessive about watching foreign-language videos, and educational video rarely oversteps the bounds of good taste and decency. We know the bad boy's name, and his initials are T. V.

TELEVISION WITHDRAWAL

You don't have to read this section unless you *really* want to know how it is that some mothers of seven can find time to write books or make patchwork quilts or run Bed & Breakfast operations while other mothers of one don't even get around to making the bed. Those who can, do. Those who watch TV (more than 15 minutes or so a day), can't.

Susan Schaeffer Macaulay (author of *For the Children's Sake*, a wonderful book on education) puts this all in perspective: "I'm not down on television, you understand. I just think it has an abominable effect on our lives!"

Let's list all the good points of having a television:

• It provides a place to put the potted plants.

• It's a free baby-sitter (that is, if we don't mind a baby-sitter who turns our children into zombies and fills them with violence and materialism).

• It keeps the kids off street corners (of course, it also brings the street corners into our living room).

• It helps us unwind after a hard day (as does a friendly massage, a family board game, or a good book).

• It keeps us up on current events (the ones the network considers important).

• It is so *educational!* All those documentaries and public TV offerings (now be honest, how much of that do you watch?)

None of us can manage our homes and families until we get the television set firmly under control. If we can't handle an inanimate box of electronics, what makes us think we can handle one or more live scaled-down versions of Tarzan?

Much has been written on how to control TV. You can now buy a clever lockout device that prevents the children from seeing anything until you, the parent, materialize with the magic key to unlock the set. People I know who have tried this tend to wimp out after a while by giving the children the key because it becomes too difficult always hopping up to lock and unlock the set—not to mention finding the key in the first place.

The easiest solution, of course, is to simply pension off the old familiar friend in an attic or sell it to a secondhand dealer and face life without TV. That mere phrase "life without TV" gets a lot of people asking the same questions Scarlett asked Rhett at the end of *Gone With the Wind* ("Where will I go? Whatever will I do?"), but if you are one of the braver ones, go ahead and join the Society for the Eradication of Television. This somewhat impromptu and free-form group has a newsletter ($5 for 10 issues, sample issue free), a speaker's bureau, and may just be the support you need to kick the habit for good. Or, if you're fence-sitting, try reading *Four Arguments for the Elimination of Television* by Jerry Mander (watch out for the new age-ish discussion of the power of imagery in the fourth chapter) or Marie Winn's *The Plug-in Drug,* both likely available from your public library. Jerry Mander deals with the physical and social effects of TV, and Marie Winn proves conclusively that it's not only *what* you watch, it's the watching itself that is detrimental, especially to children, who happen to be the biggest consumers of the stuff.

Now, being realistic, I figure most people aren't ready to give up TV entirely, no matter what the benefits of so doing. Viewers are just used to a certain amount of that kind of visual input—"addicted," if you will. That's why the networks and cable companies feel free to put out such incredibly awful stuff. But there is a way you can firmly and completely control your TV-watching, liberate yourself from the networks and cable companies, and insure that every video image in your house is one you invited. *You can buy a videocassette player that does not tune in television.*

TV-free video players are here, and here's how to get one.

NEW★★
Home Life
TV-free video systems start at $595 as of early 1990. TV-free monitors start at $250. Many models available. All discounted heavily off retail price. Free brochure.

I searched for years to find a TV-free video player (translation: a TV set without the TV), and when I did find one, through a series of accidents, was literally pushed into selling them myself. This is how it happened: When I found that this equipment was available, I put the name of the company distributing it to individuals into a previous edition of my book and thought no more of it. Then, for a series of reasons, that company was no longer able to distribute the systems. They had been using my name (without my knowledge) as the source of the order when placing the order with the manufacturer and for customers that had discovered them through my review, and thus somehow the manufacturer was thinking of me as one of their sales reps. The head of the distributing company, when he found he could no longer distribute them himself, called me and begged me to carry these players myself, so they would continue to be available to home schoolers and others interested in TV-free video. To save embarrassment to all parties, I agreed to do so.

I am telling you this so you will be aware that my commitment to TV-free video arose before we had any financial involvement with the medium! We were somewhat unsure at first whether we wanted to sell these players, having previously only sold books through our home business, but now are glad the Lord pushed us in this direction.

We have been using one of these sets for years, and are extremely pleased with both the picture quality (far better than that of a TV set) and our new freedom to mine the riches of video without the need to fear any detrimental programs entering our home. Families with a TV-free video player can study language on video, learn to play musical instruments by watching the best artists, catch up on classic films, and travel around the world in our living room, without constantly worrying if the children are watching raunchy cartoons or if the X-rated cable shows are bleeding onto our home set. And *no commercials!*

Some goodies available: forward and reverse visual search, freeze frame (great for taking notes or observing details), slow motion, and wireless remote. Most models come with all these options free. You can even get an earphone, so one student can do video studies without disturbing the others.

Now we even have TV-free monitors, so those of you who already own a VCR only need to replace your TV set, not the whole system.

Home Life offers special discount prices (hundreds of dollars off retail) on a wide choice of models, and our free catalog gives all the details of how to order through us. The more orders, the lower the prices, so send for a free catalog of these systems!

CHAPTER SIXTEEN

SUPER SOURCES FOR EDUCATIONAL VIDEO

I was afraid at first that I wouldn't be able to find enough sources for educational video to round out a chapter. Boy, was I wrong! The problem is culling the deadwood, not finding the forest. So following you will find listings of companies that offer lots and lots of educational videos, from the prim and prosy to the wild and wacky. You'll find complete academic programs, science experiments, advertising films (hey, they're free!), a kid's eye view of Japan, and lots more . . . even juggling videos!

NEW★★
A Beka Video Home School

The only complete video K–12 program. Grades preschool through 6 come as complete grades; grades 7–12 are available as individual courses. Come with textbooks and everything else you need. Used by thousands of Christian families.

For more details, see the A Beka Video Home School writeup in the Curriculum Buyers' Guide in Volume 1.

NEW★★
Art Video Library

Large, excellent selection of how-to videos for oil painting, drawing, watercolors, acrylics, and other art forms. See writeup in Chapter 1

NEW★★
Asia Society

We love their *Video Letter from Japan* (six videos) and *Discover Korea* series (total number in series TBA). Excellently-produced look at Asian cultures from a child's point of view. Extensive writeup in Worldview chapter of Volume 2.

NEW★★
Audio Visual Drawing Program

How-to-draw courses for young children taught by a retired Disney artist. Many series. Some originally aired on TV. Inexpensive. More info in Chapter 1.

NEW**
BG Science, Inc.
Electricity and chemistry video kits, $34.95 each.

Yeah, I know I said I wasn't going to mention any suppliers here that only had a few items for sale. But, as Emerson said, a foolish consistency is the hobgoblin of small minds. These are truly excellent video kits, with lots of impressive experiments laid out step by step. When you consider that the price includes all the ingredients needed for the experiments, you are even more impressed. At least I am! Details in the Science Experiments chapter of Volume 2.

Christian Films, Inc.

Located in Houston, Texas, Christian Films has been renting Christian films to churches and Christian schools since 1972. Today they have over 1,000 Christian videos, plus they have recently added over 3,500 educational videos for Christian schools and home schools.

These educational videos cover the gamut from kindergarten through high school, with some courses at the college level. These are not distinctively Christian (in fact, most were produced for public schools), but Christian Films believes many can be helpful in teaching the "difficult" subjects. For instance, your child can watch a laboratory experiment on video and see how it's done, even if you can't afford to provide him with a laboratory at home.

Some categories: language arts, child development, life science, math, world history, earth science, computer science, foreign languages, self-esteem, substance abuse, career education, ecology, geography/maps, U.S. history, comparative cultures, driver education, health, safety, biology, chemistry, physics, nutrition, and travel. As you can see, some are "hard" subjects and some threaten to be secular sermonettes. You, however, can choose which videos you want if you subscribe.

The way it works is this: you pay in advance for a subscription, which covers a set number of video rentals, including shipping both ways. You pick each video as needed, keep it and use it for up to three days, then return it. (Arrangements can be made to keep videos for longer periods.) For example, say you get a video to help explain nutrition. Maybe two weeks later you will want a travel video such as a tour of the Grand Canyon. Then you get some science videos. As each one is ordered, it is deducted from your subscription. When you deplete your subscription, you get a free video for resubscribing.

NEW**
Easton Press

I know this company purveys videos about recent history, and another firm at their address carries a BBC video course for foreign languages. But despite strenuous efforts, I have not been able to pry e'en the least tiny sample out of them. Maybe if *you* wrote to them and suggested that they send me a review sample, I can tell you about these in the next edition.

Entertainment Plus Video Club
Membership, $14.95, includes free video and 108-page descriptive catalog.

Join this club and get a free video and up to 50 percent discount on all purchases. Over 2,000 titles, including educational, inspirational, music, movies, and more. Examples: *McGee and Me* children's series from Focus on the Family, *Sandi Patti in Concert*, National Geographic specials, and so on. Send for a free brochure explaining how the club works.

NEW**
Homespun Tapes, Ltd.

All levels of how-to-play tapes for various instruments, taught by famous musicians. Leans toward country, folk (including Irish), rockabilly, jazz, and rock. Mostly fretted instruments, some woodwinds and keyboards. See Homespun writeups in Chapters 5–8.

NEW**
INC Magazine

I must be a sucker for punishment, but I keep mentioning INC. Magazine's lineup of how-to business videos, even though they have steadfastly refused to send me a review sample of even *one* of them. Some are fairly inexpensive, such as *How to Really Start Your Own Business*, which goes for less than $50. Others are ridiculously pricey, such as their Tom Peters series or their series on salesmanship.

NEW**
Home Life
Klutz Press

Juggling videos. How-to, sheer entertainment. You want 'em, here's where to get them. See writeups in Chapter 29.

NEW**
Master Books
Genesis and the Decay of the Nation, $9.95. Ayers Rock and Other Exciting Evidences, $19.95. Long War Against God, Dinosaur Mystery Solved, What Really Happened to the Dinosaurs?, Creation Evangelism, Genesis 1–11: An Overview, Ape-Men: Monkey Business, Is Life Just Chemistry?, Fascinating Design, and *Why Death and Suffering?,* $14.95 each. Special bonus offer of all 11 videos, $150. Add 15% shipping (minimum $3, maximum $14).*

Really good deals on creation science videos. I'm not sure if this offer will still be good by the time you read this, but I'm looking at a flyer that offers nine creation science videos for $14.95 apiece and one for $19.95, plus they throw in a free $9.95 value *Genesis and the Decay of the Nation* video if you buy all ten. The special bonus offer is $150 for all eleven videos. Most videos are an hour or less, with the exception being *Ayers Rock and Other Exciting Evidences for the Flood in Australia* (got that, you Aussies?), which is 108 minutes long.

NEW**
Modern Talking Picture Service
Free rental, and they even include a prepaid return envelope.

Modern Talking Picture Service is your source for FREE educational videos! Now, I know you're going to ask, "What's the catch?" No catch, except that these are industry-sponsored videos. You get to see them free because they include pitches for the products of the companies that produced them. Stock constantly changes, so I can't give you any sample titles. Here's an idea of the categories MTPS covers, though, along with a few of the hundreds of topics currently listed in those categories: Agriculture (raising alpacas, California cattle ranching). Art (glassmaking). Business (economic theory, banking, credit). Driver Education (motorcycle safety). Energy/ecology (Alaskan pipeline, endangered species). Health/Safety (asthma, cancer, how great pasta is for you, dog training, head lice). Home Economics (cooking with rice, cooking with beef, diabetes prevention). Hygiene. Marketing education (machine tool careers, manufacturing, plastics). Science (digestion, the Alaskan permafrost tundra). Social studies (how chocolate is made, Amish country, model railroading). Sports (Olympics, water safety). MTPS also has both English and German versions of a large selection of films and videos on Germany and its people, courtesy of the Consulate General of the Federal Republic of Germany. You can get a whole separate catalog of titles appropriate for elementary grades, a sports catalog, or a listing for senior citizens' groups. You just go to the index, pick a title in the category that interests you, check out its review, running time, and whether it's available in your state, and either call in your order or fill out an order form and send it in. Or you can subscribe to the Preferred Program Service, picking your preferred subject area from those listed and how often you want to receive a new video on loan (i.e., 15th of every month, every week, every 30 days, etc.). After seeing the video, you fill out the enclosed Attendance Report Card, then return it and the video in the prepaid mailer that accompanied the video. Some titles even come with discussion kits or other handouts that you are free to keep!

Unhappily, some of the titles I would most like to see still are only available on film (e.g., erupting volcanoes and earthquakes—something you don't want to see in person!), but I expect this will rapidly change, as video is becoming the educational medium of choice. In the meantime, you can still significantly enrich your home-schooling experience *for free* with Modern Talking Picture Service.

NEW**
ParentCare
Most videos priced from $14.95 to $29.95.

Catalog with huge assortment of children's videos. Disney. Sesame Street. Faerie Tale Theatre. Large sports and pastimes section includes karate, Little League baseball, soccer, ice skating, baseball, basketball, tennis, golf, biking, skateboarding, fishing, skiing how-tos. Educational video for toddlers. ParentCare thinks all parents are fat: their Parent's Corner is half exercise and beauty videos. Mr. Wizard. Mr. Rogers. National Geographic. Classic literature on video. Classic movies. Lots more! Plus an assortment of children's books, based on former Secretary of Education Bill Bennett's recommended reading list.

NEW**
Special Interest Video
Most videos are between $20 and $40.

Let's get educational here. Remember, this is the catalog with gambling videos and battling bimbos. Along with these "adult" selections, Special Interest has several pages of learning videos. Video flash cards in math and spelling. Math tutoring videos. Grammar videos. Foreign language videos. (*These* I would be interested in seeing!) SAT and college readiness. Safety habits. Preschool videos. Plus tons of sports how-to videos, exercise videos, computer training videos, how-to-play-music videos, war videos, airplane videos, railroad videos, and so on.

NEW**
SyberVision
Most videos in the $50 to $90 range. Catalog, $2.

Pricey, fancy videos. How-to sports taught by major stars; how-to business interviews with famous businessmen. Examples: Al Geiberger—*Men's Golf*, Patty Sheehan—*Women's Golf*, Stan Smith—*Tennis*, Jean-Claude Killy—*Skiing*, Jeff Nowak—*Cross-country Skiing*, Rod Carew—*Baseball*, Holman and Petraglia—*Bowling*, Dave Peck—*Racquetball*, Men's *Defend Yourself!*, Women's *Defend Yourself!* Dave Stockton—*Precision Putting*, Mike Dunaway—*Power Driving*, Hale Irwin—*Difficult Shots*. Their Role Models series of 45-minute videos includes Henry Johnson, Kemmons Wilson, Curt Carlson, Norman Brinker, John Teets, Oleg Cassini, and Rocky Aoki. The *Achievement, Self-Discipline*, and *Leaders* tape sets are all based on Stan-

ford University studies of those who excel in these attributes. A tinge of new age wishing-makes-it-so in the SyberVision advice to "saturate your own nervous system with sensory-rich images of success. "I don't mind looking at success, but personally I'd rather not be saturated with it. (Maybe it comes off if you presoak it.) All videos available in VHS or BETA.

NEW**
Vision Video
John Wycliffe, First Fruits, John Hus, Jon Amos Comenius, $59.95 each. *William Tyndale*, $79.95. *Martin Luther, Where Luther Walked, Dietrich Bonhoeffer*, $49.95 each. *John Bunyan*, $69.95. *Martin Luther: Abridged Version, Nikolai*, $29.95 each. *C.S. Lewis, Joy of Bach, Christ in Art*, $39.95 each. *Children's Heroes of the Bible*, 13-tape set, $99.95 complete. *Dangerous Journey*, 3-tape set, $59.95 complete. *New Media Bible*, $49.95 per tape or $198 per 4-tape set. Many more videos available. Add $3.95 shipping per order.

Thanks to the extreme generosity of Vision Video, our family has actually seen all of the programs listed above. Due to space constraints, I can't possibly write them all up here. You'll find detailed reviews in the Bible and Worldview chapters of Volume 2 and the History chapter of Volume 3.

These are all first-rate productions, such as you might see on TV if network executives ever darkened the doors of a church. Briefly, you have here a number of excellent church history videos, featuring famous Christians of the past: Wycliffe, Hus, Comenius, Tyndale, Luther, Bonhoeffer, C. S. Lewis, and the first Moravian missionaries (*First Fruits*). The *Children's Heroes of the Bible,* a very popular series, is 13 tapes by a Lutheran church production group that cover the entire span of Bible history with realistic (as opposed to caricaturish) cartoons. It's not always 100 percent accurate, but is more reverent and accurate than any other children's Bible series I have seen, and without any talking animals or children-transported-into-the-past foolishness. *The New Media Bible* is a fascinating reenactment of the Book of Genesis and the Book of Luke (four tapes each). Dialog is word for word from the Bible. Based on "meticulous historical, geographical, archaeological research," its purpose is to acquaint the viewer with Biblical scenery, culture, and events. *Dangerous Journey* is the old classic *Pilgrim's Progress* semi-animated. First-class art, faithful to the text. The kids liked it, even though we also had a fully-animated version from Omega Entertainment. *Nikolai* is the compelling story of a young Russian Christian boy, and a good way to introduce children to the subject of persecution without getting gruesome. *Joy of Bach* and *Christ in Art* trace the Christian influence on music and art through the work, respectively, of J. S. Bach and the old masters. Lots more: testimonials, Christian issue films, etc. Many titles are also available on 16mm film, for showing to larger groups.

ENTERTAINMENT VIDEO EVALUATION

Now that we've been so noble and educational, let's admit that we are not solely interested in video because of its educational qualities. Most of us sneak a movie now and then. This used to be a fairly safe pastime. But lately movies have become so toxic that it's not safe to expose your family to one without having it *thoroughly* checked out ahead of time. Here are two movie and video evaluation services that can help.

NEW**
Good News Communications
Movieguide. $30/year donation suggested. Bulk rates for churches, groups.

We call 'em as we see 'em. And when it comes to modern movies, we don't see most of 'em at all. (We have better things to do, like cleaning the bathroom.) All the same, we sometimes wonder if we're missing something. And what about all those old-time videos we never saw when they were movies? Some were good, some were bad, and some were ugly. We wouldn't want to unthinkingly inflict an Ugly on the children, even if it did star Errol Flynn.

Ted Baehr (pronounced "Ted Bear") is one Christian who has managed to get a toehold in the secular

media. His company, Good News Communications, produces two-minute movie reviews for radio stations and a column for newspapers and magazines. That's not too unusual so far . . . but Mr. Baehr & Co. actually have the audacity to review the celluloid from a Christian viewpoint! All movies are rated for both artistic style *and* content. Ratings run from 4+ (Excellent) to 4- (Evil).

A good chunk of these reviews are captured between paper covers in *The Movie and Video Guide for Christian Families* (Wolgemuth & Hyatt Publishers, 1990; two volumes). I'll tell you right off that I don't agree with some of the reviews, as the authors gave more points for style and took less off for explicit sexual content in some cases than I would have. Nonetheless, the section explaining how Christians used to control what went out of Hollywood and how the churches deliberately turned the reins back over to movie producers is fascinating.

Movieguide: A Biblical Look at Movies and Entertainment is a Good News Communication product designed to bring Christian reviews to you and me. The latest issues of this desktop-quality newsletter seemed to be getting more on target with their reviews. Each issue includes up to 13 well-written film reviews, plus occasional stills from the films reviewed. At least you can find out what is in the movie before you get shocked with chopped-off arms and "tasteful" orgy scenes—stuff that regular reviewers often forget to mention in their ecstasy over staging and acting.

NEW**
Movie Morality Ministries
Preview Movie Morality Guide, $25/year suggested gift. Complete set of back issues, $65, includes binder. *Recommended Movies on Video,* $18.

Somewhat more conservative than *Movieguide,* and with a more helpful rating format, is *Preview,* a twice-monthly newsletter devoted to rating new G, PG, and PG-13 movie releases. A typical issue of this black-on-ivory newsletter has reviews of four to eight current movies, rated both for entertainment value and morality. When the reviewers object to a movie, you don't have to guess why—the very specific rating system lists number of occurrences of bad language, violence, nudity and partial nudity, sexual intercourse (on-screen or implied), homosexual conduct, sexually suggestive dialogue or action, drug or alcohol abuse, and "other," a catch-all category for such items as occult themes and toilet humor.

John Evans and his reviewing staff are able to separate a movie's aesthetics and plotline from its worldview. This task is more difficult than it seems, as anyone who tries it rapidly learns. Like most traditional Christians reviewing films nowadays, they tend to lean over backwards to find *some* movies to recommend.

For those who recognize they need help picking out family films at the video store, Movie Morality Ministries has for sale both a complete set of past issues of *Preview* in a looseleaf binder (over 800 G/PG/PG13 movies released between 1982 and 1989) and their *Recommended Video Movies* booklet. The latter provides sentence reviews of over 500 secular and 150 Christian movies recommended by Movie Morality Ministries.

Videos are listed in alphabetical order and rated according to entertainment value (on a scale of 1-4), type of movie, year issued, MPAA rating, suggested viewing ages, running time, and whether they are color or B&W. Lots of classic movies are included, for obvious reasons. No way could they find 500 squeaky-clean family movies if they were limited to movies issued after 1980. Actually, some of the 500 aren't *that* squeaky-clean. Recommended Hitchcock films, for example, generally include some kind of extramarital action (not shown on screen, of course—the big H directed in the Fifties, after all!). Even so, *Recommended Video Movies* is a lot of help when wondering what video to look for among all the raunch at the video store.

CHAPTER SEVENTEEN

FUN LITERATURE

Looking for fun, wholesome books for your children to read? Look no further! Don't worry, I'm not going to pull any fast ones on you. I'm not going to try to sneak deep and important books into this chapter: The Sort of Books Our Children Should Read. For those sorts of books, check out the Literature chapters in Volumes 2 and 3. Nor will you find any phonics readers in this chapter or *any* readers, for that matter. You're looking at the Huck Finn of reading chapters. Kick off your shoes, stick a piece of straw between your teeth, lie back on the good warm earth, and enjoy your reading!

BOOKS

A Beka Books

Reading for Fun summer library (K), $19.95. *Treasure Chest* summer library (grade 1), $16.95. Add $2.50 shipping.

I know your children are going to like this, if they're anything like our kids! A Beka has come up with two summer reading libraries—one for kindergartners, the other for first-graders. Both come with oodles of books.

Reading for Fun, the summer library for kindergartners, has 55 (count 'em!) colorful little books, all packaged in an attractive case. Starting with truly tiny little phonics readers, the books get bigger and the stories get longer. Every book is short enough to be read in a single sitting, a big plus with littlest readers.

Treasure Chest, the summer library for first-graders, comes packed in (you guessed it) a treasure chest. Twelve books with full-color covers carry on the "treasure" theme with classic tales intermixed with new stories.

Both summer libraries have great kid appeal and are guaranteed to banish the reading blahs any time of the year.

UPDATED**
Alpha Omega Publications
Price per book: $1.50 and up.

Alpha Omega has assembled a good number of affordable, quality books for supplemental and enrichment reading for all grade levels—almost 250 titles with many more planned for the future. Their staff actually reads and evaluates every single one of these books for grade level readability (using the Fry Readability Formula and five other readability indexes) and the quality and appropriateness of their content. Many of the books are the original, unabridged versions. Themes include Christian character, Christian biography, historical biography, and timeless classic literature that even adults will enjoy.

Capper's Books

Capper's has been around for awhile; Laura Ingalls Wilder was reading *Capper's Weekly* before the turn of the century.

According to Capper's, "our true specialty is in our strong selection of popular children's classics." These include such titles as *Mrs. Wiggs of the Cabbage Patch*, which we are glad to report has nothing to do with Cabbage Patch dolls, *A Girl of the Limberlost*, and nature-lover Thornton W. Burgess's 1909 classic *Old Mother West Wind*. These gentle stories contrast sharply with the selfishness, nastiness, and flippishness of much of what now passes for children's literature.

Children's Book and Music Center

This enormous newsprint catalog is "the largest supply of children's books, records, and cassettes in the country." Many topics, including basic school subjects like math and reading readiness, creative arts, and physical education. The Children's Book and Music Center literature collection is three jam-packed pages of contemporary favorites. Here's where to get the compete Babar collection, or piles of books by Bill Peet, Ezra Jack Keats, Maurice Sendak, Richard Scarry, Dr. Seuss, Peter Spier, and Shel Silverstein. Also fairy tales, poetry (from Robert Louis Stevenson to Shel Silverstein), and several literature anthologies.

Apparently Children's Book and Music Center stocks more items than they list in the catalog, as a little box on the front page says, "We stock thousands of paperbacks including fiction and nonfiction for all ages. Call with your special request."

Children's Small Press Collection

The Children's Small Press Collection represents nearly 100 small progressive children's publishers. The Collection includes a wide selection of books "on the forefront of children's issues." Topics include: Activities (cookbooks, early childhood activity books, a children's organizer . . .) • Family and Human Relations (lots about divorce, fighting, and single parents) • Feelings • Fantasy and Fun • Fiction for Young Readers (all contemporary) • For the Middle Young • Resources for the Gifted (that's their title for this section, not to be confused with the company by that name) • Teen Guidance • Safety Issues • Parenting • Health and Sexuality • Science and the Environment • Teacher Resources • Nursery Rhymes and Poetry (includes *Black Mother Goose* and *Father Gander*) • Child Authors (six books in this category, up from two in the last edition) • Puppetry and Storytelling • Multicultural, Historical, and Bilingual • Conflict Resolution, Problem Solving (pacifist). Member publishers include Young Discovery Library, Advocacy Press, New Seed Press, Parenting Press, Shameless Hussy Press, Women's Press, Rainbow Press, and even Garlic Press (we kid you not!).

Chinaberry Book Service

Warm, inviting, helpful catalog of literature for children from birth through the late teens. This is a real book service, not just a glitzy pictures-with-minimal-description catalog. Each and every book is lovingly described by a mother who has read it and used it with her own children. Very large selection (the current catalog has over 80 newsprint pages), ranging from classics like *Charlotte's Web* to brand-new books. Just one example, from the writeup of *If You Give a Mouse a Cookie*:

I'm getting tired of special ordering this book! No longer do I wonder if the fact that it is available only in hardcover is enough to turn everyone off . . . EVERYONE to whom I've shown this book (and obviously those special orders) thinks this book is irresistible. It seems to be one of those books you can read a million times and never feel like hiding it from your child so you won't have to read it yet AGAIN.

It is the story of a boy who makes the mistake of giving a mouse a cookie. (The mouse is quite adorable.) Now, if you give a mouse a cookie, he's going to need some milk. (We see the boy getting the mouse a glass of milk.) But then, the mouse will probably ask for a straw. (The boy gets a straw.) Then he'll want to look at himself in the mirror to make sure he doesn't have a milk moustache. (The boy gets a napkin and holds the mouse up to the bathroom mirror so he can see himself.) . . . Eventually, the story comes full circle and the endearing mouse, who is thirsty, needs a drink of milk. And, of course, if he asks for a glass of milk, he's going to want a cookie to go with it. (By this time, the boy is completely wiped out, and the kitchen is a mess.)

Text is sparse. The colored illustrations are uncluttered, but with enough detail to keep you looking for more tidbits to chuckle over.

Chinaberry has everything from board books to Newberry award-winners to fabric-covered scrapbooks to Please Packs. Some new age, some Christian, some secular, chosen not so much for ideology (although Chinaberry has new age leanings) as for beauty, serenity, cleverness, and fun.

Christian Light Publications

Christian Light, a full-service publisher of materials for Christian schools, home schools, Sunday schools, and VBS, also offers literature they consider suitable for young children, chosen in conformity with Mennonite moral standards. Each work offered comes with a code that explains just how good they think the book is and if they recommend it with any reservations.

EDC Publishing
Find It board books, $2.95 each. What's Happening series, $3.95 each. Picture Word books, $2.95 each paperback, $6.95 each hardbound, $11.96 library bound. First Experiences series, $2.95 each or $8.95 for hardbound combined volume. Children's Picture Bible series, $4.95 each. Slot books, $8.95 each except *Mouse About the House*, $9.95. Michael and Mandy series, $3.95 each. Story Books, $2.95 each or two hardbound combined volumes, *Dragons, Giants, Witches, Princesses and Princes, Wizards*, and *Gnomes*, $10.95 each. Upside Down books, $4.95 each. Picture Classics, $3.95 or $10.95 for hardbound combined volume, *Children's Classics.*

Immense array of all sorts of educational and fun reading matter for children. EDC publishes the Usborne Books line, originally produced in the United Kingdom.

Elsewhere in this book I have mentioned a dozen or so of the more overtly educational series; now let's look at what reading matter Usborne has to offer.

Find It board books for youngest children (six months on up) are twelve thick pages apiece. Your youngster searches for the hidden animal in every picture. Stephen Cartwright's charming art illustrates this series. Included: *Find the Duck, Teddy, Piglet, Puppy, Kitten, Bird.*

Also illustrated by Stephen Cartwright, the What's Happening series for two- to six-year-olds presents common situations (*On the Farm, The Seaside, At the Zoo*) with an amusing difference. Look for hidden objects, recognize details of color and shape.

Picture Word books (*The House, The Shop, The Town*) are pages of colorful scenes containing dozens of labeled objects. Similar to the Richard Scarry approach, but with real people, not cartoon animals.

The First Experiences series, again illustrated by the inimitable Stephen Cartwright, covers *Going to the Dentist, Going to a Party* (monster costumes in this one), *Going to the Hospital, The New Baby* (a very gentle, pro-baby story), *Going to School*, and *Moving House.* Gentle story lines accompany the amusing art. Suitable for three years old on up.

The Children's Picture Bible series only covers parts of the life of Christ: *The Childhood of Jesus, Miracles of Jesus, Stories Jesus Told.* Realistic art. Ages eight on up.

Slot Books are something different. These fantasy stories are not illustrated quite as beautifully as the other Usborne books, but they are more interactive. You remove the magic carpet, space ship, or whatever from the pocket. Place it on the first page, follow the dotted line, and pop it through the slot to follow the story line. Includes: *There's a Mouse About the House, A Squirrel's Tale, The Amazing Journey of Space Ship H-20, Ted and Dolly's Magic Carpet Ride,* and *Ted and Dolly's Fairytale Flight.*

The Michael and Mandy series is another learn-to-cope-with-scary-experiences series, of which we have plenty in the USA. Covered: *Mandy and the Hospital, Mandy and the Dentist, Michael's First Day at School, Michael in the Dark, Michael and the Sea.*

The Usborne Story Books series for ages six and up is all that fairy tale stuff: *Dragons, Giants, Witches* (available separately or as a combined volume), and

Princes and Princesses, *Wizards*, and *Gnomes* (also available separately or combined). Stephen Cartwright illustrations.

Upside Down books, yet another innovative Usborne product, each contain two stories. Read one, flip the book over, and read another. These are familiar fairy tales: *King Midas* and *The Emperor's New Clothes*; *The Three Bears* and *The Little Match Girl*; *Cinderella* and *How the Elephant Got Its Trunk*; *The Frog Prince* and *The Pear Tree*; *The Pancake that Ran Away* and *Toads and Diamonds*; and *Sleeping Beauty* and *The Soldier and the Seven Giants*. All freshly retold versions of the original tales.

· Lastly, besides the myths and legends, animal stories, and others such that I just don't have room to write up, are the Picture Classics. See these described in the Classical Literature chapter.

NEW**
The Golden Key

I got my first issue of this catalog the very day I was finishing the manuscript of this book, and just had to put it in. From Cahill & Company, the people who search out such fascinating books for grown-ups, the Golden Key catalog is a treasure trove of classical and cross-cultural books. When I say "cross-cultural," I really mean it, for their collection includes a book about the last Russian Tsar and a tour of medieval Europe, as well as classic children's tales from other lands, like the Chinese version of Little Red Riding Hood. You will recognize such treasures as Kate Greenaway's *Mother Goose*, but may not have ever seen some of these gems before. Brer Rabbit as a family man? An introduction to architecture for kids that starts with the Taj Mahal, the Parthenon, and Our Lady of Chartres? How about Shakespeare in prose for kids, or Dickensian fiction by Leon Garfield? Fantasy, historical fiction, and adventure are especially well represented, with a smattering of science and art. You'll find books about nature right next to book about knights. Something for readers of all ages, from the Mother Goose set up to advanced teens and their book-snitching parents. Forgive me if I stop here, but I've got to go fill out a book order form . . .

Gospel Mission

Wholesale Christian book outlet. Their Children's Heritage line of classic Christian tales from the nineteenth century has a whole different outlook on life than modern children's literature. Personal piety and care for the poor are stressed. Lovers of Louisa May Alcott's *Little Women* series will find that warmly pious atmosphere recreated here.

NEW**
The Home School

Vast selection of children's classics, historical biography, and just plain fun stuff like Beverly Cleary's "Ramona" books. Good reading in all school subject categories, but without the drudgery usually associated with "school." Well-organized catalog is put together by the owners of a mall store catering to home schoolers. This catalog includes far more than fun reading materials!

UPDATED**
High Noon Books (division of Academic Therapy Publications)
Each set of 5 books, $12.50. Set of 10, $25. Add $2.50 shipping.

Really interesting high-lo books (high interest, low reading level) designed for preteens and teens, but also usable by any young child who can read. The books are inexpensive, and the mystery/adventure format keeps interest high.

The Tom and Ricky mystery series, one of High Noon's most successful, stars two Caucasian boys who, through serendipity and diligence, solve every mystery they meet. All the Tom and Ricky books are written at a first-grade readability level and aimed at children ages 9–14. When I tell you that there are currently nine Tom and Ricky sets, and each set contains five different books, you can see that everyone loves Tom and Ricky! The first 10 Tom and Ricky books are even available in Spanish.

High Noon's Scoop Doogan mystery series is 10 titles at a second-grade readability level for children ages 11–15. For girls, the Meg Parker mysteries are another 10 titles at the same readability level and aimed at the same age group. Also for that age group are the 10 Road Aces titles. Just slightly more advanced, Main Street Books for kids ages 12–18 feature black and Hispanic high-school students in inner-city settings.

Pressing on to third- and fourth-grade reading level and a correspondingly more mature reader (ages 12–16), we find the High Adventure series in which kids face major challenges such as tornadoes, circus fires, earthquakes, and wolves. Also at third-grade readability are the Connection Series starring inner-city kids of various races and nationalities (e.g., a Vietnamese immigrant) facing major problems, and the Numero Uno Gang mysteries, starring a multiracial "gang" (wholesome style) of blacks and Hispanics.

I could go on. There's the Life Line series with Mike and his Life Line Helicopter Service, rescuing people from all sorts of dangerous situations . . . the 9–5 mystery series revolving around kids with entry-level jobs . . . the Legal Eagle series . . . the Annie Wilkins mysteries . . . You get the idea.

Every one of these books is a fast-paced seven chapters or so, with 48 or 64 pages, perfect-bound with a spine and sized for an adult appearance. Only one plot per book, to avoid confusing the reader. Five pen-and-ink illustrations per book, none of show-stopping quality, serve to break up the print. Oh, yeah. You can also get worksheets and comprehension checkers and all that stuff for some of these series; but I'm sure you won't want to. Just when an older reluctant or slow reader is finally enjoying a whole book, let's not jump all over him with worksheets.

High Noon books all foster morals without being preachy—the heroes are good and the bad guys are bad. These are good books for younger kids too, who will enjoy the adult plots and easy vocabulary. Son Ted's verdict at the age of eight: "I like them because they're exciting."

NEW**
Ladybird Books
Books, $2.95 or $3.95 each. Flap books, $6.95 each.

From England, here is another huge series of fun books for all ages of children on all sorts of kid-pleasing and educational subjects. Start with Ladybird's Little Board Books (Baby Animals and suchlike) and First Word Books. More: Flap books—books with flaps you lift up to discover hidden objects (great fun for little kids!). Flap books include *Baby Bear's Noisy Farm* (the horse is behind the barn door, etc.), *Baby Bear's Shopping Day, Baby Bear's Hide and Seek,* and *Baby Bear's Best Friends.* Love 'em! Plus bath books. Cloth books. A set of 16 Bible Stories books for young children. Classic fairy tales. A World Wildlife read-aloud series. You'll also find several Talkabouts series. These are books to read *with* your children. You look at and discuss the pictures together. Examples: *Animals, Home, Shopping, Baby, Starting School, Bedtime, Going into Hospital.*

Ladybird also has several extensive reading series, including lots of illustrated abridgements of classic kids' literature, reviewed in Volume 2.

Ladybird also has a small number of horror books, even for young kids, that I absolutely can do without. These are done very well if you happen to like Dracula, but I just don't see the need, with all those wonderful Bible books, science books, classic fairy tales, folk tales, and children's literature!

Perma-Bound

Enormous catalog of all sorts of books bound with the special Perma-Bound process. Perma-Bound promises to make paperbacks far more durable, for far less than the price of hardbound. Much modern children's literature, some classics. Minimum order policy means you might want to co-op with other families.

CHILDREN'S BOOK CLUBS

God's World Publications
Many titles in the $2-$3 range. Many books are from publisher's discontinued stock. No obligation. Only books you order are sent. No shipping charge for orders of $10 or more.

All subscribers to any God's World publication are automatically in the God's World Book Club. Others may join simply by writing and asking to be added to the mailing list.

The good folks at God's World send out at least three catalogs a year, two of which are specifically designed for home schoolers. What you get are children's classics, reference books, and many other carefully selected books from Christian and secular publishers. Many titles are quality remainders, unavailable elsewhere, and offered at tremendous savings. Many other items, like a slipcased set of the *Little House* books for $24.95, remain available at all times. On other items old inventory disappears as new titles are added—so don't hang on to your order too long before sending it in! At present, over 700 titles are available, from over 90 publishers, with many more to be added.

The God's World Book Club should help Christian parents and others who are ready for some wholesome, stimulating reading answer the perennial question, "Whatever *shall* I find for my children to read?"

Grolier Enterprises

One morning you unwittingly open your mailbox and there it is, lurking inside. It looks innocuous enough—an ad for a children's book club. The one I got most recently said "Your child's lifelong love of reading begins with . . . 4 books for only $1.95, Plus A FREE Tote Bag."

So what's so dangerous, you ask? Grolier Enterprises' Beginning Readers' Program may do exactly what it says! Are you *ready* for a lifelong love of reading? Are you ready to have your arm jerked off every time you try to walk your children past a bookstore or a library? Reading can get to be a *habit*, you know!

The initial four books, at $1.95 for all four plus shipping and handling, are just to hook you on the program. Thereafter, every four weeks you will be sent two more books. If you want to keep them, you will pay $3.99 each plus shipping and handling. If you don't want to keep them, you will have to repack them, drive to the Post Office, and return them. This must be done within 10 days. It is, in short, a lot of effort to return the books. Keep that in mind when considering enrollment.

The Beginning Readers' Program features the likes of Dr. Seuss and the Berenstain Bears. How do I know you can get hooked on Seuss? Because those are the books my father used to teach me to read, and I wore out three library cards before I turned 15!

Grolier has a similar program, entitled Disney's Wonderful World of Reading. The ad for this one offered two free books and a bookrack, plus a chance to win a sweepstakes. Terms are the same as for the Beginning Readers' Program. The books are, you guessed it, Walt Disney productions like *Pinocchio* and *Cinderella*. You know as much about Walt Disney as I do, so I leave this offer to your judgment.

MAGAZINES

Cricket

One year (12 issues), $22.50 U.S.A., $26.50 Canadian and foreign. Single copy $1.95.

Cricket has been called "the New Yorker of kiddie lit." Each issue is a work of art: beautiful illustrations and stories written by top writers. *Cricket's* editor, Marianne Carus, is very, very picky about what goes in to the magazine. She has been known to turn down stories offered by the likes of world-famous writer William Saroyan. (Saroyan later tried again with a better story, which she accepted.)

Let's talk about awards and endorsements. What other magazine comes with a personal recommendation from Isaac Bashevis Singer? *Cricket* has won many awards for excellence, including finalist status in the National Magazine Awards competition—the only children's magazine so selected.

Of interest to home schoolers: Nancy Wallace's son Ishmael once "placed" in a *Cricket* writing competition.

The magazine's mascot is (surprise!) a cricket, who with his buggy friends, collectively known as Everybuggy, cavorts around the margins helping readers better understand the stories. Cricket also has his own adventures and his own comic strip in the back of each issue.

Stories range from Sid Fleischmann's howlingly funny McBroom tall tales to true tales about volcanic eruptions (remember Krakatoa?) and "realistic" stories about kids and their relationships, with everything in between. Many stories have fantasy themes (friendly ghosts, brave mother dragons, and the like).

God's World Publications

God's Big World (K), *Sharing God's World* (grade 1), *Exploring God's World* (grades 2-3), each $8.50 (includes teacher's guide), *It's God's World* (grades 4-6), *God's World Today* (junior high), $9.95 (includes teacher's guide), *World* (senior high and adult), $18. Bulk orders get discount. Each paper 30 issues, September to May, except *World* (40 issues).

An idea whose time has come. News for kids from a Christian viewpoint. Professionally produced, entertaining, but not superficial.

GWP has papers for all different reading levels from kindergarten to adult. The papers for children are carefully matched to their interests and abilities. Following a newspaper format, you get feature stories, reports on hot news items, editorials, cartoons, and letters-to-the-editor. One of my favorite features, "Foto File," is a page of news photos with hilarious captions underneath. Papers for the kindergarten through junior-high set also include activities for kids. A teacher's guide is included with each edition. Our kids all *love* these papers!

NEW**
Highlights for Children
Single issue, $2.95.

Yes, this is the magazine you remember reading as a young child while you waited nervously in the dentist's waiting room. It's all here: Goofus and Gallant, the role models of bad and good little boys; the Timbertoes family; hidden pictures; Our Own Pages, displaying the reader's artwork and poems; feature stories on natural wonders; children's fiction for a range of ages; dumb jokes that your kids will run around trying out on each other for weeks; crafts activities; mini-biographies of great men and women; and the famous what's-wrong-with-this-picture covers.

I'm going to be brutally honest. I never liked *Highlights* as a child. Perhaps it was the atmosphere of waiting for the dentist. Perhaps it was because I was secretly in love with Batman (not Robin) and Clark Kent (love those glasses!) and despised anything in cartoon form that didn't have some good guy biffing a bad guy or solving a mystery on every page. (Let's face it, compared to Batman, the Timbertoes are *tame*. Even compared to Clark Kent, they are tame!) Perhaps it was the subtitle, "Fun with a Purpose." A wary child with wide experience of institutionalized schooling, I was sure that nothing with a purpose could ever be fun. But I am nothing if not willing to eat my words. Yum! Crunchy! Nourishing!

So when our children, of their own free will and with absolutely no encouragement from me, sent in one of the cards for free stickers and a sample issue they found lying around the chiropractor's office, I was prepared to wait and see.

What I saw was a *Highlights* salesman hovering at our door who, putting up with my brusque-to-the-point-of-rudeness desire to get on with the lunch we were about to eat on a very tiring and discouraging day, succeeded in selling us a two-year subscription. I then saw the children falling over each other to read and reread the issues, sending away for the advertised Hidden Pictures books with their own money, driving me crazy with those dumb jokes I warned you about, and generally just loving this magazine.

The more I look into it, the more I find that the people at *Highlight's* address really know what they are doing. I have yet to see a product they turn out that isn't academically fantastic and actually interesting to all children, except those who, like me, were ruined by comic books.

There's a moral here somewhere, I'm sure. Maybe several. (1) Comic books really do rot the brain, just as our grandmothers said they would. (2) A wasted childhood can still be redeemed.

I mean, at the age of 34 I'm getting hooked on hidden picture puzzles!

Young Companion
$6/year, monthly issues.

This magazine charms others as well as myself. One reader wrote to share how delighted she was with the innocent stories designed for *older* children.

Young Companion is perhaps the only magazine for preteens and teens that does not assume the readers are into drugs and sex and rock. Style is down-to-earth and pious rather than sentimental (another plus).

An Amish production, *Young Companion* projects the unworried Christian culture of our past into the graceless confusion of the present.

CHAPTER EIGHTEEN

CHILDREN'S TAPES

The whole time I was writing this book, weird sounds kept drifting from the next room. Patch the Pirate exhorting his crew to win the Misterslippi River Race. Children's voices singing nursery rhymes. Dramatized stories, complete with sound effects like surf crashing on rocks.

The sad truth is that my daughter, Magdalene, is a cassette junkie. And much as it hurts to admit it, my son Franklin is following in her footsteps.

The shame of it all! Kids their age should be plopped in front of a TV screen, glued to the spoonfed adventures of Bert and Ernie, not singing along with characters on a cassette tape and (what is worse) actually supplying the pictures out of their own imaginations! Why, if this keeps up, our children will actually develop their memories and imaginations to the point where they might turn around and write stories of their own some day! And heaven knows that the last thing the brave new world of the twenty-first century needs is another Charles Dickens or P. G. Wodehouse to touch our hearts and bring us laughter. Life is stern and earnest. Kids should stick to wildly-oscillating graphics presenting the letter "S" and leave storytelling back in the primitive past, where it belongs.

If you believe all this, I've got a great deal on some Florida swampland . . . oops, "retirement properties" . . . that you might be interested in.

The plain truth of the matter is that "story readiness" is the great prerequisite for learning to read. Kids need to develop their ability to follow a complete story and imagine it all in their heads before reading makes any sense to them. Sure, they can learn to decode words. Yes, they can fill in the little workbook pages. But until they are "story ready," they will not learn to read with joy and fluency.

It's wonderful to spend hours reading to your children, and if you have the time, I heartily recommend it. Even in the middle of this project, I have tried to snatch time for reading a baby book to our youngest and short children's books to Magda and Franky. But in real life, many of us are too hassled to always have time for long reading sessions.

Ergo, the cassette player.

This wonderful invention can bring hundreds of storytellers and talented singers of children's music into your home. It can also make *you* a better storyteller, if you listen and learn from the pros. George Sarris's masterful interpretation of the Book of Daniel, for example, is an inspiration to our own oral Bible-reading.

From the beginning of time, children have always loved singing and stories. The Bible itself starts with a story. Jesus told stories. King David sang and danced before the Ark of the Covenant. So come on, brothers and sisters, let's get with it!

STORIES ON TAPE

Caedmon Tapes
Most cassettes and records, $8.98 each. Sets cost less per recording.

Caedmon has a vast collection of spoken-word recordings of literature—modern, classical, ancient, British, American, European and other, for people both young and old. Some recordings, like Carol Channing's performance of *Winnie-the-Pooh*, have music as well, and this is indicated by a little black musical note in the margin. (Our kids have worn out that set, by the way!) Many are abridged, the better to fit on a C-60 cassette. The selection includes novels, fairy tales, poems, legends, science fiction, and fantasy. Many works are read by the authors. Some *poseurs* are included here also, but the good outweighs the bad.

Caedmon cassettes are not narrated but "performed" by the likes of W. H. Auden, Dylan Thomas, Carol Channing, and Michael Bond (of Paddington Bear fame). The recordings are not all entertainment, though. You can get several Great Speeches sets featuring speeches that changed history, Studs Terkel's story of the Depression in the words of those who lived it, Camus reading his own novels (in French, naturally). Eggheads, in short, are in for a feast.

Caedmon's catalog is prosaic, and prices are not cheap. For diehard cassette fans, there is a way around the price boondoggle: sign up for the Library Subscription Plan. Of the four options, the one most likely to interest home schoolers is the Small Budget Children's Plan. You agree to buy each new Caedmon release in that category at a reduced rate, for a maximum investment of $55/year for 10 cassettes. In return, you get 40 percent off on all Caedmon recordings and all Arabesque recordings (classical music and opera).

NEW**
The Landmark Company
The Lighthouse Adventures cassette series, $39.95 plus $3.50 shipping.

This is the best dramatized Christian cassette series I have ever heard.

It's called *The Lighthouse Adventures*, and briefly, it's the story of Pete and Tim and how they both come to know the Lord, all on twelve cassettes neatly packed into a binder with a fancy little sheet of questions for discussion. Along the way you meet Tony, the tough guy who's into some serious stuff, ever-glib and ever-

unreliable Skip and his bonehead pal Danny, old Nathaniel Bolt the lighthouse keeper, sweet sixteen Christy, bombshell Missy—in short, a whole raft of unforgettable characters.

Unlike most Christian fiction, this series doesn't miss a beat. The acting is wonderful, as are the sound effects. The story is so gripping you might well hear the whole series through in one sitting. Our kids kept begging for "one more cassette," and we wanted to keep on going too! The discussion questions and Bible verses are just right: short, sweet, and pointed. Topics covered are important to every child: obedience, trust in God, honesty, standing against peer pressure, the dangers of showing off, true versus false friendship, and so on. Never does the story become cloying. In fact, the characterizations are so realistic that even what I regarded as faults in designing the characters (e.g., the mother's weak failure to control her sons) led to the results you would expect—all without one iota of preaching. There are more lessons in this series than the writers themselves may realize! Even the price is right.

The big question, "Will the kids listen to this more than once?" was answered immediately in my own family by them requesting the whole series a second time the moment the last cassette was over. I enjoyed it as much the second time—in fact, more, since now I saw more nuances in the plot. We played it three times on a long car trip last summer, and the kids have listened to it all the way through several times since then. I sure hope they don't wear out the tape, 'cause I'd like to hear *The Lighthouse Adventures* again sometime soon!

UPDATED**
Majesty Music
All Patch the Pirate super long-play recordings, $9.98 each. Accompaniment tapes, $35, available in reel or cassette. Music books: Captain's Copy (for choir director), $4.95 each; Sailor's Copy (lyrics and melody line only), $2.95.

Who is Patch the Pirate, and why are all these Christian kids listening to stories about him? Well, first of all Patch isn't a real blood-and-thunder pirate. Patch is the invention of one Ron Hamilton. After losing an eye to cancer, Ron was forced to wear an eyepatch. Hence the alias "Patch the Pirate." Making the most of this unhappy situation, Ron decided to dress up as a pirate and tell Christian stories. One thing led to another, and that's how we got the Patch the Pirate series.

Patch, as one would expect from a preacher in disguise, is a very straight-arrow pirate. In fact, he does nothing piratical at all except sail the sea and use sailorly talk.

The Patch adventures are parables of the Christian life. They feature really bad villains who do not roll over and play dead if you just smile sweetly at them. Patch, a Real Man, leads the crew—a welcome change from all those series of Worlds Without Adults, Amen.

Kidnapped on I-Land is an action-packed excursion into the kingdom of the nasty King Me-First. Silas Sailor, found floating on a raft by Patch and his crew, succumbs to the blandishments of King Me-First, who promises him a marvelous life on his own if Silas will just determine to always put himself first. With Silas firmly chained to him, King Me-First flies off to I-Land and flings Silas into Pity-Party Pit, a particularly dark corner of the Prison of No Sing-Sing. Patch and friends set out to rescue Silas, who is slated to become a barbecued sailor steak, courtesy of King Me-First's pet, Torch the Dragon. Silas finally decides to put Jesus first, at which point the castle disappears, Me-First shrinks into nothingness, and all is well. The whole adventure resembles John Bunyan's *Pilgrim's Progress* (on a somewhat lower literary level), and is characterized by frequent clever jokes and lots of bright, happy music.

The Great American Time Machine has Patch and his crew escorting a delegation of two from Bonkinland back through American history to discover the secret of America's greatness. The Bonkers only understand coercive power (in Bonkinland every higher Bonker gets to bonk everyone lower than him to keep them in line), and the sight of George Washington kneeling in the snow at Valley Forge and Dwight L. Moody preaching in Chicago, among other peeks into American roots, amaze them. Lots of good songs and nice effects, like the Statue of Liberty speaking with a Bronx accent.

The Patch lineup also includes *Patch the Pirate Goes to the Jungle*, *Patch the Pirate Goes West*, *Patch the Pirate Goes to Space*, *The Calliope Caper*, *The Misterslippi River Race* (these last two are favorites of our kids), *Patch the Pirate Praises*, *Quiet-Time Favorites*, *Sing Along with Patch the Pirate*. It also includes *Fun Song Favorites*, which I can't recommend because of the song, "I Want to Marry Daddy When I Grow Up." I know the people at Majesty Music just meant that song in the old, innocent "I love Daddy" way, but in this day and age where people are starting to agitate for making such things actually possible I'd rather not have my kids singing it around the house. (One possible solution: Tell your boys to sing instead, "I want to be a Daddy when I grow up," and your girls to sing, "I want a man like Daddy when I grow up.") All the above come with free 14-page read-along coloring books. For each Patch story Majesty Music has everything you need to put on a Patch musical on at your church or school.

Mind's Eye
Most cassettes $5.95 each, including *Color Book Theater*. Sets are less per cassette.

Tremendous selection of stories both classical and just plain fun. Will Rogers and other humorists, *Color Book Theater* (reviewed in the Classical Literature chapter), mystery, science fiction, history—you name it, The Mind's Eye has it. Lovely catalog for browsers.

NEW**
The World's Greatest Stories
The Prophets, Stories About Jesus, $8.95 plus $1 shipping each.

Unquestionably the best narration of the Bible we have ever heard. George Sarris, a professional actor, does far more than just read the words. He dramatizes them, breathing life not only into the speeches of the various Bible characters but also into the very prose. Example: Instead of just reading the words "Nebuchadnezzar, the king," he says them in a Middle-Eastern accent and in the tone of voice of a court attendant announcing the king. When Nebuchadnezzar gets angry, Mr. Sarris virtually breathes fire into the description. When the court officials come to Darius to weasel a law against worshiping God out of him, you can just see their slimy flattery. He does all this without adding anything to the text or taking anything away. The two tapes available so far are word for word from your choice of the KJV or the NIV. Well-chosen sound effects round out the presentation. You can tell Mr. Sarris has done his homework, really getting into the characters and recreating the temper of their times. Highly recommended.

CHILDREN'S MUSIC

Children's Book and Music Center

Immense variety of children's recordings. Includes: Mother Goose & Nursery Rhymes, Lullaby & Rest Time, Read-Alongs, Great Books Dramatized, Lots of favorite (but not classic) books on record or cassette. Plus movement recordings, foreign language recordings, and folk songs. Also books, videos, school helps, and so on.

Children's Recordings

Almost everything applauded today in children's music and stories. Categories in this large newsprint catalog include: What's New. Stories, Tales, Yarns (from *Elephant's Child* to *Charlie and the Chocolate Factory*). *Chronicles of Narnia*. Readalongs. Music and Song (Burl Ives, Anne Murray, and *Earth Mother Lullabies*, among dozens of other recordings—quite an eclectic selection!). Other Lands. Elephant Records. Raffi! and Other Canadians. Soundtracks. Sound Effects. Barry Polisar. Hap Palmer. Tom Glazer. Holiday. Mr. Rogers. Activity. Poetry. Lullabies. Even videos! The catalog also contains a Preschool Guide list of suggested recordings for this age group, a Title Index, and a list of the A.L.A. Notable Recordings carried by Children's Recordings.

A Gentle Wind
Tapes, $7.95 each; Samplers, $4.95 each. Add $2.25 shipping for snail mail or an extra 40¢ per item for first class.

Some of the most original music cassettes for kids around. You can buy a variety of Sampler cassettes for a small sum, each containing one song from a number of their cassettes. This gives you an accurate idea of what you would like to order. Choice selections: Paul Tracey's *Rainbow Kingdom*, Tom Smith's *Chip Off the New Block*, Chris Holder's *Storysinger*, and every Sampler (at the moment, there are five). Just the barest trace of New Age flavor in some cassettes, old-timey flavor in others, uniformly gentle presentation (no rock-you-out-of-your-socks screaming hype). All cassettes are high-quality and easy to listen to over and over and over again.

NEW**
JTG of Nashville
Each *Play a Tune* book, $14.95–$17.95. Add $2.50 shipping.

This doesn't quite count as children's recordings, but it fits into the genre. JTG's *Play a Tune* books are spiral-bound books with color-coded electronic mini-keyboards attached. Kids can play the songs themselves, following the color-coded notes written in simplified musical notation. You have to know how long each note should be held, since all notes are simply portrayed as colored circles with numbers inside them. Unlike other electronic keyboard books, these have slightly raised keys "for a more realistic effect." I couldn't say this made a great difference to me, but I did notice that the batteries lasted a lot longer than in another model I tried, and that the whole package held together very well in spite of rough handling by the littlest children in our family.

The series includes a really great cross-section of our cultural heritage, including *American Songs* (famous folk tunes like "This Land is Your Land"), *Jewish Songs* (I don't know about you, but I love Jewish music), *Bible Songs*, *Christmas Songs*, *Children's Songs*, *More Children's Songs*, *All Time Disney Classics*, and even (coming out just after I write this) *The Berenstain Family Favorites*, starring your old pals, the Berenstain Bears. Each song page is faced with a full-color illustration, and notes are provided where helpful. The *Jewish Songs* book has Hebrew script and translations of Hebrew lyrics below the tunes, and the *American Songs* book has historical notes. I'm impressed, by the way, that they managed to come up with so many classic Jewish songs to play on a major-C-key keyboard!

Any one of these *Play-a-Tune* books would make a wonderful travel toy for a child who can recognize colors and numbers. All together, they're a mini-education in our musical heritage.

Kimbo Educational

Kimbo has one of the largest collections of popular children's music anywhere. Nursery favorites, folk songs, sing-alongs, and so on. Hap Palmer, Raffi, Georgiana Stewart, Slim Goodbody, wake-up songs, parachute music, anything you can think of. Enormous selection, color catalog.

NEW**
Klutz Press
Kids Songs and *Kids Songs 2*, $10.95 each. Shipping extra.

First, let me tell you that these songbook/cassette combos are immensely popular. *Kids Songs* alone has sold more than 125,000 copies and generated tons of mail and testimonials. Each of these books is both beautiful to behold and easy to use. The spiral binding means pages stay open where you want them, while the jelly-proof pages of sturdy laminated cardstock are loaded with full-color cartooned illustrations. In keeping with the Klutz style, the accompanying cassette is in a net bag neatly strung through a die-cut hole in the songbook. Also in line with the Klutz tradition of going the extra mile, you'll even find a few simple musical activities you can do with your child scattered throughout these two songbooks. The whole packaging should win some kind of prize.

The songs are a family-pleasing mixture of old favorites like "Puff, the Magic Dragon," silly songs like "Chicken Lips and Lizard Hips," folk songs like "She'll Be Coming Round the Mountain," and even gospel songs like "He's Got the Whole World in His Hands."

None of the gospel songs have any specifically Christian content—even "This Little Light of Mine" has been transformed into a shapeless gonna-love-everyone song—and the Klutz version of "Twinkle, Twinkle Little Star" has the child petitioning the star to "keep watch upon the earth" and "keep it safe 'til morning light." This is on the far side of iffy as far as I am concerned. Not terribly surprising, though, considering the present New Age influence in Southern California. What *really* surprised me is the blandness of the sound on the cassettes. Both books are subtitled "A Holler-Along Handbook," and I expected the cassettes to have considerably more energy to them. Yet even "Rockin' Robin" (in book 2) didn't rock out, and I can't understand why. I'm not talking about the lack of pounding rhythm, which doesn't bother me at all, but a kind of monotonous sameness about the vocal phrasing. Everything is sung exactly on the meter and with little variation in tone. Most other popular children's music I have heard (e.g. Wee Sing and Gentle Wind) has far more sparkle. So I'm weird, so 125,000 people don't agree with me—but I just thought you should know that if you *really* want to holler along with these tapes, you'll be the one doing the hollering.

NEW**
Music for Little People
Peace Is the World Smiling, $9.95 cassette, $15.95 compact disc. Nearly 500 more musical and other offerings, most with New Age flavor. Two labels: Music for Little People for youngsters, and EarthBeat, world music for all ages.

I suppose there's some good reason a group would want to call itself the Tickle Tune Typhoon, but that name makes me want to heave a brick at whoever invented it ("you deserve a brick today"). Tickle Tune Typhoon is just one of the groups contributing to Music for Little People's most-promoted recording yet, *Peace Is the World Smiling* (another name that sends me groping for bricks).

These people mean well. Honestly. They think that wars are caused by ordinary folks in different countries harboring prejudices against each other. As if millions of Americans were sitting in our living rooms thinking hostile thoughts about "them no-good Vietnamese" in 1960. I mean, Americans are even nice to our *enemies*. We didn't exactly tromp all over Japan after World War II. Look how we helped rebuild Germany, our other major foe in that war. The rest of the world isn't trembling in fear of America. They want to move here!

It would help if the Music for Little People people were more aware of the real motives for war, such as the elite of the two sides jockeying for economic and personal advantage regardless of race, color, creed, or sex (the War of the Roses) or even, as happens, one wicked group of people aggressively attacking others who were doing them no harm (Germany v. Belgium in 1942).

The MLPers have a naive belief that pagan beliefs are conducive to peace—e.g., "Listen to the voices of the old women/Calling out the messages of the Moon and Sea/Listen to the voices of the Indian Nations," totally disregarding the warfare that raged among those same Indian Nations even before the first white man arrived in America. They also think that little kids are born loving peace and we adults need to learn from the children's wisdom (take a hike down to the local day-care center if you still believe that one!).

These are really nice people. Friendly. I like them and hate to rag them like this. But their musical offerings have become more and more New Age and less and less realistic. Pantheism. Eco-religion. "I hug the earth," I can believe. "The earth hugs me," is going too far. When the earth hugs you, you're six feet under.

The sad truth of the matter is that anything sappy about world peace sells megamillion copies nowadays. Thousands of years of human history should have taught us by now that it only takes one to make a fight (I mean, what did the English do to aggravate the Vikings?) and that if wishes were horses, beggars would ride.

The Babylonians were positive thinkers and eco-religious, and where did it get them? Fallen, fallen is Babylon the mighty, and it's not too smart to try to juice it up again.

NEW★★
New Moon Records
Each tape, $9.95 postpaid.

Most children's music is directed to kids as individuals. Here are songs that recognize children in their rightful role as valued members of a committed family.

Steve and Darlene Lester and their four sons, also known as The Incredible Luminous Universal Musical Family, have good voices and excellent instrumental backup on these family-affirming cassettes. Not surprising: Steve is a professional musician. *Only My Mama: Songs for Families with Nursing Babies,* my favorite Lester family cassette, has gems like "Don't hit the baby/Even though he hit you first," upbeat songs about nursing, parents and kids loving each other, and humorous references to the trials and tribulations of life with a family bed. A really fun cassette you'll play over and over. (For the record, Bill and I have a queensize bed that we sometimes share with our littlest baby of the moment, but even though we don't have what you could really call a family bed, we support the idea as OK for parents and little kids, as did Jesus: see Luke 11:7.) The Lesters followed this one up with a somewhat less lively and more contemplative cassette whose name escapes me at the moment, also dedicated

to nursing mamas and families that enjoy each other's company. Also available is their *Traditional Rounds, Canons, and Harmonies* tape, from which your family can learn to make beautiful music together. Very lovely singing (including the talents of their children), with such favorites as "Buddies and Pals," "Father, We Thank Thee," "Row, Row, Row Your Boat," and "*Frere Jacques,*" and a few not-so-familiar but delightful old songs. And *all the lyrics* are included (*very* important!).

Send SASE for price list that describes all their latest offerings, including any they may have come up with since this was written.

Plough Publishing House
Songs books, $12 each, hardbound. *Shepherd's Pipe* cassette $6, choral book $2.50. All cassettes and records a very reasonable $6 each. All choral books $2.50 each. Many other booklets and books. Add 12% shipping.

Here's something different—poems and songs for young children from the Hutterian Brethren. Formed as a Christian commune generations ago in Germany, the Bruderhof share Mennonite values and practice pacifism.

Popular offerings: *Sing Through the Seasons* and *Sing Through the Day* are gorgeous songbooks splashed freely with pictures that, as famous children's book author and artist Lois Lenski remarked, reflect both "the beauty and guilelessness of childhood." These *large* books (10¼ x 11") are just the size that little ones love—so big and important!

The Bruderhof also have records and cassettes to accompany their songbooks, as well as an eerily beautiful Christmas cantata called *The Shepherd's Pipe.* The singing is simple, direct, clear, and unforced.

UPDATED★★
Price/Stern/Sloan Publishers, Inc.
Wee Sing book/cassette sets, $9.95 each. Wee Sing video, $19.95 (VHS or Beta). Wee Color Wee Sing coloring book/cassette/marker sets, $9.95. Add $1 shipping per order.

Why are Wee Sing tapes perennial bestsellers in both Christian and secular bookstores? Because Wee Sing authors Pam Beall and Susan Nipp have done their homework and produced some really great products. Together these women performed the formidable task of collecting the best traditional children's music, arranging it into sensible order, and producing it with style.

Practically every family in the country with small children owns at least one of these by now, and ours is no exception. *Wee Sing Nursery Rhymes and Lullabies* has a story theme, weaving the nursery rhymes into the story of Jack and Jill going to London and attending Old King Cole's birthday party. *Wee Sing Around the Campfire* has all those songs you used to warble on summer nights around the campfire. *Wee Sing America* is a collection of American folk songs, work songs, patriotic songs, and so on. *Wee Sing Bible Songs* is all your old favorites from Sunday school. Judging solely by its title our family will probably skip *Wee Sing Silly Songs* (the kids are silly enough already!). We do have *Wee Sing for Christmas,* but were disappointed in the selection (more secular than it needed to be) and the presentation. I haven't yet heard their latest production, *Wee Sing Folk & Fun.*

Each cassette comes with an illustrated songbook containing all the songs on the accompanying cassette, plus a few extras.

Don't expect show-stopping performances on these cassettes. Some of the songs have zip, but others are presented downright blandly, particularly those sung by the children. The Wee Sing version, for example, of "Drill, Ye Tarriers, Drill" doesn't begin to compare with those done by professional folk groups (e.g., The Weavers). Our Weavers tape disappeared a long time ago, though, and our kids aren't music critics. In other words, they absolutely adore these tapes. Sarah and Magda, in particular, would play them all day long if I let them.

Wee Sing has also branched out into videos, but since it's already hard enough to tear my daughters away from the cassettes, I haven't dared to look at those.

NEW★★
Warren Publishing House, Inc.
Piggyback Songs series, $6.95 each except for *Piggyback Songs in Praise of Jesus,* $7.95. Add $2 shipping.

Let's end on an up note. Again, we're not looking at actual recordings here. It's make-your-own-music time again. And this is supereasy with piggyback songs, since all you do is sing the words of these songs to old familiar tunes. You "piggyback" the new lyrics onto the old tunes, in other words. Let me give you just one example, from *Holiday Piggyback Songs:*

> Sung to: "Twinkle, Twinkle, Little Star"
> Advent is a time to wait,
> Not quite time to celebrate.
> Light the candles one by one,
> Till this Advent time is done.
> Christmas Day will soon be here,
> Time for joy and time for cheer!

Available in this series are the original *Piggyback Songs, More Piggyback Songs, Piggyback Songs for Infants and Toddlers, Holiday Piggyback Songs, Piggyback Songs in Praise of God,* and *Piggyback Songs in Praise of Jesus.* All are in Warren Publishing House's usual open, clean format illustrated with cute line-art drawings, and all have chords over the lyrics, so you can accompany them on the musical instrument of your choice.

ENRICHMENT

CHAPTER NINETEEN

FUN FACTS & WHERE TO FIND THEM

Our kids love to learn. I don't say this to brag. It's a fact of life around here, like our tendency to let bedtime slide until midnight (homeschooled kids don't have to get up at the crack of dawn to meet the big yellow schoolbus, after all) and our taste for Peveley pineapple sherbet.

The other day I was wondering: Why do our kids, and the kids of other home schoolers I know, love to learn, when according to what the newspapers tell us, your typical American kid prefers hanging out at the mall to reading—even if he *has* learned to read?

Then it came to me. Perhaps, just perhaps, it has something to do with the reading fare we set before them. Just as kids whose parents fed them liver chips for fun food might wonder what the big deal is about snacks, as in, "Yuk! Snacks!," so kids confronted with endless rows of reading comprehension workbooks might feel the strain of reading is not worth the effort. For this we can thank the textbook companies, who for years have seen fit to swaddle the facts in their books in reams of miserably boring prose (and don't get on me for saying this—government-funded studies have said the same!).

But facts are *fun*. It's neat to discover how God made butterflies' wings out of tiny featherlike scales that come off like fine dust if you touch them, which is why you should never handle a butterfly's wings, and to see how the yucca moth can't live without the yucca plant to lay its eggs in, while the yucca plant is only pollinated by the yucca moth. It's fun to follow the saga of the fellow who invented the first steam engine, and to imagine George Stephenson's *Rocket,* a slightly later design, racing a horse-drawn carriage across the green English countryside. When all this, and much more, comes with cutaway color pictures of the butterfly's wing, the yucca moth and its symbiotic plant, and Mr. Stephenson's *Rocket,* even jaded teenagers can be tempted into stopping for a second look. Hey, even jaded *adults* whose childhood memories of "learning" centered around psyching out teachers and passing tests can be enticed into interest in this kind of attractive learning.

Government-inspected textbooks aren't all there is out there. While the textbook committees have been doing whatever it is they do, little gnomes (OK, grown men and women) have been industriously putting together series after series of you're-gonna-love-to-read-this books loaded with fun facts about everything and anything we want our kids to learn. Cultural illiteracy would be a thing of the past if every kid in the country were taught to read properly and given free access to the resources you are about to see.

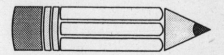

FUN FACTS BOOK SERIES

This is hot stuff: books you can scatter in front of the children and watch them read them because they *want* to. Lots of learning here; positively no strain.

NEW★★
EDC Publishing
Book prices range from an average $3.95 to $5.95 for paperback to about $12.95 for a hardback. Board books, around $3. All books full-color throughout. Shipping extra.

For an almost incredibly inexpensive price, every book of the hundreds available in the Usborne book series purveyed in the U.S.A. by EDC Publishing provides full-color illustrations and accompanying text laid out in such a way that the reader is—"attracted" is too weak a word here—*dragged* into the book. Subjects you would never have thought interesting—say, for example, how to read a weather map—become compelling reading. But maybe "reading" isn't the right word, either. Usborne books are so highly visual that reading them is the literary equivalent of watching a video.

This incredibly effective user interface didn't happen by accident. Here's the story behind it.

In the early 1970s, British parents were unable to find interesting, illustrated information books that their children would really enjoy reading at home. Textbooks were written for schools. Illustrated storybooks were written for home use. So far, never the twain had met.

At that time Peter Usborne was director of Macdonalds Children's Books. There he had a chance to put his educational theory, that explanatory books should do more than explain, into action. Mr. Usborne thought that it would be possible for a children's information book to entertain while explaining facts. So he created a little series of hardback books, called "Starters." These had humor, activities, puzzles, and colorful pages packed with information.

Originally designed for schools, Starters increasingly sold to British parents anxious to provide high-interest books to enhance their children's education. This was the start of the Usborne series.

Usborne books have certain defining characteristics. Humor is used freely, as is the element of surprise. Books are illustrated in a wide variety of styles, from cartoon to ultra-realism or even photography, depending on the subject matter. The ratio of pictures to text is extremely high. Text itself is very simple and clear, but never dumbed-down or patronizing. Books are laid out with more of a magazine-style format than a typical book format, with sidebars, call outs, labeled illustrations, cutaways, charts, and every other helpful graphic feature that could possibly illuminate the topic.

Each Usborne book takes up to three years and around $80,000 to produce. Even one of their short 32-page books can take over a year to produce. The people at Usborne books calculate that they probably spend longer producing every page of their books than any other publisher in Britain. (U.S. publishers take even longer than this, but that's because Americans are molasses-slow in producing books, not because of our superior craftsmanship!)

Perhaps the neatest thing about Usborne books is that they are not all the same. What other book series invites you to, on the one hand, *Make This Viking Settlement* (a cut-out model) and learn how to style your hair, as well as providing adorable board books to share with your baby and a virtual history encyclopedia with full-color art? Foreign language visual dictionaries . . . first learning books . . . David Macaulay-like how-it-works books . . . advanced electronics . . . Greek myths . . . the breadth of this series is astounding.

A selection of Usborne books is now being sold through home parties. If you'd like to see these books in person, contact EDC for the name of your nearest Usborne book consultant. Or just trust me that these are the best supplemental and enrichment books on the market today, and send for the catalog!

NEW★★
Educational Insights
Science Picture Library, $3.95 each book or $42 for the set.

Beautifully-illustrated reference books with laminated, wipe-clean pages. Each oversized 16-page book is designed for young readers, with big illustrations and minimal text. Pages are uncluttered, each featuring only a few illustrations as compared to the densely-packed layouts of Usborne and Young Discovery Library books.

The series includes *Marine Life, Birds, Flowers, Fish, Human Body, Dinosaurs, Musical Instruments, Trees, Animals (Mammals), Cats and Dogs,* and *Reptiles and Amphibians.*

NEW**
Ladybird Books
Books, $2.95 each.

Another terrific line of fun facts books from England. Like the Usborne books, Ladybird books come in many different series. Unlike Usborne, Ladybird purveys basic reading (look-say style) and lots of fiction (Usborne publishes fiction, but not nearly as much).

From England, here is another huge series of fun books for all ages of children on all sorts of kid-pleasing and educational subjects. Start with Ladybird's Little Board Books (Baby Animals and suchlike) and First Word Books. OK, American publishers have books like these. But what about the First Facts series for kids ages five to eight? This series includes first facts about space, animals, weather, the human body, and the earth, lavishly illustrated and with easy-to-follow explanations, as is the Ladybird habit. For even younger children, there's *Things That Go, Indoor Things, Outdoor Things, Things to Wear,* and *Things to Play With.* Plus the First Books series with the alphabet (*A is for Apple*), numbers (*I Can Count*), *Tell Me the Time, Colors and Shapes,* and *Nursery Rhymes.* And several other early learning series, plus terrific little natural history, science, discovery, and history series, reviewed in various places in Volumes 2 and 3.

Actually, Ladybird has *several* early learning series. The Ready to Learn series, the Begin to Learn series, the Early Learning series (also available in Spanish and French), and two different First Books series all introduce numbers, letters, and so on. A World Wildlife read-aloud series. Plus lots of fun fiction, classic and otherwise, as mentioned in the Fun Literature chapter.

Ladybird's How it Works series, recommended to me by a reader from Thailand (Mrs. Colleen Hale), includes *The Motor Car, Television, The Hovercraft, The Camera,* and *The Telephone.* Several other series she recommended (the Learnabouts, which sounds absolutely fascinating and includes titles on subjects from heraldry to knitting, and the Natural History series 536) aren't listed in the American catalog. I fear that the How It Works and Leaders series might be discontinued too, judging from the large number of gaps in the list of books now available at the time I write this.

Ladybird constantly comes out with new series and sometimes discontinues the old, so be sure and write for the current catalog before setting your heart on any particular series.

NEW**
Random House
Eyewitness Books series, $12.95 each. Add $2 shipping for first book, 50¢ for each additional.

The *Eyewitness* series is a set of glossy oversized volumes covering a variety of kid-pleasing subjects. Its eminently browsable layout presents information in double-paged spreads, each covering a single topic. Accompanying text provides background information; features are pointed out with arrows and explanatory text. A typical double-page spread includes maybe a dozen full-color pictures and black-and-white engravings, information about the item(s) in each picture, and lots of high-interest running commentary. The reproduction and printing on this series is top-notch, and the oversized 8¾ x 11¼" hardback books are just the right size for curling up with in a corner.

The *Eyewitness* series includes:

- NATURAL HISTORY TOPICS: Early Humans, Dinosaur, Mammal, Bird, Butterfly & Moth, Rocks & Minerals, Pond & River, Shell, Seashore, Plant, Tree, Flag, and Arms & Armor. Evolutionary approach, but not so pervading that Christian families can't use these books.

- PHYSICAL EDUCATION: The *Sports* volume.

- ANATOMY: The *Skeleton* volume covers how both human and animal skeletons work, plus lots more.

- MUSIC HISTORY AND APPRECIATION: The *Music* volume covers musical instruments, how music is made, and more.

- WORLDVIEW: The *Flags* volume covers the history and meaning of flags and banners, with country-by-country listings. A great take-off point for geography unit studies.

- HISTORY: Kids will be fascinated by the *Arms & Armor* volume, which traces the origins, working, and uses of hand weapons from the Stone Age to the Wild West. Another great take-off point for unit studies.

For a full review of each book, look in the appropriate chapter of Volumes 2 and 3.

NEW★★
World Book, Inc.

For fun facts series that are a bit more serious and a bit less entertaining, World Book offers their Science Encyclopedia, the World Book Encyclopedia, and the Childcraft series that combines children's literature with books of fun facts. These are not screamingly visual, like the Usborne and Eyewitness series, but are definitely more visual and attractively designed than any textbook series on the market. Potential problem: leftist bias pops up here and there. Third-world dictatorships, for example, are never *called* dictatorships. How does "one-party system" grab you? I mean, it's technically correct, but somehow fails to grasp the spirit of what's happening in Ethiopia. However, if you can read between the lines, World Book products have a combination of depth and kid-appeal that's really worthwhile.

NEW★★
Young Discovery Library
Each book, $4.95.

It seems that the success of the Usborne series is causing other publishers to sit up and take notice—and, more to the point, it's prodding them to produce highly visual "learning" books loaded with both facts and high-interest text.

The Young Discovery Library is one such contender for the Usborne crown. The brochure describes this new series as "colorful books of discovery for children 5 to 10." This slogan could apply equally well to most Usborne books. The difference is that the Young Discovery Library, unlike Usborne books, comes in a uniform binding: small hardcover books, 4¼ x 6⅞",

each 40 pages long. Another difference: each Young Discovery Library book has more of a traditional "book" format, with fewer inset graphics and more continuous text than a typical Usborne book. The user interface is otherwise remarkably similar; like Usborne books, Young Discovery Library books focus on the fascinating, colorful, and unusual, as well as everyday facts that children need to know.

Young Discovery Library is an international venture, involving publishers in nine countries. The series is projected as "the world's first pocket encyclopedia." Thirty-two titles are now available in the USA, with 88 more anticipated in the next three years.

Is this really a pocket encyclopedia? The books do read like miniature, highly colorful encyclopedia articles. Sections are introduced with questions, e.g., "How do the Eskimos keep out the cold?" Each book has numerous sections covering a wide range of fascinating subjects related to the main book topic. Each book also features a mini-index, and some (e.g., *Australia: On the Other Side of the World*) provide a mini-glossary as well. The publisher obviously is trying to give you "an education on the subject covered," just as he promised.

One warning: The *Crocodiles and Alligators* book graphically depicts a gazelle being attacked by a crocodile, dragged into the water, and having its leg ripped off. The only reason I can think of for this is that the series was prepared in pragmatic Europe, not in sentimental America where children's books traditionally eschew realistic violence. Typos and misspellings also do occur here and there.

Subjects chosen for the first books in this series include people (*Long Ago in a Castle, On the Banks of Pharaoh's Nile, Living in Ancient Rome, The Barbarians, Following Indian Trails*), places (*Japan: Land of Samurai and Robots, Living with the Eskimos, Living on a Tropical Island, Living in India, Australia: On the Other Side of the World, Going West: Cowboys & Pioneers*), nature study (*Crocodiles and Alligators, Undersea Giants, Animals Underground, Elephants: Big Strong and Wise, Bears: Big & Little, Animals in Winter, Monkeys Apes & Other Primates, The Blue Planet: Seas & Oceans*), and how things are made (*The Story of Paper, From Oil to Plastic, All About Wool, Metals: Born of Earth and Fire, Cathedrals: Stone upon Stone, Music!,* and *Grains of Salt*).

Young Discovery Library says that their goal is to "respond to the endless curiosity of children, to fascinate and educate." They have the fascination down pat; these books are great browsing. These glossy little hardbacks have a lovely feel to them and are tremendously kid-appealing. The facts in these books appear correct too, as one would expect when each book in the series is a collaboration between the author, the illustrator, an advisory group of elementary schoolteachers, and an academic specialist on the subject. The illustrations are glorious, each befitting the style of its particular book (medieval-style illustrations in *Long Ago in a Castle*, for example). This is one impressive little series.

FUN KNOWLEDGE THROUGH BULLETIN BOARDS AND POSTERS

NEW★★
Frank Schaffer, Inc.
Each bulletin board set, $5.95. Requires 4 x 6' blackboard. Floor Puzzles, $12.95 each.

For big, bold, and colorful, you can hardly beat a good bulletin-board visual. Little kids and special-needs students particularly respond to these oversized pictures with just-enough text to describe each piece. The Frank Schaffer catalog includes not only some of the best and brightest bulletin-board sets around, but also an excellent assortment of giant floor puzzles (little kids *love* these!), reproducible worksheets, boxed activity cards, and the like. Some especially notable items: set of three historical bulletin-board sets covers all of American history from Columbus to the computer revolution. Famous Presidents bulletin-board set features 16 Presidents along with a background illustration for each featuring an important event during his administration. *Animals and Their Babies* floor puzzle (for littlest learners) is just too sweet for words; *Animals* and *Ocean Life* floor puzzles colorfully introduce a variety of animals to slightly older children.

NEW★★
Milliken Publishing Company
Diagrammatic posters, $9.95/set. Shipping: add 10%. Minimum shipping $2.

A step removed from bulletin-board sets, but a similar concept, are Milliken's "diagrammatic posters." Each set includes eight full-color 13 x 18" diagrams or illustrations, plus four worksheets of review exercises and concise background information. If you don't have bulletin-board space, but can lay your hands on an oversized portfolio-sized binder, you can punch holes in these beauties and use them like a jumbo family al-

bum of scientific knowledge. Designed for grades 5-8—but actually usable by almost anyone of any age—the series includes *Animals, Earth Science, Electricity, Plants, Systems of the Human Body, Organs of the Human Body, Weather, Nutrition, Insects, Geology, Solar System,* and *Space.*

NEW★★
TREND enterprises, Inc.
Each bulletin board set, $5.99, comes with free Discovery Guide. Requires 4 x 6' blackboard.

As I have mentioned elsewhere in this series, you can learn an awful lot from a well-designed bulletin-board display, and TREND has some of the best. Find out the scoop on human anatomy, or the solar system, or the water cycle, or dozens of other topics, all explained with colorful, can't-miss graphics and just enough text explanation. Each set comes with a free Discovery Guide with additional background information for the topic, plus activities and (occasionally) a reproducible worksheet or two.

TRANSPARENCY WORKBOOKS

You know my feelings about most workbooks sold to public schools. "Ugh" about sums it up. The series below is an exception. Even so, I advise against making your kids wade through all the exercises. Let them read these books for fun and try out the skills as if they were playing a game. After all, the only real difference between games and classes is that you don't write reports about or get tested on games!

NEW★★
Milliken Publishing Company
Transparency/duplicating workbooks, $12.95 each. Shipping: add 10%. Minimum shipping $2.

The following offering may not be quite as user-undemanding as the others in this section, but can be as much fun to browse if you have a serious interest in knowledge. Milliken's series of transparency/duplicating books covers many high-level subjects in a visually interesting, intellectually stimulating way.

WHAT YOU GET: An 8½ x 11", quarter-inch thick book with 12 full-color transparencies. The transparencies, originally intended for use in the classroom overhead projector, work equally well left in the book as super-jazzy visuals. Each book includes background information for each transparency, plus duplicating master worksheets with exercises and questions for students to answer about each transparency. If you like, you can skip the worksheets or simply use them as stimulation for your own thinking, without writing anything down.

The series includes books for grades 4-8. Some are intended just for elementary students, some for junior-highs, and some for all ages. I would personally put the upper age limit at college rather than eighth grade. Topics include art, science, history, and geography.

Science transparency/duplicating books include: *Systems of the Human Body, Nutrition, Weather, Fossils & Prehistoric Life, Geology/Rocks & Minerals, Our Solar System & the Universe, Exploring Space, Studying Plants, Studying Insects, Envionment & Pollution* (all for grades 4-8); *Weather Science, Earth Science, The Human Body, The Solar System & Space Travel, Machines & Work, Magnetism & Electricity, Our Living World, Light & Sound Energy, Physical & Chemical Changes, Stars & Space Science, Birds, Amphibians & Reptiles, Mammals, Oceanography, Electricity, & Disease & Health* (for grades 5-8); and *Composition of the Earth, Mapping, Meterology & Climatology, Time,* and *The Universe* (for grades 7-8).

Social studies books include eight different map skills books covering the USA and its major regions,

Canada, and the world; a series of map outlines books covering all the continents; and an impressive series of historical-cultural books covering, on the one hand, U.S. history from its beginning up until 1900 (11 books) and world history with a largely Western emphasis. The latter series includes *Prehistoric Man; Sumer & Babylonia; Ancient Egypt; The Hebrews, Phoenicians & Hittites; Troy, Crete & Mycenae; Greece—The Hellenic Age; Greece—The Hellenistic Age; Rome I; Rome II; The Byzantine & Moslem Empires; Medieval Period* (two books); *The Italian Renaissance; The Northern European Renaissance; The Age of Exploration; Louis XIV—17th Century France; The French Revolution; The Age of Napoleon;* and *Russia.* The Christian history of the East is covered much better than that of the West, as the Reformation, the Counter-Reformation, and their results are largely ignored

Milliken's Art and Culture series includes *Images of Man, Images of Nature, Images of Fantasy,* and *Images of Change* (two volumes). These all feature reproductions of works by major artists, along with truly insightful commentary on the artists and their times from (unhappily) a clearly relativistic point of view.

If you have a special interest in any of these subject areas, I think you will enjoy sampling one of the Milliken volumes in your area of interest. If you like it, there are plenty more to choose from!

CHAPTER TWENTY

SUPPLEMENTAL & DRILL MATERIALS FOR ALL SUBJECTS

Ah *told* y'all that ah was goin' to get aroun' to th' subject of afterschoolin' . . .

Bill and I lived for a year in Birmingham, Alabama. This is not long enough to come by a Southern accent honestly, but it's at least long enough to know what the real thing sounds like. It's also long enough to learn to appreciate life at a slightly slower-moving pace.

I'll grant you that Birmingham residents, being city folks, don't move all that much more slowly than, say, Chicagoland residents. But out in the Alabama countryside, where we also lived for a while, everything moves more slowly. Ah mean *ever'thing,* from the folks buying corn dogs down at the local "fast"-food joint, to the cows in the meadows. "What? Me hurry?" certainly is a sensible motto when it's 95 degrees in the shade, and 90 percent humidity everywhere.

Which reminds me of the joke about the fellow from Florida and the fellow from California who were comparing states. The Floridian raved on and on about his state's wonderful beaches, wonderful resorts, great deep-sea fishing, and so on. That was all right. But when he started in on how superior Florida oranges were to California oranges, the California fellow got fed up.

"Humbug!" he declared.

"What do you mean by 'humbug'?" the Florida fellow puffed, turning red in the face.

"Just two words that summarize what I think of Florida—*humidity* and *bugs!*"

Yessir, *everything* is moving slower, including this chapter introduction. Nope, this is not an excuse for me to talk about how children who are slow in their studies can benefit from supplemental instruction. It is actually an excuse for me to talk about how taking it easy with a little bit of afterschooling can sometimes be better than throwing on a whole wad of curriculum.

By their nature, supplemental materials are easy to use. They are designed for parents and teachers to use along with regular curriculum—so they can't be long-winded and time-wasting. Often you will find concepts presented better in "supplemental" material than in "real classroom" material. The same goes for drill material. Nobody loves to linger over drilling math concepts or spelling words, so producers of this material make sure their users end up with time left over to smell the roses.

Here, then, are resources for those looking for just that little extra zing. Need to add sparkle to your child's studies, or having trouble explaining a concept? Want to make sure Junior understands what they're teaching him in school? Then check out the companies listed below . . .

SUPPLEMENTARY PRACTICE BOOKS

UPDATED*
Educational Insights

Ever since the first edition of *The Big Book of Home Learning* I have been telling people about Educational Insights' terrific assortment of supplemental and drill learning materials, as well as their products for basic learning areas. Educational Insights offers such innovative items as:

• Their BrainBoosters™ series of facts-n-quiz books. Each 32-page BrainBooster activity book is loaded with fascinating facts. Students test their own answers to the high-interest questions with a unique hand-held decoder. Series includes *Amazing Animals, Inventions and Discoveries, Puzzles and Thinkng Games, Digging into the Past, Worldwide Wonders,* and *Outer Space Adventures,* plus the new *Culture Trek, Exploring America, Prehistoric Life,* and *Undersea Adventure.*

• Wide assortment of electronic drill-n-practice teaching aids from the ever-popular Charlie, Drillmaster, Alphamaster, Rainbow II, and now the new GeoSafari. Students insert a question card and insert the probe into the right answer (Charlie) or press the right button (Rainbow II and GeoSafari) or simply type in the right answer (Drillmaster, Skillmaster, and Alphamaster).

• Kitty-Kat Bingo games drill colors and shapes, numbers, alphabet, sight words, and time-telling.

• Tons of hands-on activity kits, science experiments, geography drill, math drill, and so on.

Catalog includes hundreds of colorful, fun, and educational items. Send for it!

NEW*
ESP Publications
Basic Skills Workbooks, $1.98 each, minimum order of ten, mixed titles allowed. Jumbo Blackline Masters, $9.95 each. Super Yearbooks, $18 each. Call or write for catalog and free sample.

Huge, full-color catalog loaded to the gills with supplemental teaching aids that work beautifully at home. All are user-friendly and quite traditional in approach; the name "ESP Publications" has nothing to do with New Age.

ESP's Basic Skills Workbook series includes 178 different workbooks on just about every subject you'd ever want to learn, from grammar to music, and covering all grades from kindergarten to adult. Each of these reproducible workbooks contains 28–30 lessons and includes answer key. Topics covered are English (one workbook for each grade, plus 10 separate workbooks for skills like diagramming and parts of speech), reading and reading comprehension (12 workbooks), study skills (everything you can think of, including how to study, how to use all sorts of reference materials, how to outline, and how to find/keep a job), handwriting (set of three, all for use in third grade), spelling (set of six, including two booklets of spelling tests), phonics (set of six), vocabulary (set of nine reaches up into senior high), mathematics (10 workbooks, including advanced topics), science (11 workbooks, including one on how products are made!), early education (set of 13 workbooks), social studies, nutrition (set of five), health (set of 10, including a workbook on first aid techniques), and the human body (set of five by grade level). Each workbook can be used independently of all the others; when I refer to a "set," I'm talking about all the workbooks available under that topic heading, which often includes workbooks for many different grade levels.

Now we move on to the biggies. ESP also has a line of 78 Jumbo Blackline Master books, again covering all school subjects and age levels. Each of these books contains 96 full-page lessons that teach basic concepts. No amorphous open-ended dribbling here; ESP sticks to "concepts that are definable by rules or facts." In other words, stuff you can know you know. Concepts are introduced one at a time, reinforced through drill, and built on in subsequent lessons. The teacher's side of the lesson has the answer; the student's side does not. Pages are perforated for easy removal. "Why would I want to remove the pages?" you ask. Well, you might not. But these books *are* reproducible, and that means you have ESP's permission to legally make as many photocopies as you need for your entire class, which for parents at home means as many copies as you need for all your children. The series includes some unusual titles, such as *Learning to Draw* jumbo books for grades 3–4, 5–6, and 7–8; a jumbo *Geometry* book and another for *Algebra*; a *Human Body* series for grades 5–8 (one book for each grade) that covers important health and hygiene facts, such as nosebleeds, sinuses, and diabetes, as well as basic anatomic facts.

Finally, here are the biggest of them all (I have a funny feeling I'm telling the story of the Three Billy Goats Gruff instead of writing up a workbook line)! It's the *Super Yearbooks* for grades K–6. Each of these monster workbooks is between 560 and 864 pages, getting bigger as the kids contemplating them get older. The lesson units in these easy-to-use workbooks cover *every* basic subject in the *same order* they are usually taught in public and private schools. Complete parent/teacher instructions are included, but are hardly needed, as each page explains itself. ESP bills the Super Yearbook series as a supplement to regular class work, saying,

> If you want to help your child but you don't quite know where to begin, these YEARBOOKS are for you. You don't need special training to administer this program. You don't need to hire an expensive tutor, buy a book every month, or buy a book for each subject. There is only one purchase to make—*it's all in one very large book.*

We have used these *Yearbooks*, and can testify to their usefulness and friendliness. You wouldn't want one to be your child's entire education, but as long as you have a library card, that won't be a problem!

ESP told me to tell you to "call or write for a catalog outlining the contents of each book, plus a free sample." That's a really nice offer, so why not take them up on it?

NEW✶✶
Fearon Teacher Aids

Supplementary material for grades preschool-8, mostly designed for public-school use. Paper crafts, holiday activities, math, science, art, preschool, logic, reference skills, lots more. Thirty-six page catalog lists over 200 supplemental workbooks and other resources.

Field Educational Publishers
(formerly Xerox Educational Publishers)
Field bills you for $9.95/month for three months, or you can pay $29.84 in advance.

Field's Weekly Reader Summer Skills Library consists of a selection of the same Weekly Reader practice books used in the schools. The idea is that by working with these books over the summer, Junior can keep from falling behind, and maybe even move ahead!

Each Skills Library contains a Parent Guide, a selected set of Practice Books matched to your child's grade level, six paperback books for free-time reading, a colorful storage case, a free set of marker pens, and the indispensable Award Certificate which you can flash in front of his new teacher to show that Junior actually agitated his brains this summer instead of just roasting them in the sun. Skills Libraries are available for children entering grades 1-7. If you want to use this program for teaching this material, instead of for reviewing it, order the next-lower set. For instance, a child entering first grade orders Set A, but you could also use Set A for teaching kindergarten.

Naturally, Weekly Reader is a secular supplier and those teaching at home for religious reasons will want to keep this in mind. You do get an awful lot for your money, covering all subject areas. This set might be a good idea for helping a child at home who needs extra practice in his schoolwork too.

NEW✶✶
Gallopade Publishing Group
Most books $14.95 paper, $19.95 hardbound.

Somewhere out there is a lady named Carole Marsh who singlehandedly has written, and is continuing to write, scores of short supplemental books on every learning subject you can think of. The lady's style is brash, reminding me of the manner of a youth minister who spends all his time trying to be relevant to teens, the main audience for these books. Everything from Black History to chess. Some topics: Math for girls. Physics. French. Spanish. Latin. Shakespeare trivia. How to write well. Economics. Photography for kids. A line of sex ed books (these I can't recommend). A line of black heritage books. None of these books are what you'd call deep, but they might be enough to spark an interest in these subjects.

NEW**
Hayes School Publishing Co., Inc.

Exercises in Reading Comprehension, 8 levels, $2.95 each. *Modern Mastery Drills in Arithmetic*, 8 levels, $2.95 each. *Hayes Math Skills and Drills*, $2.95–$4.95 each. *Developing Handwriting Skills*, 6 levels, $3.50 each. *Exercises in English*, one level for each grade from 2–10, $2.95–$3.50 each. *Learning English*, grades 3–8, $3.95 each. Many more supplemental/basic series, all inexpensively priced. Friendly to home schoolers.

Clair Hayes III, the president of Hayes School Publishing, contacted me just as I was about to turn in my manuscript for this volume. It seems that a number of home schoolers have been using and enjoying his company's materials, and they thought it would be a good idea if more parents knew about them. Mr. Hayes immediately sent me a set of his exercise books, and I was sufficiently impressed to make the effort to squeeze this company into the book at the last minute.

What we have here are dozens of skill and drill series, basic skills series, and exercise series in all basic subjects. Since these are supplemental materials, they have largely escaped the lash of the public school curriculum committees. This means they can actually teach the subjects instead of instructing Jennifer in her duty to usher in world peace, end world hunger, save the environment, and become an astronaut. Imagine! Grammar without yuppie guilt. History written with regard to what actually happened, instead of as a promotional exercise for anti-Europeans. Math drills where race isn't a factor, because you can imagine "John" and "Marie" any color you want (no pictures in the book). The point of these books is to *teach students,* something the people who pick basic curriculum for public schools keep forgetting to do in their zeal for indoctrination.

Some of the series are reprints of school drill books originally published decades ago by the Benton Company of Fowler, Indiana. These have been only slightly revised. I don't know about you, but I get really nostalgic when I see that old-timey typography and simple exercises like, "On her way to school this morning, Mary Lou saw 5 robins, 1 kingbird, and 3 song sparrows. How many birds did Mary Lou see?" (Today she doesn't see any, 'cause she's being bussed.) To give you an idea of the era in which Hayes's *Modern Mastery Drills in Arithmetic* was published, consider this question: "Betty mailed two letters for her mother. On one there was a 4-cent stamp and on the other there was a 7-cent stamp. What was the total amount of postage?" Raise your hand if you remember 7-cent first-class stamps! How refreshing to see problem sets that evoke an America that really *was* kinder and gentler, in which membership in the local Pig Club (for owners of pigs) loomed large in a child's life, when movie tickets cost 45¢, and when every boy owned a whittling knife and no kid ever knifed anybody.

No effort is required to use these books at all. No teacher's guides; answer keys are usually built in, and if they are separate they only cost a few dimes. Everything is step-by-step and logically arranged. Calm common sense pervades these series.

If you'd like to give your child an old-fashioned school experience, like we had before everything became a "crisis" requiring massive societal adjustments, then check out these inexpensive workbooks.

Learning Systems Corporation

Set of 19 different language arts titles, $15. Set of 19 different math titles, $15. Individual miniworkbooks, 79¢ each.

You can't beat the price: seventy-nine-cent miniworkbooks that do a decent job of exercising your youngster in his language arts and math. The 16-page workbooks are approximately 5 x 8 inches, in two colors, professional in appearance and clever in execution.

Each skill is clearly presented in just a few pages along with exercises for practice. Because the workbooks are so small, there is no danger of boredom. Also, your learner gets an instant sense of accomplishment when he masters a new skill. Instead of just finishing a chapter, or section of a chapter, in a massive textbook, he finished a whole workbook! This sense of having completed a task is vital to keep a youngster's motivation strong.

Learning Systems Corporation's language-arts lineup includes workbooks for learning the alphabet and for practicing basic phonics skills, plus vocabulary-builders, books on syllabication, using the dictionary, punctuation, and a host of other necessary skills.

Math miniworkbooks include Time, Money, Place Value, Addition with Regrouping, Subtraction with Regrouping, Fractions, Word Problems, English Measurements, Metric Measurements, and a number of workbooks on multiplication and division of whole numbers and fractions, materials on decimals, percent, graphing, and geometry.

NEW**
The Learning Works
Activity book prices range from $3.95 to $8.95. *I Love Lists*, $19.95. *Junior Question Collection, Question Collection*, $7.95 each. *Study Skills Shortcake*, $5.95. Shipping extra.

The Learning Works has been a leading publisher of educational books for school and home use since 1976. Each and every one of their books is authored by educators. Now, as you realize by now, this can be good or bad, depending on whether the educator really knows how to teach kids or just has strange little theories about how kids ought to learn.

One good measure of an educational-book company's effectiveness is whether their books actually cover needed learning areas. It's even better if their books fill niches that other companies miss. The Learning Works come out shining on both counts. Their large list of over 100 activity books not only covers a lot of ground, but also fills a lot of holes. Major topics covered are readiness, reading (preschool through senior high), grammar and usage, creative writing, research and study skills (a *very* needed area), values and feelings, handwriting, following directions (wish I'd seen these books in time to include them in Volume 1!), holiday and art ideas, enrichment and gifted, science and computers, AIDS education, science, and math. Of this list, I'd skip the values-'n-feelings books (schools love to drag kids through this kind of navel-gazing, but parents are wise to skip it) and the AIDS books (if you live clean and avoid questionable hospital blood you won't get it, and I don't care what anyone else says).

Of course, you can consider the entire catalog to be supplemental material, since these are activity books rather than textbooks. Some of The Learning Works' list, however, are especially suited to afterschooling instruction. I am thinking of their *I Love Lists!, Junior Question Collection*, and *Study Skills Shortcake*.

I Love Lists! is a *large* resource book loaded with lists for all areas of the curriculum, plus creative ideas for putting these lists to academic use. Here are some of the lists: presidents, phobias, inventors, authors, mammals, compound words, rhyming words, things to wear on your feet, prepositions, things to write about just for fun, initial consonant blends, coins and currency, suffixes. . . . Lists are organized into sections: Language Arts, Social Studies, Science, Math, The Arts and Sports, and Just for Fun. Here are some more lists: Braille alphabet (with explanation and chart), Greek alphabet, international Morse code, sign alphabet, map symbols, mythical gods and goddesses (with explanations of who is who), units of weight and measure, Roman numerals, famous inventors. . . . Unit-study lovers will find loads of idea-sparkers here.

Question Collection and *Jr. Question Collection* present illustrated questions about literature, math, science, and social studies. *Jr. Question Collection* is for littler kids; *Question Collection* is for kids in grades 6 and up. Sample questions from the junior book: "In which direction does the sun rise?," "Whose picture is on the penny?," and "Who invented the telephone?" Useful for an instant check on your children's general knowledge, or just for fun. Answers included

Study Skills Shorcake is a slim workbook covering research skills such as reading maps, charts, graphs and time lines; taking notes; outlining; and summarizing. Learn to tackle the almanac, atlas, dictionary, encyclopedia, newspaper, and thesaurus.

The Learning Works' books for individual subject areas are reviewed in depth in the appropriate subject chapters. Just be aware that here is a source for supplemental and drill material for virtually every academic trouble area.

NEW**
Milliken Publishing Company
Reproducible workbooks, $3.50 each. Shipping: add 10%. Minimum shipping $2.

Milliken is a major educational publisher with an enormous range of reproducible and duplicating-master workbooks for K-8. "Reproducible" means you are allowed to make multiple copies for use in your own class. At home this means you can make copies for all your children. "Duplicating masters" means the pages are spirit-impregnated, therefore suitable for running off on a duplicating machine. Home users may or may not need to make extra copies, but usually will not have easy access to a spirit duplicator, so in general should choose reproducible workbooks.

Categories for Milliken workbooks include phonics, handwriting, reading comprehension, spelling, vocabulary, motivational activities, science, and math.

Milliken workbooks are not as cuddly as some others, but are still very user-friendly. You can construct anything from a quickie summer review program to a complete curriculum out of these workbooks.

Milliken's outlook, as typical for a public-school provider, is evolutionary and sometimes relativistic. This affects some subjects more than others.

Some workbook topics are available both as workbooks and as transparency/duplicating master books. The difference? Full-color transparencies and a higher price versus straight workbook format and a lower price.

We have used and enjoyed Milliken workbooks. Their math drill series, for example, is nice and straightforward—although it would benefit from timed-drill suggestions—e.g., how many minutes it should take to finish each page.

Especially useful for those who want a simple way to supplement their children's education is the new Milliken Total Workbook series. Milliken bills these as "the ideal bridge between home and school." Each workbook includes stimulating exercises in the areas of math, language arts, science, and social studies. There are two workbooks for each grade, divided by semesters, for grades 1-4. Activities range from dot-to-dot and addition problems to true/false science questions and simple experiments. To make the workbooks more attractive, each page is loaded with cheerful line drawings, some of which actually have something to do with the questions. These workbooks take a "school" approach, meaning you will want to skip the silly exercises about unscrambling words to make a sentence and such-like. Answers are in the middle of each workbook. For home schoolers this is about the cheapest way to find out what the other side is put through in school; for others, it is a convenient way to help your child practice his schoolwork—and to find out whether he really is learning what he should in school.

Milliken workbooks are available at your local teacher supply store or through their catalog.

School Zone Publishing Company

School Zone has enrichment and supplemental stuff for grades pre-kindergarten through 6. School Zone's workbooks are specifically designed for at-home

use. Each workbook covers a particular skill or subject area. These include perceptual skills, grammar, reading, math, spelling, and phonics. School Zone also has flash cards, puzzles, start-to-read books, and audio and video programs.

In the industry, School Zone has established a reputation for excellent, swift customer service. School Zone books are mostly sold in stores, but their catalog is available to all.

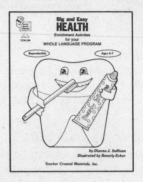

NEW**
Teacher Created Materials

A very large series of 32-96-page activity-oriented workbooks. Series covers special topics in English and other elementary-school subjects. Each is laid out in logical order and starts with a Table of Contents. Topics include arts and crafts, seasonal activities, science, make-your-own-book kits, word puzzles, language arts, graph art, social studies, and creative writing. Some representative workbook titles: *My Body, I Can Give a Speech, I Can Write a Poem, I Can Punctuate*. Reviews of a number of titles and series from this publisher are scattered throughout Volumes 2 and 3. Decent supplemental material for your home curriculum.

Western Publishing House, Inc.

A variety of supplemental and enrichment materials, from the makers of the Little Golden Books series. Lots of cheap color and activity books, starting at 99¢ and generally featuring licensed characters (e.g., Barbie, Donald Duck, Big Bird). Western has lots of activity books, lots of games, lots of children's books, lots of puzzles, and even some educational workbooks, staying in tune with the new wave of demand for home educational products. Western is a BIG producer, and their products do have that very professional, mass-produced flavor.

Of special interest to home teachers is the Golden Step Ahead book/tape series. It's instantly obvious how a "teacher on cassette" can spare Mom and Dad the effort of constantly repeating the alphabet or addition facts. So far the series includes *Beginning to Count, A to Z, Understand It* (a listening comprehension tape), and *Let's Add!* I would encourage any commercial producer reading this to think seriously about adding cassette teaching to his workbook series. Meanwhile, Western has shown they are in touch with what's going on.

Western does have a big, expensive catalog, but they much prefer to sell through stores.

DRILL, DRILL, DRILL

Put off by the word "drill"? Don't be! Repetitious practice—and especially *timed* practice—is what moves kids from just barely knowing a new fact or skill to becoming experts. Math drill, in particular, is essential, especially for home-taught kids, who tend to be great at understanding math but slow at calculations. (If you're a formal-school type, this revelation is no reason to gloat; home-taught kids are better at *everything* except this!)

So the following products are not designed so much to teach skills as to make skills second-nature. They are also not your typical awesomely boring drill materials. Our kids actually *love* these resources! Find out what makes them so special by reading the following reviews.

Educational Insights
Charlie battery model, $49.95; drill packs, $12.95 each. A.C. model, $79. *Rainbow*, $169.95; drill packs of 20 cards, $10.95 each. Many other drill materials, including an electronic tutor for geography drill.

For drill, Educational Insights has several different electronic tutors. Stick in a card and press the probe into the hole next to the answer you hope is right. Flashing lights and space-age sounds come from Charlie to let you know if you got it right or if you blew it. Rainbow, the more expensive model, has a touch-sensitive keyboard. Maxx, the most affordable of them all,

is a barrel of fun for preschoolers. If you'd like to add some zip to your drill, but can't afford a computer, one of these might be an acceptable compromise.

NEW**
Essential Learning Products
Each practice book, $2.50. Buy five and get one free. Add $2 per order for shipping ($3 in Canada). California, Pennsylania, Ohio residents add tax.

I really, really, really like these little practice 'n drill books put out by the people who publish *Highlights* magazine for children. First of all, the price is right, as you can see. Second, each book is just the right size (5¼ x 8½") for children to not feel threatened by the amount of work to do on a page. The one-step-up-from-newsprint paper is easy for children to write on with a pencil or crayon, and the illustrations (where applicable) have a nice, familiar, friendly feel. Print is nice and large. Drills have just the right amount of repetition and cover just the right questions. These books are professionally designed by people who obviously know what they are doing, and it shows.

The series includes arithmetic practice books (*Preschool Activities, Addition, Subtraction, Multiplication, Division, Fractions, Decimals, Metric, Word Problems,* and *Money*), reading practice books (*Preschool Activities* and six reading activity books for grades K through 5 and up), handwriting practice books for preschool through grade 4, phonics skills practice books (*Initial Consonants, Medial and Final Consonants, Short and Long Vowels, Vowel Combinations,* and *Blends and Digraphs*), and spelling practice books for grades 1-6. New in August, 1990: a grammar drill series. At the price, you can afford to buy the practice books you need for every child in your family!

These are the only practice books my kids have ever pestered me to let them use. I would recommend this series to every family.

NEW**
Harlan Enterprises
Games, $2.99 each. Buy four and get one free.

This can't be. It just can't be! Nobody but nobody sells educational games for less than $3!

Nevertheless my eyes are focused on a huge box full of 29 educational card games (the folks at Harlan Enterprises are nothing if not generous with their review samples!), each packed in an attractive clear plastic box. Upon closer inspection, we find that all these games have the same user interface. You get a pack of sturdy 2¼ x 3½" cards and an answer card, so kids can play without calling on you constantly for the answers. All games are played in the same way, by matching an answer on one card to a question on another. Two to four players can play either by drawing cards from a stack á la Old Maid, or by laying them facedown and turning over two at a time to try to make a match á la Concentration. Each game is printed a different color, as this is one case where the hapless parent does *not* want to mix and match!

As you can see, the Fun Games (the name of this series) were designed supremely for drilling academic facts. There is a catch, though. You can't drill *all* the addition facts, for example, with just one card pack—so if you want to drill all addition facts from 1 + 1 up to 12 + 12, you will need to get six games. Game 1 is *Addition Fun: Numbers 1 & 2*. This covers 1 + 1 up to 2 + 12. Cards demonstrate the associative property; e.g., the 2 + 3 card also displays 3 + 2. The other Addition Fun games are *Numbers 3 & 4, Numbers 5 & 6, Numbers 7 & 8, Numbers 9 & 10,* and *Numbers 11 & 12.* The Subtraction Fun games are *Numbers 1, 2, 3, 4, & 5* (1 - 0 through 5 - 5); *Numbers 6, 7, & 8* (6 - 0 through 8 - 8); *Numbers 9 & 10;* and *Numbers 11 & 12.* Multiplication Fun games are *Numbers 1 & 2* (1 x 0 through 2 x 12); *Numbers 3 & 4; Numbers 5 & 6; Numbers 7 & 8; Numbers 9 & 10;* and *Numbers 11 & 12.* Division Fun includes *Numbers 1 & 2* (1 + 1 through 12 + 2; some pairs have remainders); *Numbers 3, 4, & 5;* and *Numbers 6, 7, 8, 9, 10, 11 & 12.* Other math games include *Money Fun* (matching a card with varying numbers of dollars and coins to an "amount" card) and *Telling Time* (match the clock face to the digital time).

So much for math. You can also get *Alphabet Fun* (match "Q" to "the letter after P"), *Noun Fun* ("books" matches "common, plural" whereas "Len's" matches "proper, singular, possessive"), *Punctuation Fun* (match the sentence to the proper ending punctuation), and *Fact and Opinion Fun* ("Sunday is the first day of the week" matches "FACT," whereas "Basketball is the best sport" matches "OPINION").

On top of all these other games Harlan Enterprises also offers *Music Fun* and *State Capital Fun.* The latter is actually *two* games. The first matches states with beginning initials A-M to their capitals; the latter covers states with beginning initials N-W. *Music Fun* matches notes on the treble and bass clefs to their names.

The Fun Games were designed by a veteran classroom teacher, Tanya Harlan, who evidently understands that simple is better. You wouldn't want to use

these games to improve math calculation speed—the format does not lend itself to this—but they are fine for getting kids used to connecting basic facts together. All together, this is about the simplest and least stressful drill material I have seen.

NEW**
Hayes School Publishing Co., Inc.
Hundreds of drill and skill work booklets, most $2.95–$3.95 each.

I mentioned this company under Supplementary Practice Books (above), but many of their materials are equally well-designed for drill. Their *Modern Mastery Drills in Arithmetic* series for grades 1–8 is a reprint of a popular math drill program your father and mother may have used years ago in school. Their *Developing Handwriting Skills* series is a practice series with one level for each grade from 1 to 6. *Exercises in English* is a series of quick-drill books for English grammar, grades 2–senior high. Hayes also has drill material for spelling, reading comprehension, phonics, and a host of other basic subjects. See individual writeups under subject categories in Volumes 2 and 3.

NEW**
ISHA Enterprises
Each *Daily Grams* book, $14.50 plus 15% shipping.

Wanda Phillip's *Daily Grams* series is one-a-day English multivitamins! Each oversized paperback has 180 grammar review worksheets, designed to be used at the rate of one a day. Each lesson includes one sentence with capitalization errors to correct, one sentence that needs punctuation inserted, two general review sentences (the skills drilled in these change day by day), and one sentence-combining exercise. Exercises get more difficult as you progress through the year. For example, the first sentence-combining exercise in the volume for third- and fourth-graders merely asks you to combine the two sentences

The pencil is yellow.
The pencil is on the floor.

into one sentence, while on day 179 you are combining

A book is on the floor.
The book is about birds.
Please pick it up.

"Grams" stands for "Guided Review Aiding Mastery Skills." *Daily Grams* are written in "spiral" fashion, meaning you continue to cycle through subjects previously presented. This approach fits into the philosophy of "mastery learning."

The series includes three books. The first is for third- and fourth-graders, the second for fourth- and fifth-grades, and the last for grades 6 and up. Obviously there is some overlap between books. The most noticeable difference is that the book for third and fourth grades includes work on dictionary skills.

The average student can do a *Daily Grams* sheet in about ten minutes. This is not too much time to spend on English and grammar drill in a day. Answers to every exercise are on the bottom of the page, making grading a snap. (Naturally, you will ask your student to cover the bottom of the page while working the exercises!) I know of no simpler drill-and-practice material for English than this series.

NEW**
Milliken Publishing Company
Reproducible workbooks, $3.50 each. Shipping: add 10%. Minimum shipping $2.

Impressive array of math drill and practice workbooks from a major public-school educational publisher. Everything from early math to fractions and decimals. Needs timed-drill suggestions; otherwise a quite acceptable series useful for any child who needs a little extra math practice.

NEW**
The Providence Project
$14.95 per CalcuLadder unit. Shipping: $2 for one item, $3 for two, $3.75 for three, $4.50 for four, and $5 for five or more. Double the shipping for AK and Hi.

Learning Vitamins™ is a curriculum supplement program from the Providence Project. Its three nifty modules increase your child's handwriting abilities, alphabetizing skills, and math calculation speed.

The ReadyWriter™ exercises are designed to improve hand-eye coordination, motor skills, and stylus skills, enabling your child to write nicely without the jaggies, sloppies, or messies. What makes these stand out is the cute pictures and stories associated with the exercises. Example (from ReadyWriter level 1): "Mrs. Brown has just fixed a big batch of the Brown family's favorite dessert—brownies (naturally)! They've cooled off a bit, so now let's help her cut them. Start at the top of the page, and with your pencil 'cut' one panful at a time, from top to bottom and then from left to right. Try to make nice square brownies of the same size, and try not to cut into the middle (shaded area) of the brownies. It might be good to have some *real* brownies sometime, too!" Now tell me honestly, could your first-grader resist this?

AlphaBetter™ drills students in alphabetical sequence so they can instantly recall the relative position of any letter with respect to all the other letters. This is different from the typical method of "sing the Alphabet Song until you find the letter," which causes frustration and avoidance of look-it-up exercises. It then goes on to reference-book skills. It's a one-year unit for grades 3 and up.

CalcuLadder™ include six one-year units with 16 levels each. You get timed drill and skill review in an attractive format. This is an *inexpensive* high-potency timed-drill series, much like the highly-touted but vastly-overpriced Kumon Mathematex series from Japan. For an extensive review of this marvelous program, see the Math chapter in Volume 2.

The idea of Learning Vitamins is to provide the necessary drill in the most important (and most often under-drilled) subject areas. Children only spend a few minutes per day on the drill sheets. Each unit consists of 12 copies of 16 Level Sheets—192 exercise sheets in all. Your child works one sheet a day, repeating the sheet until he has mastered it. Upon finishing a level, you give your child an Achievement Certificate (included) and promote him to the next level (a new sheet to work on). You also get an Instructor's Handbook with each set and a set of QuicKeys,™ where applicable, for grading.

Dr. Myers holds an M.A. from Dallas Theological Seminary and a PhD. from Carnegie-Mellon. He designed the optics for the Infrared Interferometric Spectrometers on NASA's Voyager 1 and 2 space probes, is listed in *Who's Who in Technology Today,* and is the dad of eight home-schooled children. In other words, the man is well-qualified to produce good material. The artwork is really professional on these sheets, the paper is high-quality and colorful, each sheet has a Bible text relating to the skill being taught, and the prices are right. For high-potency drill material, these are a great choice.

NEW**
Timberdoodle
Wrap-Ups, each set $7.25, any 3 or more $6.25 each. Shipping 10%, $4 minimum.

Here's a case where one picture would be worth a thousand words, only I don't have a picture! Wrap-Ups are little plastic boards somewhat wider than a popsicle stick and a little longer. Both the left and right side are notched. On the left side of the stick are questions, and on the right side are answers. You take a red string tied to the top of the stick, and starting at the top question, wind the string to the notch next to the correct answer. You then loop around the back of the stick to the next question, which you match to the next answer, and so on. When you have finished wrapping the string around the stick, turn it over and see if the string lines up with the raised lines on the back of the board. If you did everything right, the string will line up correctly. As you can see, or at least imagine, Wrap-Ups are completely self-checking.

Each set of Wrap-Ups comes with 10 self-correcting boards and plenty of pieces of string. Sets available include *Preschool and Kindergarten, Addition, Subtraction, Multiplication, Division, Fractions, Antonyms, Synonyms, Homonyms, Compound Words,* and *States, Capitals, and Abbreviations.* These are a real hit with kids who otherwise would have to be dragged kicking and screaming to practice their school facts, and are especially useful with the kinesthetic "hands-on" type of learner. Try one and see what you think!

CHAPTER TWENTY-ONE

SEASONAL ACTIVITIES

As a novice home schooler, I used to wonder why so many activity books stressed seasonal themes. Now I know. It's because (1) schools feel it is their duty to teach kids about the seasons, (2) celebrating holidays is a high-interest, universally-enjoyed way to introduce children to our cultural heritage, and (3) if you're going to make something fancy out of that leftover shoebox, it might as well be a Valentine box.

Seasonal activities are a great excuse for lots of cluttering crafts, so we'll be careful to avoid resources focused on those. I'm sure you don't want your house buried under papier-maché models of the Easter Bunny, even if you as a general rule like strange rabbits who lay painted eggs.

Honoring special days is also a good way to learn a lot of interesting stuff, and a fine launching pad for spontaneous unit studies. Peanut Butter Day, for example. You can *eat* peanut-butter sandwiches, *read* about George Washington Carver, *sing* the Confederate Army folk song "Goober Peas," *plant* a peanut in a peat pot to see what will happen later, and so on. Taking the George Washington Carver motif a step farther, you can *study* about other famous black Americans, other famous inventors, other famous people involved with peanuts (Jimmy Carter springs to mind), and so on. Picking up the Jimmy Carter thread, you can study sweaters, or Southern politics, or Presidents. Non-

plussed by the sweaters? Well, what did President Carter wear all the time on national TV? Right.

All this is the exact opposite of the step-by-step practicing we were looking at in the previous chapter. That's OK: a balanced learning program should both indulge wild flights of curiosity *and* provide staid skills drills. Art and Science. Right and Left Brain (not that I necessarily believe in the neurological speculations about brain hemispheres, but it makes a convenient metaphor). Van Gogh and Isaac Newton. The grasshopper and the ant. We could go on, but let's not. Let's get into the good stuff here instead!

ACTIVITY CALENDARS AND ALMANACS

NEW**
B'rith Christian Union
Calendar of the Christian Year, $5.95. *Daily Devotional Guide for the Christian Year*, $10/year (6 issues). *Touchstone*, $13/year, $24/two years. Add $1 shipping per calendar.

I originally didn't plan to include this calendar, because I don't approve of the theology behind some of the Catholic feasts celebrated on this calendar. After spending nearly a year thinking about it, I decided to include it anyway—not because I want to convert you to "historical orthodoxy" (to which I am not even a convert myself), but because it behooves us to become aware of how Christian piety used to affect even everyday life.

Published by the same people who bring you *Touchstone: A Journal of Ecumenical Orthodoxy,* the *Calendar of the Christian Year* is a very lovely, surprisingly inexpensive actual calendar that features special dates as set by the three chief liturgical traditions: Anglican/Episcopalian, Roman Catholic, and Eastern Orthodox. For those of you who are not familiar with the idea of a liturgical year, this means that on any given day there is a Scripture reading, the name of the day on the Old Testament Jewish calendar (e.g., *29 Shevat*), and a listing of which saints or Biblical events each tradition celebrates on that day. So we find that September 16, 1989, was a day to remember Cyprian, a bishop and martyr who died in A.D. 258, Cornelius, a martyred priest who died in A.D. 253, and Ninian, a bishop called the "Apostle to Scotland," who died A.D. 432. The day before, Roman Catholics honored the day of "Our Lady of Sorrows"; two weeks later, it was the feast of Saint Michael and the Angels. Thus quite a bit of church history is woven into the year, along with (as I mentioned) quite a bit of Catholic doctrine.

The calendar is illustrated with the famous engravings of Gustave Doré, the nineteenth-century Bible illustrator.

Also available from B'rith Christian Union (*b'rith* is Hebrew for *covenant,* by the way) is a *Daily Devotional Guide for the Christian Year.* Published six times a year, it provides teaching on how people in the liturgical traditions used to/ought to celebrate the Christian holidays and feasts, lots of fascinating background history on the martyrs and events, suggested prayers, and a day-by-day Bible reading schedule. The latter has three parts:

> 1) a *daily lesson* which has been selected to develop a weekly theme or to fill out and complete the narative of the Sunday Gospel; 2) *Morning and Evening Psalms* (set respectively before and after a small "cross" symbol; and 3) a *daily chapter reading* from a schedule which covers the entire Scriptures in three years.

It's clear to me that modern Reformed Protestants also need something like this (minus the Catholic theology) to help us break out of the current fast-paced rat race and refocus on eternity. In the meantime, Catholics, Anglicans, Episcopalians, and Orthodox are the lucky ones!

Center for Applied Research in Education
Early Childhood Teacher's Almanack, $17.95. *The New Teacher's Almanack,* $18.95. Shipping extra.

Two school-year almanacs designed for classroom teachers. Something for every day of the year.

The Early Childhood Teacher's Almanack is an oversized 11 x 8½" full of monthly celebrations, natural science activities, recipes the kids can make, field trip ideas, enrichment explorations, arts and crafts, and projects. Some samples: Make finger paint, Take nature walks, Sun-dry fruit leather, Bake Doggie Crackers, Measure air pressure with a homemade barometer, Sprout seeds, Make a wind roarer, Create sand paintings, Bake natural pizza, Identify animal sounds, Walk on homemade stilts. Illustrated in old-timey style, 10 chapters from September to Summer.

The New Teacher's Almanack is an illustrated 395 oversized pages including: an annotated calendar of famous people's birthdays, holidays, special weeks, and historical events, sayings of famous people, historical facts, unusual teaching tips, biographical material written in controlled vocabulary, bulletin-board ideas, special activities and projects, sources of free or inexpensive materials, recipes for art supplies, recipes for kid-made food, games, writing sparkers, more. Same 10 chapter September-to-Summer format. Hardbound.

NEW**
Children's Small Press Collection
Tot's Agenda, $9.95 plus $1.50 shipping.

Tot's Agenda is a handy spiral-bound, hand-lettered activity calendar and record-book for toddlerhood through kindergarten. In it you can both write down your little one's accomplishments and find something fun to do together every week. There's a "handprints" page at the front and back of the book, for taking the handprint of your child at the beginning and end of the year. Health Notes, Feats to Remember, an envelope bound into the back of the book for holding photos and other keepsakes, and the special space for "Kiddie Quotes" on the bottom of each week's calendar page provide more ways to capture your memories. Opposite each weekly calendar page (you can use these spaces to write down appointments or to record achievements) is a simple, fun activity appropriate to the season, such as making a potato Easter basket in March or cutting out snowflake patterns in December. Each month is printed on a different color of paper, making the book both prettier and easier to use.

I have found that most "memories" books overwhelm me with guilt, as I constantly forget to fill in all the hundreds of forms and save all the hundreds of keepsakes that they assure me I need. *Tot's Agenda* provides just enough room for a busy mother to realistically fill with her child's memories, and just enough activities so you have a decent shot at actually doing them all. A nice gift for yourself or someone else.

NEW**
Dale Seymour Publications
Little Fingers: Creative Ideas for the Young at Art, $7.95.

A seasonal crafts program for children in preschool through grade 3 designed to teach children how to print (we're talking potato prints, not manuscript handwriting), paint, use their scissors, create paper sculptures, and so on. See complete review in Chapter 4.

Every Day Is Special
Activity calendar, $15/12 months, $2 for sample month. U.S. funds only.

Tender loving care went into this home-schooling calendar, the product of a home-school mother.

Every Day Is Special has 12 months of daily activities and neat historical facts in a calendar format. Did you know June 1 was Roquefort Cheese Day? (The day's activity suggestion: "Have a cheese-tasting party!") June 3, likewise, is Chicken Bone Day, a chance to put ye olde dry bones to use.

Activities include discussion and writing sparkers, puzzles and riddles of all kinds, activities with food (have a "rainbow lunch"), art and crafts, and on and

on. The author is widely read, knowledgeable about many fields, and incredibly creative.

Families that like discovery learning will find *Every Day Is Special* a great resource for project ideas. Everyone will find it brightens up the day. Who can be dull anticipating a Rainbow Lunch, or cheese-tasting party, or bone-cracking spree, or . . . ?

UPDATED**
Gospel Publications
Children's Calendar, $6. Sponsored *Calendar*, includes gift wrap, card, newsletters, and birthday card with small gift, $10. Free newsletter with funstuff, quiz, prizes. Materials for telephone ministries, balloon stories. Free lending library of children's Christian books.

Children's Calendar for Christian children, now printed in three colors! Each tear-off day has a poem, story, or simple activity, as well as a Bible verse for the day. Example: The story of Jenny Lind. A poem about a sick boy who printed Bible verses on balloons and floated them out his window. How to make a scrapbook of Bible Bees (e.g., "Never BEE angry"). Durable bright plastic cover, colored pages.

You can also sponsor a grandchild, neighbor child, missionary child, or underprivileged child with a *Children's Calendar*. Your $10 includes, besides a gift-wrapped calendar, a gift card with your name and address, newsletters for the child, and a birthday card with a small gift inside.

Other calendars available from this address. Write for details.

HOLIDAYS

NEW**
Anvipa Press
A New Approach to Christmas Greetings, $9.95 plus $1.50 shipping.

Christmas comes but once each year . . . but when it does, it brings Christmas cards. Learn to use this inevitable fact of life as the cornerstone of a seasonal unit-study curriculum with ViAnn Oden's *A New Approach to Christmas Greetings*. First, the obvious. Yes, this oversized book does include info on how to use all sorts of art media in decorating or creating Christmas cards. Stencils, vinyl letters, transfer type, typewriter or computer lettering, simple calligraphy, clip art, and rubber stamps are all trotted out, with information on where to obtain them and many ingenious ideas for their use. But this is not mainly a crafts book. ViAnn wants to teach your children record-keeping, purchasing, correspondence skills, art, and history. She also wants to free you from the holiday grind with new ideas for Christmas greetings, such as Christmas letters, postcards, telephone calls, cassettes, and videos. Fascinating facts about the history of Christmas greetings in both Europe and America are included as well. An organized person, ViAnn also throws in all sorts of charts, lists, and forms to help you organize your Christmas correspondence.

The book has a nice, open layout, making it friendly to use. Lots of photos and graphics lead you every step of the way. For home schoolers who enjoy unit studies, or just plain folks who want to feel in control at Christmas-time, *A New Approach to Christmas Greetings* looks like a good idea.

NEW★★
Fearon Teacher Aids
Holiday Crafts and Greeting Cards, $5.95. *Great Gifts for All Occasions*, $10.95. *Papercrafts for All Seasons*, $4.95.

Patterns and instructions for art projects, paper sculptures, and a variety of greeting-card forms for all occasions are what you'll find in *Holiday Crafts and Greeting Cards*. *Great Gifts for All Occasions* is a book of gifts you can make from "found" objects such as discarded bottles and empty cans. You supply the glue and colored paper. For kids in grades 1-6. *Papercrafts for All Seasons* is 25 art projects to celebrate the "school" seasons: fall, winter, and spring.

NEW★★
HearthSong

One of the few catalogs I have seen that emphasizes seasonal activities and family feasts. The catalog has a rather mystical feel in spots, in tune with Waldorf philosophy, but that doesn't keep it from being a great place to get holiday gear. At Christmastime, HearthSong has a handcarved Nativity set, a beautiful Advent calendar, a Nativity transparency, and ornament kits . . . plus dreidels, a book by Sholom Aleichem, and lovely menorahs! At Easter time HearthSong offers old-fashioned egg-dying kits and other holiday specialties. For birthdays: star candleholders, fancy party bags, a birthday crown, and other gear. For every day, a book on family festivals and good times.

NEW★★
TREND enterprises, Inc.
All bulletin board sets, $5.99 each, come with free Discovery Guide. Requires 4 x 6' bulletin board.

A really fun, inexpensive way to add seasonal jollity to your home is with a Trend seasonal bulletin board. As someone who has little free time, I really appreciate being able to zap up meaningful decorations without having to spend hours making them myself or having to shell out megabucks down at the mall.

This last Christmas we put up Trend's *Nativity* Christmas scene. This is a traditional Christmas setting, with Mary, Jesus, and Joseph, shepherds and wise men, a lamb and donkey, the Star of Bethlehem, and an angel overlooking the whole scene with a big "Hallelujah!" banner. The accompanying Discovery Guide actually has some simple, meaningful activities and honest explanations of the meaning of Christmas (although for various reasons I would skip donating to UNICEF—one of the suggested activities).

We also used Trend's traditional *Thanksgiving* bulletin board. I recognize some of the pictures in this set as taken from classic engravings made a century or more ago. You get Indians carrying a deer to the feast;

women and a girl tending the cooking pot; a man and his wife walking along; a Pilgrim cottage; the guests praying at the table; and a few miscellaneous oversized pictures of the items they ate. Again, the Discovery Guide adds a lot of helpful background information and ideas for expanding the Thanksgiving theme.

You can also get a secular bulletin board for Christmas (*Santa and the Elves*) or a bulletin board featuring international Christmas celebrations. Trend also has bulletin boards for other holidays, such as Valentine's Day, St. Patrick's Day, and Halloween. Every one of these comes with a Discovery Guide, making it potentially the centerpiece of a family unit study.

NEW**
Warren Publishing House, Inc.
Special Day Celebrations, Small World Celebrations, $12.95 each. Add $2 shipping.

Special Day Celebrations is over 50 mini-units for celebrating secular holidays such as Pancake Day and Cinco de Mayo, designed for use with young children. Each celebration includes background info on the event, an art activity, a song, a snack recipe, and a game or some other learning activity. *Small World Celebrations: Around-the-World Holidays to Celebrate with Young Children* has a similar format, with the focus on celebrations in other countries. This latter has a globalistic we're-all-one-big-family flavor.

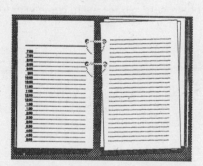

CALENDAR-KEEPING

NEW**
Fearon Teacher Aids
Quick 'n' Easy Calendar Learning, $4.95.

Workbook format includes a reproducible calendar, seasonal activity sheet, and cut-and-paste stickers page for each month of the school year.

NEW**
TREND enterprises, Inc.
All bulletin board sets, $5.99 each, with free Discovery Guide. Require 4 x 6' bulletin board.

Calendar-keepers will enjoy TREND's colorful bulletin-board calendars. The new Year 'Round Calendar Kit includes:

* 12 colorful monthly headers
* Four fill-in-the-blanks reusable monthly calendars—each a different color
* 56 weather symbols (eight each of seven symbols) for you to place on the monthly calendar
* One set of 31 numerals for daily dates
* A four-season poster with extra arrows
* A birthday poster
* 10 birthday cake symbols
* 21 birthday candles
* 28 holiday symbols
* Four special-day symbols
* Three "No School Today" headers
* One "Day Brighteners" header
* One "Special Day" header
* One "Do You Know?" header
* Five stars

How do you use it? Well, you can use the four calendar grids for separate date, weather, holiday, and special-days calendars—or combine all four functions on one calendar by posting symbols next to it on the board and connecting them to the appropriate dates with a length of yarn. The free Discovery Guide included with the kit has all sorts of clever ideas for calendar activities, plus a quick rundown of basic U.S. holidays, both religious and secular.

TREND's Monthly Calendar bulletin-board set is pretty similar. You get 78 weather symbols instead of 56, 18 holiday symbols instead of 28, and less special captions and extras. This set, however, comes with both English and Spanish month and day labels.

SEASONWARE

Now available for both IBM-compatibles and Macintosh, CE Software's excellent *CalendarMaker* program can easily be used to create your own activity calendars. See Educational Software Guide for more details!

CHAPTER TWENTY-TWO

ENRICHMENT ACTIVITIES

A treasure chest of all that's neat and nifty, but is not intended to be the primary teaching tool for a subject—that's this chapter. Here you can find the fun and the freaky, your kits and accessories for practicing concepts taught elsewhere. Afterschoolers should find this section especially useful, as should home schoolers who are looking for ways to expand their horizons.

Lots of educators today believe that kids need to learn with lots of hands-on and enrichment activities—and that is fine, as long as enrichment doesn't overpower the basics. You don't want to teach science with experiments alone, or math with coloring activities. Once your student has the basics down, though, feel free to fill in the blanks with enriching activities.

ALL-PURPOSE CATALOGS

These catalogs are your place for one-stop shopping. They collect material from many sources, organize it, and make it easy to look over and buy. Some even offer discounts!

Brook Farm Books
First Home-School Catalogue, revised edition, $8 plus $1 shipping.

Absolutely scads of unusual items, freebies, and fascinating information about home schooling. You can order more than 1,000 of the 2,000-plus listed items directly from Brook Farm Books.

Categories: Activities, Adolescence (the selection proves it's better to skip the pimpled stage and go straight from diapers to college), Art (includes sources for art reproductions), Baby & Birth (supports natural family life), Badges (buy 'em from Brook Farm Books), Beginning to Read (Richard Scarry, Dr. Seuss, and other easy readers), Biographies, Book Clubs, Books, Discount, Books, Technical, Brown Paper school books, Cards (game rules), Classics (nice large selection from different publishers, including illustrated classics and classics in beautiful bindings), Coloring Books, Crafts, Dictionaries, Education Books and Cassettes, Games, Geography, Gifted, Global Education (Donn Reed's for it), High School Subjects Self-taught, History (posters, activity units, American and Canadian), Ladybird Books, Languages, Literature (includes Marguerite Henry, Tintin, and the Tarzan series), Logic (two books), Made Simple books, Math (includes Saxon math), Music, Parenting, Radio and Recorded books (hundreds of hours of cassettes), Religion (liberal), Resources and

Teaching Aids (includes pages of freebies), Science (cosmic, fun stuff), Vocational Education (Exploring Careers series), Writing (the three best books on the subject). I left out a few of the minor categories—hope you don't mind! All is indexed for easy use.

The First Home-School Catalogue stresses challenging, constructive, informative, fun, and worthwhile items. You won't find much regular curriculum stuff here, due to the Reeds' unschooling philosophy. Think of it as a Whole Enrichment Catalog.

NEW★★
Crane's Select Educational Materials
Catalog $1, refundable on first purchase. Warbonnet kits from $15.90 to $56. Imitation bear claws, $1.90/dozen, predrilled. Shipping extra.

This catalog, put out by a home-schooling family, is a treasure chest of hard-to-find items that add extra zip and realism to your home studies. Unit study pioneers will be delighted, for example, with the large selection of Indian warbonnet kits complete with imitation eagle feathers, genuine leather, horsehair, and all other necessary ingredients. For those who want to learn more about warbonnets, there's a booklet with a short history of the warbonnet and bonnet construction tips. Wanna string some (imitation) bear claws on a string and have your very own macho native necklace? They're here. Also make-your-own moccasin kits, candle lantern kits, arrowheads, a book on how to make authentic Indian bows and arrows, and other pioneer and Indian goodies.

Moving into the space age, Crane's also has science supplies, including hard-to-find glassware and lab apparatus. Need glass tubing? Rubber stoppers? Horseshoe magnets? Chemicals for experiments? All here, and lots more.

Baskets, baskets, and more baskets: five different basket kits in all. All sorts of neat geography resources, from flash cards to games. History games. Indian coloring books. American history paper dolls. Greek and Hebrew teaching aids—for kids! Musical instrument kits. Woodworking project and how-to books. Fossil fish. Chemistry references and experiments. Many items illustrated in the catalog.

Holt Associates

John Holt's associates carry on his work, including not only *Growing Without Schooling* but the Holt Associates mail-order catalog.

Holt Associates merchandise is chosen with an eye for beauty, imagination, and simplicity. The resulting assortment is unique.

Holt Associates' literature selections are quite good, ranging from *The Bat Poet* to old favorites like the Grimms' fairy tales. For math, there is *Anno's Counting Book* and the indispensable *How to Lie with Statistics*. For science, there is *Powers of Ten*, a mindboggling book that exponentiates sizes in jumps of ten (how many jumps do you think it takes to go from "people size" to the Solar System)? For music, there is *How to Play the Piano Despite Years of Lessons*. The catalog, of course, contains hundreds more books than these, but I wanted to give you a taste of the sassiness and originality of the selections. It's worth sending away for this brochure just to read the names of the books!

Holt Associates also sells some art and music equipment, again with an eye to the gorgeous and/or unusual. We bought our Aulos recorders here, and several boxes of Cray-Pas. Holt Associates sells some expensive equipment too—violins and (on the more mundane side) pianicas and metronomes.

The emphasis on beauty makes this catalog a joy to read.

NEW★★
The Home School

Vast catalog with basic curriculum and enrichment items for all school subjects and ages. The Home School is an actual mall store selling these items, which are grouped under the major categories of Bible, Language Arts, Math, Science, History and Geography, Electives (coloring books, crafts, foreign languages, etc.), and Resources (books for parents). Basic curriculum includes name brands like A Beka and Alpha Omega, with individual worktexts or textbooks described in sufficient detail to help you make your purchase. It also includes secular publishers like Addison Wesley and D. C. Heath. Supplemental and enrichment items include such things as human body model kits, instructions for building your own flying toys, charts, maps, field guide coloring books, historical biographies (many series), games for all subjects, children's classics and other literature, and so on. Not as many hands-on items as some other catalogs, but a whole lot more basic stuff. As close to one-stop shopping for your basic home schooling needs as I've seen.

Shekinah Curriculum Cellar

All-purpose home schoolers' catalog. Thousands of items. Categories: Parent Helps, Bible, Devotional, Character Training, Phonics, Reading Skills, Literature (including biography and poetry), English and Creative Writing, Research, Reference, and Study Skills, Spelling and Vocabulary, Penmanship, Arithmetic, Consumer Math and Business, Science (including Creation Science), Health, Safety, and Manners (includes Sports, Physical Fitness, and Sex Education), History and Geography , Critical Thinking Skills, Art, Drawing, and Crafts, Art and Craft Supplies, Music, Integrated Curriculum (A Beka, Alpha Omega, Basic Ed, KONOS, Potter's Press, Weaver, and more), and Miscellaneous. Every item chosen for simplicity of use, every item described. Many unusual or hard-to-find items.

Sycamore Tree

The oldest all-purpose home schoolers' catalog. Categories: Bible, Character Development, Reading, Math, Penmanship, Grammar and Composition, Spelling, Social Studies, Science, Foreign Language, Sex Education, Physical Education, Arts and Crafts, Music, Cooking and Nutrition, Games and Puzzles, Felts, Toys, Videos, Travel, Reference Materials, Resource Materials, Parent Helps, and Curriculum (wide selection includes Weavers, Little Patriots, Konos, and Alpha Omega, among others). Sycamore Tree carries different materials than Shekinah in many areas. Emphasis is on creativity, simplicity, educational excellence, and fun.

NEW**
Timberdoodle

Home schoolers' catalog with a focus on hands-on and engineering resources. Topics in the latest catalog include: Foreign languages, fishertechnik, thinking skills, math manipulatives, math support materials, geography, science, science games, creation science, art, physical fun (here's where you can get a gym-quality mat for your home P.E. program!), Quadro, reading, Lauri materials, modalities, parent's library, home business and finances (Timberdoodle has some great stuff

from Larry Burkett), janitor's closet (professional house-cleaning supplies in family sizes), Betty Lukens felts, music, sign language, and more!

ALL-PURPOSE SUPPLIERS

These companies are major players in the enrichment arena, offering products for many different subject areas and age levels. Their products are often carried in other catalogs, but nobody carries *all* of their product line. To see everything these companies have to offer, you need their own catalogs.

Dover Publications

Over 3.000 paperbacks in all fields of interest, most priced between $2 and $5, many specially suited for home study and instruction. Everything Dover sells is a bargain—both their reprints of older books and their original publications, such as the Clip Art series. The vast selection includes something in every educational category, plus far-out stuff that doesn't fit in *any* category! And don't forget Dover's marvelous hands-on stuff—cardboard models of frontier towns and medieval castles, paper dolls, stencils, lots more. For those who want to enrich their own and their children's education, but who aren't rich themselves.

EDC Publishing

It's the British Invasion! Hey, the American Revolution and Beatlemania were just warmups. Now we're facing the fabulous Usborne Books series from England. (EDC is the U.S. importer of Usborne Books.)

Usborne books are designed entirely differently than American textbooks. Although they cover the basic subject areas (science, math, reading, history, geography, and so on), you will not find one speck of scholarly mumbo-jumbo, nor subheadings, chapter summaries, "Things to Think About," or questions to answer at the end of each chapter.

Instead of putting the student through the laborious process of memorizing bland text, Usborne Books are designed graphically to draw him in, make him *want* to learn the material and help him remember it forever. Typically a page will have one or more large, colorful illustrations with a minimum of text explaining what is happening and more text under each visual "subplot," labeling and explaining it. Example: Usborne's *How Your Body Works* uses the metaphor of the body as a machine. The section on the circulatory system shows white blood cells dressed as policemen zapping germs in the "blood river," which itself is being pumped through all the (labeled) organs. The history-book *Viking Raiders* follows the life of a Viking clan and its members through full-page pictures of the clan engaged in various activities, with each clan member named and each piece of equipment labeled—rather like a Richard Scarry book for ten-year-olds.

Do children remember this material? I've quizzed our six- and seven-year-old about anatomy and have been surprised at how much they retained from *How Your Body Works*. Of course, it helps that they *voluntarily* read these books over and over and over . . .

The more Usborne Books you buy, the more you will buy. Lasers! How films are produced! Chemistry! Natural Science! History! Whatever subject you found boring in school, there's an exquisitely-cartooned full-color Usborne book that makes the same dull old subject fascinating.

Educational Insights

Huge assortment of some of the niftiest enrichment materials around, all at incredibly low prices. Every Educational Insights product has dash and flair. Here's just one example from the enormous number of possibilities:

The *Funthinker* activity kits enrich your teaching of basic skills. Each comes in a plastic carrying case, and contains all sorts of goodies such as sing-along cassettes, stencils for tracing, storybooks, games, and even supplies such as scissors and crayons. The series presently includes *First Steps to Reading* (prereading exercises), *Learning My Alphabet, Understanding Numbers, Learning Values* (with Aesop's fables), *Beginning to Add and Subtract, Mysteries of Light* (an intriguing kit that contains a prism, a magnifier, and four color filters among many other things), and *Learning to Draw.*

I have not begun to even skim the surface of the varied and imaginative product line. See any school supply catalog, or send for Educational Insight's own, and be overwhelmed!

ACTIVITY BOOKS

Children's Small Press Collection
Big Fun Book, Look At Me, $9.95 each.

Your source for Egg Carton Tiddlywinks and over 400 other creative learning activities. Some are educa-

tional, some are just plain fun. Arts and crafts recipes. Easy arts and crafts. Early learning games. Music and rhythm. Indoor-outdoor games. Nature activities. Time and weather. Weighing and measuring. Holiday fun. Cooking fun. Similar format to *Look At Me: Activities for Babies and Toddlers* (see review in the Toys and Games chapter). Wonderful oversized pages; large, neat block print; clear directions; informative and encouraging graphics. A lot for your money!

NEW**
Warren Publishing House, Inc.
1•2•3 Art, 1•2•3 Colors, Special Day Celebrations, Small World Celebrations, $12.95 each. *1•2•3 Puppets, 1•2•3 Murals, 1•2•3 Books, 1•2•3 Games,* $7.95 each. *Theme-A-Saurus,* $19.95. Add $2 shipping.

Warren Publishing House is *the* place for activity books for preschoolers. Their lineup includes *1•2•3 Puppets, 1•2•3 Art, 1•2•3 Murals* (these are designed to be made and used in large classroom formats), *1•2•3 Games, 1•2•3 Books* (easy books kids can make), *1•2•3 Colors, Small World Celebrations, Special Day Celebrations,* and *Theme-A-Saurus,* a 600-page monster of a book filled with A to Z mini-teaching units. Each of these books has a strong hands-on flavor, with easy-to-follow directions for every activity.

MAGAZINES

Educational Services
Homeschooling At Its Best, $20/year September-May (9 issues). *Ready-Set-Learn* Enrichment Units, $6-$9 each. *Perspectives on the Past,* $16.50. *California History,* $13.50. Add 10% shipping for packets.

Homeschooling At Its Best is a home schoolers' enrichment magazine, with all materials written from a

Christian perspective. Each year's subscription covers such topics as music, art, oral speech, writing, history, physical education, and so on. The 1989-90 issues cover anatomy, world countries, hobbies, math puzzles, writing right, art techniques, and teaching tips.

Issues from previous years have been repackaged as *Ready-Set-Learn* unit studies. The series now includes units on science, creation science, world wonders, world continents, folk art, art appreciation, art history, literature, writing, and many more.

The *Perspectives on the Past* history enrichment package sequentially covers sections of American history, with time lines, history trivia and facts, quotes from the times, Inventors of the Times, Artists of the Times, Musicians of the Times, Authors of the Times, People of the Times, and so on. Enrichment activities parallel these features, as for example "Design a brochure for the Tuskegee Institute" alongside a biography of Booker T. Washington.

Kathy Means, the editor of *Homeschooling At Its Best,* has studied under Dr. Madeline Hunter and is available for home education consultation and presentations at reasonable rates. Her sister, Kim Solga, the artist who produces *KidsArt News* (small world!), does the graphics, and the magazine is produced on an Apple Laserwriter. Looks great!

74 Brand-new FREEBIES

Freebies
One year (6 issues), $6.97. Single copy, $2. Cancellation privilege within ten days of receipt of first issue.

This "Magazine with Something for Nothing" has tons of legitimate, up-to-date free and almost-free offers. Each offer has been researched to make sure the supplier has enough stock on hand to satisfy *Freebies* subscribers. The offers are written up in a style similar to mine; all ordering info is neatly appended. Example:

NO MUSS, NO FUSS
Digging in rich, brown earth gives you a satisfying feeling. But finding dirt from your indoor planting trays tracked all over your carpets makes you feel less gratified.
This gardening season, send for a sample Jiffy-7 plant starter pellet and help prevent dirty floors . . .

The review then explains the virtues of these pellets and the accompanying free brochure, and winds up with:

Send:
A Long SASE with 39¢ postage affixed
Ask For:
Jiffy-7 plant starter pellet
Mail To:
Jiffy Products of America, Inc.
Attn: Free Jiffy-7 Offer
P.O. Box 338
West Chicago, IL 60185

Each issue contains the following departments: Teacher's Page, Parent's Page, Food & Drink, Crafts, Kid Stuff, Free & Easy (simple how-to project using on-hand household items), Easter Parade, Catalog Quest (the issue I saw listed the HearthSong catalog, among others), Money Matters, Home Help, Teacher's Edition (classroom freebies), Big Spenders ("freebies" that cost up to $2 for the postage and handling), Grab Bag, Feeling Good (health freebies), Bulletin Board (a classified section), and Freebie Finders (readers ask where to find things and the *Freebies* staff answers). Several special sections are added throughout the year.

Are these freebies any good? Surprisingly, yes. One Jiffy-7 pellet might not seem too exciting, but most of the offers are really useful items. Examples: A free packet of Water-Less Crystals, enough for fifteen to thirty house plants (and the crystals stay active for up to six years!). Two product samples (buttermilk powder and baking cocoa), five coupons, and 26 recipes for 75¢. Sample of concentrated liquid wax for $1. Two plan sheets for build-and-stack storage units and understair storage for 50¢. Three pairs of plastic bunny scissors for 75¢. A teddy-bear catalog for $1. How to make a lacy Easter basket with a balloon, some yarn, water, lace, glue, and a few other fixin's (this one was on the house). A beaded bracelet kit for $1. Faux pearl jewelry set (necklace, bracelet, and earrings), $2. Zan-y-mals sewing projects for children, $2. Set of three puzzletters for you to write on and give for presents, $2. Genuine Sports Shooter eight-foot balloon, plastic air top, and mini-paratrooper for $1. Keep in mind these prices are just postage and handling: the items themselves are absolutely free.

Freebies is two-color and very attractive, with lots of graphics and zippy writing. And now that I've finished writing the review, I can finally start sending away for the dozen or so neat items that have caught my eye in this issue . . .

Shining Star
One year (four issues), $16.95. Sample issue, $4 USA, $5.95 Canadian.

Christian education magazine loaded with 80 pages of reproducible puzzles, games, and work sheets, plus teacher tips, stories, and a three-month Activity Calendar. The merciful editors include an An-swer Key in the back in case you or your little ones can't figure out the puzzles. Resourceful Sunday school leaders will find a lot here, as will those looking for handouts for children to work on during weekly worship services.

NEW**
Treasure Trove: The Newsletter for Homeschoolers
One year, $5 U.S. or $25 overseas (four issues). Published by Hewitt Research Foundation.

A Hewitt Research Foundation production, *Treasure Trove* is an a two-color enrichment magazine primarily directed at families enrolled in their program, but useful by any family. A typical issue (Fall 1989) included articles on nutrition (a simple overview of the basic food groups and some instant high-energy snack recipes), information about space technology and a touring NASA space exhibit, poetry by home-schooled children, info on how to enter Raintree Publishers Publish-A-Book Contest for 4th-6th grade children, a Pet Corner look at rodents, an Indian Picture Stones game, ideas and contacts for those who would like to volunteer for community service, a page of riddles and brainteasers, quickie book reviews, pen-pal corner, a parent's page of questions and answers, a Meet Your Teacher section, and more! Very splashy, visual layout with sprightly, memorable text. Clear, simple instructions for each suggested activity.

CHAPTER TWENTY-THREE

TRAVEL WITH YOUR FAMILY

Travel, like pasta, is a broadening experience. It's enlightening! Educational! But some might question a chapter about family travel in a book on home learning. "What's with this on-the-road stuff?" I can just hear someone ask. "Granted that travel is educational, what does it have to do with learning at home?"

My answer is that home and travel do mix. Whether your *house* is an apartment, a mobile home, or a two-story Colonial overlooking the Cape Cod surf, your *home* is where your family is. Home can temporarily be a tent in Yellowstone National Park or a Howard Johnson motel room, as long as the rest of the family shares it.

So if you pack up your family in your old RV and hit the road, you are still learning at home. And what an education! It may not extend quite from the halls of Montezuma to the shores of Tripoli, but however short the foray, travel expands the mind. Reading about Gettysburg is not the same as visiting the very battlefield on which the Blue and the Grey so valiantly contended. All the study units on Hispanic culture can never mean as much as a simple trip to a Mexican village. Even the great scenes of nature vary from location to location. To a prairie dweller, the Rockies loom quite differently in person than they did in the imagination.

To a mountain- or city-dweller, the open miles of Big Sky country literally open new vistas.

PLEASE WALK ON THE GRASS

Today it is quite possible to circle the globe and never see a thing. Hopping from airport to airport and hotel to hotel; "doing" Paris on a whirlwind tour of all the stock tourist attractions; spending your precious hours overseas shopping in a Spanish or English or American mall: this is not the way to make the most of travel.

Especially *family* travel! Hear the children complaining loudly and often when the fun family trip turns into eternity in the backseat of a car or a mere exercise in pavement-pounding. "So who cares if we get to see some famous building or natural wonder?" they will demand. "We already saw it on TV." What they are really saying is, "We are not interested in spending all day looking at things from afar. Please give us something to *do*."

The most successful family travel aims for a destination where children can *do* something: go deep-sea fishing, get art lessons from a landscape painter in the great outdoors, track beavers to their dam, feed the chickens, hike up a mountain and down again. And just possibly you, the mature adult, might enjoy some of this too!

MAGAZINES TO BROWSE

Travel With Your Children

Family Travel Times, one year (10 issues, including two double issues). $35 U.S.A., Mexico, U.S. Virgin Islands, Puerto Rico (all U.S. funds only). $39 Canadian (U.S. funds) or $50 (Canadian funds). Outside North America, $48 (air mail). Sample issue $1.

Travel-loving families get not only a family travel newsletter, but free phone travel consultations with their subscriptions to *Family Travel Times.* Founded by family travel expert Dorothy Jordon, *Family Travel Times* covers

- Planning for your vacation. For each destination covered, *FTT* gives you the needed details, including availability of cribs, highchairs, airline infant seats, and so on.

- Time together/time apart. *FTT* believes strongly in planned children's programs for children so that parents can have "adult" vacation time alone. Destination writeups describe what programs are available for each site.

- Warm welcomes. As *FTT* says, "It's not enough to be tolerated and not welcomed." *FTT* searches out hotels, resorts, and vacation sites that truly enjoy having families and are prepared to serve them.

- Sightseeing everyone enjoys. Detailed, "tried and true" advice on activities and places all family members can enjoy.

A sampling of some *FTT* articles: Adventure vacations. London/Paris update. Europe. Philadelphia. Tennis and golf vacations. San Francisco. The Baby-sitter Dilemma (no problem for those of us who manage without!). Take-along toys and games. Book reviews.

When *FTT* profiles a city (say, Chicago) they go all out. You get listings of Tours and Overviews, Views From the Top (high places where you can see the whole city), Festivals, Family Sightseeing (zoos, planetariums, parks, and so on). Each listing gives you a phone number to call or an address to write, plus date and time information on special events in that locale.

BOOKS TO READ

Adventure time! All things come to him who waits, especially if he waits reading in an armchair. Find out about strange and wonderful travel opportunities through the books below.

NEW★★
Bluestocking Press

Learning Vacations, sixth edition, $11.95 plus $2 shipping.

Ah, vacation time! Kick back and enjoy the sun . . . the surf . . . the seminar. . . . "The *seminar?*" 'Fraid so. In our relentless pursuit of self-improvement, Americans and others have discovered the joys of the learning vacation. Instead of wasting your time improving your tan on the beach, you could be in Israel on an archaeology dig! Schmoozing with Isaac Asimov in the tourist mecca of Rensselaerville, New York! Visiting the great gardens of Britain! Boating down the Amazon! Learning to weave in Canada! Attending a chamber music conference in Michigan! In the Blue Ridge mountains at a Christian writer's workshop! Off to a "cooking adventure" in France! You get the picture.

Yes, Virginia, learning is *everywhere* these days, and the writers of *Learning Vacations* have done their best to track down places where ardent learners can disappear on their vacations. With sections on Seminars and Workshops On and Off Campus, Journeys Far and Near, Archaeology-Science-History, The Great Outdoors, Arts-Crafts-Photography, Music-Dance-Drama, Museums and Historical Society Exhibits and Trips, Writer's Conferences, The World of Gastronomy, and Senior Citizens' Programs, this almost-300-page paperback has got what it takes to separate you and your tennis rackets for good. Two handy directories help you pick either programs for families with kids or programs for teens to attend on their own. A Sponsor Index and a Geographical Index help you quickly find options in the areas where you would like to vacation. Truly an "all-season guide to educational travel."

F & W Publications
Adventure Holidays, $10.95.

Looking for something spicy, something out of the ordinary, for your family vacation? *Adventure Holidays*, another annual directory from F & W Publications, lists hundreds of far-out vacations. Prices, dates, special equipment or experience required, and other essential information is provided about every adventure holiday. How about windsurfing . . . canoeing . . . hiking . . . riding . . . sailing? Too tame? All right, consider deep-sea diving or gorilla tracking, if you prefer. All this and more in the perfect resource for armchair adventurers.

UPDATED**
Travel With Your Children
Great Vacations with Your Kids, $12.95 plus $2 shipping, $9.95 for subscribers. *TWYCH's Airline Guide*, $5. *Skiing with Children* : $29 to non-subscriber, $39 Canadian; $18 to subscribers. Updated annually in fall. *Cruising with Children* : $20 to non-subscribers, $28 Canadian; $14 to subscribers. Updated annually late spring.

This is it: the "Complete Guide to Family Vacations in the U.S.," just as the subtitle claims. Written by Dorothy Jordon, founder of TWYCH™ (Travel with Your Children) and Marjorie Cohen, the author of six other travel books, *Great Vacations with Your Kids* gives you the low-down on getting ready, getting there, what to take, how to plan your days, and (the heart of the book) amost 500 pages of intimate reviews of just about every place in America that a family would want to spend its vacation. After rapidly handing us the dope on all-suite hotels, budget motels, home exchange schemes, condominiums, bed and breakfasts, and hostels, including agencies that specialize in booking these setups, the book gets down to business with separate chapters on adventure vacations, city vacations (what to see and where to stay), resorts, sports vacations, farms and dude rances, camping and cabins, cruises, and a catch-all "none of the above" section. You'll find specific details, including addresses, phone numbers, and even the name of the managers of the hotels/resorts/dude ranches/etc. reviewed in this book. Every vacation site is examined in terms of its family-friendliness, which in today's age-segregated world often translates into separate programs for you and the kids. Each entry includes an "in their own words" section where the facility owners put in their own 10 cents' worth about their wonderfulness, a description by the authors of the facility's main features, a "for

kids" section describing what activities and arrangements for children are offered, an "accommodations" section telling what is available, and a "rates" section giving sample rates. Unless you're staying at Uncle Joe's, don't leave home without it.

TWYCH's *Airline Guide* (updated annually) packs all you need to know about air travel with children into just four large pages. A chart of all 60 major national and international airlines tells you at a glance if car seats are OK, if the airline provides children's meals, diapers, or bibs, if families with children get special seating, and other essential information.

There's more! TWYCH's *Skiing with Children* and *Cruising with Children* guides tell you all about the specific services and family amenities of (respectively) 140 ski resorts in the U.S., Canada, and Europe and more than ninety ships representing over thirty cruise lines. This is extremely detailed, helpful information presented in report sheets which you may purchase separately or together.

Skiing with Children and *Cruising with Children* are updated annually. Lots of additional information on skiing and cruising respectively, as well as in-depth descriptions of the resorts and cruises. If you subscribe to *Family Travel Times,* the magazine published by TWYCH, you get discounts on these books. See *Family Travel Times* review above.

PLACES TO STAY

You can travel for its own sake, jetting about here and there. Or you can pick a destination you want to visit, go there, and stay there.

The following listings provide places to stay, mostly with a rural flavor, and people to meet, likewise.

NEW**
Adventure Guides, Inc.
Farm, Ranch, and Country Vacations (40th anniversary ed.), $12 postpaid or $13 if you want it sent first class mail. Free newsletter, *Family Vacations at Ranches in the Rockies,* send SASE.

If we ever have time for a real family vacation, this is the book I'll go for first. It's 224 pages of vacations far away from the city, with more than 200 selections, lots that fit budgets of well under $1,000 per week for a family of four, including meals and accommodations. (The rate can be three times that amount at the fanciest resorts covered in the book.) You'll get to choose from a broad selection of destinations coast to coast: working farms and ranches, ranch resorts and lodges, farm inns, dude ranches, B & B farms, and so on. Each entry tells you the rate, dates the place is available, how to make your reservations, how to get there, whether children are welcome and what activities if any are provided for them, and gives you a nice chatty description of the place. You know author Pat Dickerman knows the subject and has visited these farms and ranches—this is the 40th annual edition of the book!

UPDATED**
Christian Life Workshops

The Hospitality Handbook, $14.95 (includes 3 copies of *The Guest Room Directory*). *The Guest Room Directory* (sold only in sets of 3), $8.95/set. Add 10% shipping ($2 minimum, $5 maximum).

These two books started out life as *The Christian Bed & Breakfast Directory* and grew out of home-school speaker Gregg Harris's desire to see Christian families revive Biblical hospitality. *The Hospitality Handbook* is a concise introduction to guest-room hospitality. Gregg tells you how to prepare your guest room (or a child's room vacated to serve as a guest room), how to serve a comfortable breakfast, how to handle arrangements and avoid potential legal hassles, and how to organize your records. *The Guest Room Directory* lists hundreds of families (alumni of Gregg's seminars) who are willing to offer their guest rooms to travelers. It explains the basic rules of guest etiquette, how to contact your potential hosts, and everything else you need to know. Each listing in *The Guest Room Directory* tells you where each host is located, how many adults can sleep comfortably there, what kinds of rooms are available, and how to contact the host family.

UPDATED**
National Homeschool Association

This new group has taken over responsibility for running the home schoolers' travel directory that first saw the light of day as the *Growing Without Schooling Travel Directory*. The last edition listed over 200 contacts, mostly alternative-education-minded folk. Write for current price and more info.

Michel Farm Vacations

Room and 2 meals (country breakfast and evening meal): per week, $235/person; per weekday, $35/person; per weekend day, $42/person. Lunch on farm or box lunch for tour, add $5. House with kitchen facilities: per week, $150/person; per weekday, $20/person; per weekend day, $25/person. Under-4's, free. 30% discount on children aged 4-12. Single occupancies, add 20%.

Central booking agent for farm vacations on over 20 host farms in the Harmony, Minnesota, area. Wide variety of winter and summer sports nearby. You get room and board on the host farm, including lots of homemade bread, homemade soups, homemade sausage. Treat your kids to the sight of cows being milked and machinery at work, or spend some time feeding and getting to know a calf, a sow and her piglets, chickens, or other animals which will be penned in small enclosures for your convenience.

Choose from 14 vacation tours in advance. Guided driving tour of the Harmony area Amish settlement, with time for shopping for Amish furniture and crafts (guide rides in your car—$22-$30/car). Niagara Cave Tour. Historic Lanesboro, with special dinner in town. Ernie Tuff Museum. Scenic drive includes visits to museum, cave, and park. Rochester, including the Mayo Clinic. Lake City, including a possible ride and dinner on the paddlewheeler Hiawatha. Shopping or skiing in the Red Wing area. Northeast Iowa tour, with visit to Bily Clocks and the house where Antonin Dvorak composed the *New World Symphony* . Norwegian-American museum in Decorah. Golfing on one of seven courses. Hiking, biking, or cross-country skiing (this is free). Trout fishing. Canoeing. Deer hunting on several of the host farms.

Oak Leaf Bread and Breakfast

With bed & breakfast: $30/two people, $8/each additional person (up to 6), $5 for each additional person (up to 12). $250/five days of family reunion or retreat without breakfast. Children under 5 free. Traveling animals stay in the barn.

Southeastern Kansas is the place for this working ranch operation with registered cattle and a "marvelous hog operation." Oak Leaf B&B has "all the stuff of which farms are made: chickens, milk cows, garden, barns, hay lofts, mud, and dogs." Pet the buffalo. Gather the eggs. Help milk the cow. Work in the special kids' garden, or play volleyball, badminton, croquet, and horseshoes. Visit the on-site country art gallery with offerings from local artists and craftspeople, or try your hand at a variety of herb and flower crafts.

Your hosts, a Mennonite couple, provide gracious service and "the best cinnamon rolls in three counties, maybe four," according to their employers. Not to mention the homemade sausage with good coffee and cabbage, for the non-German palate.

Three state parks and reservoirs are within driving distance, if you just absolutely can't bear to stay out of the car.

Stay in the house, or in the completely furnished guest house that can sleep up to 12 people.

Oak Leaf recommends that you plan a longer stay if you really want to see the ranch in operation. Unscheduled and spontaneous people will enjoy it best.

VIDEOS TO SEE

I predict that travel video is going to really boom, and soon. What is clogging up the shelves in your local travel agent's office, however, is *not* travel video. It's sell-the-vacation video. That's an important difference!

Travel videos try to give you an experience of what it's really like to be in a different place. They make an attempt to educate you about the country (or state, or province, or city) and its customs and topography. You get to meet some of the locals close up, and see the scenery. Really good travel videos even share some of the place's history with you.

Here's the one source I have so far found that qualifies as real travel video. If you know of any others, have them send me some review samples and I'll see what I can do about getting them into the next edition!

NEW**
Quantum Communications
Each Traveloguer video, $29.95. Shipping, $3 first tape, 75¢ each additional. 10 or more tapes purchased at once, shipping is free.

Too many travel videos are the updated equivalent of Uncle Harry's slide show of Europe, long on tourist attractions and short on descriptions of the real countries and their people.

Not so with the Traveloguer Collection! These 60-minute videos are adapted from films produced by real "traveloguers." Traveloguers are independent film producers who spend years studying what makes a country unique, as well as spotting the best film shots. They then present their films to live audiences of thousands throughout North America. The best of these films of European countries have been brought together into the Traveloguer Collection.

Videos can be a risky business, not to mention a risqué business. Makers of travel videos sometimes like to linger on the seamy, nightclub side of a country, and heaven knows we don't need to bring any more of this into our homes. So I asked the people at Quantum Communications to allow me to review their entire 17-video series. I was really impressed! Not only is this some of the most spectacular film footage I have ever seen, narrated by people who obviously know what they're talking about, but these videos have tremendous educational value (again setting them apart from other travel videos series). The videos teach you *geography,* as every visit to a new part of the country is introduced by highlighting the parts you are about to visit on a video map, and the videos each make a point of showing you each country's distinctive terrain. The *culture* and *history* are introduced, through visits to dozens of important cultural events and historic sites. The traveloguers also make a point of introducing us to interesting craftsmen and businesses in each country, and showing us in detail how several local crafts are made (e.g. Swedish wooden horses, Irish porcelain baskets). You find out about the day-to-day life of both urban and rural inhabitants, and what they do for sport and entertainment. The traveloguer narrator gives you a verbal picture of the social and political structure of the country while showing you examples of government buildings and state institutions. You are also treated to a trip down the major waterway of each country, and taken to the home of a typical inhabitant. Lest all this sound dull and dry, let me hasten to assure you that these are tremendously entertaining videos, put together with a lot of intelligence and wit. I won't soon forget the spectacle of the kilt-clad Scotsman doing his best to hurl a 300-pound telephone pole end-over-end! (That's a national sporting event, believe it or not!) You get a real "feel" for countries that previously were just names on a map. The videos come in impressive, durable gold-stamped cases that will look lovely on your shelf. And on top of all this, you get a free companion reference guide with each videotape purchased directly from Quantum Communications. It's a gold-imprinted pocket-sized booklet with a map locating the places visited on the video, a representative recipe of the country, a brief history of the country, cultural pointers for visitors, and a recommended reading list for further study of that country.

I can heartily recommend 14 out of the 17 Traveloguer videos. The remaining three require more serious consideration, for the following reasons. *Eternal Greece* starts with a squirrely sequence featuring a girl posing as Gaia, the earth goddess, and presents paganism throughout in rather too glowing terms to make Christians comfortable. (This is not at all true of the other videos in the series, by the way—they mention each country's Christian heritage in very positive terms.) The *Americans in Paris* video also has a brief nightclub sequence (the only one in all 17 videos), and if you know anything about Paris nightclubs, this is not something you want the children watching. *¡Si Spain!* also has a brief shot of a portrait of the nude wife of a Spanish nobleman. Said portrait created a scandal at the time it was painted, and it doesn't really belong on a family video. I'm telling you about this only so you are forewarned. I don't want you getting the impression that the rest of the videos suffer from these problems. Even in the case of the Paris and Spain videos, these are only lapses in what are otherwise fine videos. In general, the traveloguers have done a commendable example of showing us what is worth showing and depicting a society honestly, without dragging us through its seamy side or pushing any propaganda.

The folks at Quantum Communications are pretty confident about this video series, to the point of saying, "If you don't agree that the Traveloguers stand heads above any country tour you've ever seen, you can send them back and we'll refund your money." They're pretty safe; you won't want to send them back. These are videos you can watch again and again, learning more and enjoying them more each time.

TRAVEL GAMES

EDC Publishing, Inc.
Car Travel Games, Air Travel Games, $3.95 each.

Clever books of things-to-do for children age seven and over. The games and puzzles, etc., all depend on close attention to the colorful pages, so these are not good choices for the car- or air-sick child. Many of the games included could be played just as well at home.

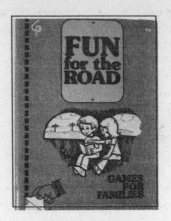

Gazelle
Fun for the Road, $2.95 postpaid.

Inexpensive book of travel games. Games do not depend on looking at the book's pages—a plus for those prone to motion sickness.

NEW★★
The Learning Works
Build a Doodle Travel Pack #1 and *#2, Dinosaur Travel Pack #4,* $8.95 each. *Travel Game Pack #3,* $14.95. Shipping extra.

Learning kits to amuse your kids while on the road. Each Travel Pack includes two books, a box of crayons, and a reusable storage bag. The *Build a Doodle* travel packs are an especially neat idea. You get one book of 32 step-by-step line drawings and one doodle pad. The line drawing of a telephone, for example, is built up in five steps. First the child copies a foreshortened rectangle. Then he adds two little squares on top of his drawing. Next comes two semicircles for the mouth- and earpieces. Next a curve connects them, making the handset. Finally he adds a dial and a telephone cord. Each step of this process is presented as a separate drawing, so the child can see exactly what he needs to add at each step. As a bonus, each doodle drawing has a suggested activity. The activity for telephone says, "Add something to show that the telephone is ringing." The line-art book never gets drawn in, so it can be used by many children. All you need to do is keep providing more scratch paper when the doodle pad runs out!

ARMCHAIR TRAVEL

For travel software, Blue Lion Software's *Ticket to . . .* series is all I have run across that really counts. The series includes *Ticket to London, Ticket to Paris, Ticket to Spain,* and *Ticket to Washington* (the city, not the state), plus a new foreign etiquette program, *R.S.V.P.* They run on IBM and compatibles, Apple, and Commodore. For more info, check out the writeup in the trusty Educational Software Guide in Volume 3. Meanwhile, for those who don't have a computer or who just like View-Masters, here's another way to take a peek at life in lots of other places.

Worldwide Slides
Most View-Master packets, $3.25 apiece. Battery-operated projector, $19.95. 3-D Viewer, $3.95. Add 10% shipping.

Do you remember that Christmas you got your first View-Master? Sure you do. Wasn't it fun to click the switch, advance the reel, and see the beautiful color display?

Most of us ended up with packs of cartoon reels as children. But View-Master also developed hundreds of packets of travel reels to go with their viewers. These are now available from Worldwide Slides.

The typical three-reel package includes 21 3-D images, all lovely pictures of famous or important sights. Some packages available: Scenic USA, Alaska, Eskimos of Alaska, Alabama, Grand Canyon, Tour of Canada, Maritime Provinces, Library of Congress, Paris, France, Castles in Europe, Puerto Rico, Luxembourg, Athens, Norway , Disneyland. This is just the tip of the iceberg.

With a View-Master projector, the whole family can travel from your living room. Or get the inexpensive standard viewers, point at a light source, and travel!

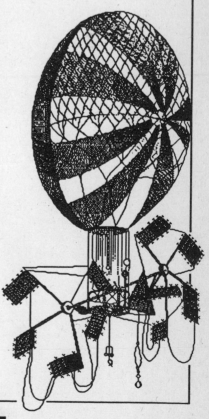

SPECIAL CASES

CHAPTER TWENTY-FOUR

HELPING YOUR "LEARNING DISABLED" CHILD AT HOME

Once upon a time there was a kingdom of rabbits. Big rabbits. Little rabbits. White rabbits. Brown rabbits. Rabbits that liked to sit and twitch their whiskers. Rabbits that liked to roll in the meadow on sunny days.

Then one day a hungry-looking rabbit came to the rabbit kingdom. As always, the rabbits took him in and politely asked him what job he would like to do.

"I want to teach the slow rabbits to run faster," he said.

The rabbits had to stop and think about this. They had never really paid much attention to who ran fast and who ran slow. The main point, for them, had always been getting home safely, and it didn't matter whether you did it by outracing a dog or by freezing in a clump of weeds or by knowing where all the hidey-holes were.

Still, teaching the slow rabbits to run faster seemed like a good idea. What could it hurt? After all, any rabbit would enjoy running faster. So the rabbits agreed to make the strange rabbit Head Teacher of the slow rabbits.

"I will need to be paid for my work," the stranger replied. "One carrot a week per pupil." That sounded reasonable enough. So the strange rabbit, whose name was Barnum, became the first rabbit teacher.

At first his class was pretty small. There were only two rabbits in the whole kingdom who everyone considered slow runners. This bothered Barnum, because

he had to spend so much time looking for food. Two carrots a week weren't enough for even the scruffiest rabbit to live on, let alone a famous teacher of speed racing! So he had an idea. He announced that he was going to test the rabbits for speed defects. They would all run a race, and the ten who ran the slowest would get speed lessons.

All rabbits love a race, so Barnum had no trouble at all running his test and adding another ten rabbits to his class. Now he had enough carrots, but he felt that with so many pupils he needed an assistant. To make sure there were enough carrots for both his assistant and himself, he set up another race and picked up another twenty rabbits for his class.

In Barnum's class the rabbits were really working out. He broke down running into two hundred basic steps, each of which his students had to master in sequential order before they could advance to the next one. This made many of the rabbits confused. They couldn't remember all the details. So he made those rabbits attend extra classes and hired another assistant. Of course, in order to pay for the assistant, he had to set up yet another race and pick up more rabbits for the classes. Then the extra rabbits needed more teachers. After a few rounds of this, almost forty percent of the rabbits were in Barnum's classes.

The races were becoming more and more desperate. Rabbits didn't want to go into Barnum's class and be called "Slow Tail" by the other rabbits. Some rabbits began to cheat, jumping the gun at the beginning of the race. Some parents even approached Barnum's helpers and asked them to tutor their children *before* a race, so the children wouldn't have the humiliation of being assigned to a class. The tutors gladly agreed. Some even began suggesting that *every* rabbit should take the special classes, starting at the age of two days, lest they possibly develop speed problems later. There was talk of all-day speed classes; of summer speed school; of mandatory preschool speed training. Those were heady days for speed trainers, whom the other rabbits held in the highest respect, as they were sacrificially devoting themselves to rescuing rabbit children from speed defects.

A few rabbit parents began to wonder why the rabbit kingdom all of a sudden was so full of slow runners when in the old days almost every rabbit had been able to get home safely, and most of them could even run pretty fast.

Meanwhile, the rabbit population began decreasing. Barnum's pupils had so much to think about whenever they tried to run that any half-blind, senile fox could catch them. When it had finally gotten to the point that foxes and weasels were simply hanging around the outside of the rabbit holes, knowing they could catch almost anyone who ventured out, the king of the rabbits held a meeting. "Who is to blame for this?" he thundered. "Why have the rabbits in my kingdom become so slow?"

Barnum was right there with an explanation. "It's minimal brain defects, genetic defects, visual-processing problems, and lack of gross motor skill readiness, O Your Majesty!" he chanted, looking proud of himself for having invented so many big words and phrases.

The king didn't buy this. "So why are our rabbits so mentally and physically crippled only since *you* came along?" he wanted to know.

"None of this is my fault, Your Serene Highness!" Barnum replied, deeply offended. "It's not my fault that these rabbits have poor family backgrounds, watch too much television, and are exposed to all sorts of air and water pollution before birth! I'm doing everything I can to help. And besides, none of those rabbits in the old days knew anywhere near as much about running as I do. Our grandrabbits probably had lots of speed defects too. We just didn't know as much about speed defects and how to help them back then."

"You may or may not know a lot about speed defects, but it's clear that you know nothing at all about curing them, when most of your pupils can't even put

their noses out to sniff the air without getting eaten," said the king. "Such a bunch of dispirited, unconfident rabbits I never have seen. If speed defects really exist, but can't be cured, then your teaching work is a waste of time. If they don't exist, it is also a waste of time. So out you go, and we'll go back to the old way of concentrating on getting home safely, not on speed."

Barnum left in a huff, along with a number of rabbit parents and children who had become accustomed to following his authority more than that of the rabbit king.

But a fox was waiting outside the hole, and we can't be sure that any of them got very far. . . .

It took a little time for the rest of the rabbits to get used to the idea that speed was not the most important thing in life, but once they did, everything went back to normal. Once again, rabbits sunned themselves and twitched their whiskers without worries. Once again, most rabbits made it safely home. And a lot of fat foxes got very hungry!

LABELING KIDS FOR FUN AND PROFIT

It's a good thing people are so much smarter than rabbits. Or are we? Ever since Binet and Simon inadvertently invented the world's first IQ test, schools have spent a disproportionate amount of time labeling students rather than teaching them. Few spoke out against this practice. The prevailing wisdom quickly became that if a child didn't learn, it was *his* fault. Not the teacher's. Not the school's. Not the curriculum's. The only "solution," such as it was, was to label the student as early as possible and strap him into special courses that plodded ever-so-slowly through the standard curriculum.

Government funding was redesigned to pay schools three or four times as much for each labeled student. Once government funding was in place, the number of labeled children mushroomed miraculously, to the point where some writers talk about 25 or even 40 percent of all students as having some form of "learning disability."

That was the bad news. This is the good news. The experts are wrong—again. IQ tests are *not* a predictor of success in life. Neither is the ability to sit for hours in a classroom seat. "Special" kids are mostly *not* "special," just mistrained and/or mistaught. Even children with organic learning problems do *not* need to spend their childhood years struggling with data doled out in teeny-weeny portions.

So the resources in this chapter will not look much like those you might expect. Here are no dumbed-down easy readers or inch-by-inch math programs. Instead, we will look at *child training, reading, games, art,* and a few unique resources especially designed for parents who would like to strip off their children's labels altogether.

HELPING YOUR LABELED CHILD

Step one in helping your labeled child is to *reject the label.* Unless the school, or whoever labeled your child, can demonstrate that an *organic* problem exists, they're just saying, "We don't know why Johnny doesn't learn and we aren't interested in finding out." If Johnny has crossed eyes and can't see the blackboard, or his earwax is the consistency of concrete, then obviously he will have learning problems until his eyes get uncrossed or his ears get cleaned. But if Johnny is labeled "learning disabled" or "retarded" or "developmentally delayed" these so-called diagnoses have no *medical* significance at all.

Albert Einstein's teachers thought he was stupid and would have called him learning disabled if the term had been around back then. But Mr. Einstein was merely disinterested in their teaching; there was nothing wrong with *his* brain.

So if your child is doing poorly in school, consider the following possibilities:

(1) He is bored.
(2) He has a poor teacher.
(3) He is being taught by a poor method.
(4) He is being taught in a way unsuited to his learning style.
(5) He is very bright and has contempt for his classes.
(6) He is very bright and is trying to "fit in" with the gang by acting stupid.
(7) He is a thorough chap who doesn't like to race on to new items until he has digested the old. (But school leaves no time to digest the old.)
(8) The class is graded subjectively, and the teacher doesn't like him.
(9) He is not well-disciplined and rather than dealing with his bad behavior, the school prefers to label him "hyperactive."

These nine possibilities are just the tip of the iceberg. The bottom line, when dealing with physically normal children, is this: shall we give up and blame them, or consider their failures *our* failures and keep searching for the solution?

BOOKS AND BOOKLETS ABOUT "LEARNING DISABILITIES"

We'll talk in the next chapter about what to do if your child has genuine physical handicaps or brain damage. First, here are some excellent resources with the real facts about "learning disabilities."

Education Services
A Biblical Psychology of Learning, $8.45 postpaid.

How can you prevent learning problems? How can you motivate a labeled child? These are common questions parents and teachers ask. Dr. Ruth Beechick's excellent *Biblical Psychology of Learning* preempts all these questions. Beginning with the importance of first establishing a proper heart attitude through parental discipline and nurture, Dr. Beechick spurns the manipulative trickiness of much modern learning theory. By answering the most important question, "Why do children and other people learn or refuse to learn?" she provides a road map for the lesser questions as well. Highly recommended.

Holt Associates
Everyone Is Able—Exploding the Myth of Learning Disabilities, $3.95 plus $1.50 shipping.

If you would like to find out why intelligent people are questioning the whole premise of "learning disability," and why you should fiercely resist your child being branded with this label, this booklet from Holt Associates provides the ammo. Hear from the "other experts"—parents of labeled children (or whose children would be labeled if the mainstream experts got their hands on them) and specialists within the schools who see what the LD label does to children and education. These are real-life stories. Many articles were written especially for this booklet. The quality of the writing as a whole is thoughtful, but not dispassionate. Must reading.

Reading Reform Foundation
The Magic Feather, $16.95 plus $1.70 shipping.

From the book jacket: "His parents called him bright and curious—his teachers called him hopelessly retarded. A million kids are similarly judged every year. His parents fought the schools and proved the tests wrong. You can too."

Bill and Lori Granger, a prolific husband-wife writing team, have a son, Alec, who at age six could read several years above his grade level. When a routine school test diagnosed Alec as having an IQ of 47, the Grangers at first pooh-poohed it, and then trotted out Alec's precocious reading ability. Unmoved, the school psychologist who gave the test said Alec would have to be deposited in a Special Education class. But unlike other parents, the Grangers dared to fight the test-worshiping "experts."

The Magic Feather is the story of Alec's narrow escape from the Special Ed net (his parents ended up

placing him in a Montessori school) and an exposé of the special ed industry.

Some juicy quotes from the book jacket:

While perhaps 3 percent of all school-age children might benefit from Special Education, nearly 11 percent of the nation's schoolchildren are currently confined in Special Ed programs—*more than four million children*.

In some school districts, racial and ethnic segregation are enforced by using the Special Ed program as a dumping ground for unwanted students.

For each child successfully captured by a Special Ed program, a school district may receive *four thousand dollars* in government monies.

As the Grangers say, "We learned some startling things. We have found that the process that pins such labels on children is at best expedient and at worst outright fraud . . . Nobody knows what a 'learning disabled' child is, and the difference between him and another called 'emotionally disturbed' or 'retarded' may be nonexistent. What they share is that they did not 'fit in' in a regular classroom . . . Nearly one out of eight kids in school are in Special Education today . . . This is too many and educators know it."

More than an exercise in consciousness-raising, *The Magic Feather* is a resource book for parents who want to fight the system from within, and a list of good reasons for those who want to get out. I'm not sure it's in print any longer—check your local library for it first.

Pantheon Books (check your library for this one—it was published in 1975)
The Myth of the Hyperactive Child and Other Means of Child Control. Large book with bibliography, appendix, footnotes, and index.

Here in Missouri we are saddled with an early childhood education pilot program enticingly labeled "Parents as First Teachers." Part of this program, beside the group meetings supervised by "experts" and the in-home visits to check on the parents, is a strong emphasis on early screening of children to catch cases of "developmental delay." Its proponents hope that this presently-voluntary program will soon become compulsory in every community in the U.S.A.

In view of this push to force children into early childhood screening, you owe it to yourself to learn why diagnostic screening is *not* helpful and why the "scientific" labeling process is a bunch of self-serving hooey. The book that will do this for you is Peter Schrag and Diane Divoky's scrupulously-researched *The Myth of the Hyperactive Child.*

Authors Schrag and Divoky are serious journalists who regularly write for major national media. Diane Divoky recently contributed the *Encyclopedia Britannica* entry on Home Schooling.

BALANCE AND VISION

If you have a labeled child and are searching for answers, sooner or later you're probably going to run into the "developmental" approach to solving "learning disabilities."

Whereas public school special ed experts like to blame learning problems on such invisible bogeymen as "minimal brain dysfunction," the developmentalists claim that learning problems arise from children missing important developmental steps. Their solutions range from "neurologically organizing the child's brain" to "teaching the child to properly visually process information."

This is all OK so far. What you need to watch out for is developmentalists' tendency to blame not only *learning problems* but even *sinful moral choices* on a child's failure to progress through normal developmental stages. For example, one otherwise good book written by a Christian developmentalist says, "Without an adequate way to take in information, store it and maintain a visual picture an individual perishes in his mind, soul and eventually his spirit." This would appear to mean that children who have visual-processing handicaps (or blind children, for that matter) are doomed and damned until they can get expert training. I spoke to the author and he tells me this is not what he meant to convey and that he will revise this section in the next edition of his book. In the meantime, however, such language can be spiritually misleading—especially since some developmentalists like to point to the large percentage of juvenile delinquents who are neurologically imbalanced or impaired in their visual-processing functions in order to "prove" their theories that developmental lacks "cause" children (who are otherwise naturally good in their view) to turn into criminals.

I believe the developmentalists are confusing cause and effect. The Bible says that if you don't use your talents, you lose them (Matthew 25:28-30). Self-focused children aren't interested in other people or the world around them; such children could very well miss out on developmental stages that depend on focusing on things and people outside yourself. Lazy children won't concentrate, and thus fail to progress at other skills. Rebellious children won't persevere at a task, and thus fail to improve their visual-processing skills. Etc.

This doesn't mean that all children who have trouble learning are especially sinful. It *does* mean that children who have trouble learning have no more right to sin than the rest of us, and that in some cases sin can even be the cause of the learning problem.

OK. Now you know developmentalists sometimes get overenthusiastic about their programs' ability to conquer crime and eradicate the common cold. You know that these programs can help with specific learning problems but that they are *not* a new way of salvation. Now let's talk about some developmental programs that can help your child with his technical skills.

NEW**
Keys to Excellence
I.Q. Booster Kit, $69 plus $4 shipping. Workbooks alone, $24.95 plus $4 shipping for set of 4.

For those of you who like to prevent problems before they start, let me recommend the excellent perception-training workbooks from Keys to Excellence (formerly Perception Publishers). These go by the name of I.Q. Boosters, and that's just what they are! These really cute and stimulating workbooks provide a complete, graded series of developmental tasks that actually increase your child's ability to concentrate visually and aurally, his concentration and perception skills, and even his ability to draw neat lines! They are offered two ways: (1) As part of the I.Q. Booster Kit, which also includes four cassettes on how to develop the early learner and a set of 151 fun activities that will further develop his physical abilities. (2) The workbooks may be purchased separately as a set of four. Because of their design, they will appeal most to preschool and early elementary children. Author Simone Bibeau sticks to her subject of expertise and does *not* make any exaggerated claims for perception training. I highly recommend her program.

National Academy of Child Development (NACD)

Based on the theories of Robert Doman, NACD provides individualized therapy and advancement programs for all kinds of special-needs and gifted children. The main theory informing the program is Mr. Doman's theory of "neurological dominance." The idea is that your brain is divided into two halves, one of which should be dominant. You should be right-eyed, right-handed, and right-footed (or left-eyed, left-handed, and left-footed). Otherwise, the two halves of your brain will end up spending too much time zapping signals back and forth and you will be confused and awkward. Mr. Doman also strongly stresses the developmental stages. The typical NACD child (if there is such a thing!) is given a number of developmental exercises, plus some academic materials and some special therapy directed to his special problems. In the case of our son Teddy, who among other problems had a very low sense of touch, we were given stimulation exercises using a vibrating massage device, among other things. Teddy also was extremely weak, so we were given physical therapy exercises.

NACD has done some amazing things with severely brain-damaged children, comatose children, Down's children, and other children with major organic problems. Their program is quite expensive, and you will have to bring your child in to be evaluated. NACD staff fly around the country to major cities. They offer cassette training courses in their philosophy. Most of the material on those cassettes is excellent, if you keep in mind the caveats I mentioned above!

UPDATED**
Vision Development Center
The Learning Connection, $14.95. Plan A: workbook, deposit, and lease of all materials/supplies for 8 weeks, $375. Maintenance kit (to use after the first 8 weeks so child does not regress), $75. Plan B: workbook and purchase of all materials/supplies, $475. Plan C: consultation/evaluation, $25. Add $50 for each additional child to cover consultation/evaluation fee and workbook.

Next, there's the Vision Development Center, run by Steven Shapiro. Steve has written a book, *The Learning Connection,* that explains his theory of the importance of "visual processing." This inexpensive book includes an eight-week course of useful developmental exercises. He also has produced a home kit, the Stepping Stones Home Course Program, which includes the special vision-training equipment and exercises provided on-site by the Vision Development Center.

For Mr. Shapiro, "vision" is not just whether your child can see clearly. It's the ability to *process* and *remember* what he or she sees. He also makes some interesting points about what he considers the unhelpfulness of "learning styles" theory and the public-school style of special-ed placement. The technical side of his program appears to produce good results. The section of his book on how vision-processing skills relate to spiritual understanding is presently not the best, but it will be revised in future editions.

The home course concentrates on developing visual skills and connecting them to coordination, perception, and auditory skills. Sounds pretty fancy, right? No, we're not talking about testing kids' eyes to see if they need glasses. We're talking about teaching the eyes to work together, to work with the hands (handwriting) and rest of the body (general coordination), and to get the info that reaches eyes and ears into the brain, where it can do some good.

Most children with reading and other school problems are actually suffering from bad educational methods. Intensive phonics and better math programs are the cure for these ills. But kids who can't concentrate, have trouble focusing on the paper (although their eyes check out OK), don't remember what you just told them two seconds ago, and so on may indeed benefit from a developmental program focusing (excuse the pun!) on vision, such as VDC offers.

VDC has been primarily a walk-in consultation center. The home program was added on for parents who don't happen to live in Tulsa. From what I've seen of it, it looks fundamentally sound. You first fill out an evaluation form for your child. This involves rating him from 1-5 in several skill areas, and testing him visually in several ways, as well as filling out a brief educational and medical history. To this you might attach some of your child's latest schoolwork. You then get a phone consultation. If you opt for more than this, you will get • an instruction manual for coordination, perception, and auditory exercises • an instruction manual for vision exercises • student workbook with progress chart • instruction video • materials kit including focusing lenses and flipper, red/green glasses and pictures • and focusing targets. You may choose to rent or purchase these items. In any case, you keep the workbook.

The exercises are easy enough to do, but require a willingness to invest some time with your child, as is usual in programs of this sort. Kids adore the attention! For your child, the unusual materials and variety of exercises should be fun. The whole course, incidentally, is designed to last just eight weeks.

VDC's brochure has some impressive testimonials from a a teacher, two parents, and a 33-year-old computer teacher who "can now read and comprehend a book from the Bible in 2 or 3 sittings rather than 25 or more readings."

ALLERGIES

NEW**
Bluestocking Press
The Impossible Child, $9.95 plus $2 shipping.

"There is a subset of children who appear to learn well and easily on one day, but not on another. They seem unable to function consistently well in school. They often act appropriately but suddenly, for no apparent reason, their behavior can exasperate the most patient teacher or parent. Other children appear unable to learn or behave most of the time. Some are too active; others are too tired. . . . Many have recurrent headaches, leg aches, or digestive complaints."

Any of this sound familiar? Then *The Impossible Child* might hold some answers for you. The purpose of this book is to show you how to detect if your youngster is experiencing an unsuspected allergic reaction, and what to do if he or she is. The book does not lay the blame for all bad behavior at the feet of allergies. It does, however, point out that some kids get high on some foods, or bummed out by molds and pollens, and that we all have a much harder time functioning properly under such circumstances.

This is not a superficial book, in spite of its easy-reading style. You are given specific facial or body clues to tip you off to a possible allergic reaction—e.g., red earlobes. The book also includes numerous before-and-after examples of children's work and considerable detail about specific allergies and how to spot and treat them.

Is behavior modification therapy the solution to non-allergy-caused behavior problems? Author Doris Rapp says yes. I say no. This fairly major disagreement aside, I think this is a good book. We do owe it to our kids to find out if they suffer when exposed to chemicals, pollen, pets, or dairy products. However, no way can the vast increase in kids' rotten behavior today be blamed on allergies. Allergies may indeed provide extra pressure, but even a splitting migraine does not have the power to force any of us to bite, spit, and swear unless we let it. Allergies can, however, severely hinder the learning process—and mainly for that reason I suggest that if your child sometimes acts "impossible," you should try observing him or her for allergy symptoms as spelled out in this book.

EMOTIONAL HANDICAPS

An awful lot of what passes for "learning disabilities" or (the more technical term) "emotional handicaps" is simply bad behavior. People today don't like to believe in sin, so the poor child is labeled instead of simply being taught that he really *must* behave. His parents are told he is "hyperactive" or that he suffers from "attention disorder deficit" or "emotional handicaps" or even "minimal brain damage" (they mean damage so minimal that no physical examination will ever uncover it). Then, to solve this problem, he is put on drugs or segregated from the other children.

Of course, not all seemingly hyper behavior is sinful. Little boys and tomboys *need* to run around from time to time and make a lot of noise—two needs to which school definitely does not minister, except on the playing field! But if you happen to know any children who leave a trail of broken and scattered possessions (their own and other people's), who ignore adults' commands, who yell and fuss and bite, who wiggle and refuse to pay attention when you are trying to tell them something important, who call other kids names, who lie, cheat, or steal, and in general make life miserable for everyone around them, there's hope for kids like that. These kids don't need Ritalin. They need training in how to be *good,* backed up with encouragement for good behavior and sanctions that say, "I really meant what I said" for bad behavior.

I think most of us know how to encourage good behavior and discourage bad behavior, if we put our minds to it: Be swift and consistent, stern and loving. Easy to say, hard to do! Now that we've mastered that, we need good rules for the kids.

Nine times out of ten, kids with serious behavior problems don't really know *what* the rules are at their house, and neither do their parents. I don't mean that there aren't any rules, just that the rules seem to be constantly changing from day to day as the little rascals discover new ways to create mischief! The problem in this situation is that the parents are reacting to problems as they arise instead of preventing problems by consciously training the kids to become responsible. If this is your situation, the resource below will help tremendously.

NEW**
Christian Life Workshops

21 House Rules Preschooler's Training Kit, Rules for Friends, Uncommon Courtesy for Kids, $10.95 each or $14.95 for set of coloring book, posters, and instructions. *Training Grounds in Child Discipline* video rental $25 plus $50 refundable deposit, video purchase $75, cassette tapes $12.95. Add 10% shipping ($2 minimum, $5 maximum).

A great resource for parents who recognize that academic success starts with self-disciplined children is Gregg Harris's wonderful *21 House Rules Preschooler's Training Kit.* Available from Christian Life Workshops, it provides a framework of totally reasonable rules for behavior that children themselves will agree with! Rules like, "We obey our Lord Jesus Christ . . . We do not hurt one another with unkind words or deeds . . . When someone is sorry, we forgive him . . . When we have work to do, we do it without complaining . . . When we take something out, we put it away." Following these simple rules will eliminate 80 percent of the parent-child strife around your house. Of course, *you will have to obey the rules too!* The kit comes with a reproducible training manual/coloring book that illustrates all 21 rules (some great drawings by Gregg's son Joshua), a laminated (jelly-proof) 21 House Rules Master Sheet to post on your fridge or bulletin board, 21 individual rule posters, and complete instructions. Over 3,000 satisfied families have used it. Very highly recommended.

Rules for Friends is just exactly what every family needs to keep "socialization" from becoming a social disease! Following the same format as CLW's *21 House Rules Preschool Training Kit, Rules for Friends* trains your children how to treat their friends and lets the children's friends know what is expected of them when they visit your home. This one is designed for somewhat older children.

Just out is the brand-new *Uncommon Courtesy for Kids,* co-authored by Gregg and Joshua. This "training manual for everyone" introduces the concept of courtesy to both kid and adult readers, then gives Six Man-

ners of Speech, Four Words to the Wise, Five Rules for Public Transportation, Six Ways to Be Considerate to Adults, Six Table Manners, Phone Manners, How to Take a Phone Message, Seven Rules for Going to Church, Eight Rules for Traveling in the Car, Four Awkward Things That Happen to Everybody, and more! Each set of rules is illustrated with examples of people of all ages following (or not following!) the rules. Parents are also told how to train kids gently in these rules. Knowing what a wicked world this is, Gregg also includes instructions in when *not* to obey or follow adults. You'll get a lot more out of *Uncommon Courtesy* if you get the complete kit, which includes not only the basic coloring book manual but a laminated poster summarizing all the rules and individual "rules" posters, plus instructions in how to use these materials to help your kids actually learn to be courteous. *Very* highly recommended!

Finally, Gregg's *Training Grounds in Child Discipline* workshop is available both in video and audiocassette formats. In 90 minutes you'll learn how to *train* your child to be "faithful in small things" rather than reacting to problems. Extremely highly recommended.

SOCIAL DISABILITIES

Often the worst thing about "learning disabilities," at least as far as those who have them are concerned, is the negative social reaction of other people to LD kids. Little things like hearing them say, "Get lost, retard!" Never being invited to birthday parties. Eating alone in the cafeteria every day. Having no one to play with.

Even gifted children can suffer this same kind of outcast status (minus the "retard" labels). But before anyone manages to turn social disabilities into a booming new industry, here are my thoughts on the matter.

Aside from the peculiar problems faced by kids who just aren't members of the dominant ethnic group (e.g., the only Jew in a class of rednecks, the only Gentile in a class of Jews, a black kid in a white class, a white kid in a black class, etc.) and kids who get picked on because of their physical appearance, there is also the situation of the kid who is an outcast because the group is corrupt in its behavior and he refuses to go along with the slamming of fat kids, drug use, sexual language, or whatever. Kids who are victims of prejudice or outcasts because of their own integrity will always be with us as long as there is sin in the world, and no amount of training can prevent these situations, although an alert school administration can keep them in check. But there are two other possible reasons a kid might be a social outcast:

(1) Ignorance. He simply does not know the social conventions. Since young children have scant sympathy for others in the typical peer-group setting, he is more likely to be ridiculed and left out of things than to find another child who will show him the ropes.

(2) Self-centeredness. He loves himself too much to be sensitive to other people's expectations, and hence never learns the social conventions.

Children who are genuinely slow at learning will often be slow at learning social conventions as well. Children have social conventions more rigid than those of any adult, and when one of their number transgresses the unwritten rules, vengeance follows swiftly. The solution here is for the parents to be sure to teach the child how to behave around other people before they ever let him loose on the world. A simple course in basic courtesy, kindness, and how to say nice things to people in a non-manipulative way is indicated. Plus instruction on the basic rules of decorum for your particular community.

The psychotic personality type, who you may recognize as the kid so full of self-esteem he couldn't care less about anyone else, can't be convinced that he ever is at fault. This type of child will have tremendous problems getting along with anyone until he learns to stop worshiping himself. He might look terribly sad and talk constantly about how other people mistreat him, but he is the cause of most of his own troubles. This child needs a spiritual rebirth—I'm not going to kid you that educational band-aids will solve his problems. Once his own selfish nature has been replaced with the love of Christ, then he can be gently taught to consider others before himself, to not resent slight af-

fronts, and to pay attention to the social cues others give him. I have seen this process work from its beginning to its end, and can testify that the worst social outcast, when born again and instructed from the Bible in righteous social graces, can even become popular and well-loved.

NEW★★
Academic Therapy Publications
No One to Play With, $10 plus $2.50 shipping.

Betty B. Osman's pioneering book *No One to Play With* deals frankly with the problem of the "living disabilities" which affect many children with so-called "learning disabilities." For youngsters who lack confidence both in the classroom and on the playground, life may not be easy in any area.

No One to Play With is excellent on diagnosis, but spotty on cures. Christian parents, for example, may not appreciate the suggestion that LD children "may require far more concrete and graphic presentations [of sex] than many local school boards deem appropriate." I also can't share the author's faith in behavior modification as the cure for all poor behavior. Where this book shines is (1) in its realistic appraisal of a problem too many of us ignore, and (2) in the compelling case histories which, if nothing else, create empathy for the victims of living disabilities. You may recognize your child, or yourself, in the story of Freddy, the withdrawn TV-watcher who avoided other children, or in the saga of Susan, whose own brother and sister called her names at home. Distractible George; Jimmy, who was never included in games; Jeff, whose parents were divorced; ornery Danny, who always "had to" pick fights; and a host of other children pass before your eyes, along with the tale of what the author did to help each of them and why it worked. She also covers the situation of gifted kids with learning disabilities and LD adults.

NEW★★
Christian Life Workshops
21 House Rules Preschooler's Training Kit, Rules for Friends, Uncommon Courtesy for Kids, $10.95 each. Add 10% shipping ($2 minimum).

For kids whose social disabilities come from not understanding the basic social laws, these kits are a lifesaver. See complete review above under "Emotional Handicaps."

ARTS AND CRAFTINESS

One other big reason children get labeled is that schools are not set up to minister to kinesthetic learners. For those of you unfamiliar with learning-styles terminology, "kinesthetic" learners learn best by doing, whereas "visual" learners remember best what they see and "auditory" learners remember best what they hear. Kinesthetic folks make the best piano players, car mechanics, artists, bakers, gardeners, clowns, and rodeo artists, to name just a few categories! They tend to not enjoy sitting still, and would rather be doing something than listening to and watching other people.

Now, even kinesthetic types need to develop concentration. So why not give 'em interesting hands-on projects? And what could be more interesting than arts 'n crafts?

NEW**
S & S Arts & Crafts

There are hundreds of arts 'n crafts suppliers out there, but I'm only going to mention one in this issue. The reason is that S & S Arts & Crafts not only has terrific prices and a huge variety of different materials and kits, but their kits are especially designed for success. Hundreds of senior citizen centers, special ed programs, day camps, and other organizations use S & S kits. Thus, kits are flagged as to age level, and some are rated especially useful for "special needs" clients. (S & S has a special *Healthcare Therapy Masterbook* version of their catalog, if you're interested.)

Most kits come in sets of 12 to 25, which poses no problem for families with several children, since kids enjoy making the same project more than once and you'll have freedom to throw away mistakes. At a price ranging from 10¢ to around $2 per project, a kit with 12 projects might only cost a couple of dollars anyway.

For those who want a bigger challenge, you can simply buy the art foam, mosaic tiles, macrame cord, or whatever other art supply you want at a very attractive price, and then make up your own projects.

S & S sells some kits that are overtly Christian and some New Age unicorns, Halloween vampires and devils, and pagan tribal decorations. The latter are a distinct minority in the catalog, and will probably remain so as long as parents continue to buy the better choices S & S offers.

ARE YOU GAME?

Another way labeled children can *quickly* recover their self-confidence is to prove their abilities in a different arena. This was first pointed out to me in a book, *Deal Me In!: The Use of Playing Cards in Teaching and Learning,* from Jeffrey Norton Publishers. The author, Dr. Margie Golick, contends that playing cards are a high-interest educational tool as well as a means of social entry for children who lack physical prowess or social skill. Some skills she claims card games can develop: rhythm, motor skills, sequencing, sense of direction, visual skills, number concepts, verbal skills, intellectual skills, and social skills. After a lengthy introduction presenting her case for card games, she gets down to cases with more than five dozen games, plus card tricks and logic games. Every card game is summarized, learning skills enhanced by the game are summarized, and then you get the rules: rank of cards, basic overview of the game, bidding (if appropriate), object of the game, rules of play and scoring, comments, and necessary vocabulary for play.

The book includes several indexes to help you find the game you want, and some psychotherapeutic moralizing by the author. She approves of gambling and swearing, and of course some parents disapprove of card games entirely. However, whether or not you decide to get this particular book, Dr. Golick is absolutely right that success in games is not only potentially educational, but a potent means of reviving a child's confidence in learning new things. In fact, labeled kids *often* are better at games than their straight-A compatriots! Hank the Hunk might be great at football, though not at math; Wendell the Weedy might be a slow starter at reading, but beat the socks off everyone else at marbles.

That in mind, you might also want to turn to the Best Basic Toys chapter and check out some of the kids' games listed there.

ORGANIZATIONS THAT OFFER HELP FOR LABELED KIDS

Citizens Commission on Human Rights
Free brochures: *How Psychiatry Is Making Drug Addicts out of America's School Children* and *Ritalin: A Warning for Parents.*

The special education label can become a self-ful-filling prophecy, not only because of how it under-mines a child's scholastic confidence but because of the dangerous misuse of drugs on labeled children. CCHR's pamphlet *How Psychiatry Is Making Drug Addicts out of America's School Children* explains why and how healthy children with no organic disorders are unreasonably labeled and put on drugs, and how this sometimes leading to real brain damage or irreversible handicaps.

CCHR's follow-up pamphlet, *Ritalin: A Warning for Parents*, lists 15 little-publicized but important possible side effects of Ritalin use and withdrawal. It also briefly discusses Thorazine, the "chemical lobotomy."

"If a teacher, psychologist, psychiatrist or a school employee is trying to force your child or a child of a friend or relative into 'therapy,' CCHR may be able to help," says their brochure. CCHR has chapters in most major American cities and in Mexico, U.K., Canada, Austria, Holland, Norway, Sweden, Denmark, Switzer-land, France, Germany, Italy, Australia, and South Africa.

The Orton Dyslexia Society

If your son does cute little things like write *Z* backwards and read *saw* for *was*, and if you are teach-ing him at home, just ignore it. If, however, he is en-rolled in school and the pressure is on to *do* something because for heaven's sake this child is *dyslexic*, don't panic. Get in touch with these folks.

True dyslexia is just a different way of processing information and doesn't need to be "cured." Dyslexics are often geniuses who only need the right teaching method to turn them loose on the world. Dr. Samuel Torrey Orton did pioneering work in developing these methods, and the society carries on his work.

It's very likely that your little one is not dyslexic at all, but just learning and making normal mistakes. Most so-called dyslexia is actually the fallout from teaching the look-say method of reading in which children are required to memorize the shapes of ev-ery word in the language. This type of "dyslexia" can

be instantly cured by a good phonics program, of which there are two dozen in the Reading section of Volume 2.

In 1975 the Michigan Reading Clinic examined over 30,000 allegedly dyslexic children. Of all the 30,000 only *two* children were found to be unable to learn to read.

Since the Orton Dyslexia society uses multisenso-ry, intensive phonics, which works equally well with dyslexics and nondyslexics, it can't hurt to send for a list of their materials.

MATERIALS THAT COULD HELP

UPDATED★★
Academic Therapy Publications
Free *Directory of Facilities and Services for the Learning Disabled*, send $3 per copy to cover postage and handling and ask for order #0092-3256. *Helpmates*, order #628-2, $7.50

Academic Therapy Publications' motto is "special materials for special needs in today's education." They have combined their previous brochure line into a new book, *Helpmates. Helpmates* includes: *Helping Your Child at Home with Reading, Helping Your Child at Home with Arithmetic, Helping Your Child at Home with Spelling,* and *Helping Your Child at Home with Handwrit-ing,* plus new material of the sort commonly dispensed to classroom teachers on television, sibling rivalry, a sex ed reading list (ugh!), and a substance abuse read-ing list (double ugh!). The old brochures told parents the most common reasons a child might have a prob-lem with the subject in question, and gave dozens and dozens of really practical tips for reinforcing these sub-jects in a fun way using things found in every home. The new book has updated these topics so that they apply to both "learning disabled" and other children.

Also from Academic Therapy Publications is their free *Directory of Facilities and Services for the Learning Disabled* (well, *almost* free; you have to enclose $3 per copy for postage and handling). The *Directory* is now in its thirteenth edition and contains scads of useful information about facilities serving these children: size of staff, services offered, types of problems handled, ages served, fee type, and year established, all listed by state for convenience. The body of the *Directory* is state-by-state listings of more than 500 facilities and services for these children. If you are not terribly excited about the services of experts, the *Directory* also includes a comprehensive listing of companies offering specialized materials for labeled children and their teachers, national organizations and agencies serving this community, educational journals, college guide for LD students, and more. An alphabetical index and index by service provided finish off the book, which closes with an area code map so parents can easily call any interesting references.

Academic Therapy Publications has recently acquired Ann Arbor Publishers, a producer of visual-tracking workbooks. Many of the workbooks are reusable, using a specially patented pen and processed paper, so the student's writing disappears after a week or so.

Lastly, Academic Therapy Publications is the publisher of High Noon Books, a line of more than 100 high interest/low reading level novels. Intended to tempt the older slow reader, these paperback books are designed to look "adult." The plots are grown-up but also clean and wholesome, unlike so much modern reading material for children. Do "modern kids" still like to read this sort of book? Well, *I* had to read the sample books Academic Therapy sent in brief snatches since my sons kept disappearing with them when I wasn't looking!

Educators Publishing Service

Parents' Packet, $6. Language Tool Kit, $21. Teaching Box, $92; accompanying storybooks, $14.50. *A Guide to Teaching Phonics*, Orton Phonics Cards, $8 each. *Reading, Writing and Speech Problems*, $5. Lots more. Free shipping on prepaid orders. Special Language and Learning Disabilities catalog available.

Educators Publishing Service has a nice little brochure offering "Home Use Materials for Students with Learning Difficulties." EPS carries a number of Orton books and packets, plus Orton Phonics Cards and Orton-Gillingham Language Kits. You can also get reference books on learning problems, including Dr. Orton's classic *Reading, Writing and Speech Problems in Children*.

The *Parents' Packet* of articles from the Orton Dyslexia Society Reprint Series tell what dyslexia is, how to diagnose it, and how to remedy it using the Orton-Gillingham method. The booklet ends on an uplifting note, profiling eminent achievers who have had dyslexia.

Language Tool Kit of 119 cards and a teacher's manual can be used by a parent for teaching reading and spelling to a student with a "specific language disability." The *Teaching Box* is a very highly structured, step by step program for children with severe learning difficulties. You get 69 groups of 3 x 5" cards, separated by dividers. Two accompanying books explain how to use and supplement the cards, and explain dyslexia. One pack of phonogram cards is enclosed, and you can buy a set of 14 storybooks to accompany the program.

There's lots, lots more that I have no room to describe. Hey, why don't you send for the brochure?

CHAPTER TWENTY-FIVE

HELPING YOUR SPECIAL CHILD AT HOME

At school, "Special Education" is a euphemism for classes for students labeled slow or learning disabled. In most cases there is nothing "special" about it, except getting specially teased by all the kids who aren't labeled "special"!

At home, Special Education becomes truly special. For the first time, the labeled child gets a chance to show he or she *can* achieve. Parents tend to be remarkably unwilling to accept dogmatic limitations on their children's future. We keep plugging away and hoping for the best, unlike the "experts" whose little charts tell them Johnny will only be able to achieve this far and no farther. Like all sincere amateurs, parents have a stake in discovering a better method, and the hope to believe it might be out there somewhere. Another way to put this is that parents believe in miracles. Smart of us: miracles still happen, you know!

SPECIAL KIDS BELONG AT HOME

Let's now assume that there is solid medical evidence that something is wrong with your child's brain and/or body. What then?

Popular prejudice to the contrary, these are the very children who need most to be taught at home. Very few professional therapy programs provide hours of individualized therapy every day, and those that do are prohibitively expensive. In the family, on the other hand, a special child can receive hours of instruction and help *without* being made to feel abnormal.

The materials you will want to use depend on your child's special problems. Look in the School Supplies chapter in Volume 1 and the Preschool sections of Volume 2 and you will find loads of colorful, noisy, hands-on, grabbable learning devices. Many materials designed for early childhood education work well with special children. Make it as much fun as you can for yourself—pick stuff you would enjoy playing with too! If you are able to take your time and let your child learn at his own pace, this takes off a lot of pressure.

Our first son was born premature and had to spend five weeks in intensive care. Ted was very slow in his physical and muscular development as well. On first diagnosis, one nationally known neurologist predicted that Ted most likely had the fatal disease of spinal muscular atrophy, and if not that, he at least would be handicapped for life. We called in the elders of our church and had them anoint Ted with oil in the name of the Lord. Ted did *not* have spinal muscular atrophy, as it turned out, and neither is he a cripple. Nor is he mentally retarded, another pleasant prospect that was held out to us.

When the experts were busy trying to discourage us about Teddy's chances, my reaction was, "Even if they are right, I bet he *still* can succeed!" Today's "normal" kids are busy retarding themselves, lolling around in front of the TV set and wasting their lives trying to impress their peers. A "retarded" child who worked hard at his studies should be able to beat a "normal" kid who never puts forth any effort. Ditto a "handicapped" child who exercises vs. a "normal" kid who lounges around all day. In fact, when a "handicapped" child really works hard, sometimes he or she even beats the "normal" kids who are trying!

They said little Wilma Rudolph would never walk again, but Wilma's mother was determined enough to spend her one weekly day off sitting for hours on the bus, taking Wilma to get therapy. Wilma walked. Then Wilma ran. Then Wilma won the Olympics.

FOR KIDS WITH REAL SPECIAL NEEDS

NEW★★
The Attainment Company

Debra Evans, the author of several Crossway books on womanhood and mothering, sent me a very nice catalog called Options. It's "an exclusive selection of gifts for people with special needs," published by the Attainment Company. On the cover is an attractive picture of a young woman with Down's Syndrome sitting by a basket of apples. Inside are all sorts of products designed to help mentally-handicapped teens and adults gain independence in their shopping, cooking, eating out, grooming, housekeeping, and so on. Many of these products are also good for people who have trouble, for whatever reason, with communicating intelligibly. The catalog is uniformly respectful of the abilities and needs of those who can benefit from its products, and is targeted at their families and friends.

NEW★★
Betterway Publications
The First Whole Rehab Catalog, $16.95.

Thousands of sources for adaptive equipment and specialized supplies and services for people with physical, vision, or intellectual limitations. The book describes and illustrates systems and devices that can simplify the basic tasks of daily living, make house-hold chores easier, increase your mobility, make it easier to communicate, help in your job, and enhance your recreational opportunities. Major categories include Daily Living, Personal Care, Access, Communication, Mobility, Transportation, Health and Fitness, Recreation, Education and Vocation, Catalogs, and Publications and Media. More than 250 black and white photographs. Lots of appendices: support groups, independent living centers, legal resources, accessible travel, and sports opportunities.

NEW★★
C.H.I.C.K.S.

I recently received a press release announcing "the formation of a national group dedicated to the belief that homeschooling is for every child." Named C.H.I.C.K.S., which stands for "Christian Homeschoolers Instructing Challenged Kids for His Service," this new group hopes to provide

1) A network of Christian educators who feel a desire to include their "special" kids in their homeschooling programs.

2) Books and magazines that might prove useful.

3) Programs that will welcome and accommodate themselves to our children. (YMCA, libraries, sports programs, etc.)

4) For those who desire to be included, a listing of families describing their children and the types of disabilities that they are trying to accommodate. Other families with similar problems will be able to correspond to inform and encourage.

5) Access with professionals who are willing to help us in our desires to see that our children are well-educated and that we are informed of all that is available to help us in promoting their further development.

6) Knowledge that there are others that you can pray with, talk to, and work together with at the times when you question your decision (or your sanity, *or both*).

7) Conventions or seminars to help us continue to grow and learn.

C.H.I.C.K.S. is "still in the planning stages," so now is the time to write and express support or interest, if you are so inclined.

NEW**
Dale Seymour Publications
The Special Artist's Handbook: Art Activities and Adaptive Aids for Handicapped Students, $18.95.

Every now and then you come across a resource so well done, and so obviously needed, that you wonder why nobody ever came up with something like it before. *The Special Artist's Handbook* is one such resource. In this oversized quality paperback, author Susan Rodriguez provides:

• A section on handicaps that explains myths, prejudices, and misconceptions; characteristics of exceptionalities and how to respond to each of them in the art classroom; and a sign language guide covering the most-needed words for art instruction. Exceptionalities covered are mental retardation, socially and emotionally disturbed, learning disabled, physically handicapped, sensory losses, and gifted.

• An A-Z section of craft activities. from Apples and Oranges (working with clay) to You're a Doll! (making a paper doll that has your features). Not only are these activities exceptionally clever and well-designed for teaching special students lessons other than crafts (e.g., the I Can See Right Through You! craft based on X-rays of human anatomy), but each activity comes with adaptations spelled out for each exceptionality, in which the author explains what to do to make the activity more accessible or educational for each special-needs group. The activities themselves are described quite clearly, starting with a list of materials, teacher preparation necessary, basic direc-

tions, suggestions for further development, and photographs of final products produced by some of the author's special-ed students.

• The section on adaptive aids and materials is a Godsend for parents and teachers of special-needs children. Here you'll find easy-to-implement, clever ideas for overcoming difficulties. Does your child have trouble holding narrow objects? Try pushing a foam hair curler over pencils and brushes. No arm movement? Try tucking brushes into a headband and painting with head movements! Also included: aids to organization (especially needed by some students), resources that help in sewing and cutting, and adaptive aids for visually handicapped and blind students, and a recipe file of materials that appeal to the senses of smell, touch, or sight.

• Section 4, "The Art Classroom," explains how to set up your art area for safety and maximum educative potential and encourages visits to art museums.

• The whole book is topped off with a glossary of special-education terms and (very helpful) a general index to the entire book.

The layout of this book couldn't be any easier to use. Everything is just where you need it, with no need to flip back and forth. Any parent or teacher of a special-needs child can really benefit from the information, activities, and ideas tucked between the covers. Highly recommended.

NEW**
Hear An' Tell
Cassettes, $7.95 each. Flash Cards, $4.95 each. Game Boards, $6.95 each. Teaching manual $4.50. Little Lamb woolly puppet, $9.95. Illustrated storybooks, $3.95.

Goldilocks, Little Lamb, and *Cinderella*, three language-learning and activity kits, now come in all-English formats, especially for use by special-needs children. Hear an' Tell founder Patricia Al-Attas, a speech pathologist by training, says, "These English kits have been well received by teachers in special education. . . . I have even had people with 'special needs' children track me down, literally showing up on my doorstep." What's all the hubbub? Try looking at the Hear an' Tell listing in Chapter 9.

Rifton: Equipment for the Handicapped

As I said, school supply houses and firms that cater to preschoolers are good places to start, especially those that carry Montessori materials. For physical therapy, Rifton Equipment for the Handicapped has the stuff. Exercise chairs, bolsters, wedges, play equipment, and so on—it's all here. Prices are acceptable for the quality, and it's possible that insurance may pay for some of it if you get a doctor's prescription. We've used similar equipment of our own manufacture, and it did Ted a lot of good.

LEARN TO READ REGARDLESS OF I.Q.

Ball-Stick-Bird
Two sets: books 1–5 and books 6–10, each set $74.95; includes Instructor's Manual. Add $3 shipping.

Ball-Stick-Bird, a phonics program invented by research psychologist Dr. Renee Fuller, differs tremendously from every other phonics system. For one thing, it was designed to teach certified, institutionalized retardates to read (people with an IQ of 60 or less). For another thing, it worked. No other phonics program, not one, has ever made its debut under such difficult circumstances.

Dr. Fuller's approach is sufficiently unorthodox. Instead of "Sam sat on a fat cat"-style primers, her readers start off at a rated fourth-grade level. The reason is that she is playing to a student's need for stories that make sense. Similarly, she introduces the capital letters first, since they can *all* be constructed from a "ball" (circle or portion thereof), "stick" (straight line), and "bird"(v-shaped slanted lines). Color-coding these basic forms to make the difference between the strokes even more dramatic, beginning with capital letters presented in a carefully planned sequence, and requiring the student to "build" each letter out of its forms (thus involving all four sense modalities) Ball-Stick-Bird goes out of its way to make basic phonics mastery painless.

But—and here comes the rub—other phonics programs also feature simplified approaches to reading.

Yet nobody dares take them inside institutions for the mentally handicapped and expect success.

Ball-Stick-Bird gets its punch from, of all things, a really different story approach. Dressed up in the cutting-edge formula of a science-fiction story, Dr. Fuller presents some heavy-duty moral applications. Her Good Guys and Bad Guys star in fables about human nature: the lust for power, the foolishness of sloganeering, how experts use their authority to stifle criticism of their actions, and so on.

It is easy to see why "labeled" people—like the "mentally retarded" and "special education" children—lap up these stories. Dr. Fuller tells it like it is. She literally gives them the words that explain their experience as the powerless victims of "experts."

I should mention that Ball-Stick-Bird can be used with any person or child mentally old enough to follow a story. Dr. Fuller's contention is that Story Readiness, not some mystical amount of Motor Skill Readiness, is the real preparation for reading, and that successful reading itself grows out of the basic human desire to understand one's own life as a story.

Dr. Fuller says that IQ tests fail to measure "our human ability of story creation—perhaps our greatest abstract ability." In other words, people of *whatever* I.Q. level *all* understand and need stories.

Now, I don't know what you will think of Dr. Fuller's theories, so just let me tell you what they do in practice. At first her Ball-Stick-Bird curriculum was meant for bright dyslexic students, like Dr. Fuller herself. (She had taught herself to read with the *Oz* books of L. Frank Baum, and had personal experience of the power of a good story in creating enough motivation for a student with learning difficulties.) However, soon members of her staff of psychological services at Rosewood Hospital Center, Maryland's main institution for the retarded, began begging her to try the series out with severely retarded students. When Dr. Fuller finally made the experiment, in the words of *The Journal of Developmental Education,* "the results defied all conventional wisdom; students with IQs in the 30s, and sometimes lower, were learning to read and write." Along with their newfound literacy, these students were also blossoming in other areas, gaining for the first time the self-confidence to attempt independence.

Dr. Fuller couldn't believe this, so she began a series of studies. The amazing result of her studies was that, again in the words of *The Journal of Developmental Education,* "there was no significant correlation between IQ and the ability to learn to read with comprehension." Did you catch that? *No* significant correlation between IQ and the ability to become literate.

The point here is that human beings are not animals who need "training" (in the sense that dogs are "trained" to jump through a hoop) so much as beings created in the image of God who are *born* able to reason and understand stories. Thus, your labeled child does not need Pavlovian conditioning; he needs to be treated like a reasoning being. That is what Dr. Fuller, with her science-fiction readers featuring classic conflicts between statist "bad guys" and freedom-loving "good guys," has done. These are not trivial stories; they have levels of meaning an adult can enjoy—especially a retarded adult who has been treated like a dependent child for years. Not that you need to be retarded or over 13 to use these books. A four-year-old who manifests "story readiness" (e.g., the ability to sit and enjoy a story from start to finish) can learn to read from them.

From a Christian perspective, this makes great sense. If the spirit of a man is truly independent of his physical brain, there is no reason why any human being, however "mentally deficient," should not be reachable through the basically spiritual medium of stories—especially stories that help him make sense of his own life. Like, for example, the original, unbowdlerized Bible stories. Let's start thinking about it . . .

NEW**
Educators Publishing Service, Inc.
Reading: The Right Start, $8.50 postpaid.

If you are willing to take the time to cut out magazines for pictures of objects whose names start with m or b; if you are able to take the time to make dotted letters for your children to trace; if you'd like to hunt for objects to place on a tray so your child can figure out which one you remove; then you really only need this book, and you've got yourself a complete readiness and phonics course for $8.50 (plus the cost of a bottle or two of Elmer's Glue).

Mrs. Gould, a reading consultant in New York City for 35 years, has put together a book that is one part educational philosophy, one part a "How-To" section on how to teach reading and reading readiness with games and activities, and part an introduction to her Structured Reading Program (not available, unfortunately, from EPS).

For children with learning problems, Mrs. Gould's approach is one of he best. She starts with the problem areas: audio perception, visual perception, memory, concentration, and eye-hand coordination. Based on her years of experience in tutoring children with these problems, and flavored with anecdotes from those tutoring sessions, she lays out before you a step-by-step sequence for making sure children are able to follow the directions and instructions they get in a reading program. These kids are often hard to deal with, but Mrs. Gould gets around that by making games out of the exercises they need to perform. She follows this up with her Structural Reading Program approach, in which the *structure* of the English language is made clear by step-by-step phonics and by strictly limiting the vocabulary read to only words that follow the structure. Again, this may not be necessary with average kids, but can make all the difference in the world to kids with reading difficulties.

Regardless of whether you decide to use the Structured Reading approach or not, you will find this book interesting. Mrs. Gould is strongly against teaching the alphabet letter names to young children, believing that children only gain insight into the structure of English through knowing the sounds of the letters. She also passionately pleads for teaching children to read *before* they start school. Her argument is that "natural readers" will tend to teach themselves some mistakes that could cause problems later, and slow children need the extra early intervention to keep them from failing in first grade and consequently giving up on learning. She undermines her point somewhat by calling for schools to provide this early intervention, since as her own examples point out, it is the experience of being compared to other children in school that causes slower children to feel inferior. Otherwise, her discussion of why in her estimation there is a "critical period" for learning to read provides much food for thought, especially for followers of the better-late-than-early and un-schooling philosophies.

I wonder if EPS could be persuaded to carry the Structured Reading materials that go along with this book: the Learn-to-Read books, Early Reading Activities kits (so you don't have to spend your family vacation putting together readiness games), and pupil and teacher books. It would be handy to have all of them in one place.

TEACHING KIDS ABOUT HANDICAPS

NEW★★
The Learning Works
We All Come in Different Packages, $8.95. Shipping extra.

Information and activities to increase sensitivity to people with handicaps. Covers communicative, physical, mental, and learning handicaps—I mean *everything*, from epilepsy and dwarfism to aphasia. The book itself was actually illustrated by a dwarf, but no big deal is made of this, other than a casual mention in the chapter on "Little People."

This is a teacher's book with some reproducible worksheets bound in. The book explains each of the handicaps and dispels myths. Children are encouraged through simple activities to put themselves in the shoes of those with handicaps. Quite a lot of learning opportunities here: sign language, Braille, how to deal with an epileptic seizure, and so on, along with consciousness-raising activities like trying to construct a puppet with one hand in your lap. You wouldn't want to do every single thing in this book at home, but it is a very good, complete, involving, and caring resource.

Missionary Vision for Special Ministries
Free literature and programs for your group, church, school, neighborhood, or home. Donations welcome.

What does it feel like to be blind . . . or crippled . . . or different-looking? How should you treat someone who is physically different? With games, activities, and songs, blind Christian missionary Ruth Shuman shares ways to break down the walls between "handicapped" and "normal" people.

Materials available from this ministry include: Blindfold Experiments, Children's Book List of recommended reading about handicaps, Teasing Really Hurts, Put Yourself in Their Place, Yes or No — How Would You Respond? and Toppling Stereotypes About the Handicapped. MVSM's materials provide a realistic picture of handicapped life and give guidelines for conducting positive relationships.

PROGRAMS THAT MIGHT HELP

National Academy of Child Development
Miracles of Child Development, 6-hour cassette program with note outline, developmental profile, and data reporting forms for home use, $50. *Learning Disabilities: What Do the Labels Really Mean?*, 2-tape set, $18. More tapes and books available.

Founded by Robert Doman, a nephew of the Glenn Doman who runs the Institute for Achievement of Human Potential and who wrote those books on teaching look-say reading to your baby, NACD specializes in home therapy programs for the really hard cases. Children who have suffered severe brain damage, or who have neurological problems, or fits, or physical handicaps, are thoroughly diagnosed by NACD's staff and then presented with a home program tailor-made for them. NACD is expensive (hundreds of dollars a year per child) and many of their methods are severely criticized by the medical establishment. They do have some spectacular success stories, however, and their philosophy of optimism at least keeps them trying to achieve results, whereas medical experts seem to be getting more and more pessimistic these days. We were members of NACD for a while, and Ted just loved his program (all except the knee bends).

NACD programs are a lot of work for the parents and are highly patterned. You do exercise A for two minutes three times a day, and listen to tape B for three minutes twice a week, etc. NACD is also into the "dominance" theory of brain organization, whereby the goal is to be right-handed, right-footed, right-eyed, and right-eared, or conversely left-handed, -footed, -eyed, and -eared. Thus your child may end up wearing an eye patch or ear plug to assist him in "switching over" from right to left, or vice versa. NACD also believes strongly in the stages of development, and enrolled teenagers and even adults sometimes wind up crawling around like babies until they improve their coordination in that stage.

You can order NACD's introductory tape set, *The Miracles of Child Development*, for $50. The tapes are fascinating and inspirational, but take them with a grain of salt. B-mod is not the answer for all childhood discipline problems as Mr. Doman believes, though his suggestions for motivating children, and especially his stress on praise and encouragement, are well worth hearing.

Learning Disabilities: What Do the Labels Really Mean? challenges parents not to rest until they find out what is *really* wrong with their children. Mr. Doman explores some common sources of children's problems (hearing/sight problems, memory problems, neurological imbalance and so on) and offers practical suggestions for unearthing and remedying these problems.

I really appreciate NACD's philosophy that labeling counts for nothing; it's solving the problem that counts. This is also the only remedial organization I know with the optimism to strive for bringing handicapped and labeled children up to or beyond *normal* (not handicapped) functional levels.

UPDATED★★
Blue Bird Publishing
Home Education Resource Guide, $12.95 postpaid.

The *Home Education Resource Guide* lists dozens of organizations that serve the handicapped and their families, plus listing magazines, recreation opportunities, and educational resources especially designed for those with physical impairments. Plus the *Guide* lists hundreds of specialized resources for researchers and home-school leaders, many of which are not included in my book because of their limited audience. If your child has been labeled, or has an actual handicap, the *Guide* can help you find people who can help. New edition was revised in 1989.

SPECIAL TRAVEL OPPORTUNITIES

NEW★★
New Horizons, Inc.

Reader MaryLou Sandretto sent me the catalog of this non-profit agency that specializes in the travel, vacation, and recreational needs of the handicapped community. They serve people with cerebral palsy, muscular dystrophy, developmental disabilities (Down's and other forms of retardation), and blindness, among others. The agency provides all travel, including trips to attractions, and restaurants included in the program, rooms for the duration of the stay, admission and ride coupons to all attractions, and professional staff. They do not provide special services, nurses, or therapists, except as prearranged. Clients must provide their own medication in individual packets marked by day and time for dose. Staff will observe the taking of the medication, but by law the client must take it himself. Client to staff ratio is 3:1.

Wheelchair clients are welcome, and clients with ambulatory difficulties will have a staff person with them if their pace is much slower than that of the rest of the group. Non-verbal clients "can be accommodated easily, especially if they have Modified American Sign Language skills," but also even if they don't. Disruptive clients will be sent home, but only after consulting with the home program and as a last resort.

Outings in the past have included

- Cape Cod vacations (whale-watching, shopping, swimming, dune buggy rides, barbecue, croquet, Jarts, kick-ball, and rainy-day crafts and hobbies)

- A week in Bermuda (tours and shopping, swimming, dancing, movies, lots more)

- A week in London (medieval feast, dancing, eating out, shopping, tours)

- Washington, D.C. and Hershey, Pennsylvania (tours, Space Museum, National Zoo, chocolate factory tour)

- Southern California (Hollywood, Knott's Berry Farm, Universal Studios, Disneyland, San Diego Zoo)

- Cruise to Nova Scotia

- Vermont Mini-vacation

- Nashville and Memphis (Elvis tour, Opryland, riverboat jazz, etc.)

- San Francisco

- Hawaii

- and more!

Perhaps the most useful program is their "Old-Fashioned Christmas at a New England Country Inn," designed to "provide a warm and loving old-fashioned Christmas for those of us who are without families to go to." This includes a traditional Christmas complete with munch-out Christmas dinner, sleigh or hay ride, Christmas carols, and Christmas gifts individually chosen for the client by staff members.

Prices are very low for all these amenities, but reservations are first come, first served, so if this kind of vacation sounds like a good idea for you or someone you know, send away for the brochure and sign up early.

CHAPTER TWENTY-SIX

HELPING YOUR GIFTED CHILD AT HOME

Here it is, straight up: I don't believe in Gifted and Talented programs. That doesn't mean, however, that I don't believe in gifted and talented *kids*. After all, my own children are gifted and talented! And so are the children of all my friends! And so is just about every child I have ever met!

The question is, "Gifted and talented at *what?*" Here we immediately have a problem. In the old days the answer was simple. Fast readers and math whizzes were gifted. So were kids who could memorize lots of facts. Those students got "tracked" into more advanced classes, where they studied traditional material at a higher level. Fast-track kids might be studying trigonometry while slow-track kids wrestled with fractions. Both tracks were aimed at the same material—the slower kids just took longer to get there, that's all. And most of us realized that God handed out other gifts besides the ability to memorize Shakespeare at supersonic speed.

WHAT IS GIFTEDNESS?

Giftedness, insofar as it means anything at all, is really *intellectual focusedness*. The truly gifted child is not necessarily brighter, just more determined to think things through. When other kids might choose a pick-up game of baseball, he prefers to arrange his butterfly collection in correct taxonomical order. While every-one else is admiring the band parade, she is thinking up a new kind of music. He or she is experiencing what we used to call a *calling*.

The nagging creative inspiration is a spiritual gift—whether from God or elsewhere. Both great men and wicked men have found themselves driven by a focused inner compulsion. Giftedness, then, may imply spiritual sensitivity more than mental acuity.

Is it just a coincidence that school G&T programs focus so heavily on occult and pagan themes? *Dungeons and Dragons* units are common, as are activities in which children role-play pagan worship. I worry about this. Surely spiritually sensitive children are the *last* ones who should be exposed to occult influences.

GIFTEDNESS AT HOME

If giftedness really is focusedness, then *any* child turned on to learning is gifted. And where better to encourage this enthusiasm than at home? You can enrich your enthusiastic child's education with safety at home, using the same materials the best G&T programs use, or substituting others of your choice. In this way you can ensure that creative thinking doesn't become an exercise in lack of compassion (Christians know you can pray instead of picking people to throw out of hypothetical lifeboats) and that training in political strategies does not evolve into training in challenging one's parents.

You can also avoid the heady arrogance of having your child labeled "gifted," which is just the counterpoint to the pain felt by the child labeled "slow." One can't be Lord of the Roost unless one has lesser beings to lord it over. One can, however, be as excited about learning as one pleases without putting anyone else down. There is enough room in the world for all of us, and enough worthy tasks for us all to work on.

Enthusiasm for learning was never meant to be the province of an elite. Though your child may not be considered "gifted and talented" by the school district, he is gifted and he is talented. His natural enthusiasm may have been blunted by passive entertainment and peer dependency, but if you throw a tablecloth over the TV and liberate him at least temporarily from the clutches of his peers, his creativity and intelligence will amaze you.

MAGAZINES

UPDATED**
Challenge
One year (5 issues, August through April), $20. Single issue, $4.50.

Nicest-looking, easiest to use magazine for teachers of gifted kids. Issue layout is clean, inviting, and enhanced with clip art. Articles are intelligently designed, with goals, objectives, resources, and so on easily locatable.

Challenge has been updated to include more material for parents and kids. Most activities and units can easily be used at home. This is a change from the past, when the editorial content was directed squarely at the classroom teacher.

Each issue contains many teaching units, activities, and teaching tips. Examples: "Native Americans, An Integrated Arts Approach," "Can You Solve a Mystery?" and "The Great Pizza Project." Lots of fun activities for kids are also included. These are usually of the puzzle and brainteaser variety, in big bold print with lots of graphics.

Challenge has the same outlook as classroom G&T programs. In past years, a disproportionate amount of energy went into articles asking children to role-play pagan worship, just like they do in public-school classrooms all over America. In just one issue, for example, the Native Americans unit required children to "create and perform a chant appropriate for a Native American corn ceremony." The Mythology unit suggested children could "design a temple for a god/goddess and construct a model." The article "A Celebration of Life," a report on a death ed unit given to public-school eighth-graders, displayed a large Yin/Yang symbol at the top of the page. This (probably unconscious) New Age emphasis was repeated to some extent in all issues I saw. Syncretism (affirming all religions as equally valid) appeared consistently in articles and activities that touched on religion. The editor tells me that syncretism won't be an emphasis in future issues, but I'm adapting a "wait and see" attitude.

Challenge is a published by Good Apple, the producers of an array of magazines for teachers, including *Shining Star*, a magazine for Christians.

Creative Kids
New reader subscription price, $17.97 (8 issues, October through May). Sample copy, $3. Canadians and foreign subscribers, add $6/year for postage; pay through U.S. banks or by postal money order.

Magazine by and for "creative students." They are safe in this standard, as dullards by definition do not send in articles for publication. Loaded with all sorts of activities, art, poetry, puzzles, mazes, reviews, and so on, *Creative Kids* is edited by adults, but entirely kid-written. Activities may be reproduced for classroom use.

UPDATED✶✶
The Gifted Child Today (GCT)

New reader subscription price, $23.97. Sample issue, $5. Canadians and foreign subscribers, add $6 per year for postage and pay through U.S. banks or by international money order.

The Gifted Child Today is "The World's Most Popular Magazine for Parents and Teachers of Gifted, Creative, and Talented Children." *GCT* contains practical advice, home and school activities, special columns about computers and so on, reviews of books and resources for "gifted" kids, a calendar of meetings about same, an annual directory of summer camps and programs for same, interviews with "experts," and on and on.

The layout is a cross between that of a professional journal and a regular magazine: lots and lots of smallish type, but also quite a few graphics. This may suit *GCT*'s more scholarly approach, which is less geared to providing step-by-step classroom units and more directed to the "Why?" and "How?" of educational philosophy.

The company also has its own mail-order bookstore of games 'n stuff for "gifted" kids and their parents. See the Brainstretchers section of this chapter for more details.

NEW✶✶
Highlights for Children

Don't forget good ol' *Highlights* when you're thinking about magazines for gifted elementary-aged kids. Just because they don't wave a hat around and announce that their readers are especially gifted, it doesn't mean that *Highlights* articles and their kid-contributed pieces aren't just as good as those launched with a lot more hype.

What about gifted teens? My guess is that truly gifted older children read *adult* magazines and can do very well without all this "gifted" hype.

Prism

One year, 6 issues, $19.95. Sample copy, $4. U.S. funds only.

Billed as "a nationwide network of communication for the gifted and talented," *Prism* is a forum for gifted kids in grades 7 through 12. The editors hope that by connecting these kids together, some kind of synergy will produce cultural revolution. *Prism* is currently distributed to public-school districts and private schools in the USA.

Prism has garnered compliments from Carl Sagan, astronomer Frank D. Drake, Florida Governor Bob Graham, and Phyllis Diller.

The stories, poems, and articles submitted by these "gifted" children often express a spirit of loneliness. "Why does everyone treat me like a nerd? Why do all the girls ignore smart kids and like big stupid jocks? Why doesn't anyone understand me?" To combat this feeling of isolation, *Prism* functions like a mail-order support group, with an extensive Pen Pal section in every issue and editorials on how to handle giftedness.

BRAINSTRETCHERS

EDC Publishing

Most Usborne oversized paperback books cost between $2.95 and $6.95. Hardbound versions run from $6.95 on up. Library bindings available for some volumes. *Picture Puzzles, Brain Puzzles, Number Puzzles*, $3.95 each.

Every book in EDC's Usborne line is suitable for gifted ed. Stimulating and colorful, Usborne Books sparkle with enthusiasm for learning. The line includes a Young Engineer series (three volumes), Technology series (five volumes), Computers series (12 volumes), Electronic World (three volumes), Explainers series (15 volumes), scads of science and math entertainment, natural history by the bushel, the Time Traveller history series (four volumes), and too much more to mention. Just get the catalog.

The Usborne Brainbenders series is three full-color puzzle books for kids aged eight and up—or so they say. Our seven- and six-year-olds like them. Brainteasers of all sorts abound in these high-quality, inexpensive paperbacks. According to *Games and Puzzles* magazine, the series is "This year's perfect present."

UPDATED**
Educational Insights
BrainBoosters,™ $5.95 each. Decoder (works with all BrainBoosters), $1.50.

You've never seen anything like this before. Educational Insights' BrainBoosters™ line is six colorful, spiral-bound 32-page books jam-packed with brain-stretching activities. The ad says, "Eye-popping two-page spreads brim with information, extension activities, and ten topic-related questions." The ad has it straight. The books are gorgeous.

But eye-appeal is not the biggest deal here. Brain-Boosters™ comes with an amazing self-checking apparatus called the Decoder. Kids twiddle each of the ten dials to a circle, triangle, or square in order to answer the ten questions on the left-hand page. The right-hand page has clues in case you had trouble answering the questions, and also a panel of seemingly random circles, triangles, and squares. Place your Decoder over the panel and the correct answers appear in the Decoder's little see-through boxes.

Most books in this series—*Amazing Animals, Inventions and Discoveries, Digging into the Past, Worldwide Wonders, Outer Space Adventures, Prehistoric Life, Culture Trek, Exploring America, Underseas Adventures*—concentrate on teaching children facts in an interesting way. The brainstretching here comes from following clever clues to find answers. *Puzzles and Thinking Games* takes the BrainBoosters™ concept one step further with all kinds of colorful picture riddles, analogy puzzles, and other real mind-benders.

The BrainBoosters™ series gets *my* nomination for This Year's Perfect Present. To see it is to buy it.

 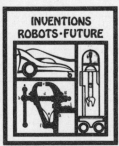

NEW**
The Learning Works
Enrichment Series books, $9.95 each.

Series of eight books for gifted education, each containing three mini-units for gifted education. Activities are coded according to Bloom's taxonomy. If you don't know what this is, the book will explain it. Each unit includes lots of background information on the subject being studied, plus pre- and post-tests with answer keys. Tone is clever without being hysterical or self-satisfied. Each page or two introduces a single topic with its background information, illustrations, and a few suggested activities. Some activities are open-ended—e.g., "Write a different ending for this [Mayan] myth," while others require research of specific answers *not* necessarily included in the text.

I haven't seen every book in the series, but the one I did see didn't have any obvious pro-pagan bias, as is so common in gifted materials. The emphasis on actual cognitive knowledge is also refreshing. Students are expected to actually learn something in these books. Series includes *Mythology, Archaeology, Architecture; Weather, Electricity, Environmental Investigations; Monsters, Mysteries, UFOs; Castles, Codes, Calligraphy; Inventions, Robots, Future; Egyptians, Maya, Minoans; Advertising, Communication, Economics;* and *Pirates, Explorers, Trailblazers*.

UPDATED**
Midwest Publications

Public-school materials directed at improving thinking skills. Midwest's materials are nongraded and can be used with students of all abilities in grades K–12, but gifted students seem to be especially attracted to these materials. The line includes workbooks on Syllogisms, Word Benders, pattern 'n puzzle Brain Stretchers, matrix-puzzle software, and so on. Midwest endeared itself to me by question 15 in its *Inductive Thinking Skills* workbook, which begins, "Larry lives in Iowa. He doesn't like school." The problem proceeds with Larry trying to talk his folks into moving to south Texas so that he won't ever have to go to school again (we don't go to school when it's warm, and it's *always* warm in south Texas). If you can't figure out what's wrong with Larry's reasoning, you'd better buy this book.

Midwest's *Building Thinking Skills* series (see Thinking Skills chapter in Volume 2) is an ideal starting point, but they also publish additional books like the Mind Benders and Math Mind Benders series to keep gifted students challenged and excited. And then there's their Apple software line—see the Educational Software Buyer's Guide.

Midwest's publications seem to really do the job of improving the accuracy of a student's thinking and exposing him to new possibilities within the confines of logic. Tested students show great improvement. See the Midwest reviews in the Logic chapter for more info.

Resources for the Gifted, Inc.

Kathy Kolbe began Resources for the Gifted as a frustrated mother. When regular programs didn't respond to the needs of her two children, Kathy Kolbe decided to create brain-stretching alternatives to standard school fare. After the major publishers told her there was no market for materials specifically designed to teach thinking skills, she started publishing them herself. Mrs. Kolbe soon built her business into the world's largest producer of learning aids for gifted children.

RFG carries a full line of gifted/talented materials in every category. They are all stimulating, entertaining, and expensive. Suitable for kids from prereaders to high-school seniors, they use a lighthearted approach to encourage creativity and emphasize the teaching of problem-solving skills. RFG encourages parents to use the materials with kids of all ability levels.

Timberdoodle

One-stop shopping for the best thinking skills material. Timberdoodle carries Midwest Publications *Figural Mind Benders*, games, and probably most of the other worthwhile entries in this section by the time you read this. A Christian home business, Timberdoodle weeds out the iffy stuff and offers the rest at good prices with great service.

WFF 'N PROOF Learning Games Company
Game prices vary from $4.50 to $22.50.

You want games that raise IQ? You've got it. All WFF 'n PROOF games involve heavy thinking and clever deduction. All follow the rules of logic ("If A is not B, and C is not B, then is A necessarily C?") Children who regularly play these games show measurable increases in IQ. For more info, send for a brochure, order the Timberdoodle catalog, or see the detailed reviews in the Computer, Math, and Science chapters of Volumes 2 and 3.

PART VII

JUST PLAIN FUN

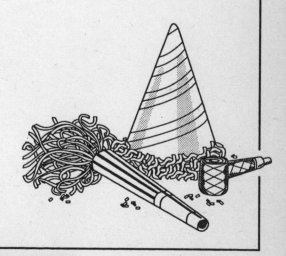

CHAPTER TWENTY-SEVEN

JOKES, RIDDLES, & BRAINTEASERS

Any of you with children over the age of three or four know how the little ones, medium ones, and teenage-sized ones all love jokes and riddles. Any of you married to an engineering or computer graduate also know how *these* folk love screamingly bad puns and jokes. And just about everyone loves puzzles.

I could tell you that riddling builds IQ and that puzzles are great perception and fine-motor-skill training. It's true. But life was much nicer when folks did this sort of thing for fun, instead of as an effortful attempt at self-improvement (or child improvement).

I have this terrible feeling that someday soon teachers will start testing kids on how fast they can put together a puzzle, and don't want any share of the blame when this happens.

So, for no really sound educational reason at all, here's a whole chapter full of jokes, riddles, and brainteasers.

WEIRDO COMPANIES

Many of the products mentioned in this chapter are unusual, but the following companies are really unusual, as in, "Let's make reservations for these dear people at the nearest rubber room."

Jonson Specialties

Did I say "unusual"? Jonson Specialties has it all: stick-ons, balloons, lollipops, giveaway toys, games, rings, flag picks, pens, pencils, pencil tops, toy animals, treasure chests, and even vending machines and capsules. Short-lived but inexpensive yo-yo's. Twist balloons. Eraser collections. Most items come in packages of a dozen to a hundred, so are well suited for party gifts.

NEW**
Klutz Press
Dumb Glasses, $10/4 pairs. Rubber rodents and vinyl vermin, $7.50. Icky-Poo Balls, $5.50 each. Icky-Poo String, $4. Glow-in-the-dark wardrobe: shoelaces, $1.95; bow tie, $4; earrings, $2.50; more. Shipping extra.

It would be lying to say you *need* any of this stuff. But if you *want* (heaven knows why!) a set of weird glasses, Klutz has 'em. Four sets, to be precise. Groucho Marx, X-ray goggles, venetian blinds, and Boing-Boings, the ever-popular popping eyeballs on springs.

For reasons known only to themselves, the people at Klutz also offer a cigar-boxed set of horrendously ugly critters (I'm taking their word for it), including rubber mice, four-inch roaches, and glow-in-the-dark slugs. More: Icky-Poo , in both string and ball form. I've never seen this stuff, thank goodness, but am told that it will stick without residue, cling to and crawl down walls without marking them (except latex walls: on them it leaves shadows), won't gum up your hair or rugs, washes out with soap, and feels *gross*.

For the *really* strange among my readers, Klutz also carries glow-in-the-dark wardrobe items. Supposedly these will make you the life of the party during blacked-out stage performances. If so, why doesn't Klutz carry glow-in-the-dark gloves? Sounds suspicious to me. But what can you expect from the people who are attempting to start a "Lawn Cow" fad?

NEW★★
Signals

The public TV equivalent of the Wireless catalog (see below). Signals is, in its own words, "A Catalog for Friends and Fans of Public Television." These people like to think of themselves as artistically elite, so you'll find C. Escher watches and T-shirts, Frank Lloyd Wright silk scarves, and a video chat with Georgia O'Keefe, among other items. They also like to think they are smart, so you'll find Mensa quiz books (Mensa is a group exclusively for high-IQ types) and a book called *Can You Pass These Tests?* that includes tests for New York City cab drivers, Texas public school teachers, air traffic controllers, and so on.

Now we get to the serious stuff for serious pretenders. University T-shirts—from the University of Moscow, Paris Sorbonne, Oxford University, and other places that most Americans can't get into in real life. Lots of ballet and opera videos. Videos for all those PBS shows, like "Fawlty Towers" (you can also get the scripts separately), "Monty Python" (book also available), "Dr. Who," "Miss Marple," "Sherlock Holmes" (new version), "Prisoner," "Jane Austen," "Mr. Rogers," etc. Plus all those trendy the-world-is-about-to-end-so-get-your-rain-forest-T-shirt-now videos. Some useful stuff: design kits for home layouts, landscapes, and decks. Julia Child cooking videos. If you're smart you'll skip the "expert" advice on everything from pregnancy and codependency to motherhood (oops, I meant "parenting").

This may not sound very funny so far, but you can also pick up a Last Chance Garage T-shirt with its own printed-on grease spots (for slumming with the natives, don't you know) and a tour of Great Britain hosted by a Monty Python regular. A Periodic Table of

Desserts (or one of Veggies, or Fruit and Nuts) makes a nice conversation piece for your wall. I wonder how many parents will have the guts to buy the "if you love me, read me a story" T-shirt? And I wonder how many of them will turn off their PBS specials to do so?

Wireless

Just plain zany. Catalog put out by the perpetrators of "Prairie Home Companion." How-to music books mingle with *Swedish Humor and Other Myths* and radio humor cassettes. Lots of Scandinavian ethnic gifts with a humorous twist and educational items. If you're looking for a truly unusual gift for that eccentric someone, you'll find it here.

BRAINTEASERS

NEW★★
Dale Seymour Publications
Plexers and *More Plexers*, $5.95 each.

What in the world is a "plexer"? As you might guess, "plexer" is derived from the word "perplex." These are books of fiendishly clever pictorial puzzles, mostly made up of letters. You have to decide what word or phrase the letters bring to mind. Look to the direction, size, and positions of the letters for clues.

Here's an example of a plexer:

THEHABIRDAND

The answer, of course, is "A bird in the hand." Yuk, yuk!

Not surprisingly, my six- and nine-year-old captured these books the second they arrived in the house. Also not surprisingly, my husband and I fished them out the minute the kids went to bed. I don't know if solving these plexers made us any smarter, but it sure was a lot of fun!

NEW★★
Dale Seymour Publications
Eye-Cue Puzzles, set A and set B, $10.95 each.

Regular jigsaw puzzles are for wimps. You want a *real* challenge? Try the *Eye-Cue Puzzles* from Dale Seymour! First, open the box. You'll find four little zip-loc bags, each containing eight square puzzle pieces adorned with colorful geometric designs. Your job is to "match color and design elements, placing the squares edge to edge" in order to form one of the 10 possible configurations. These range from four-in-a-row to the fiendishly difficult hollow square. With four puzzles sets per box, and 10 configurations into which you are attempting to fit each puzzle set, a little simple math tells us that you have here 40 shots per box at a room in the funny farm. Set B looks a little more user-friendly to me, but then, I struggle with the *easy* configurations! And one last thing: no solutions are provided. For a set of sample solutions you have to send a self-addressed stamped envelope to the publisher. A great gift for people with finely-honed spatial skills; a quick trip to gooney-land for those without.

Educational Insights

Educational Insights BrainBoosters are mind-stretching, colorful booklets with questions to answer and a special decoder to find out how you did. See complete review in Chapter 28.

NEW★★
Essential Learning Products Company
Hidden Pictures Books, $2.95 each.

From the people at *Highlights* magazine, here's a whole line of Hidden Pictures books. You know how these work. Inside of a complex line-art drawing that looks like a regular scene, all sorts of pictures of objects are hidden. The lines on the trunk of the tree might conceal the outline of a sparrow, for example. To make it easier, some books list the objects you are searching for. Kids love these puzzles and will work at them for hours. Adults can get sucked in too. I spent an hour helping my four- and five-year-olds locate

some of the tougher missing objects. Some of the books include extra games and mind-bending riddles. The series includes *Hidden Pictures Plus Fun for Masterminds, Hidden Pictures Plus Brain Teasers, Hidden Pictures Plus Brain Stretchers, Hidden Pictures Plus Brain Benders, Hidden Pictures Plus Thinking Fun, Hidden Pictures with Picture Clues and Other Games, Hidden Pictures and Other Challenges, Hidden Pictures Favorites by John Gee, More Hidden Pictures Favorites and Other Fun, Hidden Pictures for Beginners, Hidden Pictures and Other Fun,* and *Hidden Pictures Plus Other Puzzlers.*

Official Publications
Children's Fun Puzzles, $5/year (6 issues). *Superb Fill-It-Ins, Superb Crosspatches, Featured Fill-It-Ins,* each $15/year (12 issues). *Variety Crosspatches, All-Number Fill-It-Ins,* each $7.50/year (6 issues). *Superb Crosswords, Deluxe Crosswords, Preferred Crosswords,* each $15/year (12 issues). *Crossword Treat,* $7.50/year (6 issues). *Superb Variety Puzzles, Crossword Varieties, Leisure Word-Finds,* each $9/year (6 issues). *Variety Word-Find Puzzles, Superb Word-Find Puzzles,* each $15/year (12 issues). *Superb Word-Twists, Soap Opera Word-Find,* each $7.50/year (6 issues). Add $1.50 postage outside U.S.A.

I don't know how they do it. Official Publications publishes all sorts of puzzle magazines, including *Children's Fun Puzzles.* Now, how do they come out six times a year with dozens of crosswords, mazes, find the twins, connect the dots, picture puzzles, mysteries, memory quizzes, and even a puzzle on the cover for less than $1 per issue?

This is the *only* puzzle magazine that readers have raved to me about. Large, easy-to-read format, challenging puzzles (including some of the same sort adults delight to solve), all designed for the 7- to 12-year-old set.

Also from Official Publications (are you ready?): *Superb Fill-It-Ins, Superb Crosspatches* (variety of fill-ins, different diagrams and topics), *Featured Fill-It-Ins* (easy 80+ puzzles, since you only have to fit the given answers in to the right squares), *Variety Crosspatches, All-Number Fill-It-Ins, Superb Crosswords, Crossword Treat, Deluxe Crosswords, Preferred Crosswords, Superb Variety Puzzles, Crossword Varieties* (assortment of crosswords and word games for all levels), *Leisure Word-Finds, Variety Word-Find Puzzles, Superb Word-Find Puzzles, Soap Opera Word-Find* (would I make that up?), and *Superb Word-Twists* (a literally kinky new kind of word-find). Between 66 and 130 puzzles per magazine. Now you're prepared for the next time you're in the hospital.

NEW**
Penny Press
Bargain Bags, $4.95 plus $1 shipping. *Selected Logic Problems, Logic Problems, Favorite Logic Problems,* $2.95 each. *101 Puzzles in Thought and Logic, My Best Puzzles in Logic & Reasoning,* $3.95 each. Add 75¢/volume shipping. Monthly puzzle magazines, $15/12 issues. Bimonthly magazines, $11.50/6 issues. Quarterly magazine, $7.50/4 issues.

I owe this entry to my mother-in-law, Mrs. Betty Pride. She came to visit us while I was revising the *Big Book,* and brought along an issue of *Original Logic Problems,* a quarterly puzzle magazine from Penny Press. This magazine has some awesome matrix logic puzzles (if you have to ask what those are, see the Logic chapters in Volumes 2 and 3), and Bill and I sat up late one night figuring one of them out. The Penny Press lineup includes *Approved Crosswords, Classic Crosswords, Family Crosswords, Joy of Crosswords, Merit Crosswords Plus,* and *Variety Puzzles and Games.* Their bimonthly magazines are 114-pagers: the *Approved Jumbo Issue* (crosswords and variety puzzles) and *Variety Puzzles Jumbo* (variety puzzles only). *Original Logic Problems* only comes out quarterly, probably because it takes that long to come up with 45 of these super brain-stretchers in every issue!

Penny Press also sells books full of logic problems. *Favorite Logic Problems* is the book for those who like to take it easier. Its 128 pages of not-too-tough (by Penny Press standards!) matrix puzzles have the charts already printed for you. *101 Puzzles in Logic and Thought* and *My Best Puzzles in Logic & Reasoning* make you create the solving charts.

For those who like to sample first, Penny Press's Bargain Bag includes one issue each of every one of their magazines except *Original Logic Problems.*

WFF 'N PROOF Learning Games

What company has managed to integrate Chicago schoolchildren where the federal, state, and local governments failed? Answer: WFF 'N PROOF Learning Games Associates. It seems that some of our university profs are actually producing something useful—a series of educational games that really gets kids involved.

The game that got dozens of Chicago schoolkids, black and white, to voluntarily board buses and spend their Saturday mornings nerding math is *Equations.* This deceptively simple pre-algebra game consists of a set of numerals and operations. One player sets a goal. Then everyone in turn tries to pick a resource from the remaining pool that will (1) not allow the goal to be reached in one or less steps and (2) not make reaching the goal impossible with the remaining resources. From here the description gets more complicated. Suffice it to say that it takes only 15 minutes to learn to play *Equations,* but a math major like me or my M.I.T.-graduate husband Bill could spend weeks playing it without getting bored. In Chicago kids play *Equations* in the Academic Games League. At home, they can play it with you, or (thanks to the folks at WFF 'N PROOF) with the family Apple.

Nobody can play *Equations* without sharpening their thinking and their arithmetic skills. Boys tend to love it more than girls, but everywhere it's been tried the math skills have gone up and the absentee rate down.

WFF 'N PROOF has a pile of other games for science, language, grammar, logic, and set theory. All stress abstract thinking. The WFF 'N PROOF Game of Modern Logic has been shown to increase I.Q. scores by more than 20 points in avid users.

CHAPTER TWENTY-EIGHT

PUPPETS, VENTRILOQUISM, AND MAGIC TRICKS

He trapped us at the shopping center. It happened like this:

"He" was a lanky, pallid-faced teenage boy who appeared to be losing the war on pimples. "We," the Pride family, were wandering around a shop I'll call Aunt Gertie's, looking at their knick-knacks and trying to find where they stored the Fimo clay. This young gentleman was standing behind a counter, evidently about to eat a lunch consisting of greasy French fries and a large strawberry shake. My mind was running on the probable connection between this typical American diet and his typical teenage complexion, when suddenly the boy put aside his food and began making cards appear, disappear, and change color. Our kids were mesmerized as he turned foam bunny mamas and papas into dozens of little foam bunny babies, changed nickels into quarters, tore dollar bills in half and put them back together, recovered quarters from their hiding places in our children's hair, and similar feats of magical skill.

Not only did this lad have hidden depths as a magician (I discovered he performed professionally at children's parties), he was quite a salesman as well. About twenty dollars of our hard-earned loot disappeared into his cash register before we staggered out into the fresh air.

Needless to say, our older children spent the rest of that afternoon practicing their new magic tricks on anyone they could get to watch them. Since then, they have branched out into basic ventriloquism and puppetry, with results guaranteed to amaze and amuse!

Below are resources for all three of these classic high-interest educational teaching methods—puppetry, ventriloquism, and magic—plus a source for clown supplies. Stick on your rubber nose and enjoy!

PUPPETRY

NEW★★
Fearon Teacher Aids
Fingerlings, $6.95.

From the lady who brought you *Magic Mixtures* (see Chapter 4) comes this book of finger-puppet patterns for eight basic finger puppets—slip-ons, ring fingers, cylinders, finger-hole puppets, glove-finger puppet, snap-ons, pom-pom, and nutshell finger puppets—plus ideas for turning them into 100s of characters. Includes 25 original stories, rhymes, and activities, and directions to improve your finger-puppetry skills. How to make puppets, stages and props from "found" materials. How to make finger-puppet gloves. The author thinks that "Finger puppets, also called fingerlings, can provide a wide variety of valuable learning experiences for young children." I'm not convinced that we need to struggle to find educational value in finger puppets—hey, they're *fun*! And if you want to know more than you thought there was to know about fingerlings, this is the book.

NEW★★
Fearon Teacher Aids
Paper-Bag Puppets, More Paper-Bag Puppets, $6.95 each. *Bagging It with Puppets*, $12.95. *Pom-Pom Puppets, Stories, and Stages*, $11.95.

Grab a paper bag and make a puppet! Patterns for puppets correlated with typical school studies such as the zoo, the farm, favorite stories, and holidays (*Paper-Bag Puppets*) or community helpers, seasons, and more favorite stories (*More Paper-Bag Puppets*). These aren't huge grocery-bag puppets, but cute little lunch-bag puppets. No stories, just patterns for puppet heads and faces. You trace the puppet's face on regular paper or photocopy it and then transfer it to construction paper. Cut out the pieces, paste them on a paper lunch bag, and that's it!

Bagging It with Puppets is intended to be more educational. These are fairly involved patterns that end up producing one puppet character per alphabet letter, plus one for each long vowel. These very clever puppets each use a lunch bag as the body base. Characters include Doctor Dan (or Donna), X-Ray Boy (his skeleton shows), and Kooky Kookaburra. Winnie Witch and Ogie Ogre are balanced by Amy Angel. Count on

taking a lot of time to make these puppets. I'm not saying this isn't fun, but this is not the quick way to learn to read!

Pom-Pom Puppets, Stories, and Stages is just what it sounds like. 64 original stories and poems, lots of pom-pom puppets patterns, and patterns for stages for your pom-pom puppet shows. The educational twist here sneaks up on you in different ways, like counting monkeys on bikes in "Molly's Bicycle Adventure," or listening for *p* sounds in "Pigs in a Puddle."

NEW★★
Lauri, Inc.
Lace-A-Puppet, $9.95. Lace-a-Saurus, Lace-a-Pet Puppet, $6.50 each. Extra laces, needles available.

Every kid's first puppets. Kits include precut felt body shapes, plastic needles, yarn, and small geometric felt pieces for decorating your completed hand puppets. Just lace round 'n round the edges, through the precut holes. Cute, simple designs. Lace-A-Saurus and Lace-a-Pet Puppet kids each come with three puppets and large plastic needles—enough for each of three kids to have his or her own. The Lace-a-Puppet set (our favorite) comes with six puppet "people," for even more value. Designed for ages 5–9, but we've used them (under supervision) with kids as young as three years old. Recommended.

NEW★★
The Learning Works
Make Amazing Puppets, $3.95. *Puppets for Dreaming and Scheming*, $15.95.

Creative ideas for making puppets; your choice of plain vanilla instructions or the whole nine yards. *Make Amazing Puppets* is an inexpensive book of creative ideas for puppet-making out of found materials. Would you believe you can make a puppet out of paper plates? Envelopes? Cups? Cereal boxes? Amply illustrated instructions spell out hundreds of clever ideas. Plus ideas for special effects and puppet stages. Just opening this book is enough to get you inspired. Don't let the witch and bat puppets on the cover turn you off; such characters hardly appear at all in the book. A really good book otherwise.

Puppets for Dreaming and Scheming costs four times as much. Is it worth it? Probably only for schoolteachers and others who frequently use puppets in their work. It has ideas for making fancier puppets, plus scripts, lessons, patterns, and construction techniques. Lots of ideas for how to teach school lessons with puppets, plus some actual lessons. Make hand, glove, rod, pop-up, shadow, string, and stick puppets. If all this fails to slake your thirst for puppet construction, you also get a bibliography of references and resources.

NEW★★
Maher
Vent puppets, $22.95 and up. Mopkins, $39.95, optional hat another $5. Bird Arm Illusion, $39.95.

Argh! They're coming at me! They're weird, wacky, furry, and feathered! It's the invasion of . . . the Maher Ventriloquism Puppets! Armed with turning heads and mouths that open and close, here are 33"-high sheepdogs and rabbits; blue, brown, green, or red Grumletts (don't ask me to describe a Grumlett); bees, buzzards, skunks, and foxes; Fancy Feathered Friends;™ Dinostar,™ a just-hatched stegosaurus who can clap or wiggle his arms; people puppets of various ages, sexes, and races; and a lovable, huggable, adoptable Mopkins who comes with his own headband, sunglasses, kerchief, adoption papers, managerial contract, legends of the Mopkins, and instruction booklet. But my personal favorite is the Bird Arm Illusion. It looks like a bird puppet is perched on your arm. Your hand is clearly visible. Yet the bird is completely under your control. I'll say no more for fear of spoiling this trick, but this might be the ultimate puppet.

NEW★★
Show Biz Services
Catalog, $3.

Large line of soft puppets, plus everything else the family entertainer could possibly want. Show-Biz supplies other puppet and ventriloquism companies, so that should give you an idea of their size. Don't miss this catalog!

Son Shine Puppet Company
Puppets from $15 to $99. Teaching materials and dialogs, many under $5. *Son Shine Gazette*, monthly newsletter, free sample copy.

Everything you can imagine having to do with puppets, all designed for use in puppet ministries. Patterns for creating your own muppet-style puppet with a changeable face! Stage plans! Dialogs! How-to books! Pre-recorded puppet music and soundtracks! Larger than lifesized costumes! Children's church lesson units! And, of course, lots and lots of puppets.

Extremely affordable and fun for kids are Son Shine's new patterns and precut kits for making Almost Anything Puppets. The materials packet includes precut fake fur for one long-mouth puppet and one wide-mouth puppet, each 12 inches tall, plus extra fur for the ears, etc. If I understand the catalog listing right, you can get both pattern and materials for only $5.99. And unlike most puppet projects, Almost Anything Puppets can become almost anything your child imagines. See the photo on the previous page for some examples!

Also available from Son Shine: The Son Shine Gazette. This bimonthly newspaper is a "children's ministry resource shopping guide." A typical issue includes scripts and ideas for puppetry, dramas, object lessons, and teaching tip, as well as updates on Son Shine's speakers' schedule and their puppet lineup.

Son Shine conducts puppet training seminars for beginning and advanced puppeteers, as well as teachers interested in learning new techniques and teaching ideas. Contact Randy and Glenda Hoyle at Son Shine for more info.

NEW★★
Warren Publishing House, Inc.
1•2•3 Puppets, $7.95 plus $2 shipping.

Here's a collection of simple, clever puppets you can make for children ages three-six. Each is constructed of materials commonly found around the home and is presented as a specific character with his own song or poem. Some come with patterns; most can be made simply by following the clear instructions and looking at the illustration. Like other Totline books from Warren Publishing House, *1•2•3 Puppets* has a friendly format that is easy to follow.

Some examples of the puppets: Fish Envelope, Dinosaur Sock, Popsicle Stick Car, Abe Lincoln Tongue Depressor, Clothespin Pancake Man, and Butterfly Straw. A delightful collection with 55 puppets in all.

VENTRILOQUISM

Teddy and Joseph wanted to learn to "throw our voices like a ventriloquist." I wasn't sure whether ventriloquists really threw their voices, or if they used some special gadget, but was willing to have the boys find out. They came home from the library loaded with books on ventriloquism, all of them just awful. Raunchy routines for X-rated clubs. Diagrams for models that would take an expert woodworker 200 hours to put together. Sad-sack advice about how to get into show biz.

Then I remembered our Maher catalog. Flipping through it, we found dozens of comedy dialog books with *clean* dialogs, an entire how-to course, instructions on how to build all kinds of dummies, how-to tapes taught by experts on special issues like "Developing Characters' Voices," and the book we finally ended up getting, *Ventriloquism for the Total Dummy*. This $7.95 book comes with a little hand puppet and some really good advice for the beginner. If you want to get into ventriloquism, start with it. Now, for supplies and further instruction on the art of VENTing your feelings (ventriloquist love puns!), look below.

NEW★★
Laugh-Makers: A Magazine for Family Entertainers
Subscription, $18 (6 issues). Single issue, $3.

Trade magazine for laugh-makers. Dan Ritchard, author of *Ventriloquism for the Total Dummy,* says, "The articles are interesting, and the ads are extremely helpful for people trying to track down supplies."

Maher

Anyone who is the slightest bit interested in visual teaching will love Maher's free catalog of ventriloquist dolls, puppets, and visual instruction (balloon, chalk talk, clowning, etc.) For the novice, Maher has a unconditionally-guaranteed home-study ventriloquist course (30 lessons for $79.95). Maher's selection also includes dialogues, scripts, cassette tapes, books, and novelties. But best of all is the Christian emphasis of Maher's inventory. It seems that a goodly chunk of the world's practicing "vents" are Christians engaged in it as a ministry, and they've written all sorts of books of gospel dialogues and how-tos for Christian ventriloquism.

Maher also offers deluxe vent figures that they rebuild from commercially-produced dolls. These have a lot of features for a base price of less than $190. Add-on features, such as winkers, raising eyebrows, and spitting (some people want that!), cost extra. For young folks Maher has some animal characters (Eagle, Buzzard, Sheep Dog . . . and Grumlett!) for $44.95 each, or rebuilt commercial figures for $69.95. Catalog of Knee Pal professional dolls costs $2 (refunded with order). Prices of these dolls start at $224.95.

Maher Workshop
Catalog, $2.

Once you have learned to amaze your friends with ventriloquism, it's time to think about investing in a deluxe dummy of your very own. Maher Workshop, a business completely unrelated to the Maher Studios (see above) in spite of the identical name and similar interest in ventriloquism, has "the most complete selection anywhere of figures with Personality and Audience Appeal." Chuck Jackson handcarves his basswood figures and adds a lot of quality touches, which is why the Junior Series starts at $469 and the Standard Professional Series starts at $599. Special effects can be added to the Pro figures, such as raising eyebrows, winking, and shaking hands. Fifteen-year warranty, 100 percent satisfaction or money back within first two weeks. Recommended by missionaries and pastors. Figures available in all colors, both sexes, and all ages.

NEW**
Show-Biz Services

Ventriloquism: Magic with Your Voice, $12. *Ventriloquism for Children and Adults* video, $25. Dummies, $200 and up. All prices postpaid. Catalog, $3.

Show-Biz services started out as a comedy-writing service, so they have oodles of comedy scripts for entertainers. Along the way, they branched out into ventriloquism, magic, balloon sculpture, and clowning supplies. Show-Biz is now one of the biggest wholesale magic outlets in the country.

Owner George Schindler is a real expert on these fields of entertainment. He has written a book *Ventriloquism: Magic with Your Voice* for beginning ventriloquists, two on beginning magic (see the Magic section), and one on beginning balloon sculpting. You might want to check these out. His firm also has records, videotapes, and audiotapes for ventriloquists (he says the *Ventriloquism for Children & Adults* video is good and covers all the basics), plus soft puppets.

If you want to wear a funny wig and rubber nose and do a ventriloquism act full of magic tricks while surrounded by dozens of clever balloon sculptures, this is the place.

MAGIC TRICKS AND SKILLS

My husband Bill has been doing simple magic tricks for years. He learned his skills at Moody Bible Institute, believe it or not, at a class conducted by Open Air Campaigners. These people go into the inner cities and gather groups of kids to hear a gospel message. With an audience of street kids, you learn really fast to use high-interest teaching methods; thus the OAC bag of tricks includes magic and ventriloquism.

So don't get spooked by the word "magic." Yes, I know that professional performers of magic tricks sometimes like to wear black capes and other ghostly gear. But we're not looking at a collection of occult material here. This is trick magic, puppeteering, ventriloquism, and other fantasy fun completely unrelated to witches and goblins. Christian street preachers use these materials to get the crowd's attention. You can try them at home to charm the kids and develop your own dexterity.

Hank Lee's Magic Factory
Catalog, 270-plus oversized pages, $6. Magic of the Month Club, $12/year.

What workshop is full of magical things and populated by elves? You're thinking of Santa's, right? Well, the mythical Mr. Claus has real-life competition. Hank Lee's Magic Factory in good old Boston is staffed by such imps as Elmo, Joe-O, Bob-O, Phono ("Still answers the phone at night and on weekends"), and Byte-O ("The computer elf"). Hank Lee's catalog has an immense selection of magic tricks, equipment, props, and books. I find it easier to follow than Tannen's (see below). Let me warn you, though, once you pick it up you will have trouble putting it down! The descriptions of the magic tricks make fascinating reading, and the layout makes browsing a delight. Now who wants a pair of soft dice that changes colors and produces baby dice . . .

To make it even easier for you to blow all your hard-earned shekels on magic, Hank Lee has invented a Magic of the Month Club. Members get a membership card, "Noosletter" subscription, and discounts of 10 to 40 percent off selected books and magic, plus previews of the hottest new stuff.

And for the really dedicated magic fan who also owns a computer, Hank Lee has set up a magic bulletin board. Call (617) 484-8750 between 5 P.M. and 8 A.M. Eastern time. The password is HANKLEE. You can leave orders using your credit cards, leave questions and messages (questions will be answered as EMAIL for the next day), check out the latest magical goodies, and so on.

Louis Tannen Magic, Inc.
850-plus-page hardbound catalog, $8 postpaid U.S.A., $10 foreign. Summer Magic Camp, $350. *Magic Manuscript* magazine, $18/year (6 issues), $3.50 for sample copy. Foreign and Canada, add $7/year for surface mail, $34/year airmail.

Another fabulous magic catalog: typeset, indexed, and illustrated. Tannen's catalog includes close-up magic, magic for kids, stage magic, silk magic, card magic, coin magic, and some heavy-duty illusions for professional magicians. The book section is huge. Tannen's fifteenth catalog was the 1985-87 edition, so you know they've been around for a while.

Tannen also runs a Summer Magic Camp for boys and girls ages 9 to 18. Held on the grounds of LaSalle Academy (which I *think* is in New York State), the camp fee includes a Magic Supply Kit (retail value $50) as well as the magic instruction. Campers get "a rigorous schedule of evening shows, celebrity performers, and finale appearances by the campers." Well-known magicians serve as guest teachers and lecturers. You've got to admit that this camp sounds like a serious-minded prankster could get something out of it.

And if you should be looking for a full-color magic magazine, Tannen publishes the world's only. *Magic Manuscript* has news, reviews, interviews with the pros, and pictures of people making rings of fire or chopping lovely ladies asunder (temporarily, of course).

NEW★★
Magic Moments with Class, Inc.

A catalog of magic tricks and illusions for educators. You can teach various school lessons with the tricks. All of their "simple and fun" tricks come with instructions and suggested lessons for K–8. Sometimes the connection between magic and education is fairly easy to figure out, as with the Atomic Bulb you light up in your hand or some other unplugged-in location. (This one introduces a unit on electricity, natch!) Others are a bit more farfetched. Some are downright fascinating. The Tornado Tube, for example, lets students observe the action of a tornado vortex in a tube of liquid.

Catalog offerings are: magical science novelties, optical illusions and wonders, energy toys and puzzles, science novelties, educational games and puzzles, science discovery kits, and a large selection of books and tapes (some evolutionary). Of the non-magic items, perhaps the most intriguing is their "incredible workable wax-candle-making kits" with wax that softens in warm water. Kit comes with three wax squares, sticky wax, black accent wax, plastic knife, prewaxed wick and wicking rod for candles. Age 4 and up.

NEW★★
Show-Biz Services
Presto! Magic for Beginners, $6.95. *Magic with Everyday Objects,* $6. Catalog, $3.

From the guy who wrote the two books on magic listed above, here is a huge line of magic supplies. Show-Biz is a wholesale supplier of magic goods to other companies, like Hank Lee and Tannen's, but also does some retail sales. Basic how-to books, tapes, and videos can be had here, as well as the tricks that will amaze Uncle Henry at your next family get-together.

CLOWNING

Everyone loves a clown. So be the person they love! All it takes is a fake nose, some grease paint, a funny wig, and an ability to fall down without getting hurt. I can't help you learn to fall without breaking any bones, but I can show you where to get the rest of this stuff. See below!

NEW★★
Lynch's
Catalog, $5.

The ad in *Juggler's World* says, "We Carry A Complete Line Of: Make Up • Clown Wigs • Clown Shoes • Woochie and Other Clown Noses • Sequin Fabrics and Trim • Rhinestones." Unit study fans will instantly figure out all sorts of uses for these items, and now the rest of us know where to get our clowning gear.

NEW★★
Show-Biz Services
Basic Balloon Sculpture, $6. Catalog, $3.

It's all here! Rubber noses. Clown makeup. Funny wigs, breakaway wands, tables, trays, and other props. Much more! Also balloon sculpture materials, in case you're the kind of clown who likes to leave the audience holding something besides an aching belly (from laughing so much). George Schindler's *Basic Balloon Sculpture* is your guide to this fascinating art. I hear that a balloon sculpture video will also be available soon. How-to-clown videos? That, I couldn't say . . . but I think it would be a great idea!

CHAPTER TWENTY-NINE

HOBBIES

Around here we believe very sincerely in hobbies. All work and no play makes Jack a dull boy. Hobbies need to be kept in bounds, of course, except in the serendipitous cases where a hobby blossoms into a business. Is your future business idea below? Read and find out!

GENERAL HOBBIES

NEW★★
Alpha Omega Publications
Catalog, $2.50.

Alpha Omega's *Horizons* catalog is a terrific one-stop shopping source for hobby kits for kids. This full-color catalog for home schoolers has acrylic, oil, and watercolor painting kits; three different calligraphy kits; a resource guide to help you start a cottage industry with your calligraphy; two fabric printing kits; several woodcarving and whittling sets plus lots of books about carving, whittling, and making saleable folk toys and wild animals; books about rock, coin, and stamp collecting; books on basketmaking, sewing, knitting, country flower drying, patchwork, balloon sculpture, paper toys, paper dolls, and origami. Large color pictures show you what you're getting, snappy text tells you what you're getting. This is in addition to their lines of classic kids' books, phonics materials, entire K–12 LIFEPAC curriculum, science equipment, child-training helps, books for parents . . . you get the idea? A don't miss catalog.

BASKET-MAKING

See? You don't need to go to public school to learn all the really important things in life. Here is a source that can get you started on the craft of basket-weaving. And in case you might be inclined to scoff at this humble hobby, let me tell you that a few weeks ago I got a letter from a lady who makes baskets in her spare time, fills them with gifts for busy executives, and has made a very successful business out of this!

NEW★★
Crane's Select Educational Materials
Catalog $1, refundable on first purchase. Basket kits range from $8.95 to $16.95. Shipping extra.

Crane's has not one, not two, not three, but *five* different basket-weaving kits. Baskets are a variety of shapes and functions, and are made using a variety of techniques. The inexpensive Homestead Basket is made using the "weave and chase" technique. The impressive 10 x 14" *Jeremiah's Basket* is much larger, but quite easy to make, with a cross-woven square bottom and "stop and start" sides fashioned from a variety of materials. Most beautiful, in my opinion, is the classic *Egg Basket,* made with three-point lashing and ribbed construction. A wall basket and gathering basket are also available.

NEW★★
HearthSong
Pine Needle Basketry Kit, $14.50. Shipping extra.

So you forget to sign up for Basket Weaving 1 in high school. It's not too late—HearthSong will be happy to teach you this traditional Native American craft, or at least enough of it to make one basket out of traditional native American pine needles. Kit includes pine needles, raffia, a tapestry needle, and the booklet How to Make a Pine Needle Basket, with all the scoop on how to do it, including how to stalk the wild pine needle.

Making a basket was a big hit at our house. Son Joseph, age eight, was the first to try it, and his success inspired Sarah, age six, and Ted, age ten, to make baskets of their own. Although the instructions only promise you that enough materials are included for one basket, we found that with judicious stretching, there was enough for two small baskets in one kit.

How it works: You stitch the pine needles together using raffia as "thread." Combinations of different decorative stitches make the basket pretty and personal. The instructions are very clear about how to make those stitches. I didn't have to help the children at all.

Pine needle basketry has the virtue of being an inexpensive hobby. Once you have learned the basic stitches, you may find you have most of the ingredients just lying around your yard. Our son Ted disappeared into the backyard soon after the kit arrived and returned in triumph bearing a double handful of usable fallen pine needles from our own trees. Even if

you have to buy the needles (extra supplies are available from the company that manufactures this kit), they are not terribly expensive.

PAPER HOBBIES

NEW★★
Montessori Services
Elementary Papermaking Kit, $32 plus shipping.

The Egyptians did it. The Chinese did it. Medieval monks did it. They all did it the hard way, just like you will. What did they do? They made sheets of paper by hand. Here's how they did it. Take organic fibers, such as old rags or wood shavings, pound the mess into pulp, stick it in a vat, mold it, dry it on felt, and follow a lot of other steps I am not at liberty to divulge. If you do it right, eventually you have a sheet of paper . . . and you learn why mass-produced paper was such a giant leap forward in the history of mankind.

Montessori Services' Elementary Papermaking Kit includes almost everything you need: directions explaining the process, a vat, two molds, linter (cotton fibers to make into pulp, about 40-50 sheets' worth), four felt pieces on which to dry the pulp, and two sponges. You also get instructions on traditional techniques for dyeing and layering paper, plus suggestions that link papermaking to the study of nature, ecology, and history. You supply the blender with which you pulverize the hapless cotton, and any inks or dyes you may want to use to marbleize or otherwise glorify your final product. A fun project for as many as four children per kit, or for one very patient kid who enjoys doing the same thing, with variations, over and over again.

NEW**
Learning at Home
Marbleizing kit, $12.

Now that you have made some paper, you can marbleize it. Marbleizing is the ancient and honorable art of producing abstract, swirling designs on paper. The designs resemble marble patterns, hence the name. You may have seen marbleized endpapers on old library books.

Learning at Home's marbleizing kit is imported from Japan. The kit contains six tubes of paint in basic colors. The enclosed directions are in English with that charming Japanese flavor.

NEW**
Flax Art & Design
Marbleizing kit, $16. Faux Finish Marbleizing Kit, $13.40 each color. Video, $19.95. Shipping extra.

A fancier marbleizing kit for paper and fabric marbleizing is available from Flax. This comes with two onces of Marble Thix powder (I haven't the faintest idea what this is for), four two-ounce bottles of acrylic paint (blue, red, green, and yellow), eight eye droppers (for plopping the paint gracefully into the water), two marbling combs (for swirling the paint gracefully about once it is dropped into the water), and complete instructions.

Push the marbleizing concept one step farther with the Faux Finish Marbleizing Kit. This little number lets you marbleize all over *any* paintable surface, including picture frames, cardboard boxes, and Uncle Joe's kitchen table. Each kit covers about 12 square feet with (we hope) the lovely look of real marble. You get four ounces of basecoat color, four ounces of marbleizing colors, one ounce of veining color, two ounces of extender, two ounces of thickener, one sponge, veining feather, a polyester sponge brush, and instruction booklet. The stuff itself is non-toxic and washes up with soap and water until you let it dry, at which point you'd better hope you did the project right. Choice of Tiffany Rose, Florentine Green, and plain old Black. In case you, like me, feel a bit apprehensive about attacking your antique furniture with a poly sponge loaded with marbleizing compound, Flax also offers a 56-minute VHS video on the gentle art of marbleizing.

Flax also has instant marbleizing-in-a-can (nine colors!), pre-marbleizing sheets from France, self-adhesive vinyl rolls of 11 designer faux finishes, pickling stain, overgrainers and mottler brushes, and even what they claim is "the definitive book on graining and marbling."

FABRIC HOBBIES

Fabric art has one big advantage over other forms of art: it's *useful*. Everyone has to wear clothes. Fabric art also is one easy avenue into a home business, if you have special artistic talent. People love T-shirts with clever designs and slogans. Sneaker art also can be quite successful. Other types of clothing are a more iffy business proposition, but are still fun to decorate even if you are the only one who will wear them. You can rubber-stamp quilts, tie-dye scarves, and screen print fabric to sew into throw pillows. You can put your own designs on curtains, tablecloths, and place mats. The noble wife of Proverbs 31 might have done something of this kind, as she wove with clever fingers and supplied the merchants with sashes, besides decorating her bed coverings and dying her family's clothes.

NEW**
Alpha Omega Publications
T-shirt printing kit, $22.95. Fabric screen printing kit, $41.95. Shipping extra.

I had to mention these kits because the catalog pictures were so beautiful. The T-Shirt Printing Kit comes with everything you need to get started in what could turn into a money-making hobby. Includes frame, squeegee, three colors of ink, tracing paper, photo-emulsion, sensitizer, five textile patterns, monogram alphabet, and instruction book. The Fabric Screen Printing Kit needs only soap and water cleanup. Step-by-step illustrations show you how to make your stencil, print your patterns, and make them color-fast for washability. Kit includes three colors of ink, detail brush, plastic spreader, three stirring sticks, plastic fabric squeegee, frame with screen, five exclusive Design with Jennifer textile patterns, monogram alphabet, two tracing sheets, *Design with Jennifer Idea Book*, and instruction book.

NEW★★
Daisy Kingdom
Catalog, $2.

I saw the ad in *Rubberstampmadness* (OK, Roberta?) and knew I had to put this company in here. Daisy Kingdom has come up with a new kind of rubber stamp that "not only gives wonderful results on fabric, but works great on paper, too!" They sell everything you need to stamp on fabric: Daisy Kingdom fabric stamping ink, felt pads, permanent fabric markers, fabric paints, a 16-page booklet (How to Rubberstamp on Fabric), and lots more. Catalog is 52 pages, full-color. This is a fabric art even a young child can manage.

NEW★★
Flax Art & Design
Fabric Paint kit, $23.75 each set. Screen printing kit, $37.95, available in either fabric or craft version. Tie-dye kit, $16.50 (specify small, medium or large children's T-shirt). Shipping extra.

Three more fabric hobbies for those who yearn for a T-shirt collection to match Imelda Marcos's shoe collection . . .

First, fabric painting. Flax has two sets of textile paints that do *not* need to be ironed on. Paint 'em on straight from the bottle's pen tip, let 'em dry at room temperature (it takes 4-24 hours, depending on whether you live in hot, dry Arizona or cold, wet Washington State). The word is that these non-toxic colors won't wash off or otherwise disappear on you once they are set, but I haven't tested them myself to tell you for sure. Set 1 includes glossy paints and metallic glitter paints. Set 2 is "shimmering iridescents."

Second, screen printing. Screen printing is a process whereby you can make multiple colorful prints of your lovely designs. One main application of this hobby is to print on—you guessed it—T-shirts. Another, more beloved of "real" artists, is to print on art paper. (The reason for this is that you can get hundreds of dollars for an art print on paper, but I've never heard of anyone paying hundreds of dollars for a T-shirt.) Flax's kit comes with four-ounce bottles of black, blue, and red inks, photo emulsion, sensitizer, screen filler, detail brush, plastic spreader, three stirring sticks, squeegee, frame with screen, five patterns, idea/instruction book, monogram alphabet, and tracing sheets.

Third, tie-dying. You remember how this was done. You tied a T-shirt in knots, dumped it in a vat of boiled-up dye, let it simmer, and then retied it, repeating the process in another vat of dye, and so on. The whole process was very artistic, which is to say, tedious, messy, and unpredictable. The Tulip tie-dye kit Flax sells abandons these time-honored steps. As far as I can see from examining the outside of this kit, you are actually *not* performing the honorable sixties' art of tie-dying, but rather cheating by spraying water all over a painted-on design, thus simulating the real thing. Kit comes with seven bottles of different colorfast dye colors, one water spray bottle, an idea/instruction booklet, and a children's cotton/polyester T-shirt. (See? Only *kids* are brave enough to wear these things now! Never trust anyone over sixteen . . .)

RUBBER STAMPS

Rubber stamping has got to be one of the most fun ways to feel artistic, be creative, and express yourself—even if you can't draw a stick figure! Believe me, if you think rubber stamping is nothing more than whanging a stamp on a pad and pressing it on a piece of paper, you are in for a surprise. Rubber stamping is becoming a serious (whoops, wrong word), um, *genuine* art form. See below!

All Night Media
Stamp-A-Story,™ $19.50. Stamps on Wheels,™ $10.50 each, includes handle, stamp wheel, and ink cartridge. *101 Ways to Stamp Your Art Out,* $1.50. Shipping, $2 continental U.S., $5 to AK, HI, U.S. Territories, and foreign countries. Catalog, $2.

Delightful, whimsical, strange, beautiful, educational, rococo—what is all the above? The All Night Media collection of rubber stamps and accessories. All Night Media offers three types of stamps. The first is a collection of more than 300 individual stamp designs, each mounted on a beautiful wood block. The blocks are beautiful because each has a full-color picture of the stamp on it, complete with shading and highlights, so you can see which stamp you are picking up without turning it over and squinting at the rubber whorls. A wonderful assortment covering everything from cats and teddy bears to more sophisticated nature designs and classic Winnie-the-Pooh. Next up, All Night Media offers sets of rubber stamps. These stamps are mounted on a rubber base and are really good values. One favorite set is Stamp-A-Story,™ a collection of 33 stamps including Mom, Dad, kids, and pets along with fun props—a skateboard, a ladder, a car, and even an airplane, to name a few. Finally, the third type of stamps are Stamps on Wheels.™ These are available in pad-inking or self-inking varieties. Both types are fun, featuring designs such as dinosaurs, bear pawprints, and more, but the self-inkers are particularly wonderful. With an ink cartridge built-in, you can roll endlessly to make streamers, gift wrap, or decorate your stationery.

All Night Media also offers a full selection of inkpads and stamping accessories to bring out the hidden artist lurking within you. Items like rainbow inkpads, Color Brushers™ so you can paint on different areas of your rubber stamps for dazzling multicolor effects, color pencils especially made for coloring in rubber-stamped images, embossing powder to produce raised images, glitter glue to highlight your work, metallic inkpads, and Stamp & Wrap™ paper especially for use with rubber stamps of all kinds. If you can't find what you're looking for in their lovely glossy catalog, it must not exist.

NEW★★
Good Stamps
Catalog $2, refunded with first order.

Paper supplies for serious stampers. Quantity amounts of business cards (two sizes), post cards (two sizes), gift tags, greeting cards (two sizes), bookmarks, envelopes and stationery, and various types of cut-out cards. Items available in an assortment of colors, including parchment and brites. Free paper swatch book.

NEW★★
His Footeprints
Catalog, $3.

This is it: your one-stop shopping source for rubber stamps. Twelve-year-old home schooler Lindsay

Foote bought Ann Ward's rubber stamp business (you remember Ann: she's the author of the *Learning at Home* preschool–grade 2 curriculum reviewed in Volume 1), and has put together an amazing, impressive catalog with stamps from Stampendous, Personal Stamp Exchange, All Night Media, Sonlight Impressions, and Prints of Peace. This is a *big* selection—I'm talking a 100+ page catalog with every stamp design printed in it, and stamps arranged according to topics. You can also get stamping tips, a complete selection of stamping accessories, inks, pads, and everything you could want!

NEW★★
Prints of Peace
Bible Folks: Old Testament Kit, $10.95. Other stamps, $3.50 and up. Catalog, $1.

Another one for you, Roberta. Prints of Peace has Christian stamps! These include a little puzzle-piece person with the slogan "God knows where you fit in" and a kneeling lady with the message "God is only a prayer away." Lots more inspirational stamps. Stamp kits have stamps mounted on a neoprene-foam block and packed in a sturdy clear plastic case. These include a variety of useful subjects, such as a folk art potpourri (wonder if it works on walls?), a musical instruments kit, and some neat Bible Folks kits. The Old Testament Bible Folks kit includes the Ark of the Covenant, cherubim, a chariot with horses, Goliath, dancing Israelite family, Moses with his staff, a woman with a jug, a boy, and a praying priest with hands lifted up to the Lord. Total selection includes teacher stamps, office stamps, Christmas and Easter stamps, humor stamps, and all-occasion stamps, plus full-color greeting cards. Really nice artwork.

Rubberstampede

Beautiful rubber stamps. The selection is eclectic, with offerings ranging from a mother bunny trundling her baby rabbits in a carriage to a piece of pizza to aid in teaching fractions. Cartoons and animals are intermixed with serious art. The catalog is large and contains every stamping accessory your little heart could desire. You can get personalized stamps and custom stamps and Rainbow Pads and uninked pads and metallic inks and stamp holders and stamp sets (Betty Boop or Teddy Bears, to name just two).

Rubberstampede's Alpha Bears™ set sells for $12.95 and has been a big hit with teachers.

Rubberstampmadness
One year (6 issues) $18, sample issue $3.50. Back issues, $4 each. Canada: $20/6 issues. Foreign: $35 air mail, $20 surface mail.

Introducing the biggest . . . the most frequently published magazine for rubber stamp artists! Tabloid-sized magazine printed on strong white paper has news, tips, and some positively ginchy ads. One back issue tells you all you ever wanted to know about carving stamps from erasers; another covers stamping on fabric. Extensive reviews of current rubber-stamp catalogs. What's Doin', mail art listings, classifieds, special themes and features. A quick browse through the ads shows that rubberstamping is not only alive and well, but in danger of becoming a recognized art form. Time to get in on the ground floor, right?

GET TRAINED

NEW**
Life-Like Products, Inc.

This very low-key model railroading catalog is mostly devoted to over 100 tips for creating and adding to the realism of your layout. These range from how to make a platform for your set to how to make a realistic abandoned freight car (right down to the vandal's graffiti!). The rest of the newsprint catalog shows the accessories, railcars, and sets this company offers. They urge you to buy their products at your local hobby store, but allow that if you can't find these kinds of goodies in your area that they might be able to help you directly. This means you'd better specifically ask for a price list when requesting the catalog, since the catalog itself does not contain prices.

I'll say this for Life-Life: they have a *very* complete selection, right down to real live teeny bits of coal for your coal cars. Tunnels. Grass mats. Trees of all sorts (I *love* model trees!). People. Signs. Lights (even a blinking traffic light!). Buildings in various scales, from a Pizza Hut to a lighted general store and even the old village church. Action accessories. Train sets. Itty-bitty widgets like track nails and hook-up wire. Track. Locomotives. If you can't find what you want here, chances are they told you how to make it in the "Tips" section.

Now here are two associations for model railroaders:

National Model Railroad Association
Teen Association of Model Railroading

GET A HORSE

NEW**
Klutz Press
Rope Set, $24 plus $3 shipping.

I haven't seen this set, and it wouldn't do me any good if I did, because I promise you that I lack the co-ordination to do any Will Rogers stunts. If you, however, feel up to trying your hand at rope spinning, Klutz has the one and only book on the subject plus a rope spinner's lariat made of, in their own words, "100% cotton braided cord with the right length, flexibility and special 'honda' to keep the loop running freely." What small Japanese cars have to do with capturing dogies is beyond me, but the Klutz folks assure us that the instructions and photographs in the book will give you the right stuff to master the basics plus a few more advanced moves. Set includes rope and book.

TIE THE KNOT

Boy Scouts used to specialize in knot-tying. Now anyone, regardless of age, sex, or condition of physical co-ordination, can learn to tie great knots. See below.

NEW★★
Klutz Press
The Klutz Book of Knots, $9.95 plus $3 shipping.

So well-designed I could knot believe it . . . The catalog says "*The Klutz Book of Knots* is a unique concept." Ain't it the truth! Here's how to tie 25 popular knots, from the classic sheepshank to the trucker's hitch and the package knot. But this is more than a mere book. It's 22 full-color laminated pages of heavy card stock with die-cut holes through which you can insert the included blue and red nylon cords to practice the illustrated knots. Even a five-thumber like me can tie some great knots when it's made this easy.

JUGGLING

It's great aerobic exercise! It's training in gross and fine motor skills! It's hand-eye coordination to the nth! It's socialization skills! It builds confidence! It flattens your stomach and builds up your shoulders! It's slightly balmy and definitely humorous. It's . . . juggling!

I can't juggle worth beans, but all the same I love it. (UPDATE: Since I wrote those words, I *have* learned to juggle. See Home Life writeup below for the products that made this miracle possible!) This has got to be the perfect physical education program for home-schooled kids, especially those who live in cold or damp climates where kids have to stay indoors a lot. The same boy who tries to sneak out of doing 20 situps a day will juggle for an hour and think nothing of it. The same girl who thinks jumping jacks are "too much work" will jump all over the place trying to keep three beanbags in motion. So go ahead . . . Amaze your friends! . . . Break a little furniture! . . . Bruise a few oranges!

NEW★★
Home Life
Juggling Step by Step video, full-color VHS: ½-hour version $25, two-hour version $49.95. *The Complete Juggler* book, $10.95. Flutterflies scarves (three nylon scarves with complete directions in self-mailer), $7.95 ($2 off retail). Many other juggling items available. Add 10% shipping USA/Canada, 25% overseas ground, 60% overseas air mail.

Before you tell me that juggling is just for those with special talent, and that you tried to learn once but failed, let me explain that I know *exactly* where you're coming from. I, too, tried to learn to juggle with *Juggling for the Complete Klutz*. I, too, failed miserably. (Bill did learn to juggle a little with that book, so it does work for *some* people.) But recently we discovered a wonderful wholesale source of juggling equipment and how-to videos that make it possible for a Total Klutz like myself to learn to juggle. The day we saw the video, I was able to juggle three scarves briefly. A week later I was just starting to juggle three balls. Now I can juggle three balls or beanbags for 20 catches fairly consistently (my record is 100+ catches), juggle three rings for 10 catches, and Bill and I can "steal" three juggled beanbags back and forth. I'm even working on juggling circus-style clubs! What accomplished this miracle? The *Juggling Step by Step* videos and *Complete Juggler* book, both by the amazing Professor Confidence, Dave Finnigan.

This is *the* way to start juggling, for all us not-terribly-coordinated types. Believe me, you'll look on juggling in an entirely different light after watching this tremendously entertaining and educational video! In *Juggling Step-by-Step* you meet Professor Confidence (a smooth fellow in top hat and tails who introduces the lessons and performs many of the moves), Won Israel (a colorful little clown), Amy (a beautiful Filipino girl), Andrew (an incredibly talented young juggler), and Robert (a Huck Finn-type kid). Each of these has a particular speciality: balls, clubs, rings, scarves, devil sticks, diabolo, and team juggling are some of the topics covered. Again, after the first lessons on basic moves, you are expected to pick up more advanced moves from simply watching the tape. Exception: the section on juggling with torches (!) includes some wise safety tips (although they left out the most important one, in my opinion—don't even *think* of trying to juggle with torches unless you have asbestos skin!).

The video is available in both a less-expensive ½-hour version and the full two-hour version. The ½-hour version gives you a basic introduction to juggling scarves, beanbags, balls, rings, and clubs. The full two-hour version includes everything on the ½-hour version, and then goes on to more advanced routines with clubs, balls, unusual equipment like cigar boxes and hats, and even flaming torches! You'll also be introduced to team juggling, juggling with many objects, multiplex juggling, two-in-one-hand, and lots more. The instruction sequences include routines by some really great jugglers, including some not featured on the shorter version. These videos are a quantum leap in juggling education. Since not every single move on the video is explained in detail, I recommend you also get the *Complete Juggler* book. It includes detailed illustrated directions for all the moves on the two-hour video and comes with three colorful pressed-fiber scarves, for practicing scarf juggling. (The scarves are not the greatest quality; our Flutterflies scarves are much better.)

You see your mistake? You tried starting with beanbags (or balls, or oranges). Here's what you should do; pitch the beanbags and try our juggling scarves. These "training wheels of the juggling world" can repair your sagging confidence, and as an added benefit they won't knock over vases. Once you have mastered scarves, *then* move on to beanbags, but *only after watching the video several times.* Juggling is just too hard to learn from a book for most of us; we need to *see* how it works. Even a juggling friend can't show you the moves in slow motion, but the video can (and does)!

NEW**
Klutz Press
Juggling for the Complete Klutz, $9.95. Klutz Juggling Bags, $2 each or $5/set of 3. Juggling Chicken, $6 or $15/set of 3. Juggler's Convention video, $29.95. Lots more juggling items available. Shipping extra.

Our family has a new hobby. Juggling. Or, to be more accurate, *trying* to juggle. What got us started was the classic *Juggling for the Complete Klutz.* This is the book that launched Klutz Press—the drop heard 'round the world. (For non-jugglers, the "drop" is what happens when you are trying to juggle and miss.) *Juggling for the Complete Klutz* has sold a million copies in the last ten years, partly due to its attractive packaging and partly due to its upbeat contents. The book comes with three square juggling beanbags in a handy net that you tie through a die-cut hole in the book to keep them all together. Inside are simple instructions for how to juggle, with non-threatening line drawings of an aging hippie attempting same and often failing. We all can identify with the poor spaced-out-looking guy whose beanbag ends up in Mom's soup . . . or down a sewer grate . . . or up in the chandelier. The authors definitely don't expect too much from you.

But—let's be honest here—however little the authors of *Juggling for the Complete Klutz* expect, it's too much for me. Bill can juggle three beanbags for several rounds. I can't even do it *once.* (*This was true at the time I wrote it, but things have changed. See Home Life writeup above!*)

As a matter of fact, Klutz has more objects to juggle than you can shake a stick at. See above. My personal favorite is the Juggling Chickens. Somehow I expected these to be rubber, like the fowls on Groucho Marx's "You Bet Your Life," but in real life they're aerodynamically-sound polyvinyl, which means rather hard and stiff. Use 'em for sight gags if juggling is too hard.

Besides a tasteful set of juggling chickens, I also bought Bill the *Juggler's Convention Video: 1989* for his 38th birthday. What a hoot! This professional video record of the highlights of the International Juggler's Association convention has some incredible routines from the first, second, and third-place finalists in the regular and juniors competitions, plus team juggling routines, novelty acts, and more. Over an hour of so-cially unredeeming fun. Expect to lose a lot of oranges to strange accidents after watching this video if you don't have regular juggling stuff on hand!

Klutz also has several how-to juggling videos. *Who? Me? Juggle?* introduces you to a few basic moves. The rest of the tape is then given over to footage of people of various ages, sexes, and sizes juggling. I per-sonally liked the *Juggling Step-by-Step* video better (Home Life has it at the same price), and Bill and the kids second me in this.

STAMP AND COIN COLLECTING

Need I say anything? Is there anyone out there who never started a coin collection (all the old ones in your change) or a stamp collection (saving the stamps off Aunt Rosie's postcards from Italy)? This kind of stamp and coin collecting is free, and simply for fun. More advanced forms of the sport become increasingly ex-pensive. They also yield serious educational opportu-nities, as stamps in particular usually commemorate historically significant places, people, or events. A pad-dleboat stamp might instigate a unit study on river-boats, the Mississippi, and Mark Twain. A stamp from Antigua might send you to the globe to find that tiny island. This is lots of calorie-free fun.

Collecting for the sake of investing is definitely more dicey, and no more or less fun than gambling usually is, minus the murky lighting and sleazy ladies. Stamp and coin collections also drop drastically in val-ue during times of recession or other disasters, so I'd advise you to collect the real moola (gold and silver) instead of fancy coins with high prices and low weights, if you're mainly looking for an investment. Or

even spend the money on a hobby that produces items of monetary or entertainment value. After all, if you can juggle you can always make a living, but the world is not full of employment opportunities for people who spent too much money on collectibles!

NEW**
Postal Commemorative Society

These people sell some absolutely gorgeous stamp sets. I know because several of my children signed up for several of the sets. Here's what happens: You get a brochure detailing the offer—say, gold replicas of each of the famous mint mistakes, plus accompanying card with a color print of the stamp and historical informa-tion. Sign up for the series and you are deluged with other offers, not to mention the stamps you promised to buy. Cancel at any time, but you'll miss out on the special collecting case. This is high-class stamp collect-ing made easy. I doubt that you'll make serious money on investing in these sets (thousands of other people are buying them, after all), but if you have lots of mon-ey to spend on a harmless, non-aerobic hobby, it's an option.

Universal Publishing Company

Universal handles promotional activities for sever-al companies specializing in collectibles. For example: send $1 in U.S. funds to JOLIE COINS, Box 399B, Roslyn Heights, NY 11577-0399 for seven different pieces of genuine foreign paper money from around the world and a free catalog. For the same amount you can get 30 different cat or dog stamps from around the world and a price list from CAT & DOG STAMPS, P.O. Box 466, Port Washington, NY 11050. Or, if you'd prefer six different U.S. Lincoln head cents, each at least 50 years old, send another $1 to JOAN ALEXAN-DER, P.O. Box 7M, Roslyn, NY 11576. Universal says, "These offers are excellent collection starters, party fa-vors, treats, and educational materials for both young and old."

None of these companies sends approvals or sells the names and addresses they receive, so why worry? This is as close to a freebie as I've found in the stamp 'n coin fields.

CHAPTER THIRTY

THE BEST BASIC TOYS FOR YOUR CHILD

Everything is educational these days. Those blocks we played with as kids are now promoted as training tools for fine motor skills. Riding a tricycle now means getting instruction in directionality and other important perceptual skills. Even looking at comic books has been found to be great for visual discrimination training (pick out Superman—there he is—well done!), sequencing, left-right progression, etc., etc.

Americans, the most do-your-own-thing people on the face of the earth, seem to be suffering a bad case of the educational guilties. This has deep psychological overtones, I am sure, but since I hate books that natter about deep psychological overtones, we will just pass on to the practical question:

"Doesn't anyone want to have fun anymore?"

Does a toy *have* to be educational before Ma and Pa Yuppie will buy it? Are yuppies the only people with kids and money? These questions are far beyond the scope of this book. But advertising claims are not beyond the scope of this book, and I think you ought to know that, when it comes to modern toys, lots of words are being fluffed up around a very little bit of real educational value.

Beware, beware, beware! Get to know what the ad jargon really means. Here's a little test to see how you are doing so far.

"The product develops gross motor skills" means:
  A. It teaches teens to become bad drivers.
  B. In order to use it, you are forced to make loud, whirring noises.
  C. It is supposed to develop your general coordination.
  D. All of the above.
  E. None of the above.

Which of the following actually develops fine motor skills?
  A. Eating fried rice with chopsticks at Fast Food Eddie's Chinese Takeout.
  B. Making spitballs.
  C. Writing "I will not make spitballs" 500 times on the blackboard.
  D. All of the above.
  E. None of the above.

"Your children's perceptual ability will be enhanced" could be said of:
  A. Taking a nature walk.
  B. Reading a comic book.
  C. Listening to the Boogie-Woogie Bugle Boy from Company B.
  D. All of the above.
  E. None of the above.

"Children will have hours of fun playing with it" is

  A. An absolutely true statement based on at least 1,000 hours of product testing with kids in real-life situations.

  B. An outright lie—99 percent of kids would rather watch TV.

  C. Marketing talk for, "Here's a way to get the kids out of your hair without paying a baby-sitter."

  D. All of the above.

  E. None of the above.

"The product has great educational value" means

  A. "Our marketing manager has determined that we can raise the price $5 if we say it's educational."

  B. "The two teachers we asked liked their free samples just fine."

  C. "There's still a sucker born every minute."

  D. All of the above.

  E. None of the above.

In real life, virtually *anything* can be touched, tasted, smelled, and looked at, and most things can be shaken and listened to as well. Just because my baby daughter tries to teethe on my shoe as she plays about the floor does not mean shoes should be sold as a "tactile stimulus experience." Every house has things to look at and listen to and taste and smell and feel. Good toys and games aren't "experiences": they are something to *do*.

TOYS, PRO AND CON

At the same time as the educational toy market is bulging to eight times its previous size, a movement is afoot to talk parents out of buying any toys at all. "Toys are childish!" voices cry. (True, of course.) "Children should use *real* tools and do *real* work instead of fooling around with expensive trinkets."

It's bad enough that toys cost so much, and even worse if you have to feel guilty about buying them. Should we feel guilty about buying toys, or (more consistently) stop buying them altogether? Are Junior's Lego bricks a harmful influence?

After giving the matter deep thought, and riffling through more toy catalogs than I care to mention, I think I've found some helpful guidelines.

Passive toys, toys that do things without having anything much done to them, are worthless. In this category put talking dolls, battery-operated miniature cars, and the TV set, as long as these items are used as designed. If the talking doll is used as a regular doll and not limited by the extent of her built-in vocabulary, if the minicar's battery falls out and it can be propelled about the floor on pretend journeys to Alaska, if the TV is turned into an aquarium, then they become useful.

Toys that duplicate adult tools are only useful if it will be years and years before your children are ready for the real thing. What is the sense of buying Junior a toy typewriter when, for the same price, you could get a real used typewriter that he could really learn to type on? Why get Suzy her own tiny set of breadpans and mixing bowls when she can help you with your real baking? Our ten-year-old son, Teddy, washes the (real) dishes in our (real) kitchen sink for $5 a week, and with the money he saved he bought his own used IBM Selectric typewriter. Joseph, our eight-year-old, loves to make cakes with our (real) mixing pans and electric beater. Sarah, our six-year-old, figured out how to install and remove drill bits from Dad's manual drill when she was four years old. Magda, our five-year-old, *loves* tools and is always hovering over the tool caddy every time we have a project. Both boys, and now Sarah, help Dad screw together bookcases and do other carpenter work. It would be too much for a seven-year-old to wield an adult-sized hammer, though, so we bought Ted a good set of children's tools when he was that age, and Joe will soon get one also.

Open-ended construction toys and art materials are good for fantasy play. Under this heading come all sorts of building blocks and construction kits: Legos, Duplos, Tinker Toys, Erector sets, Lincoln logs, and so on. These are the products that really will give Junior "hours of fun," since they are limited only by his imagination. I do not include kits that only build one particular item, like a castle or a Frontier Town, in this category. These are fun only while the project lasts, and then you have to either store them for years or throw away hours of Junior's work.

Board games and other family games are great relaxers. This does not apply to the "wipe out your opponent" sort. Competitive games have their place, but I have never seen any happy results from families playing them. You can change a competitive game into a cooperative game by making the goal to have everyone win, which is how we do it. We don't stop playing until everyone is "home." Games whose only purpose is to produce one "winner" and many "losers" and that teach you nothing along the way belong in the trash.

For children, play is learning. For adults, play is relaxation. If you relax too much, you get limp and sloppy. If you never relax, you get ulcers. The proper balance of play and work produces healthy bodies and minds. "A cheerful heart doeth good like a medicine" (Proverbs 17:22).

ALL-PURPOSE TOY AND GAME COMPANIES

Childcraft

Childcraft's motto is "Toys That Teach." Their catalog is big, bright, and filled with an assortment of educational toys, equipment, and books in all subjects. Childcraft has lots and lots of play equipment and giant building materials: Big Waffle Blocks, giant cardboard blocks, a Combi Kit that can make toys big enough to ride on, the Quadro construction kit that makes a gym, and lots more. There's something in every price range, but yuppies will feel more comfortable with the prices than bargain-hunters. The selections have good educational and play value.

NEW**
Child's Play Educational Toys, Inc.

A new company with a really fine lineup of educational toys. I recognize some excellent games from Aristoplay and Educational Insights, Lauri puzzles, and Brio trains. Beyond that they carry hundreds of items I haven't seen before, but that look wonderful. Unique construction blocks that flex and pivot. Crafts kits. Art supplies. Dramatic play. Fractions, Letters. Math. Geography. Brainy games. Science. Engineering. Nature study (I might send for their Butterfly Garden). Two games to teach fractions through the themes of Fruit Soup and Vegetable Soup. Rainbow Foam Paint. Preschool activity toys. Full-color catalog has good prices, easy-to-follow layout.

Constructive Playthings

Constructive Playthings has two catalogs: a school catalog, loaded with institutional playground equipment and heavy-duty playthings, and a Home Edition. The latter has hands-on stuff only (no books or workbooks). I've seen a lot of catalogs, but this one has several unique crafts that tempted me. The no-spill tempera markers also are a good idea. We struggled with a set from another company that had paintbrush tops attached to bottles, out of which the paint stubbornly refused to flow. Constructive Playthings tests all its products to avoid lemons like that. You may also be interested in the large selection of family games, the free toy guide, or Constructive Plaything's Jewish Education catalog. Lots of reasonably-priced items for ages birth to eight, many under $5. Better prices than other companies.

Lane Nemeth, Discovery Toys® President

Discovery Toys, Inc.
80% of toys cost less than $15.

Lots and lots of toys sold as having educational value. The product line for littler kids is mostly chunky, bright, colorful plastic toys. These are definitely high-quality items, designed to take abuse and come up smiling. Prices are not bad either.

Discovery Toys sells *only* through home demonstrations. Their product line is constantly changing to reflect the best available in the toy market. Discovery Toys products are imported from all over the world, and the country of origin is mentioned in each of the catalog entries which your local educational consultant shows you. In case you're not quite sure about what a particular toy is good for, each item is described in terms of its "Educational Play Value." Every item is beautiful, every item is educational, and most are not to be found anywhere else.

Discovery Toys does *not* send their catalog to the general public, preferring to deal only through local representatives. You may buy toys at a toy party, or order through your rep's catalog.

By hosting a Discovery Toys demonstration, you can get a commission on the toys sold and perhaps even half off one of the most-wanted items (*Children's Encyclopedia*, several neat and expensive construction sets . . .). Discovery Toys is also looking for people to do the selling at their home demos.

Growing Child

Would you like to bridge the generation gap? Growing Child offers a large selection of classy playthings, with an emphasis on classic toys that you might have played with and that can be handed down to your grandchildren. This is not another yuppy catalog: the prices are reasonable. All catalog items are age-graded and developmental.

Growing Child is not a bunch of aging nostalgia buffs either. You can find many of today's best toys along with the old-time favorites like nesting blocks and counting frames. Goodies like Dr. Drew's blocks, a Noah's Ark puzzle with interchangeable pieces, and Lauri puzzles are scattered throughout the catalog. And Growing Child has a large selection of children's literature, including several pages of award-winners.

UPDATED**
HearthSong

"A Catalog for Families." I've watched the Hearth-Song catalog grow from black-and-white with line-art illustrations to its present full-color, beautifully-photographed version. This is one of the few catalogs in which almost every item tempts me! The reason is that the people at HearthSong focus on natural products (wool instead of acrylic, wood instead of plastic), timeless toys and crafts (tin spinning tops, yo-yos, blocks, knitting, basketry . . .), creativity (lots of natural art supplies!), and family togetherness. HearthSong also understands the value of imaginative free play. Their idea of dramatic play props includes lengths of colorful cotton gauze that the child drapes any way she wants, instead of one-size-fits-all masks and other props that limit you to one character. Similarly, their play space is a set of wooden frames and large colorful fabric pieces that kids can arrange and rearrange, instead of a plastic cabin like so many other companies offer.

HearthSong products are not just toys. They are make childhood a wonderland—something like a very loved and protected Victorian Era child might have experienced, but more up-to-date. Just beautiful.

Just For Kids

Definitely yuppy catalog of toys and clothing. Colorful, many pages, rather more frivolous and decorative items than other catalogs. No bargains here: some expensive toys like the Rocking Kitten ($139.95) or the Emigrant Doll Family ($149.95). Good service.

NEW**
Klutz Press

Klutz is not an all-purpose toy catalog, but they do sell lots of classic toys along with lively instructions on how to use them. See individual reviews under toy and game categories.

Toys to Grow On

Toys to Grow On has a big, beautiful color catalog. So do lots of other companies. Ah, but who else sells kits designed to provide 99 hours of fun for . . . Babies, Toddlers, Preschoolers, and School-Age Kids? Each kit is $44.95, thus putting it out of *my* reach, but perhaps not out of yours. And there are such items as a Hermit Crab Lab (including two crabs and extra shells), a build-it-yourself roller coaster for marbles, minigolf with marbles, *Tot Trivia*, etc., etc. For more solidly creative types, there's pages and pages of collage kits, fancy paper kits, paints and paint aprons, butcher-block paper by the roll, double-sided easels, sticker fashions kits, and lots more. Plus their dramatic play props.

Toys to Grow On has an amazing amount of hustle. Who else has a Never Forget Birthday Club? Who else gives away a No-Choke Testing Tube (it lets you know whether any given object is small enough to be swallowed by a young child) *free* with any order? Who else has a chatty company newsletter bound into their catalog, with enticing article titles like, "Why Is This Man Skating Away With Your Toys?" Who else gives away $50 gift certificates to customers who send in interesting tidbits that get published in the catalog? Who else tells you how to gather a variety of insects in next to no time (hold an open umbrella underneath a low branch of a bush and *shake!*)? Hustle isn't everything, but in a country where people dress for success it's bound to help.

BEST BLOCKS

Blocks are the perfect first toy. They are utterly open-ended—you can make anything from blocks! They provide good practice in coordination, cooperation, and that essential skill, learning to take disappointments gracefully, as every tall tower sooner or later falls down. Inventing and implementing new ideas is part of what sets man apart from the animals, and blocks are a child-sized way to work out new ideas. And, best of all, most block styles are completely unbreakable!

Here are a variety of block sets, from the classic alphabet block to fantasy village blocks. Most are hard, or even impossible, to find in local stores. Enjoy your choices!

NEW**
Ames Corporation
Wagon Blocks, $18. Building Blocks, $22. Spelling Blocks, $28. Add $2 shipping.

All I know about this company I got off their card in a business-to-business card deck. They sell three sets of blocks: wagon blocks, for ages one to three (although the picture looked like some of these had parts too small for youngest children), building blocks for ages four and up, and spelling blocks for ages five and up. The spelling block are smaller-sized blocks with capital letters on all sides. The building blocks are unusually-shaped blocks with holes drilled through them, and a slight resemblance to Tinkertoys. The wagon blocks picture was too murky to make out. All blocks are made from mahogany, an extra-durable wood, and touted as being heirloom quality.

UPDATED**
Dr. Drew's Blocks
72 blocks with drawstring bag, $34.95; with wood tray, $54.95. 108 with wood tray, $54.95 (this set is their best seller). 288 with cardboard box, $99.95. 36 with wood tray, $24.95; with cardboard box, $14.95. 32 with drawstring bag, $17.95. Add 10% shipping ($2 minimum).

Here's the block set that inspired this section. See the picture, and you'll know why!

Dr. Drew's blocks are made out of hardwood, not your typical soft pine. This means they clack together in a satisfying fashion and they don't immediately develop a leprosy of dings and dents like common blocks. Dr. Drew's blocks are also slim and rectangular (3 x 2 x ½"), so even babies can grasp them easily and adults can build terrific constructions (see the accompanying photo). The blocks come in a natural, splinter-free finish that go with any decor except Recent Plastic. They are truly a "discovery" toy, limited only by your imagination and the size of the set you purchase. The whole kit and caboodle comes with a durable and attractive canvas bag, so you have someplace to put them (most other sets come with a cardboard box that immediately generates into a ragged eyesore). Now you know why Dr. Drew's Blocks received a "Toy of the Year" award from the Parents Choice Foundation.

Oh yes: the inventor, Walter F. Drew, is a for-real Ph.D. and early childhood educator. He would say that the simplicity and uniformity of his blocks make it easy for children to discover number relationships and basic geometric patterns and to develop their creativity through construction and free play. He would also point out that all ages can play with the blocks together. I will just say that these blocks are *fun*!

We've owned a variety of these sets, from the biggest to the smallest, in cardboard boxes, bags, and wooden trays. My advice is to go for their best-seller, the set of 108 in the wood tray. The wood tray makes it much easier and neater to pack away, as well as teaching all sorts of basic sorting and arranging skills, and you get enough in the set to build some really great constructions. A family heirloom you can pass on to your grandkids!

NEW**
Flax Art & Design
Archiblocks, $60 a set. Choice of Greek or Santa Fe.

I don't know if the following unique block sets can really be called *basic,* but they certainly are different. Based on the idea that to rebuild the past is ever to remain a child, what you have here are two sets of what can only be called building blocks of history. The Greek set includes 58 maple blocks shaped like Doric columns, triangular pediments, and assorted rectangles. The Santa Fe set has 76 blocks including arches, posts, a ladder, and dowels for sticking through holes in a rectangle, thus simulating guns pointing out of the Alamo or something like that.

Having never had a chance to play with this set, the following comment may be sour grapes. Still, I wonder if either set includes enough blocks for really open-ended play. Seems to me that once you've built the mini-Greek temple portico, that's about all you can do with the Greek set. The Santa Fe, having more blocks, has a few more possibilities, but you'd really need two sets to get things moving. At the price, that doesn't look too realistic for most of us.

NEW**
Growing Child
Blocks in a Box, $69.95, or $59.95 for *Growing Child* subscribers. Engraved nameplate, add $5. Other block sets available.

You remember the alphabet block sets from our youth, with letters, numbers, and animals inscribed on the sides. This is a nicer version. You get 64 1¾" square "practically indestructible" hardwood alphabet blocks with rounded edges. Two sides are embossed. Bright, non-toxic colors. Counting all six sides of each block, you end up with 248 alphabet letters, 64 numerals, eight mathematical symbols, and 64 different labeled pictures of birds and animals. Sharper, crisper letter outlines than the old-fashioned version. The whole set fits in its 8½" square unfinished wood box, and you can carry it around easily thanks to the two brass handles on the sides. Optional engraved nameplate.

NEW**
HearthSong
Castle Blocks, $54. New Village Blocks, $46. Shipping extra.

For years I longed to get my hands on Hearth-Song's Village Blocks set. These are 70 pieces, 1" to 2" across, some more-or-less cubic and others more-or-less triangular, cleverly cut with grooves and arches so that when you put them together you get the effect of doorways, windows, and roofs. Twenty of the pieces are colored, for a cheerful effect. The whole set fits in its (included) cloth storage sack.

When my review set arrived, my suspicions were justified. The children immediately took Village Blocks to their hearts and began creating towns, castles, cathedrals, and other delightful creations. Every one from the one-year-old to the ten-year-old has spent hours happily playing with these blocks. Definitely a Best Basic toy.

Not wanting to press my luck, I didn't ask for a review set of HearthSong's Castle Blocks. These 60 maple blocks have the same user interface as the Castle

Blocks: different-shaped pieces that go well together, some grooved and arched, others not. Red roof blocks (some triangular cones) and large cylindrical bases make the "castle" effect. Blocks range in size from 1½" square to 4¾" long—somewhat more chunky that the Village Blocks. For kids in love with princesses and knights, this looks like an alternative Best Basic toy.

BEST PUZZLES

Puzzles, like blocks, are an essential first toy. Like blocks, puzzles foster fine motor skills and spatial perception. Also like blocks, they don't "teach" these skills so much as provide a motivating way for kids to practice them on their own.

For sheer educational play value, nobody beats the two puzzle companies below.

NEW**
Lauri, Inc.
Fit-A-Space, $9.50. Chubby Puzzles, Beginner Puzzles, Picture Puzzles, $5.50 each. Large Pattern Puzzles, $12.95 each. A-Z Panels, $6.50 each. 1-10 Panel, $3.50. Perception Puzzles, $5.50 each. Shape and Color Sorter, $10.95.

I love Lauri puzzles! Lauri puzzles are all made out of colorful crepe foam rubber. This means they are fun to look at, have an intriguing texture, are quiet to use, don't slip when you're working on a smooth surface, and even smell nice! They also come in all sorts of innovative styles, for everyone from preschoolers on up. Example: Fit-A-Space is circles into which you fit 52 mix-and-match shapes of different colors. Chubby Puzzles are first puzzles for little kids with two to four pieces each, plus frame. Each puzzle is 8" square and comes with a removable pattern board. Beginner Puzzles are the next step up. Each has five to 10 large pieces and makes a very pretty picture. Picture Puzzles (Lauri has 33 of them) come with 11 to 23 pieces. These are lovely, colorful puzzles of such things as Noah's Ark and an astronaut taking a space walk. For more advanced puzzlers, Lauri has Large Pattern Puzzles (32 to 93 pieces) in fun pictures like a fantasy castle, a train, and a merry-go-round.

Thinking "education"? Lauri's new Shape and Color Sorter is the best I have ever seen. Twenty-five pieces of double-thick crepe foam rubber can be sorted by either shape or color. They come with a base board and five colored pegs. I also wouldn't be without

Lauri's A-Z Panels (both capitals and lower-case) and 1-10 Panel. Children fit the crepe foam alphabet letters (or numbers) into the frame. Perception Puzzles are foam rubber with cutouts of slightly different shapes into which you fit pieces that are all of similar objects. E.g., the School of Fish Perception Puzzle includes 12 fish of different colors and shapes. Fit-A-State and Fit-A-World map puzzles teach geography. Lots, lots more!

Pacific Puzzle Company
United States puzzle: Small $23, medium $40, large $65. Continents: Europe, Asia, Africa $19 each; North, South America $16 each; set of 5 continents, $80. Dymaxion World puzzles: small $22, large $45. Bible Map puzzles: Early Bible Lands, New Testament Palestine, Old Testament Palestine $18 each; Roman World, $20; complete set of 4, $70. Alphabet puzzles (upper-case, lower-case), $25 each. Number puzzle, $12. Geometric shapes puzzle, $18. Stenciled animal puzzles: $5 each. Intertwining animal puzzles, $12.50–$24. Natural People Puzzle,™ $12. Other puzzles available. Many puzzles available with knobs (20¢/knob, $3 minimum). Shipping: $3 first puzzle, $1 additionals. Canada, AK, HI add 50% more shipping. Inquire for foreign shipping rates.

Exceptionally high-quality line of geographical, educational, and novelty puzzles. Pacific Puzzle Company uses the best materials available, including imported birch plywood, and (for their geographical puzzles) the nicest full-color maps they can find. Puzzle shapes are carefully cut to truly represent the shape of the state, country, letter, or whatever.

Now, let me tell you about what exactly Pacific Puzzle Company has to offer. Beyond the usual United States, world, and continent maps (all impressively crafted and really solid), there's the Dymaxion™ puzzles. These 20 triangular shapes fit together to present the world. However, unlike other map puzzles, you can put it together correctly dozens of different ways, depending on which viewing angle you choose to highlight. Or, for little folks, you can get a Beginner's U. S. puzzle. Same accurately-cut state shapes, simpler format. State pieces are plain, bold colors with no printing. The puzzle backing is printed with state outlines and names and the location and name of each state capital.

Pacific Puzzle Company's solid wood alphabet and number puzzles use the contrasting colors of natural birch and mahogany to spotlight letters and numerals. Unlike crepe rubber puzzles I have seen, these leave the center holes of the characters empty (e.g., the two holes in the letter "B" and the middle of the "O"), making them safe for young children. A knobbed geometric shape puzzle is also available.

Now, back to the unusual. PPC's Natural People Puzzle™ is 50 stylized person-shaped cutouts in a drawstring bag. There's a catch: the pieces only fit together *one* way, making it a popular challenge for adults and older children. This puzzle is also made of birch and mahogany.

Stenciled animal puzzles are just that: country-style stencils on natural birch. Only 12 pieces apiece, these lovely designs are for younger children.

There's more, but I'm sure you get the idea. Now, price. Some of Pacific Puzzle Company's offerings seemed pricey to me at first blush. After all, $20-$45 is a lot to pay for a map puzzle when you can get a cardboard puzzle for $1.29. Ah, but these are more than puzzles—they are *artwork!* Develop your children's artistic taste and respect for beauty at the same time as their puzzle solving ability with these elegant puzzles.

Timberdoodle

Timberdoodle is now the exclusive source for Pacific Puzzle Company's Bible Lands puzzles. Timberdoodle sells both Pacific Puzzle Company and Lauri puzzles at discount—write for their current prices.

BEST CONSTRUCTION TOYS

If you're an obsessive-compulsive type, I can tell you right now that construction toys will bring much sorrow into your life. Piles of parts scrunching underfoot. Strange objects poking you under the sofa cushions. Half-finished models littering the halls. If you can't live graciously with a certain amount of continuous mess, don't even think of buying construction toys for your kids.

We all like to theorize, of course, that Junior will learn good organizing habits and put his toys neatly away. This can happen, but don't forget Junior's little brothers and sisters, who have *not* learned good organizing habits. Not that you will be able to prove who is responsible for scattering the Erector set to kingdom come. When you find the inevitable mess, fingers will be pointing in all directions, and sure enough, the culprit will turn out to be Mr. Nobody.

Since Construction Toy Pickup is going to be a favorite sport at your house for years to come, it makes good sense to either (1) limit the arena to a special playroom well-stocked with large boxes, or (2) settle on a few favorite construction toys instead of turning the whole house into Lost Part Junkyard, Inc.

We all have our personal favorites, of course, but for sheer versatility and long-lasting play value, the following two sets are hard to beat.

NEW**
LEGO Shop at Home Service

#260, *Idea Book*, $3.25. #2312, DUPLO Block Set, 39 pieces, ages 2–5, $13.75. #2770, Furnished DUPLO Playhouse, ages 2–5, 58 pieces, $69. #760, Storage Cabinet, age 5 and up, $54. #6066 Camouflaged Robin Hood Outpost, 221 pieces, age 7 and up, $22. #6704, Black Falcon's Fortress, 435 pieces, age 8 and up, $35. #6317, Trees and Flowers Accessories kit for LEGOLAND Town, 24 pieces, ages 6 and up, $4. LEGO bricks, 62 pieces, specify color, ages 3 and up, $4.50. #8054, Motorized TECHNIC Universal Building Set, 206 pieces, ages 8 and up, $47. #8890 TECHNIC Idea Book, 52 pages, $4.50. These are just sample prices; the catalog has hundreds of kits. Free shipping.

This has got to be the favorite construction toy of home schooling families. From the Duplo kits for preschoolers, with their big chunky pieces, through the "regular" Lego bricks beloved of elementary-school kids, to the new motorized LEGO Technic series for preteens and up, there's quite literally something for everyone. The LEGO line now includes hundreds of accessory kits for everything from fantasy play with knights and castles to futuristic space stations. Boats. Trains. Cars. Planes. Buildings. Trucks. You're going to lose some of the pieces, so how handy that you can get replacement pieces from this Shop at Home Service!

By the way, for *serious* LEGO brick fans: the Traveloguer Collection of European travel videos from Quantum Communications has a sequence on the Denmark tape where you get to visit an entire amusement park constructed of LEGO bricks. You can also see the bricks being made in the factory. Fascinating!

NEW**
Timberdoodle

Quadro set, regularly $400, discounted to $315. Baby Quadro, regularly $200, discounted to $175. Shipping extra.

Quadro is "the world's first large scale construction kit." Kids can bolt the large red plastic pipes, different-colored panels, and black connector pieces together themselves, and the resulting structures can hold people who weigh up to 220 pounds. Construction possibilities are limited only by the child's imagination. Designed for both indoor and outdoor use, Quadro can be made into a number of different play gyms, desks, houses, bookshelves, slides, and other utilitarian structures. Kids can also bolt it together into fantasy planes, castles, cars . . . whatever they can think of.

Timberdoodle only offers the Universal Quadro kit, which is the top-of-the-line model. It includes 57 connectors, 12 short tubes, 48 medium tubes, six long tubes, 10 color panels (four black, two yellow, two blue, two green), four indoor wheels, 160 bolts, four wrenches, and a Mini Design Kit. This latter is a 1:5 scale version of the big Quadro kit, and is included so your child can try out his construction ideas in small scale before going to work with the big kit.

Baby Quadro is a new set of 232 elements, on a smaller scale than the normal Quadro kits. It comes with four half panels and shorter tubes, plus two wheels and four rollers, so the kiddies can have fun pushing around their new creation. Baby Quadro comes with directions for building 11 different things, from a table with chair to an airplane, but of course you can make many more projects than these.

Quadro sets are all compatible, even Baby Quadro and the Universal set, and warranted for one year, which is about as good a guarantee as you can get on outdoor play equipment.

Now comes the $400 question: Do we own a Quadro set? We do not, but I trust the people we know who have had Quadro sets for years, and none of them are complaining.

Timberdoodle also sells some incredible fishertechnik engineering construction kits, which more than give LEGO Technic a run for its money. All their fishertechnik kits are sold at significant discounts off manufacturer's retail price, by the way. Top stuff!

BEST PAPER DOLLS

Sure, you can get paper dolls at the supermarket. But there's life beyond Fashion Francie and her wonderful swimsuit wardrobe. See below!

UPDATED**
Paper Soldier

Catalog, $4.

A source for wonderful antique pop-up books, paper dolls and soldiers, and all sorts of other neat things. Many one-of-a-kind items (collectibles), plus the best paper dolls currently in print. Example: Collectible paper dolls from The Enchanted Forest Series, at $6 a set. This includes Beauty and the Beast, Little Red Riding Hood, Goldilocks and the Three Bears, and Rapunzel. Each package includes the character named, plus one or more supporting characters from the story (e.g., Grandma and the wolf), six colored outfits, and six black and white outfits. Historical paper dolls: Henry the Eighth and his wives, for example. Dress-up dolls for little kids (teddy bears, baby mice, etc.). Reprinted paper dolls. Collectibles. Fashion dolls of various eras. Modern paper dolls, e.g. Princess Diana and Prince Charles. Plus lots of paper soldiers, paper dollhouses, paper airplanes, paper buildings. If you like scissors, this is your company.

BEST REAL DOLLS

I grew up not liking dolls. My idea of a doll was a plastic-smelling, hard lump with a perpetual phony smile and a figure that was some German manufacturer's idea of a nice, healthy baby—e.g., incredibly fat. The face was that of a creature never seen in this world—partly adult with its facial proportions, partly child with mouth pursed in a perpetual sickening "goo." Not exactly something I wanted to hug to my heart. The reaction was more like, "I wish I'd been given pajamas instead." This bias against dolls persisted long enough to also render playing house guilty by association, and so on into ingrained tomboyhood.

Alas and alack! Oh, sniff and sorrow! If only I had been given some better dolls to play with! Perhaps I could have been married to some nice young man and had seven kids . . . instead of—wait a minute! I *did* get married to a nice young man! I *do* have seven kids!

So maybe playing or not playing with dolls is not such a big thing psychologically after all. Freddie is not going to turn green or move to the weird part of San Francisco just because he likes to go to bed with his sister's rag doll. Janie's entire future does not depend on being protected from plastic German dolls sent by loving German aunts. All the same, a cuddly, cute, meaningful, lovable doll beats one that isn't. Hence the award-winning entries below.

NEW**
HearthSong
Bunting Baby Kit, $18, choice of blue or pink, specify skin color. Real Doll Kit, $28, specify skin and hair color. Baby Doll Kit, $34, specify skin and hair color. Mini Kit, $13, specify skin color. Mini Baby Doll Kit, $14, specify skin color. *Making Dolls*, $10.95.

Want to make natural fiber dolls for the young 'uns? HearthSong sells not only the dolls themselves (prices and sizes vary), but a kit to make your very own 12" natural fiber baby doll and a book about doll-making. Keep in mind that I haven't seen either of these, now, still, the catalog descriptions and illustrations look enticing. *Making Dolls*, the catalog informs us, is "rich with full color photos and simple diagrams which show readers how to make 17 different types of dolls," including a cuddly baby doll, large baby doll, finger puppets, gnomes, dollhouse dolls, and so on. HearthSong's own Bunting Baby Kit comes with cotton

velour for the hood and body, carded new wool filling, cotton knit for head and hands, thread, tubular gauze, embroidery thread for features and decorations, pattern, and instructions. Result: one cuddly baby doll.

HearthSong also offers a Real Doll kit (all the ingredients for a 16" doll) and Baby Doll Kit (life-sized 20" doll with hair). Those who just need instructions and the hard-to-find cotton-knit for skin (it comes with a pattern silkscreened onto the knit) and tubular gauze for the inner head can order the Mini Kits.

We bought HearthSong's wool-filled First Doll a few years ago, and I want to warn you now: when they say "hand-washable" they mean *hand* washable! We put the doll in the washer with some Woolite, and got back a sad little bag full of hard woolen lumps. Don't let this happen to you! Apart from this tragic experience, the doll was a real hit with my then-three-year-old daughter. (And, never fear, we dug out the wadded-up stuffing and replaced it with nice fresh wool lint from our dryer the next time we washed our Superwash wool mattress pad. Happy ending!)

UPDATED**
Pleasant Company
Doll and book, $74. Doll with hardcover book, $80. Doll with Keepsake Edition paperback set (6 books), $100. Doll with Keepsake Edition hardcover, $140. Books, $5.95 each paperback, $12.95 each hardcover. Basic accessories, $20. Other accessories, mostly $16–$20 each. Twelve Months of Traditional Pastimes, $15/month. Shipping extra on everything except Twelve Months subscription.

The American Girls collection from Pleasant Company is an entirely different approach to dolls. These are role-play dolls for girls ages seven to 14. Each has tons of delightful accessories and an entire six-book series introducing her character.

Kirsten is a Swedish pioneer girl who comes to America with her family in the mid-1800s. She is the doll we tested. Samantha is a rich nine-year-old Victorian orphan, living with her grandmother in turn-of-the-century New York. Molly is from a more modest, but not poor, background. Her story centers around life in America during the Second World War.

The 18" dolls are absolutely beautiful, as befits their price! They have cuddly cloth bodies and posable vinyl arms, legs, and head. Each comes fully dressed in historically-accurate garments (except for the Velcro closures!) and with at least one book. The Keepsake Editions are worth getting, if you can manage it, as the boxed set is not only much more attractive and a good way to keep the books nice, but it comes with a built-in bow and gold-tone bookmark clip. Romantic!

So you have a doll and at least one book about her character. Now the fun *really* begins! First, you can get a basic accessories kit, featuring items mentioned in the books. In Kirsten's case, that included an embroidered *hankie* to tuck into her apron pocket, a wooden *spoon* and *spoon bag,* a *sunbonnet*, and an *amber heart* on a cord to hang around her neck. Then, for each book in the six-book series, there are special accessories. A slate bag with chalk (it really works!) and other supplies, all in a calico bag (Kirsten). A Summer Amusements kit with a tuffet, paint set with palette, brush, and six tiny tubes of watercolor paint, and a doll-sized sketchbook for you to paint in (Samantha). Capture the Flag gear kit includes whistle, armband, flag, canoe paddle, letter, picture, and a bean can full of creepy crawlers (Molly). These are just a few of the dozens of accessory kits available.

These are not cheap, crummy items, like the kind of doll accessories you find in too many stores, but solid props with accompanying historical information. Your girls can really get into *learning* about the historical periods while dreaming themselves into the lives of these dolls. The girl-sized outfits now available from Pleasant Company (e.g., Saint Lucia Dress in sizes 6X, 7, 8, 10, 12, 14, and 16) let them play-act the part as well.

To take the process even further, Pleasant Company now has a Twelve Months of Traditional Pastimes subscription program. It starts with a paper dolls kit—Kirsten, Samantha, and Molly paper dolls plus old-fashioned paper clothes and accessories and historical information. Other months' offerings include a Theatre kit (star in three plays, one for each girl, all packed in a lovely ribbon-tied box), family album, old-fashioned games, a cookbook, a diary, embroidery sampler, Victorian valentines, knitting Nellie, weaving loom, lanyard kit, and straw ornaments. If ordered separately, items vary in price.

Some people might think this is too much money to spend on toys. Considering the fine moral values and even acknowledgment of Christianity built into all three series, considering the innocent pleasure these toys give girls at that impressionable preteen age, and considering that you can get a doll, Keepsake Edition books, accessory kits, and Twelve Months subscription for less than the cost of one college credit, the price does not seem excessive to me for anyone who has the money to spend on a girl they love.

In fact, my children's only negative criticism of this series was, "Why don't they have an American *Boys* collection? Like a Daniel Boone doll, or Jim Bowie doll?" I'll pass on your suggestion, kids!

BEST DOLLHOUSES

Every little girl wants a dollhouse of her very own. Even me, although I was a strange child who never played with dolls if I could help it! Dollhouse people and their furniture were different. Playing with such a small-scale world gives children a way to practice feeling domestic responsibility, and to act out the roles they are trying to learn. They can practice being the architect, interior decorator, mommy, and daddy. A child is lord of his or her little play world, which makes a welcome change from the reality of always being under the tutelage of others.

NEW**
HearthSong

Three Story Dollhouse, $235. Living Room, Bedroom, Children's Room, Bathroom, Kitchen, Dining Room sets, $29.95 each. Piano, $16.95. Rustic Cupboard, $25.75. Dollhouse Cookstove Set, $22.50. Dollhouse Dishes (30 pieces), $13.25. Dollhouse Kitchenware (16 pieces), $10.95. Dollhouse dolls, $9.95 each.

This is the ultimate, the supremo, the top of the line, the poshest-of-the-posh dollhouse you would ever want to get. No, it's not carpeted with tiny oriental rugs, or illuminated with cunning little electrical gadgets or any of the other whiz-bang expensive stuff that you find in other high-end dollhouses. What we have here is solid play value. I say this without having tried one in person—the catalog pictures make it clear enough what the kits contain and how they work.

As with other HearthSong products, this dollhouse is designed for open-ended play. It comes with an attic pulley for hauling toy objects up and down, sliding wall panels, stairway, rope ladder, and attic clothesline. You put it together without tools—an important point, since we still have the pieces of a discount dollhouse sitting in our garage which we discovered needed cutting out, gluing, nailing, and painting *after* we bought it.

Made of birch plywood with a natural pine frame, the HearthSong dollhouse is reassuringly traditional in feel, while incorporating today's preferred open, hands-on feel. This is not a dollhouse to sit back and admire, but one to get involved with.

It's a pity that all the lovely furniture, without which the dollhouse is just four big rooms and a large attic, costs so much. I'm not saying that it's overpriced, because you get an awful lot in each of those durable, all-wood sets. For example, the Bedroom set includes a double bed with bedding, a closet, set of shelves, and

two night tables. It's just that I'll probably never be able to buy one until the kids are bringing *their* kids to visit us—and by then I fear I'll be too creaky to get down and play with it myself!

NEW**
Paper Soldier

Inside a Tudor House, Inside a Victorian House, $12.50 each. *How to Make Dolls' Furniture,* $3.50. *The Victorian Parlor,* $2.95. *Shaker Paper House,* $10. *Cut and Assemble Paper Dollhouse Furniture,* $3.95. Lots more. Shipping extra.

This is for those of you with teeny-tiny budgets drooling fruitlessly over the HearthSong dollhouse. Paper Soldier sells *paper* dollhouses. Let's start with *Inside a Tudor House* and *Inside a Victorian House.* These paper toys come with two large, full-color wall sheets and a floor base. Slot the sheets together to make the rooms, then cut out the eight sheets of furniture and accessories. These are full-color on one side, black-and-white on the other. The theory is that you can color in the B&W side. Anyway, you also get five cut-out people and historical information as well.

The Victorian Parlor is just what it sounds like. Printed on heavy stock in black and white, it's a completely furnished parlor including family. You cut and color. *Shaker Paper House* is a book that opens up to make the stand-up walls of four tiny rooms. You furnish them with the paper Shaker furniture included. *How to Make Dolls' Furniture* is a reproduction of a Victorian classic. Lavishly illustrated. *Cut and Assemble Paper Dollhouse Furniture* provides you with four rooms of mission-style furniture to put together with scissors and glue. Ultra-fancy models from France in 1:250 scale, of L'Arc de Triomphe, Chateau Chenonceau, and Paris Opera, and other gorgeous French buildings. Many more paper models, including historical buildings like Monticello, German castles, and so on.

BEST PAPER AIRPLANES AND OTHER WIND TOYS

NEW★★
Family Learning Center
The Old Fashioned Paper Airplane Book, $2.95 postpaid.

Every little boy, and many a little girl, loves to spend hours folding paper airplanes. Why not add some variety to this classic kid-pleasing activity? Here are instructions for how to fold a variety of old-fashioned paper airplanes using common notebook paper. Includes instructions for an Arrow Plane, High Flyer, Star Cruiser, Daddy's Favorite, Bi-Wing Glider, Gliding Jet, Soaring Eagle, and Pete's Plane.

Into the Wind Kites

A kite of beauty is a toy forever . . . Kites, I daresay, are one of the few fun things left that haven't been packaged as "educational." However, kite flying is no longer sheer frivolity either. Men with muscles of steel now spend their free time hauling stunt kites about, or being hauled about by same, as a sport. Two-string stunt kites have been clocked at speeds in excess of 90 mph while still going through precise maneuvers.

Gentler sorts can still laze about in the grass watching their kites float about in the bonny blue. New kite materials make the devices both compact and lightweight, so you can stuff them in a bag and take them along for your family picnic.

Into the Wind has a selection of kites that range from elegant simplicity to downright weird. Some kites are shaped like stars, some like manta rays, some like shoeboxes. You can get a Sky Shark (it looks like Jaws aloft), an eagle, butterflies, parrots, and other extravagant, colorful creatures. Dragon kites have long, long tails and Precision Star Cruisers have each other (you can stack six on a line). Airfoils! Amazing Flying Bird that winds up and flaps his wings! Windsocks! Airplane Kites! Wind Fish! Fighter Kites! Kitemaking materials and accessories! A little further afield in the field of flight, Into the Wind also has a pile of boomerangs.

Don't think this all means lots of money either. A 6½' wingspan nylon Rainbow Delta costs only $19, and a Rainbow Octopus kite is just $5. Well-heeled types can manage to spend $100 or more on a single kite, but most offerings in this catalog are in range of the average kite fanatic.

Into the Wind's *Pocket Guide to Kiteflying* sells for a mere 25¢ and can help you fly a kite like an expert. Into the Wind has materials for kitemaking too.

NEW★★
Paper Soldier
Scale model planes, $2 to $15. Jack Armstrong specials, $2.50 each. Shipping extra. Catalog, $4.

In a more historical vein, here's a lineup of model historic aircraft made out of paper. I love this catalog hype: "Hey Kids! Be the last one on your block to own these penny weight flying planes from Jack Armstrong and Wheaties. If you missed out 40 years ago, here's another chance." Dozens of other paper models series, both American and German, and some rare Polish models. Full color. Plus paper locomotives and other ground-bound transportation.

BEST CLASSIC GAMES

The best games in life are free, like tag. Others require slightly more equipment, like hopscotch (ya gotta have chalk and a sidewalk). Kids teach other kids these games. But it's not always easy to find the basic equipment for some of the great classic games. Dimestore jacks are invariably crummy, and lots of toy stores don't even carry marbles or yo-yos.

So who ya gonna call? Klutz Press, that's who! These people have devoted themselves to making the world a fun, and sometimes silly, place to live. In this they have succeeded admirably.

One comment: The reason these games are in the Toys chapter and not the Educational Games chapter is that I'm not going to waste your time pretending that jacks is educational. It's a game, that's all. Ditto marbles, yo-yoing, and kooshing. (If you don't know what a koosh is, you'll find out in a minute.)

MARBLES

NEW★★
Klutz Press
The Klutz Book of Marbles, $6.95 plus $2 shipping.

Klutz Press is the definite winner here. Look no farther for your first set of marbles and a book that explains how to use them. *The Klutz Book of Marbles* comes with a net bag containing 15 of the most beautiful marbles I have seen, *and* a fabric drawstring pouch in which to keep them. The book itself is the usual spiral-bound laminated-cardstock Klutz production, with full-color cartoon illustrations explaining every step of marble lore. You get a brief introduction to the sport, then straight on into 16 classic marbles games, from the tournament game of Ringers (as played in the annual National Marbles Tournament) to less-familiar games like Black Snake and Bridgeboard.

JACKS

NEW★★
Klutz Press
The Klutz Book of Jacks, $6.95 plus $2 shipping.

Learn how to handle your jacks successfully and lots of new and old games to play with them. Games include Plainsies, Pigs in the Pen, Cherries in the Basket, Washing Jacks, Speed Jacks, Scatter, Slugsnail, Seisnialp (backwards plainsies), Goats on the Mountain, Dog Paddle, and Shooting Stars (a cross between juggling and jacks).

The Klutz Book of Jacks comes with 14 colored metal jacks in a net bag, a rubber ball, and a fabric drawstring pouch in which to keep them. The book is spiral-bound for ease of use. Pages are made of laminated cardstock and covered with full-color cartoon illustrations, some humorous and some educational. As a pigtailed girl I played jacks without this book (it *can* be done), but at the price, why try?

KOOSH

NEW★★
Klutz Press
The Official Koosh Book, $9.95. Extra koosh ball, $4.95. Mondo koosh, $9.95. Add $3 shipping to total order.

So koosh-playing is not a "classic game" yet. It will be.

First, the question, "What's a koosh?" The answer: "A rubber Tribble with the frizzies." *The Official Koosh Book* will teach you over 30 games and activities to do with this odd creation. Most require teams, partners, or enemies, such as Lacroosh and Bop the Brother. You can do things with a koosh that you can't with a regular ball or Frisbee. Some of the games also can be played with regular balls or Frisbees. It all depends on how hard your hands are and whether you're into kooshiness or not. For solo activities, you can also juggle kooshes or play hopscoosh with 'em, just like you can with regular stuff like beanbags.

The Official Koosh Book comes with a pink-blue-and-purple koosh ball, so you can see it and be amazed at its obvious wonderfulness. Warning: The kids will all want one or more koosh balls of their own. Solution: Klutz will be happy to sell you either a "normal" koosh ball (insofar as there can be anything normal about kooshes) or a supersized Mondo koosh. (They will also be happy to sell you a set of pink flamingos for your front lawn, but I'm not responsible for that.)

An application Klutz didn't think of: Teaching little kids to catch. Deb Deffinbaugh of Timberdoodle first pointed out to me that kooshes are easier to catch than regular balls, and she's right. She didn't mention that little kids like to try to snack on them, but that's all right too, as long as they don't actually bite off any of the rubber frizzies. A new Basic Toy for the Nintendo generation.

YO-YO

NEW✶✶
Klutz Press
The Klutz Yo-Yo Book, $9.95. *No-Jive Yo-Yo*, $15. *Smothers Brothers Signature Yo-Yo*, $25. *Silver Bullet*, $25.

The Klutz Yo-Yo Book has sparked a minor yo-yo revival at my house, thanks to its hardwood American maple yo-yo and challenging tricks—$9.95. There's more—*lots* more.

I should also mention that most Klutz books are wire-bound on heavy card stock, making them both durable and easy to use. Really helpful illustrations (colored where necessary) and down-home instructions showing how to use your jacks, yo-yo, marbles, nylon cord, beanbags, aerobie, plastic jump rope, bubble apparatus, hacky sack, harmonica, koosh ball, seed packages, magic props, card deck, and so on in more clever ways than you ever dreamed possible!

Every child will find *something* here to be good at.

Klutz continually comes up with more new whydidn't-someone-do-this-before products (including some that are more strictly educational, such as their *Kids Gardening*), so be sure to send for their latest consumer catalog.

"Seaweed" and "Royal Majesty"

CLASSIC TOYS

Clark County Crafts
Carrousel riding horses, $18 each. Quantity discounts. Custom badges, 75¢ each (minimum of 4 badges).

Looking for an old-fashioned stick riding horse with personality and pizzazz? Clark County Crafts, an Oregon home business, may have what you're looking for. What you get is a hardwood dowel with a stuffed "horse head" mounted on it. Each horse is crafted from different combinations of fabric and uniquely accessorized. Face fabric may be corduroy, calico, or plush fur. The mane might be wool yarn, worsted acrylic, cotton, silk, or fringe. Eyes can be felt circles or acrylic "glass"; the essential halter is cording. All this in any of a rainbow of color combinations, and each with its own name. "Seaweed," for example, is a lovely green with silk ears and has ball fringe for a halter.

Also available is a custom flag/banner service. Send a picture or drawing of what you want, including outside dimensions, and they'll give you a free estimate. Banners are one-sided, but flags are two-sided and can have different designs on each side.

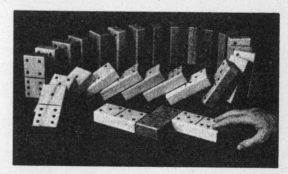

World Wide Games
Marble roller, $98.50. Table cricket, $169.95. Box hockey, $168.50. British ring toss, $32.50. Shoot-the-moon, $24.95. Maori Sticks, $6.75. Pommawonga, $12.75. Pic-E-U-Nee, $13.95. Backgammon, $87.50. Large Dominoes, $59.95. Hindu Pyramid, $12.50. Sponge Polo, $99.95. Wykersham, $49.95. *New Fun Encyclopedia*, $64.95 (set of 5 volumes).

If you like wood, you'll love WWG's games. They have marble mazes and table cricket and box hockey and British Ring Toss (toss rubber rings at hooks on a board). They have Shoot-the-Moon and Maori Sticks and Pommawonga and Pic-E-U-Nee (one-handed Ping-Pong). Backgammon. Building blocks. Solid cherry wooden toys. Large Dominoes. Hindu Pyramid. Sponge Polo. Wykersham. Etc. The prices are fairly outrageous, but these are heavy-duty, handcrafted toys meant mainly for public use, as in playgrounds and cruise ships.

WWG also has books about games, such as the *New Fun Encyclopedia*. And for people who like to play in huge swarms, there are six-foot Earthballs and the ever-silly Parachutes.

CHRISTIAN TOYS

UPDATED**
Rainfall Inc.
Praying Praise dolls, $19.95 each. "Fruit of the Spirit" shape sorter, $13.99. "Full Armor" set, $23.99. Bible Peel & Play, $4.99 each. Bible Play-Alongs, $3.99 each. Color 'n Dial, $9.99. Refills, $5.99 each. Suggested retail prices.

Rainfall Toys has a fairly complete line of open-ended Christian toys, from dolls to Bible videos.

"Joy," "Love," and "Christian" are cute 16" praise dolls. For the benefit of the uninitiated, a "praise" doll is one designed to "capture the joy of prayer." They come packaged in an on-the-knees praying position, with hands devoutly folded. Joy and Love are girls; Christian is a boy. These are just plain dolls with pretty clothes and hair—no electronic messages, no Bible verses on cassette, no moving lips.

The "Fruit of the Spirit" shape sorter is a regular shape sorter—baby sticks objects through the properly-shaped hole in order to get them inside, then pulls the ring to dump them all out again. In the new, improved version of this shape sorter, each shape is labeled with a Christian virtue—e.g., "goodness," and the shape has some connection with the virtue. "Long-suffering" is shaped like a cross, "gentleness" is a lamb, and "love" is a heart. What is "peace"? You guessed it—a dove!

Rainfall's "Full Armor of God" play armor is just that—classic plastic play armor for your child to wear, with each piece emblazoned with a motto from Ephesians 6. The breastplate, for example, has "Righteousness" written large across it; the helmet sports the

word "Salvation." You'll have to explain the significance of the Christian tags to your children, as otherwise the little rascals will simply whang away at each other with the plastic swords and shields without learning any spiritual lessons.

Also in the Rainfall line:

- Bible Greats dolls, 7½" high action figures, each costumed and packaged with an accessory and a story booklet. Combo packs include more extras, such as two lions for Daniel and the Big Fish for Jonah. Bible Play-Alongs are story cassettes to accompany Bible Greats. These are nice toys, if not terribly durable. I'd stick to my Bible instead of the storybooks and cassettes if I were you.

- Bible Peel & Play sets each include two background scenes, play boards that set up as an easel, 30 full-color reusable, washable vinyl pieces to stick hither and yon, instructions, and Bible story sheet. Presently available: The Great Flood, From Slave to Ruler (Moses), and Jonah and the Big Fish.

- Rainfall's Noah's Ark set has 112 detailed pieces, including Noah and his family, the ark, and lots of pairs of animals. A great value.

- Color 'n Dial lets you crank the 22-foot roll of stories to color, presenting one scene at a time. This refillable rugged plastic case also includes molded crayon tray, eight crayons, crayon sharpener, and crayon storage box. Refill scenes available are The Prodigal Son, Jesus' Miracles and Parables, They Came Two by Two, A-Z Things We Know, Count and Color, and Color Things That Go.

- Various stuffed critters include Psalty, the tennis-shod humanized hymnbook, and the ever-wimpy Gerbert, as seen on Family Channel, plus lots of accessories for the fans of these creatures.

- Rainfall's two *Choices* games are reviewed in the Character Education chapter, and the *Piano Play-Book* in the Music chapter. Love that *Piano Play-Book*!

All Rainfall toys are very sensibly priced and as durable as you can expect. A real alternative to He-Man and Nintendo.

CHAPTER THIRTY-ONE

EDUCATIONAL GAMES FOR ALL AGES

This is not a complete guide to educational games. Nobody could even *list* all the educational games out there without taking up most of the space in this book! In this chapter I have, with only a few exceptions, settled for listing companies that publish many educational games. These are the categories: Cooperative Games, Board Games, File Folder Games, Card Games, Make-Your-Own Games, and Ungames. For educational software games, look in the Educational Software Buyer's Guide. For games that teach any given subject, look in that volume and chapter. You'll be amazed how easy it is to have a good time and learn at the same time!

COOPERATIVE GAMES

Family Pastimes

Cooperative games and books about same, educational puzzles, game plan kits. Also wholesales to home businesses (take note!). Some action games (a la table hockey) and plans to construct same. Example: Huff 'n' Puff game is won by puffing ball across table without dropping it into trap. Non-macho types use the little squeezers provided. New age flavor to some games.

Warren Publishing House/Totline Books
1•2•3 Games, $7.95. Add $2 shipping.

Subtitled "No-Lose Games for Young Children," 1•2•3 Games is a collection of non-competitive games for groups. Charming format, easy instructions.

BOARD GAMES

UPDATED**
Aristoplay

Educationally appealing, gorgeous board games loaded with extras. Versatile (most can be played on many different levels of difficulty). Fun. Challenging. Reviews of these games are scattered throughout the four volumes of *The Big Book of Home Learning*. Their new games in this edition include *Pyramids and Mummies* (archaeology), *The Game of Great Composers* (music history and appreciation), *Friends Around the World* (worldview, brotherhood from a liberal perspective), and *Some Body* (a terrific human anatomy game). Aristoplay's lineup also includes *Music Maestro* (recognizing modern, classical and medieval instruments, orchestra readiness), *Made for Trade* (Early American history game that teaches economic principles), *By Jove!* (mythology game), *Artdeck* (learn to recognize modern masters), *Where in the World?* (geography), *Dinosaurs and Things* (evolutionary look at the Big and the Ugly), *Good Old Houses* (architecture game), *Main Street* (commercial architecture), and several historical card deck games.

Educational Insights
Listening Lotto-ry: $12.95 each for Set A (basic sounds) or Set B (more complex sounds). Kitty Kat Card Games, $6.95 each. Kitty Kat Bingo games, $10.95 each (includes 65 cute little Kitty Kat counters). Primary Math Games, Intermediate Math Games, each $24.95/set of 3 included games. Plus 'n Minus Games, $9.95. *Thinkfast!, Gotcha!, Capture the Flags,* $5.95 each. *Presto Change-O,* $19.95.

Send for this catalog! Educational Insights is the most innovative, creative manufacturer of school learning materials around. Board games galore. Phonics and math records. Puzzles. Trace 'n Write Handwriting. Science kits. BrainBoosters.™ Human Body Kits. Electronic tutors. All priced ridiculously low, all colorful, all fun. Completely wipes out the competition.

Now, what does Educational Insights have in board or card games? How about Listening Lotto-ry, in which students match the sounds they hear to the objects on the picture cards? Kitty Kat Card Games teach upper/lowercase alphabet recognition (*Katnip!*), beginning consonant sounds (*Meow!*), and numeral/set recognition (*Whiskers!*). Kitty Kat Bingo games cover color and shapes, numbers, or the alphabet. Or how about a nice math game? Primary Math Games is a set of three games—*Sum Buddies* for basic addition, *Minus Maze* for subtraction, and *Time Out* for time-telling—all colorful and actually fun to play. Plus 'n Minus Games is math drill made painless as students must add and subtract to find their way around the game board. The double-sided board (one for addition, one for subtraction) comes with a reproducible activity workbook. Intermediate Math Games consists of *Prehistoric Times* (multiplication), *Dinosaur Division* (division), and *Ballpark Figures* (estimating skills). *Thinkfast!, Gotcha!,* and *Capture the Flags* are high-speed math competition using all four basic arithmetic processes: addition, subtraction, multiplication, and division. *Presto Change-O* helps kids learn to make change as they collect an allowance, do chores for cash, and blow their stash on treats.

Educational Insights is always coming out with something new, so send for their latest catalog and stay on top!

Rainfall, Inc.
Bible Challenge, $14.99. *Choices* (children's or adult's version), $14.99 each.

Bible Challenge is a Scripture knowledge game based on Scripture itself, not on trivia like, "What is the shortest verse in the Bible?" The two *Choices* games both present ethical problems for the players to answer with the help of Scripture. Unusual, thought-provoking format. Kids' version has a colorful gameboard and less "heavy" questions.

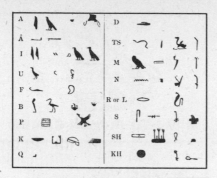

FILE FOLDER GAMES

UPDATED**
Shakean Stations
Twelve-game sets, $14.95 each. Twenty-Four-game set, $21.95. Seven-game sets, $13.95 each. Puzzle games, $5.95. Twenty manila file folders, $1.50. Twelve string tie envelopes, $1.50.

Delightful, inexpensive "file folder" games. You cut out the colorful game board portion and mount it on a legal-size file folder, then laminate or cover with clear contact paper (this last step is not essential, but it does help the game last longer). Play pieces are stored in a string-tie manila envelope that you mount on the back of the file folder. The whole process takes next to no time, and you end up with a long-lasting game for under $2, and in some cases less than a dollar.

Shakean games are sold in sets of 5, 7, 12, or 24. *Reading Unlimited*, the only set of 24 games, covers phonics from alphabet recognition through syllabication. Games sold in sets of 12 include: *Smart Start*, a set of reading readiness games; *Sports of Sorts*, vocabulary and word-building skill games with a sports theme; and *Meaning Go-Round*, beginning comprehension skill drill with an amusement park theme.

Classroom games (which can be played with as few at two or as many as 36 players) come in sets of seven, for grades 1-4. These are *Everybody Plays* and *Play It Again*. Both these sets concentrate on phonics and language arts.

Shakean Stations' *Puzzle Games* set comes with five game boards and 22 word lists for practicing specialized skills, such as matching states and their capitals or working on antonyms and homonyms or drilling math facts. You pick the list you want to work on, and write each word twice, once on the puzzle square and once on the corresponding game board. Players put the puzzle together by matching the problem (like the capital of Alaska) to the solution (Juneau). Each puzzle

is self-correcting, and if you cover it with contact paper (available in any school supply catalog) it should last and last.

CARD GAMES

Ampersand Press

Inexpensive, clever card games that teach about the food chain (*Predator* and *Krill*), flower lifestyle (*Pollination*), electricity (*AC/DC*), comets (*Good Heavens!*), and so on. Their Science Participoster has lots of clever puzzles to fill in, and people have been raving to me about it. Rumor: Look for a weather game or sea game from these people soon.

UPDATED**
Educational Insights
I.Q. Games, $7.95 each game.

A really neat concept in educational card games, I.Q. Games is a set of six quiz games, each coming with a special device called the Scorekeeper. The Scorekeeper has a surface with holes for tallying points for up to four players. You peg in your score, sticking little yellow pegs into the tens and ones places to register a score up to 99. The Scorekeeper also has a slanted base, with room between the tally surface and the base to insert a pack of game cards. You put the cards in clue side up. Try to figure out the answer using only the first clue on the card. If you can, you get five points. If not, you pull out the card a little farther, revealing the second clue, which is only worth four points, and your opponent gets to try to answer. Besides the clues (including one picture clue), each card has a "Now You Know" section with fascinating facts about the card topic. These games are really fun to play and do motivate the players to learn a lot of facts quite quickly! Set includes *Animals of the World, Famous Places of the World, Dinosaurs & Prehistoric Life* (slightly evolutionary), *U.S. Geography, World Geography,* and *U.S. History.*

Jeffrey Norton Publishers, Inc.

Deal Me In, subtitled *The Use of Playing Cards in Teaching and Learning*, is more than directions for a slew of card games. The author, Dr. Margie Golick, contends that playing cards are high-interest educational tools as well as a means of social entry for children who lack physical prowess or social skill. Some skills she claims card games can develop: rhythm, motor skills, sequencing, sense of direction, visual skills, number concepts, verbal skills, intellectual skills, and social skills. After a lengthy introduction presenting her case for card games, she gets down to cases with more than five dozen games, plus card tricks and logic games. Every card game is summarized, learning skills enhanced by the game are summarized, and then you get the rules: rank of cards, basic overview of the game, bidding (if appropriate), object of the game, rules of play and scoring, comments, and necessary vocabulary for play.

The book includes several indexes to help you find the game you want, and some psychotherapeutic moralizing by the author. She approves of gambling and swearing, and although her comments on these subjects do not take up any significant part of the book, I didn't want you to buy it and then accuse me of not warning you! By and large a helpful resource that could use some light editing in the next edition.

NEW**
Safari, Ltd.
Each card game, between $2.95 and $9.95.

Tons of quiz, lotto, and rummy-style educational card games, many under exclusive license from the Smithsonian Institution. American history quiz and rummy. Presidential quiz, rummy, lotto, and playing cards. Art appreciation quizzes and rummy. U.S. Space rummy and quiz. Natural science card games: *North American Wildlife, Endangered Species Rummy, Animals of the Zoo Rummy, Snakes Rummy, Hidden Kingdom Animal Rummy, Mineral Rummy,* more. Lotto games: *Dino Lotto, Ocean Lotto, Jungle Lotto, Presidential Lotto.* Quiz games: *Dino Quiz, Ocean Quiz, Jungle Quiz, Presidential Quiz, American History Quiz, Space Exploration Quiz.* Pick-Up Pairs games (otherwise known as matching games): *Dino Pick-Up Pair, Ocean Pick-Up Pairs, Animal Pick-Up Pairs.*

The Lotto and Pick-Up Pairs games are simple enough for young children. Rummy games are more advanced. Some of the quiz games require specialized knowledge that most of us don't have (at least before studying the game cards!).

All Safari, Ltd. games are museum-quality. In fact, museums are a big source of Safari sales!

Learning at Home sells a number of Safari games and other products.

MAKE-YOUR-OWN GAMES

NEW**
Fearon Teacher Aids
Make Your Own Games Workshop, $7.95.

Another volume in Fearon's highly successful *Workshop* series, *Make Your Own Games Workshop* has patterns and instructions for more than 30 games of all kinds. Paper games. Cardboard box games. Pegboard games. Spinner games. Recycled junk games (would you believe Pasta Word Pour?). Skill levels needed to play these games vary from total beginner to advanced players. Some action games, some strategy games. Unlimited variations possible. Constructing these games is easy: each is designed to use readily-available objects found around the home and takes less than an hour to put together. Some are virtually "instant" games—just photocopy the game sheet in the back and be ready to play. Many games have educational value, drilling such skills as word perception and arithmetic (Word Quoits and Number Quoits) or geography (U.S.A.).

The *real* purpose of *Make Your Own Games Workshop,* however, is not to amaze you with the cleverness of the authors, but to unlock your creative ability to invent your own games. I think this is great. Anything that helps us stop thinking of ourselves as helpless consumers of whatever big companies choose to produce is worth knowing about. A really mind-opening book.

UNGAMES

NEW**
Learning at Home
Kids' version, Teen version, Family version, $8 each, all pocket games. Christian version board game, $16. Original version board game, $14.50.

Learning at Home carries almost every version of the fabulously successful Ungame, so called because it's more of a communication tool than a traditional game. Here's how the Ungame works. Each game comes with two card decks of questions: lighter and more serious topics. Draw a card and answer the question. Questions ask you to relate your experiences or opinions on a particular topic in two or three sentences. The pocket form is just the card decks in a carrying case. The board-game version also has a playing board with areas for different emotions (excited, angry, happy, worried, affectionate, lonely, successful, frustrated) and a path that lets you draw cards, ask questions or make comments, or move to the emotion areas. Nobody wins or loses; the object is to get to know the other players.

The reason this game works is that (1) everyone loves to talk about himself! and (2) the game respects the difference between social sharing (the lighthearted questions) and more serious sharing (the second card deck). Nobody wants to be trapped into baring his soul right off to a group of strangers. For this reason, the Couples version, which Learning at Home wisely has decided *not* to carry, doesn't quite make it. This has a bunch of questions submitted by marriage counselors, psychologists, and the sort of couples who admire these guys. B-o-r-i-n-g navel-gazing. The other versions are much more interesting. Here are some sample questions from each version.

KIDS' VERSION:
- Annie has a talent for dancing. What is one of *your* talents?
- Mark and Matt are good friends. How would *you* describe a good friend?

TEEN VERSION:
- Share three things you think you need in order to be happy.
- If you were the parent, how would you feel about having yourself for a child?

FAMILIES' VERSION
- Share a funny thing that happened to you when you were a child.
- What family holiday experience has left you pleasant memories?

ALL AGES VERSION (ORIGINAL VERSION):
- Complete the sentence: Something interesting I have learned about life is . . .
- What would you like to receive on your next birthday?

CHRISTIAN VERSION:
- Tell about a time when God answered one of your prayers.
- "Therefore encourage one another and build each other up . . ." (1 Thessalonians 5:11). Say something that will encourage and build up each of the other players.

You can think of some uses for these games, I am sure. Family night? Family reunions? Parties? Icebreaker at a support-group meeting or Bible study? You tell me!

INDEXES

INDEX OF AMERICAN SUPPLIERS

A Beka Book Publications
Box 18000
Pensacola, FL 32523-9160
1-800-874-BEKA (2352) M-F 8-4:30 CST VISA,MC
(904) 478-8480 Ext. 2062
Fax: (904) 478-8558
Free catalog, order form, and brochures.
Christian texts and supplies.

A Beka Video Home School
Box 18000
Pensacola, FL 32523-9160
1-800-874-BEKA (2352) M-F 8-4:30 CST VISA, MC
(904) 478-8480 ext. 2062
Fax: (904) 478-8558
Free brochure.
Home school video program.

ABC School Supply
P.O. Box 4750
Norcross, GA 30091
(404) 447-5000 weekdays. VISA, MC

Fax: (404) 447-0062
Free catalog. Returns: Within 30 days. 15%
service charge if company not at fault.
School supplies pre-K-6.

Ability Development
Box 4260
Athens, OH 45701-4260
(614) 594-3547 VISA, MC, C.O.D.
Free catalog.
"The Suzuki Place"

Academic Therapy Publications
20 Commercial Boulevard
Novato, CA 94949-6191
1-800-422-7249 for location of nearest distributor.
(415) 422-7249
Fax: (415) 883-3720
Directory of Facilities and Services for the
Learning Disabled.
Other parent/teacher resources and remedial
educational materials.

Advance Memory Research, Inc. (AMR)
2601 Ulmerton Rd., E.
Suite 106B
Largo, FL 33641-3822
1-800-323-2500 VISA, MC, AmEx, D Club,
C Blanche
FL: (813) 539-6555
Free brochure. Call toll-free for info.
Foreigh language and speaking courses.

Advanced Training Institute of America
see Institute in Basic Life Principles

Adventure Guides, Inc.
36 E. 57th St.
New York, NY 10022
1-800-252-7899 VISA, MC.
(212) 355-6334
Free newsletter with large SASE.
Farm, Ranch, and Country Vacations.

Al Menconi Ministries
A1 2139 Newcastle Avenue
P.O. Box 969
Cardiff by the Sea, CA 92007-0969
(619) 436-8676 M-F 8:30-4:30 PST. VISA, MC,
C.O.D.
Fax: (619) 436-1648
Publisher of *Media Update Newsletter*.
Music evaluations.

Alexandria House, Inc.
468 McNally Drive
Nashville, TN 37211
(615) 831-0180 Check or M.O.
Fax: (615) 781-8767
Free shipping on prepaid orders.
Christian guitar course.

All Night Media, Inc.
Box 2666
San Anselmo, CA 94960
(415) 459-3013. Check or M.O.
Catalog $2. Stamp Cadet Membership, $4.
Rubber stamps and accessories.

Alpha Omega Publications
P.O. Box 3153
Tempe, AZ 85281
1-800-821-4443 Ask for Dept. OMP
AZ: (602) 438-1092
Fax: (602) 438-2702
Free catalog.
Christian curiculum.
Home school program.

American Bible Society
1865 Broadway
New York, NY 10023
1-800-543-8000 Credit card orders only. VISA,
MC.
(212) 408-1499
Fax: (212) 408-1512
$20 minimum.
Handling charge on credit card orders $1.95.
Foreign language Bibles.

American Classical League
Miami University
Oxford, OH 45056
Check or M.O. U.S. funds only.
Membership organization for teachers of Latin,
Greek, and classical humanities. Workshops,
newsletter, etc.

American Institute of Music
MPO Box 1706
Niagara Falls, NY 14302
(416) 225-1001
Music education home study curriculum.

American Map Corporation
46-35 54th Rd.
Maspeth, NY 11378
(718) 784-0055 9-5 EST weekdays. VISA, MC,
AmEx.
Free catalogs. Returns: Within 30 days on lan-
guage materials only.
Maps. Language courses.
Anatomy manual.

Ames Corporation
P.O. Box 1032-D
Selma, AL 36702
1-800-328-0228 VISA, MC.
Free brochure.
Mahogany wood building blocks.

Ampersand Press
691 26th St.
Oakland, CA 94612
(415) 832-6669 Check or M.O.
Free brochure.
Science games.

AMR
see Advanced Memory Research

AMSCO School Publications
315 Hudson St.
New York, NY 10013
(212) 675-7005
School books.

Andy's Front Hall
P.O. Box 307
Vourcheesville, NY 12186
1-800-759-1775 (orders only). Ask for the order desk. VISA, MC, C.O.D.
(518) 765-4193
$20 minimum on credit card orders. Returns: Defective merchandise.
Folk instruments and music.

Anvipa Press
160-D N. Fairview Ave. Suite 226
Goleta, CA 93117
(805) 683-4552 Check or M.O.
A New Approach to Christmas Greetings book.

Ares Publishers, Inc.
7020 N. Western Ave.
Chicago, IL 60645-3426
(312) 743-1907, Ext. 5 Check, (U.S. only), M.O., VISA, MC.
Back issues $5 each.
The Ancient World. Scholarly journal of antiquity.

Aristoplay, Ltd.
P.O. Box 7028
Ann Arbor, MI 48107
(313) 995-4353 VISA, MC. School P.O.'s net 30.
Fax: (313) 995-4611
Free color catalog.
Refund or exchange of damaged or defective games.
Lovely, classy, award-winning educational games.

Art Extension Press
Box 389
Westport, CT 06881
(203) 227-6637 VISA, MC.
Free brochure.
Art history and appreciation.

Art Video Library
1389 Saratoga Way
Grants Pass, OR 97526
(805) 474-1938 VISA, MC.
Art instructional videos to rent or buy

Asia Society
725 Park Ave.
New York, NY 10021
(212) 288-6400 Check or M.O. or school P.O.
Free brochure and materials list.
Excellent videos about children's lives in Japan and Korea.

Attainment Company
504 Commerce Parkway
Verona, WI 53593
1-800-327-4269 VISA, MC.
Fax: (608) 845-8040
Options catalog.

Audio Forum
96 Broad St.
Guilford, CT 06437
1-800-243-1234 VISA, MC, AmEx, DC, CB
(203) 453-9794 CT, AK, HI
Fax: (203) 453-9774
Free catalogs. Returns within 3 weeks, full refund.
Spoken word cassettes.

Audio Visual Drawing Program
1014 North Wright St.
Santa Ana, CA 92701
Check or M.O.
Free brochure.
Art courses in book and video.

Aylmer Press
P.O. Box 2735
Madison, WI 53701
(608) 233-2259
Video and Learning video.

B & I Gallery Specialists
609 Lincoln Terrace
Moorestown, NJ 08057
(609) 235-4943 Check or M.O.
Gallery™ art appreciation game.

B'rith Christian Union
4637 North Manor Ave.
Chicago, IL 60625
(312) 267-1440 Check or M.O.
Liturgical year calendar.

Ball-Stick-Bird Publications, Inc.
P.O. Box 592
Stony Brook, NY 11790
(516) 331-9164 Check or M.O.
Free color brochure.
No returns.
Reading system for labeled children.

Basil Blackwell, Inc.
American International Distribution Corp.
64 Depot Road
Colchester, VT 05446
1-800-445-6638
Fax: (617) 494-1437
Publisher.

BDA&M
9350-F Snowdon River Pkwy.
Suite 243
Columbia, MD 21045
1-800-228-8258 for credit card orders. VISA, MC, AmEx.
Hexaglot electronic foreign language translator.

Bear Creek Publications
2507 Minor Ave E.
Seattle, WA 98102
Check or M.O.
Publisher *No Bored Babies* book.

Berlitz
866 Third Ave.
New York, NY 10022
1-800-223-1814
NY: (212) 702-2000 Great Britain: 0323-638221
Foreign language courses and accessories.

Bethany House Publishers
6820 Auto Club Road
Minneapolis, MN 55438
(612) 829-2500 Check or M.O.
Basic Greek in 30 Minutes a Day.
Christian publisher, many other books.

Betterway Publications
P.O. Box 219
Crozet, VA 22932
1-800-522-2782 8-6 EST. Check or M.O.
Publisher.

BG Science, Inc.
13725 Drake Dr.
Rockville, MD 20853
(301) 460-1275 Check or M.O.
Free brochure. Returns: No questions asked within 30 days.
Video science labs.

Blue Bird Publishing
1713 E. Broadway #306
Tempe, AZ 85282
(602) 968-4088 VISA, MC.
Free brochure.
Publisher of home-school and home-business books.

Bluestocking Press
P.O. Box 1014
Placerville, CA 95667-1014
(916) 621-1123 VISA, MC. U.S. funds only.
Free info with large SASE and 2 first class stamps.
Series of books on what to read and where to find it. Special report on how to sell educational products to home schoolers and other alternative educational markets.

Bob Jones University Press
Customer Services
Greenville, SC 29614
1-800-845-5731 weekdays. VISA, MC, C.O.D.
Free catalog. Orders and info on toll-free line.
Returns: Resalable condition, with permission, within 30 days.
Christian texts and school supplies.
Christian Student Dictionary.
Reading list K-12.

Bolchazy-Carducci Publishers
1000 Brown Street, Unit 101
Wauconda, IL 60084
(708) 526-4344 VISA, MC, AmEx.
Free catalog includes ordering info for many other magazines, publishers. Must request buttons catalog separately. Returns: Resalable condition, within 30 days.
Huge array of Latin and Greek materials—books, filmstrips, music, even buttons! Scholarly books on the classics, some in German. Waldo Sweet's "Artes Latinae" programmed text, cassettes, readers, workbooks, filmstrips.

Bright Ring Publishing
P.O. Box 5768
Bellingham, WA 98227
(206) 734-1601 (office) (206) 733-0722 (home)
Fax: (206) 675-9503
Craft courses and supplies.

Brook Farm Books
P.O. Box 277
Lyndon, VT 05849
The First Home-School Catalogue.

C.H.I.C.K.S.
15846 West Parkway
Detroit, MI 48223
Home-school organization for parents of special kids.

Caedmon Tapes
1995 Broadway
New York, NY 10023
1-800-223-0420 VISA, MC.
NY: (212) 580-3400
Free 94-pp. catalog.
Spoken-word recordings, all categories, including children's recordings.

Calvert School
Tuscany Road
Baltimore, MD 21210
(301) 243-6030
Fax: (301) 366-0674
Free brochure with detailed outline of subjects and topics.
Home-school program.

Cambridge University Press
32 East 57th St.
New York, NY 10022
(914) 235-0300 Check or M.O.
Free brochure.
Free shipping on prepaid orders.
Allow 3-4 weeks for P.O. delivery.
UPS shipping available at extra cost.
Latin course for children.

Capper's Books
616 Jefferson
Topeka, KS 66607
1-800-777-7171, ext. 107 VISA, MC.
Free catalog.
Authentic old-timey pioneer stories.

Carden Educational Foundation
P.O. Box 659
Brookfield, CT 06804
(203) 740-9200
Free catalog. Returns: 30 days, resalable condition, call first.
Complete private school curriculum.

Center for Applied Research in Education, Inc.
P.O. Box 430
West Nyack, NY 10995
Guided research units.

Challenge
Box 299
Carthage, IL 62321-0299
1-800-435-7234 VISA, MC, or school P.O.
(217) 357-3981
Magazine for gifted children.

Charles Coyle
P.O. Box 2186
Ann Arbor, MI 48106
Check or M.O.
Roman Coins and Culture classical journal.

Chasselle, Inc.
9645 Gerwig Lane
Columbia, MD 21046
Free catalog.
School supplies.

Child's Play Educational Toys
P.O. Box 452
Fishkill, NY 12524
(914) 223-5515 VISA, MC, C.O.D.
Free catalog. Returns: Resalable condition or damaged/defective items within 30 days.
Educational toys catalog.

Childcraft Education Corp.
20 Kilmer Rd.
Edison, NJ 08818
1-800-631-5657 9-6 M-F EST. VISA, MC, AmEx.
NJ: 1-800-624-0840
Free color catalog. Returns: With permission, within 30 days, unused.
Educational furniture, toys, and games.

Children's Book and Music Center
P.O. Box 1130
Santa Monica, CA 90406-1130
1-800-443-1856 M-Sat 9-5:30 PST. VISA, MC.
CA: (213) 829-0215
Catalog $1.
You may call the toll-free line for assistance in choosing materials.
"The largest supply of children's books, records, cassettes in the country."
Wide selection of books, thousands of tapes, musical instruments.

Children's Recordings
P.O. Box 1343
Eugene, OR 97440
VISA, MC, or school P.O.
Free newsprint catalog. Returns: Defective merchandise or damaged in shipping.
Contemporary children's records, tapes, and videos.

Children's Small Press Collection
719 North Fourth Avenue
Ann Arbor, MI 48104
1-800-221-8056 VISA, MC, or school P.O.
MI: (313) 668-8056
Free catalog.
Children's books, records, and games from almost 100 small publishers.

Childshop
P.O. Box 597
Burton, OH 44021-0597
Check or M.O.
Catalog $1. Unconditional guarantee.
Children's woodcraft plans and kits.

Chinaberry Book Service
2830 Via Orange Way, Suite B
Spring Valley, CA 92078-1521
1-800-777-5205 M-Sat 9-5 PST. VISA, MC.
(619) 284-0902
Large newsprint catalog $2. Satisfaction guaranteed.
Extremely detailed children's book catalog. New Age flavor.

Christian Book Distributors
Box 3687
Peabody, MA 01961-3687
(617) 532-5300 VISA, MC.
Free sample catalog. Returns: Shipping mistakes, defective products.
Membership $3/year. You don't have to be a member to order.
Discount Christian books/Bibles.

Christian Character Concepts
13732 Meadow Lane
Flint, TX 75762
(214) 894-6619 Check or M.O.
Free brochure with SASE.
Character curriculum. Spanish.

Christian Education Music Publishers, Inc.
2285 West 185th Place
Lansing, IL 60438
(708) 895-3322 Check or M.O.
Free catalog.
Music reading course.

Christian Films, Inc.
P.O. Box 2512
Houston, TX 77252
1-800-621-8880
TX: 1-800-831-8324
Educational videos.

Christian Life Workshops, Inc.
P.O. Box 2250
Gresham, OR 97030
(503) 667-3942 Check or M.O.
Brochure with SASE. Returns: 100% refund, except shipping and handling.
Home-school workshops on tape. Books. Organizer. Seminars. *Bed & Breakfast Directory*.

Christian Light Publications
1066 Chicago Ave.
P.O. Box 1126
Harrisonburg, VA 22801-1126
(703) 434-0750 VISA, MC.
Fax: (703) 434-0769
Free catalog.
Science equipment, curriculum, and school supplies, Mennonite-approved books.

Chroma Corporation
P.O. Box 1025
Edmonds, WA 98020
(206) 672-4710 Visa, MC.
Fax: (206) 775-7196
Free brochure.
Color-coded guitar learning system.

Citizens Commission on Human Rights
5265 Fountain Ave., Suite #2
Los Angeles, CA 90029
(213) 667-2901
Pamphlets warning against "therapeutic" drugging of children.

Clark County Crafts
3124 Ayres Holmes
Auburn, CA 95603
(916) 888-0781 Check or M.O.
Free price list with large SASE.
Carousel riding horses, custom badges.
Quantity discounts.

Classical Bulletin
Ares Publishers, Inc.
7020 North Western Ave.
Chicago, IL 60645-3416
Check or M.O.
U.S. funds only payable to *The Classical Bulletin*.
Magazine.

ClassicPlan™
20969 Ventura Blvd., Suite 213
Woodland Hills, CA 91364
(818) 883-4093
Fax: (818) 347-0541
Free brochure. Returns: Within 30 days.
"Art immersion" program.

Constructive Playthings
1227 E. 119th St.
Grandview, MO 64030
1-800-255-6124 VISA, MC.
MO: (816) 761-5900 Fax: (816) 761-9295
Free home catalog. Free toy guide for parents.
Free catalog of Jewish educational materials.
Play furniture, toys, school supplies pre-K-3.

Conversa-phone Institute, Inc.
One Comac Loop
Ronkonkoma, NY 11779
(516) 467-0600 Check or M.O.
Fax: (516) 467-0602
Sells through distributors.
Recorded courses, self-help.

Cornerstone Curriculum Project
2006 Flat Creek
Richardson, TX 75080
(214) 235-5149 Check or M.O. Free brochure.
Innovative subject curricula.

Covenant Home Curriculum
3675 N. Calhoun Rd.
Brookfield, WI 53005
(414) 781-2171
K-12 curriculum. Quarterly tests.

Crane's Select Educational Materials
P.O. Box 124
Bedford, IN 47421
(812) 279-3434 Check or M.O., C.O.D.
Supplemental teaching materials catalog.

Creative Kids
P.O. Box 6448
Mobile, AL 36660-0448
1-800-476-8711 VISA, MC, AmEx, Discover.
Fax: (205) 478-4755
Unconditional guarantee.
Magazine by/for talented kids.

Cricket
Box 300
Peru, IL 61354
1-800-435-6850 Check or M.O. or they bill you.
IL: 1-800-892-6831
Children's magazine.

Daisy Kingdom Rubber Stamps
134 N.W. 8th
Portland, OR 97209
Check or M.O.
Full-color catalog $2.
Rubber stamps and supplies for fabric (and paper).

Dale Seymour Publications
P.O. Box 10888
Palo Alto, CA 94303
1-800-872-1100 CA: 1-800-222-0766 VISA, MC.
(orders)
(415) 324-2800
Fax: (415) 324-3424
Free catalog. Returns: In resalable condition, within 30 days, call first.
Publisher.

Davidson's Music
6727 Metcalf
Shawnee Mission, KS 66204
1-800-782-7664 VISA, MC.
MO: (913) 262-4982
Free catalog. Returns: In new condition.
Music learning.

Dick Blick
Dick Blick Central
P.O. Box 1267
Galesburg, IL 61401
1-800-447-8192 VISA, MC, AmEx.
West: P.O. Box 521
Henderson, NV 89015
East: P.O. Box 26
Allentown, PA 18105
Georgia: 1117 Apharetta St.
Roswell, GA 30075
Send order to address closest to you.
Catalog $3.
Art and craft supplies.

DIDAX, Inc.
One Centennial Drive
Peabody, MA 01960
(508) 532-9060 Check or M.O.
Fax: (508) 532-9277
Free catalog.

Discovery Toys
2530 Arnold Dr., Suite 400
Martinez, CA 94553
1-800-426-4777
(415) 370-7575
Fax: (415) 370-0289
Home distributors, party plan.
Toys with "educational play value."

Dover Publications, Inc.
31 East 2nd St.
Mineola, NY 11501
Check or M.O.
Free catalogs. Returns: Within 10 days.
Reprint bookseller. Good selection.

Dr. Drew's Toys, Inc.
P.O. Box 1003, Dept. H
Boston, MA 02205
(617) 282-2812 Check or M.O.
Free flier.
Thin rectangular hardwood blocks.

Easton Press
47 Richards Ave.
P.O. Box 5707
Norwalk, CT 06856-9926
VISA, MC.
Video History of Our Times
Elite books and tapes.

EDC Publishing
Division of educational development corporation
P.O. Box 470663
Tulsa, OK 74147
(918) 622-4522 VISA, MC.
Catalog $2.00 ($2.00 coupon enclosed). Returns: after 60 days, less than 12 months, resalable condition, 15 percent restocking charge, written authorization.
Usborne books.

Educational Insights
19560 S. Rancho Way
Dominguez Hills, CA 90220
1-800-933-3277
(213) 637-2131 or 979-1955
Fax: (213) 605-5048
Producer of innovative, hands-on materials for
grades K-12.

Educational Services
Kathy Means
175 Gladys Ave, #7
Mountain View, CA 94043
(415) 961-4414 Check or M.O. payable to
K. Means.
Free brochure with SASE. Satisfaction guaranteed.
Publisher of *Home Schooling at Its Best,* Ready-
Set-Learn enrichment units.

Educators Publishing Service
75 Moulton St.
Cambridge, MA 02138-1104
1-800-225-5750 VISA, MC.
MA: (617) 547-6706
Free brochures. Indicate grade level you need.
Language arts and parent helps.

EKS Publishing
5336 College Avenue
Oakland, CA 94618
(415) 653-5183 Check or M.O. or C.O.D.
Free catalog. Returns: In perfect condition, up to
6 months.
Biblical/prayerbook Hebrew texts, teaching aids,
and games for all ages.

The Elijah Company
P.O. Box 12483
Knoxville, TN 37912-0483
(615) 691-1310 Check or M.O.
Returns: In resalable condition, within 30 days.
Home school distributor of *How to Tutor, Alpha-
phonics, Keyboard Capers, Type It, Spelling
Dictionary,* Star Shirt.

EMC Publishing
300 York Avenue
St. Paul, MN 55101
1-800-328-1452 VISA, MC.
Free catalog. Returns with permission.
Foreign language resources catalog.

Entertainment Plus Family Video Club
P.O. Box 9550
Jackson, MS 39286-9550
1-800-647-2284 VISA, MC, Discover.
Free brochure.
Family video club.

ESP Publishers, Inc.
1201 E. Johnson Ave.
P.O. Drawer 5080
Jonesboro, AR 72403
1-800-643-0280 VISA, MC.
AR: (501) 935-3533
Fax: (501) 972-1121
Free catalog. Refund: No questions asked.
Textbooks, workbooks, cassette programs,
filmstrips.

Essential Learning Products Co.
2300 W. Fifth Ave.
P.O. Box 2607
Columbus, OH 43216-2607
(614) 486-0631 MC
Fax: (614) 486-0631 Ext. 14
Free brochure. Returns: Return with note within
30 days.
Math and language arts practice books.

Every Day Is Special
1602 Naco Place
Hacienda Heights, CA 91745
(818) 961-4630 Check or M.O.
Activity calendar for home schoolers.

F & W Publications
see Writer's Digest Books

Family Learning Center
Rt. 2, Box 264
Hawthorne, FL 32640
(904) 475-3243 Check or M.O.
Returns: Resalable condition, within 30 days.
Home-school curriculum and widgets.

Family Pastimes Games
RR 4
Perth, Ontario K7H 3C6
CANADA
(613) 267-4819 Check or M.O.
New, expanded newsprint catalog $1.
Board and action games.

Fearon Teacher Aids
PO Box 280
Carthage, IL 62321
1-800-242-7272 VISA, MC.
(217) 357-3900
Fax: (217) 357-3908
Free catalog.
Publishers.

Field Publications
Weekly Reader
245 Long Hill Road
Middletown, CT 06457
1-800-848-1882 VISA, MC.
Free brochure. Returns: 15 days, they pay fourth-class postage.
Summer Skills library.

Films Incorporated
5547 N. Ravenswood Ave.
Chicago, IL 60640
Videos to accompany EMC foreign language programs.

FLAX Art & Design
1699 Market St.
P.O. Box 7216
San Francisco, CA 94120
1-800-547-7778 VISA, MC, AmEx. Orders only.
24 hours, 7 days.
(415) 468-7530 8-4:30 PST M-F.
Returns: Resalable condition, original packaging, within 30 days.
Art instruction and supplies.

Frank Schaffer Publications, Inc.
23740 Hawthorne Blvd
Torrance, CA 90505
1-800-421-5565 VISA, MC, or school P.O.
Fax: (213) 375-5090
Sold in teachers' supply stores and catalogs.
Colorful and entertaining workbooks, puzzles, etc. for preschool and elementary grades.

Freebies
P.O. Box 20283
Santa Barbara, CA 93120
Check or M.O.
Fax: (805) 962-1617
Magazine.

Fun Technicians
P.O. Box 160
Syracuse, NY 13215
(315) 492-4523
$3/issue.
Ventriloquists' trade magazine.

Gallopade Publishing Group
Main St.
Historic Bath, NC 27808
(919) 923-4291
Check or M.O. or school purchase order.
Free brochure. Satisfaction guaranteed.
Publisher.

Gazelle Publications
5580 Stanley Drive
Auburn, CA 95603
(916) 878-1223 Check or M.O.
Fax: (916) 888-8627
Free brochure (long SASE appreciated).
Returns: 100 percent satisfaction guaranteed.
Home-school books.

GCT. Inc.
P.O. Box 6448
Mobile, AL 36660-0448
1-800-476-8711 VISA, MC, AmEx, Discover.
Fax: (205) 478-4755
Free catalog.
Returns: Within 60 days for complete refund.
Gift/talented magazines and resources.

A Gentle Wind
Box 3103
Albany, NY 12203
(518) 436-0391 9-5 EST. VISA, MC.
Minimum charge order, $14. Returns: Free replacement of defective tapes, within 15 days. Exchange of undamaged tapes, within 15 days.
Original children's music.

Gerard Hamon, Inc.
P.O. Box 758
721 West Boston Road
Mamaroneck, NY 10543
1-800-331-4971 VISA, MC.
(914) 381-4649
Free catalog.
Foreign books and periodicals.

God's World Publications
P.O. Box 2330
Asheville, NC 28802-2330
1-800-476-8924 VISA, MC.
Fax: (704) 253-1556
Samples and catalogs available.
Satisfaction guaranteed.
Christian newspapers for K-12.
Ask about God's World Book Club.

Golden Key
Federalsburg, MD 21632-0339
1-800-333-6583, Ext 24 (orders) 24 hours 7 days.
VISA, MC, AmEx. Minimum charge order $15.
1-800-462-3955 (customer service)
Book catalog.

Good News Communications
P.O. Box 9952
Atlanta GA 30319
Check or M.O.
Publishes *Movieguide*.

Good Stamps
30901 Timberline Road
Willits, CA 95490
(707) 459-9124 VISA, MC. Minimum charge
order $15.
Catalog $2, refundable with first order.
Satisfaction guaranteed.
Rubber stamps and supplies.

Gospel Mission
Box M
Choteau, MT 59422
(406) 466-2311 VISA, MC.
Fax: (406) 466-2140
Free catalog.
Returns: No returns for properly filled orders.
Wholesale Christian book outlet. 30% off retail.

Gospel Publications
P.O. Box 184
Jupiter, FL 33468
(305) 747-2461 Check or M.O.
Free newsletter for children.
Children's Calendar. Materials for telephone
ministries, balloon stories.
Free lending library of children's Christian books.
Free children's correspondence course (include
$1 to help with postage).

Great Christian Books
1319 Newport Gap Pike
P.O. Box 3499
Wilmington, DE 19804-2895
(302) 999-8317 VISA, MC.
Fax: (302) 999-9786
Membership $5/year U.S., $8 Canada, $12
overseas.
Discount Christian books.

Grolier Enterprises
Sherman Turnpike
Danbury, CT 06816
Club plan.
Beginner Books for kids.

Growing Child
P.O. Box 620
Lafayette, IN 47902-1100
(317) 423-2624 VISA, MC, AmEx
Fax: (317) 423-4495
Satisfaction guranteed.
Toys, books, records, and videocassettes.

Hammond Inc.
515 Valley St.
Maplewood, NJ 07040
1-800-526-4953 Check or M.O.
NJ: (201) 763-6000
Returns with permission.
Geography and other school supplies.

Hank Lee's Magic Factory
125 Lincoln St.
Boston, MA 02111
(617) 482-8749 24 hours, 7 days. VISA, MC,
AmEx, Discover.
Catalog $6.
Professional magic apparatus, wholesale/retail.

Harlan Enterprises
P.O. Box 145
Brownfield, TX 79316
(806) 637-8190 Check or M.O.
No returns.
Simple drill games.

Harrisville Designs
12 Main St.
Harrisville, NH 03450
(603) 827-3334 VISA, MC, school P.O.
Free brochure.
Personal looms for children.

Hayes School Publishing Co., Inc.
321 Pennwood Ave.
Wilkinsburg, PA 15221-3398
1-800-245-6234 VISA, MC.
PA: (412) 371-2370
Free full-color catalog. Minimum phone order $15.
Supplemental materials.

Hear An' Tell
320 Bunker Hill
Houston, TX 77024
Check or M.O.
Fax: (713) 784-7689
Free brochure. Returns: Resalable condition.
Foreign language programs.

HearthSong
P.O. Box B
Sebastopol, CA 95473
1-800-325-2502 VISA, MC, AmEx, Discover.
Fax: 1-800-872-0331
Free 40-page full-color catalog.
"A catalog for families."

Hewitt Research Foundation
P.O. Box 9
Washougal, WA 98671
Check or M.O. Free catalog.
Innovative home-school materials.

High Noon Books
20 Commercial Blvd.
Novato, CA 94949-6191
1-800-422-7249 VISA, MC, AmEx
(415) 883-3314
Free catalog. No returns.
Call or write for address of one of their Canadian distributors.
Hi-lo mystery stories with moral principles.

Highlights for Children
P.O. Box 810
Columbus, OH 43216-0810
Magazine.

His Footeprints
26461 Fresno Dr.
Mission Viejo, CA 92691-1512
Check or M.O.
Catalog $3.
Rubber stamps and supplies.

Holt Associates
2269 Massachusetts Ave.
Cambridge, MA 02140
(617) 864-3100 VISA, MC.
Catalog for SASE and 45¢ postage.
Books of interest to home schoolers.
Music and art supplies.

Home Life
P.O. Box 1250
Fenton, Mo 63026-1250
Fax: (314) 225-0743
Check or M.O.
Free catalog. Returns: Resalable condition, 60 days.
Home education and family books. Organizers.
TV-free video players. Juggling equipment.

The Home School
3131 Smokey Point Dr.
Arlington, WA 98233
(206) 659-6188
MC, Visa. Free catalog.
Returns: 30 days, resalable condition, postage prepaid, accompanied by copy of original sales order or register receipt. Special order items and cassettes can't be returned for refund.
Home school curriculum and supplies.

Homespun Tapes, Ltd.
Box 694
Woodstock, NY 12498
1-800-33-TAPES VISA, MC, COD (USA only)
(914) 679-7832
Fax: (914) 246-5282
Free catalog.
Music instruction on audio- and videocassettes.

Hoover Brothers Educational Equipment and Supplies
P.O. Box 1009
Kansas City, MO 64141
(816) 472-4848 MC, C.O.D.
Catalog $7.50.
School supplies.

Hosannah
2421 Aztec Road N.E.
Albuquerque, NM 87107-4224
Foreign language Bible cassettes.

Hugh O'Neill and Associates
Box 1297
Nevada City, CA 95959
Check or M.O.
Nice people.
Publisher, *Big Yellow Drawing Book.*

INC Magazine
38 Commercial Wharf
Boston, MA 02110
1-800-234-0999 (subscriptions)
(617) 227-4700 (editorial)
Business magazine.

Institute in Basic Life Principles
Box 1
Oak Brook, IL 60522-3001
(708) 323-9800
Fax: (708) 323-6394
Seminars. Supplier of ATIA curriculum.

Instrument Workshop
8023 Forest Dr. N.E.
Seattle, WA 98115
(206) 523-6129 6-7 AM, 7-9 PM Pacific Time.
VISA, MC.
Free list of catalogs.
Old time keyboard instrument kits, plans, tools.

International Linguistics
3505 E. Red Bridge Rd.
Kansas City, MO 64137
1-800-237-1830 VISA, MC, Institutional P.O.
MO: (816) 765-8855
Returns: 30 days.
Foreign language courses.

Into the Wind Kites
1408 Pearl
Boulder, CO 80302
(303) 449-5356 M-Sat 10-6, credit card orders
only. VISA, MC, AmEx, Discover.
Fax: (303) 449-7315
Complete refund or exchange. You return prepaid
and insured.
Kites and accessories.

Isha Enterprises
5503 East Beck Lane
Scottsdale, AZ 85254
(602) 482-1346 Check or M.O.
Free brochure with SASE.
Grammar materials.

Jeffrey Norton Publishers, Inc.
Suite RCC-103
96 Broad St.
Guilford, CT 06437
1-800-243-1234 VISA, MC AmEx, DC, CB,
institutional P.O.
CT, AK, HI: (203) 453-9794
Fax: (203) 453-9774
Free catalogs.
Returns: within 3 weeks, unconditional.
Various cassette-of-the-month plans.
Spoken-word cassettes, videos.

Jonson Specialties
Box 357
Cedarhurst, NY 11516-0357
1-800-221-6714 VISA, MC, AmEx.
NY: (718) 327-5965 8-5
Fax: (718) 868-1202
Free catalog. Satisfaction guranteed.
Toys and rewards.

JTG of Nashville
1024C Avenue South
Nashville, TN 37212
(615) 329-3036 MC or VISA.
Fax: (615) 324-4028
Free catalog. 90 day guarantee.
Play a Tune™ Books series.

Just for Kids
Winterbrook Way
Meredith, NH 03253
Toys and games. Expensive.

Keys to Excellence
Perception Publications, Inc.
1814 W. Seldon Lane
Phoenix, AZ 85021
(602) 946-6454 Check or M.O. or order from
school supply.
Readiness workbook series.
Cassette training for parents to help their children
achieve academically.

KidsArt
P.O. Box 274
Mt. Shasta, CA 96067
(916) 926-5076 VISA, MC.
Free catalog. SASE appreciated. Satisfaction
guranteed.
Kids' art magazine. Kid Prints home program for
teaching fine arts.
Imaginative art supplies.

Kimbo Educational
P.O. Box 477
Long Branch, NJ 07740
1-800-631-2187 VISA, MC. Free color catalog.
NJ: (201) 229-4949
Fax: (201) 870-3340
Records, cassettes, filmstrips, read-alongs, and
videos, especially early childhood and movement.

Klutz Press
2121 Staunton Ct.
Palo Alto, CA 94306
(415) 857-0888 VISA, MC, C.O.D.
Fax: (415) 857-9110
Free catalog.
How-to books for juggling, yo-yo, marbles, etc.

KONOS
P.O. Box 1534
Richardson, TX 75083
(214) 669-8337 Check or M.O.
U. S. funds only. No phone orders.
Free brochure and order form.
Curriculum, time lines, "how to" tapes, writing
tapes, seminars.

Ladybird Books, Inc.
49 Omni Circle
P.O. Box 1690
Auburn, ME 04210
1-800-523-9247 Check or M.O.
(207) 783-6329 Fax: (207) 783-6130
Books on a variety of subjects for a variety of ages.

Laissez-Faire Books
942 Howard St.
San Francisco, CA 94103
1-800-326-0996 VISA, MC 9-6 M-F 12-5 Sat. PST.
(415) 541-9780
Free catalog. 30-day unconditional guarantee.
Libertarian bookseller.

Lakeshore Curriculum Material Center
P.O. Box 6261
Carson, CA 90749
1-800-421-5334 CA: 1-800-262-1777. VISA, MC,
AmEx.
Info: (213) 537-8600
Free catalog.
Returns: Within 30 days, unused goods.
School supplies preK-3, special ed.

Landmark Company
1580 Raven Hill
Wheaton, IL 60187
(312) 690-9978 VISA, MC.
Lighthouse Adventures tape series.

Lark In the Morning
88 Page
Box 1176
Mendocino, CA 95460
(707) 964-5569 Check or M.O.
Catalog $2.50.
Rare/unusual instruments, books.

**Laugh-Makers: A Magazine for Family
Entertainers**
see Fun Technicians

Lauri, Inc.
P.O. Box F
Phillips-Avon, ME 04966
(207) 639-2000 Check or M.O.
Fax: (207) 639-3555
Free brochure.
Crepe rubber products.

Learning At Home
P.O. Box 270
Honaunau, HI 96726
(808) 328-9669 VISA, MC.
Free catalog.
K-12 books and workbooks.
Math manipulatives, science and art supplies.
Curriculum and teaching guides.

Learning Systems Corporation
P.O. Box 201
Wyncote, PA 19095
(215) 453-3538 Check or M.O.
Catalog $1. All sales are final.
Miniworkbooks, skillforms.

Learning Works
P.O. Box 6187
Santa Barbara, CA 93160
1-800-235-5767 Check or M.O.
(805) 964-4220
Fax: (805) 964-1466
Free catalog. Returns: Resalable condition within 10 days.
Supplemental materials.

Legacy
204 N. El Camino Real
Suite E 718
Encinitas, CA 92024
1-800-848-0206 VISA, MC.
(619) 943-9564
Fax: (619) 431-0489
Free catalog. Party plan sales.
Character building materials.
Children's videos, audios and toys.

LEGO Shop at Home Service
P.O. Box 640
Enfield, CT 06082-0640
(203) 763-4011 VISA, MC.
Free catalog. Satisfaction guaranteed.
Duplo and LEGO construction sets.

Leonardo Press
Box 403
Yorktown Heights, NY 10598
(914) 962-7856 or 962-5890 Check or M.O.
Free catalog.
Spelling and math programs.
School-tested.

Life-Like Products, Inc.
Attn: Dock 2
1600 Union Avenue
Baltimore, MD 21211-1998
Model railroading supplies.

Logos Language Institute
Christian Mission Center
P.O. Box 374 UMHB
Belton, TX 76513
(817) 939-8320
Foreign language materials

Longman Publishing Group
95 Church St.
White Plains, NY 10601
(914) 993-5095 Visa, MC, AmEx.
Fax: (914) 997-8115
Free catalog.
Publisher.

Loucks Music, Inc.
P.O. Box 150946
Nashville, TN 37215-0946
(615) 833-6159 Check or M.O.
The Recorder Factory. Sacred instrumental music.

Louis Tannen Magic, Inc.
6 West 32nd St., Fourth Floor
New York, NY 10001
(212) 239-8383 VISA, MC, AmEx. $15 minimum.
Catalog $6 plus $5 UPS.
Magic supplies, book, magazine.

Lovebug Press
P.O. Box 25262
Sarasota, FL 34277-2262
(813) 371-6104 Check or M.O.
Returns: In resalable condition, within 30 days.
Children's art activity book.

Loyola University Press
3441 North Ashland Ave.
Chicago, IL 60657
1-800-621-1008
(312) 281-1818
Fax: (312) 281-0555
Reading course in Homeric Greek.

Lynch's
939 Howard St.
Dearborn, MI 48124
(313) 565-3425 Check or M.O.
Catalog $5, refunded on first order more than $25.
Clowning supplies.

M/L International Marketing, Inc.
Box 152537
Tampa, FL 33684-2537
(813) 933-7065 VISA, MC, AmEx.
Ask about payment plan.
Basic Library of the World's Greatest Music.

Magic Moments with Class, Inc.
P.O. Box 761
Horace Harding Station
Little Neck, NY 11362
(516) 365-7279 Check or M.O.
Returns: Prior notification, defective merchandise only, within 10 days.
Creative toys and games.

Maher
P.O. Box 420
Littleton, CO 80160
(303) 798-6830 VISA, MC.
Free catalog.
Ventriloquism and other entertainment supplies.
Unrelated to Maher Workshops (below).

Maher Workshops
P.O. Box 1466
Cedar Ridge, CA 95924
(916) 273-0176 Check or M.O.
$2 info pack.
Ventriloquism and other entertainment supplies.
Unrelated to Maher (above).

Majesty Music
P.O. Box 6524
Greenville, SC 29606
1-800-334-1071 M-F 8:30-5. VISA, MC, school or church P.O.
(803) 242-6722
Free brochure.
Patch the Pirate cassettes, books, scripts.

Mandolin Brothers, Ltd.
629 Forest Ave.
Staten Island, NY 10310
(718) 981-3226 VISA, MC, AmEx, Disc., Optima.
Fax: (718) 816-4416
Minimum credit card order, $50.
Free catalog.
Refund: 3 days, original carton, new condition.
Stringed instruments and books.

Metropolitan Museum of Art
Special Service Office
Middle Village, NY 11381-0001
1-800-635-5355 Credit card orders. VISA. MC, AmEx. $15 minimum.
(718) 326-7050 Customer service.
Free catalog.

Michael Olaf - Montessori Shop
5817 College Ave.
Oakland, CA 94618
(415) 655-7100 VISA, MC.
Catalog, $1.
"The Montessori Shop." Innovative materials for all ages.

Michel Farm Vacations
R.R. 1, Box 914
Harmony, MN 55939
(507) 886-5392 Check or M.O.
Free color brochure shows area sights of interest. 20% deposit, balance due 2 days before arrival at farm.
Refunds: cancellation received 14 days prior to starting date.
Farm vacations.

Midwest Publications
Critical Thinking Press
P. O. Box 448
Pacific Grove, CA 93950
1-800-458-4849 VISA, MC.
(408) 375-2455
Fax: (408) 372-3230
Free catalog.
Thinking-skill materials for better academic performance.

Milliken Publishing Company
1100 Research Blvd.
St. Louis, MO 63132-0579
1-800-325-4136 MO. 1-800-333-READ. VISA,MC, C.O.D.
(314) 991-4220
Fax: (314) 991-4807
Free catalog. Available catalogs: K-8, 7-12, computer software, Reading, Early Childhood.
Home education products Pre-12:
Curriculum centered workbooks, theme units, software, early childhood products, children's literature w/guides.

Mind's Eye
P.O. Box 6727
San Francisco, CA 94101
1-800-227-2020 VISA, MC, AmEx.
CA: (415) 883-7701 Fax: (415) 883-1849
Free gorgeous catalog.
Stories on tape.

Missionary Vision for Special Ministries
Ruth Shuman, Director
640 West Briar Place
Chicago, IL 60657
(312) 327-0489
Free resources on understanding handicapped folk.

Modern Learning Press
Rosemont, NJ 08556
(609) 397-2214 VISA, MC.
Free brochure.
Art prints and resource guides.

Modern Talking Picture Service
500 Park Street North
St. Petersburg, FL 33709
1-800-243-6877
(813) 541-5763
Fax: (813) 546-0681
Free loan educational videos.

Montessori Services
228 South "A" St.
Santa Rosa, CA 95401
(707) 579-3003 VISA, MC, C.O.D.
Free catalog.
Early childhood supplies. Books, art supplies,
nature and science.

Moody Correspondence School
820 N. LaSalle St.
Chicago, IL 60610
1-800-621-7105 VISA, MC.
IL: (312) 329-4166
Free catalog. 15-day free trial.
Self-study adult Bible courses.
Dispensational.

Motivational Art Training
9300 Beecher Rd.
Pittsford, MI 49271
Check or M.O.
No phone orders.
Christian Art Manual.

Movie Morality Ministries
1309 Seminole Dr.
Richardson, TX 75080
(214) 231-9910 Check or M.O.
Recommended Movies on Video book. *Preview
Movie Morality Guide* (twice monthly).

Museum of Fine Arts—Boston
Catalog Sales Dept.
P.O. Box 1044
Boston, MA 02120
1-800-225-5592 (orders) MC, Visa, AmEx.
(617) 427-7791 (customer service)
Free catalog.
Mail-order museum gift shop.

Music for Little People
P.O. Box 1460
Redway, CA 95560
1-800-345-4446 VISA, MC, AmEx, Discover.
Fax: (707) 923-3241
Free catalog.
Returns: Full credit or refund within 30 days.
Cassettes, videos, CD's, musical instruments,
new age emphasis.

NACD
P.O. Box 1001
Layton, UT 84041
(801) 451-0942 VISA, MC.
Free catalog, brochure.
Satisfaction guranteed.
Physical therapy/behavior modification programs,
tape sets.
On-site evaluations.

National Homeschool Association
P.O. Box 58746
Seattle, WA 98138-1746
(206) 432-1544
National home-school information clearinghouse.
Home schoolers' travel directory.

National Model Railroad Association
4121 Cromwell Road
Chattanooga, TN 37421
Model railroading association.

New Horizons, Inc.
P.O. Box 652
Belmont, MA 02178
(617) 489-4226 or 5323 Check or M.O.
Free catalog.
Vacations for handicapped people.

New Moon Records
P.O. Box 203
Joshua Tree, CA 92252
(619) 366-9684 Check or M.O.
Cassettes of original family music.

North Dakota State Dept. of Public Instruction
Division of Independent Study
State University Station
Box 5036
Fargo, North Dakota 58105-5036
(701) 237-7182 Check or M.O.
No payment plan.
Refunds: First two weeks. Processing fee of $5 retained.
High school correspondence program.

North Light Books
1507 Dana Ave.
Cincinnati, OH 45207
1-800-289-0963 VISA, MC.
Fax: (513) 531-4744
Free Catalog.
Returns: 30 days, resalable condition.
Publisher.

Oak Leaf Bed and Breakfast
Love Agricultural Resources
Rt 1, Box 113
Elk City, KS 67344
(316) 755-2908 or 633-5260 Check or M.O.
Free brochure with SASE.
2,000 acre working ranch.

Official Publications, Inc.
P.O. Box 937
Fort Washington, PA 19034
Check or M.O.
Fax: (212) 980-4776
Free brochure.
Puzzle magazines.

Optasia Fine Art Design
P.O. Box 369
Fruitport, MI 49415
(616) 865-3148 Check or M.O.
Fax: (616) 865-3032
Beautiful postcards, note cards to color.

OptimaLearning Language Land
88-D Belvedere St.
San Rafael, CA 94901
1-800-672-1717 VISA, MC.
CA: (415) 459-4474
Free brochure. Returns: Within 30 days. Language for Tots™ series.

Orton Dyslexia Society, The
724 York Rd.
Baltimore, MD 21204
(301) 296-0232
Help for people with dyslexia.

Pacific Puzzle Company
378B Guemes Island Rd.
Anacortes, WA 98221
(206) 293-7034 VISA MC. U.S. funds only.
Free catalog.
Refund or exchange if dissatisfied.
Beautiful hardwood puzzles.

Paper Soldier
8 McIntosh Lane
Clifton Park, NY 12065
(518) 371-9202 Check or M.O.
Catalog $4.00.
Antique and new paper toys and models.

Parent-Child Press
P.O. Box 767
Altoona, PA 16603
(814) 946-5213 VISA, MC. Minimum credit card order $10.
U.S. funds only.
Montessori philosophy, art materials.

ParentCare Ltd.
2515 East 43rd Street
P.O. Box 22817
Chattanooga, TN 37422
1-800-334-3889 24 hours 7 days. VISA, MC.
Free catalog. Returns: Defective merchandise.
Video catalog.

Pearl Paint
308 Canal St.
New York, NY 10013
Catalog $1
World's largest art and craft discount center.
12 locations (NY, NJ, VA, FL).

Pecci Educational Publishers
440 Davis Court #405
San Francisco, CA 94111
(415) 391-8579 Check or M.O.
Free brochure.
Reading program and Super Seatwork

Penny Press
6 Prowitt Street
Norwalk, CT 06855
Check or M.O.
Logic problem puzzles.

Penton Overseas, Inc.
2091 Las Palmas Dr., Suite A
Carlsbad, CA 92009-1519
1-800-748-5804 CA: (619) 431-0600
FAX: (619) 431-8110
Visa, MC, AmX.
Free brochure.
Foreign language voculary development.

Perma-Bound
Hertzberg-New Method, Inc.
Vandalia Rd.
Jacksonville, IL 62650
Perma-bound books. Over 13,000 titles.

Pleasant Company
P. O. Box 497
Dept. 8272
Middleton, WI 53562-0497
1-800-845-0005 VISA, MC, AmEx.
(608) 836-4848
Fax: (608) 836-4403
Free catalog.
Free *The American Girls* newsletter "for any American girl, ages 6-11."
American history dolls, accessories.

Plough Publishing House
Hutterian Brethren
300 Rosenthal Lane
Ulster Park, NY 12487
(914) 339-6680
Fax: (914) 339-6685
Hutterite books, songs about/for children.

Pompeiiana, Inc.
6026 Indianola Avenue
Indianapolis, IN 46220
(317) 255-0589 Check or M.O. U.S. funds only.
Pompeiana Newsletter. Current fads translated into classical Latin, plus student activities.

Postal Commemorative Society
47 Richards Ave.
Norwalk, CT 06856
Stamp collecting materials.

Praise Hymn, Inc.
P.O. Box 1080
Taylors, SC 29687
(803) 292-1990 Check or M.O. U.S. funds only.
Returns: Permission only. 10% restocking charge.
Christian music courses, band method.

Price/Stern/Sloan Publishers, Inc.
360 N. La Cienega Blvd.
Los Angeles, CA 90048
(213) 657-6100 VISA, MC.
Fax: (213) 855-8993
Free brochure.
Widely available in bookstores.
WEE SING series.

Prints of Peace
P.O. Box 717
Camino, CA 95709
Check or M.O.
Catalog $1.
Rubber stamps and greeting cards.

Prism
P.O. Box 030464
Ft. Lauderdale, FL 33303-0464
(305) 563-8805 Check or M.O.
Fax: (305) 563-8853
Sample copy $4.
Magazine by/for gifted kids.

Providence Project
P.O. Box 1760
Wichita, KS 67201
(316) 265-0321 Check or M.O.
Learning Vitamins.

The Putnam Publishing Group
390 Murray Hill Parkway, Dept. B
East Rutherford, NJ 07073
Visa, MC.
Books on sign language.

Quantum Communications
3301 West Hampden Ave., Suite N
Englewood, CO 80110
1-800-521-5104 VISA, MC, AmEx.
(303) 781-0679 Fax: (303) 761-8556
Free brochure. Satisfaction guaranteed.
Traveloguer videos.

Rainfall Inc.
1534 College Ave. S.E.
Grand Rapids, MI 49507
1-800-437-4337 VISA, MC.
(616) 245-5985 Fax: (616) 245-2127
Free brochure for large SASE.
Bible games and toys.

Random House, Inc.
400 Hahn Road
Westminster, MD 21157
1-800-733-3000 VISA, MC, AmEx. Orders only.
1-800-725-0600 Inquiries and customer service
Fax: (301) 848-2436
Include state sales tax.
Shipping: $2 first book, 50¢ each additional book.
Returns: Resalable condition.
Publisher.

Reading Reform Foundation
P.O. Box 98785
Tacoma, WA 98498-0785
(206) 572-9966 NY chapter: (212) 307-7320
Check or M.O.
Book list, $2.
Membership $25/year.
Resources on reading debate.
Prophonics.

Reformed Presbyterian Church of North America
Board of Education and Publication
7418 Penn Avenue
Pittsburgh, PA 15208-2531
(412) 241-0436 Check or M.O. or they bill you.
Free catalog.
Quantity discounts for bookstores and churches.
Psalm books, cassettes.

Resources for the Gifted, Inc.
3421 N. 44th St.
Phoenix, AZ 85018
(602) 840-9770 for inquiries. VISA MC. Touchtone
phone: 950-1088, wait for tone, then press
664066 (toll-free).
Free catalog.
Returns: 60 days, resalable, you pay postage.
Kathy Kolbe Thinkercise materials.

Rhythm Band, Inc.
PO Box 126
Fort Worth, TX 76101
1-800-424-4724 VISA, MC.
(817) 335-2561 Fax: (817) 332-5654
Free color catalog.
Musical instruments for children.

Rubberstampede
P.O. Box 1105
Berkeley, CA 94701
(415) 843-8910 10-4 M-F Pacific Time VISA, MC.
Free catalog.
Rubber stamps, of course!

Rubberstampmadness
P.O. Box 6585
Ithaca, NY 14851
(607) 277-5431 Check or M.O.
Sample issue $3.50.
Rubber stamp magazine.

S & S Arts and Crafts
Colchester, CT 06415
1-800-243-9232 8 AM—9 PM EST M-F, 8-noon
EST Sat. VISA, MC, or school P.O.
CT: (203) 537-3451
Fax: (203) 537-2866
U.S. funds only.
Open account: 3 credit references, prepay first
order. $25 minimum order. No C.O.D.
Arts and crafts projects.

Safari Ltd.
P.O. Box 630685
Miami, FL 33163
1-800-554-5414 VISA, MC
(305) 621-1000
Fax: (305) 621-6894
Free catalog. Returns: Within 10 days, call first.
Educational games.

School Zone Publishing Company
1819 Industrial Drive
P.O. Box 777
Grand Haven, MI 49417
(616) 846-5030 Check or M.O.
Free catalog.
Home learning workbooks, flash cards, puzzles,
video- & audiocassettes, readers, pre-K-6.

Shakean Stations, Inc.
P.O. Box 68
Farley, IA 52046
(319) 744-3307 VISA, MC.
Free 8-page color brochure.
Inexpensive file folder games.

Shar Products
P.O. Box 1411
Ann Arbor, MI 48106
(313) 665-7711 VISA, MC, C.O.D.
Free color catalog.
Stringed instruments, accessories, supplies.
Videos.
Suzuki materials. Huge list of sheet music for
strings.

Share-A-Care Publications
Rt. 2, Box 77-E
Reinholds, PA 17569
Check, M.O. or COD. U.S. funds only.
Free brochure. Send large SASE. Returns:
Permission required, resaleable condition, 30 days.
Grades 1-8 art program.

Shekinah Curriculum Cellar
967 Junipero Drive
Costa Mesa, CA 92626
(714) 751-7767 Check or M.O.
Catalog $1.
Refunds: Resealable condition, within 15 days.
Co-op buying plan.
"Quality books and teaching aids for home
educators."

Shining Star
Division of Good Apple
Box 299
Carthage, IL 62321
1-800-435-7234 VISA, MC.
Free catalog. Returns: Permission required.
Christian educational materials, magazines.

Shorewood Reproductions
27 Glen Road
Sandy Hook, CT 06482
(203) 426-8100 C.O.D., will bill subscription orders
of 5+ prints.
Fax: (203) 426-0867
Art prints.

Show-Biz Services
1735 East 26th St.
Brooklyn, NY 11229
(718) 336-0605 Check or M.O.
Catalog $3. Satisfaction guaranteed.
Ventriloquism, puppetry, magic, and balloon
sculpture supplies.

Signals
P.O. Box 64428
St. Paul, MN 55164-0482
1-800-669-9696 (orders) VISA, MC, AmEx,
Discover.
1-800-669-5225 (cust. service)
Fax: (612) 290-9320
"A Catalog For Fans & Friends Of Public Televi-
sion"

Small Business Press, Inc.
7515 Greenville Ave., Suite 510
Dallas, TX 75231
(214) 739-0058 VISA, MC
Free brochure. Returns: Within 10 days.
I Want to Paint a Zebra book.

Society for the Eradication of Television (S.E.T.)
Box 10491
Oakland, CA 94610
(415) 530-2056
Free sample.
Subscription $5 for 10 issues.
Newsletter, News and Notes from All Over.
Bumperstickers.
Educational organization.

Son Shine Puppet Company
P.O. Box 6203
Rockford, IL 61125
(815) 885-3709 Check or M.O. C.O.D. to
institutions.
Free catalog. Free sample copy of newsletter.
Returns: With authorization.
Puppets, costumes, accessories, newsletter.

Special Interest Video
475 Oberlin Ave. South
Lakewood, NJ 08701-1062
1-800-522-0502 24 hours 7 days. VISA, MC,
AmEx, Discover.
Free catalog. Returns: within 30 days.
Video catalog.

Speedy Spanish
36107 S.E. Squaw Mt. Rd.
Estacada, OR 97023
Check or M.O.
Spanish instruction with Christian content.

Summy-Birchard Inc.
Warner Brothers Publications, Inc.
265 Secaucus Road
Secaucus, NJ 07096-2037
(201) 348-0700 Fax: (201) 348-0301
Divisions: Suzuki Method International and Sum-
my Birchard Music.
Educational music publishers.

SyberVision
Fountain Square
6066 Civic Terrace Ave.
Newark, CA 94560-3747
1-800-227-0600 VISA, MC, AmEx.
Catalog $2. Quantity discounts. Returns: Within
60 days.
Unique cassette language courses, sports and
self-help videos.

Sycamore Tree
2179 Meyer Place
Costa Mesa, CA 92627
(714) 650-4466 (info) (714) 642-6750 (orders)
VISA, MC.
Fax: (714) 642-6750
Catalog $3. Includes $3 rebate good toward first
purchase.
Full-service home-school supplier.
Home-school program.

Teach Me Tapes, Inc.
10500 Bren Road East #115
Minnetonka, MN 55343
1-800-456-4656 VISA, MC
(612) 933-8086 Fax: (612) 933-0512
Free Brochure. Returns: Within 30 days.
Teach Me foreign language tapes.

Teacher Created Materials
5445 Oceanus Drive, #106
Huntington Beach, CA 92649
1-800-662-4321 (USA)
1-800-541-4906 (Canada).
Visa, MC.
(714) 891-7895
Fax: (714) 892-0283
Supplementary materials for public schools.
$2.50 postage & handling for orders under $25.
10% for orders over $25.00. Min. order $10.
Foreign & Canada add 20% for postage & handling, U.S. funds only.
Student activity workbooks.

Teen Association of Model Railroading (TAMR)
% Lone Eagle Payne
1028 Whaley Road, Route 4
New Carlisle, OH 45344
Model railroad association.

Timberdoodle
E. 1610 Spencer Lake Road
Shelton, WA 98584
(206) 426-0672 Check or M.O., or COD.
Free catalog.
Returns: 60 days, resalable condition.
Educational materials.
Fischertechnik kits.

Toad's Tools
P.O. Box 173
Oberlin, OH 44074
Check, M.O., C.O.D. Catalog, $1, refundable on
first order.
Returns: 30 days.
Topnotch kids' tools.

Toys To Grow On
P.O. Box 17
Long Beach, CA 90801
1-800-542-8338 24 hrs, 7 days. VISA, MC, AmEx.
$10 minimum.
(213) 603-8890
Fax: (213) 603-2991
Free catalog. Returns: Within 30 days.
Mail-order toy catalog.

Travel With Your Children (TWYCH)
Family Travel Times
80 Eighth Avenue
New York, NY 10011
(212) 206-0688
Family travel magazine. *Skiing with Children, Cruising with Children* annual directories.

TREND Enterprises, Inc.
P.O. Box 64073
St. Paul, MN 55164-0073
1-800-328-0818
MN: (312) 631-2850
Fax: (612) 631-2861
Stickers, wipe-off books, bulletin board cut-outs, flash cards, games, more.

Universal Publishing Co. of Port, Inc.
P.O. Box 226
Port Washington, NY 11050
(516) 944-6038
SASE for list of hobby offers.
Publisher of *The Sample Sleuth.*

University of Calgary Press
2500 University Dr., N.W.
Calgary, Alberta T2N 1N4
CANADA
(403) 220-7578 Cheque on Canadian or U.S. bank, postal M.O., VISA, MC.
Fax: (403) 282-6837
French classical language study newsletter.

Vic Lockman
P. O. Box 1916
Ramona, CA 92065
Check or M.O. Minimum order $6.
Cartoon booklets. *Cartoon Catechism for Young Children, Biblical Economics in Comics.*

Vision Development Center
6218 S. Lewis, Ste. 106
Tulsa, OK 74136
(918) 742-0072 VISA, MC.
Free brochure.
Full refund of deposit for rented materials returned on time in resalable conditon.
Developmental program for overcoming learning problems.

Vision Video
2030 Wentz Church Rd.
Worcester, PA 19490
1-800-523-0226 VISA, MC, C.O.D.
(215) 584-1893
Fax: (215) 584-4610
Free catalog. Returns: Within 30 days.
Church history and Bible story videos.

Visual Education Association
581 W. Leffel Lane
P.O. Box 1666
Springfield, OH 45501
1-800-543-5947 VISA, MC.
OH: 1-800-243-7070 Fax: (512) 324-5697
Free brochure.
Flash card sets in all subjects!

Warren Publishing House, Inc.
Totline Books and Newsletter
P.O. Box 2250
Everett, WA 98203
1-800-334-4769 VISA, MC.
Fax: (206) 481-1926
Free catalog. Refunds: 30 days.
Materials for preschool, kindergarten.

Wenger Corporation
Music Learning Division
P.O. Box 448
Owatonna, MN 55060
1-800-843-1337
MN, AK, HI, and Canada: (507) 451-1951 collect.
Coda catalog $4 and worth it.
Music software and accessories.

Western Publishing Company, Inc.
Dept. M Sales
P. O. Box 700
Racine, WI 53401
(414) 631-5202 Check or M.O.
Fax: (414) 631-5035
Workbooks, kid's books, video-cassettes, coin collecting supplies, puzzles.

WFF 'N PROOF Learning Games
1490-FS South Blvd
Ann Arbor, MI 48104-4699
(313) 665-2269 VISA, MC, C.O.D.
Free catalog.
Games for school subjects.

William Morrow and Company
105 Madison Ave.
New York, NY 10016
(212) 889-3050
Publisher.

Wireless
Minnesota Public Radio
274 Fillmore Ave. East
St. Paul, MN 55170
1-800-669-9999 VISA, MC, AmEx, Discover.
Fax: (612) 290-9320
Free catalog. Satisfaction guranteed.
Many strange things.

World Book, Inc.
Educational Services Department
Merchandise Mart Plaza
Chicago, IL 60654
(312) 245-3456 Check or M.O.
Orders over $25 may be billed.
Encyclopedia. Workbooks. Learning aids. Posters.

World Wide Games
Colchester, CT 06415
1-800-243-9232 VISA, MC, AmEx.
CT: (203) 537-3451
Free catalog. Satisfaction guranteed.
Wooden games and puzzles.

World's Greatest Stories
George W. Sarris
P.O Box 2021
South Hamilton, MA 01982
(508) 468-1556 Check or M.O.
Free flyer with SASE.
Dramatized Bible cassettes.

Worldwide Slides
727 Washburn Avenue South
Minneapolis, MN 55423
Check or M.O.
Pana-Vue catalog $1, refunded on first order.
Minimum 5-packet order.
Free View-Master™ catalog.
View-Master™ slides.

Writer's Digest Books
1507 Dana Ave
Cincinnati, OH 45207
1-800-289-0963 VISA, MC
Fax: (513) 531-4744
Free catalog.
Returns: 30 days, resaleable condition.
Publisher.

Young Companion
Pathway Publishers
Route 4
Aylmer, Ontario, CANADA N5H 2R3
Check or M.O.
Magazine for Amish teens.

Young Discovery Library
P.O. Box 229
Ossining, NY 10562
1-800-343-7854
(914) 945-0600
Fax: (914) 945-0875
Check, M.O., or purchase order.
Publisher.

INDEX OF FOREIGN SUPPLIERS

Realizing that you overseas and Canadian readers prefer to shop in your own countries, I asked every distributor listed in this book for a list of their non-USA distributors. The results, while scanty, might be of help to some of you. The American company is listed first, with its distributor's name (and address, where available) second.

As you can see, any of you who are interested in starting an importing business featuring American home-education materials have a wide-open market. Most other countries do not have as well-developed home-schooling movements as the U.S.A., and consequently Americans are blessed with more than our fair share of innovative products designed for home use. Why not even things out a bit? And when you get your business going, let me know so I can list it in the next edition!

ASIA/PACIFIC

Betterway Publications
Graham Brash (PTE) Ltd.
227 Rangoon Road
Singapore 0821

AUSTRALIA

Children's Small Press Collection
The Book Garden
Unit E3 Cnr. Windsor Rd.
Castle Hill N.S.W. 2154
02-634-2558

Conversa-phone Institute, Inc.
Lift Australia Pty. Ltd.
P.O. Box 401
Unit 8-1 Vuko Place
Warriewood, NSW 2102

Gospel Mission
Koorong Books Pty Ltd.
17 Ryedale Road
West Ryde, NSW 2114

Midwest Publications
Hawker Brownlow Education Pty. Ltd.
235 Bay Road
Cheltenham, Victoria 3192
Fax: 61-3-553-4538

Milliken Publishing Company
Encyclopaedia Britannica (Australia) Inc.
Britannica Center 12 Anella Ave.
Castke Hill NSW 2154
02-680-5607 FAX: 02-899-3231

North Light Books
Kirby Books Ltd.
Private Bag No. 19
P.O. Box Alexandria, NSW 2015
2-698-2377

Rainfall Inc.
Care and Share
3 Harley Crescent
Condell Park, N.S.W., Bankstown 2200
(02) 7073111

Son Shine Puppet Company
Children for Christ
Mike Dunsworth
288-290 King St., 1st floor
Newtown, NSW 2042

Teacher Created Materials
Hawker Brownlow Educ. Pty. Ltd.
235 Bay Road
Cheltenham, Victoria 3192

Vic Lockman
Light Educational Ministries
PO Box 101
Booleroo Centre,South Australia 5482

Vision Video
Australian Religious Film Society/Esdras Giddy
Blenheim Road and Warwick Street
(02) 888-2511 Fax 011-61-2958-2812

AUSTRALIA/NEW ZEALAND

Learning Works
Hawker Brownlow Educational Pty. Ltd.
235 Bay Road
Cheltenham, Victoria 3192
Australia
03-555-1344

CANADA

Alpha Omega Publications
Academic Distribution Services
528 Carnarvon St.
New Westminster, B. C. V3L 1C4
(604) 524-9758

American Institute of Music
American Institute of Music (home office)
Suite 106, 5803 Yonge St.
Willowdale, Ontario, M2M 3V5

Betterway Publications
Raincoast Book Distribution, Ltd.
112 East 3rd Ave.
Vancouver, B.C. V5T 1C8
(604) 873-6581

Bright Ring Publishing
Monarch Books of Canada Limited
5000 Dufferin St.
Unit K, Downsview, Ontario M31 5T5

Conversa-phone Institute, Inc.
Distribution Fusion III
5455 Rue Pare Suite 101
Montreal, Quebec H4P 1P7

Discovery Toys
Discovery Toys Canada
1132 South Service Road
Oakville, Ontario L6L 5T7
1-800-268-5160

Educators Publishing Service
66 Scarsdale Rd.
Don Mills, Ontario M3B 2R7
(416) 755-0591

Gospel Mission
Valley Gospel Mission
Box 412
Sardis, British Columbia V2R 1A7

Kimbo Educational
Monarch Books of Canada
500 Dufferin St.
Downsville, Ontario M3H 5T5
(416) 663-8231

Midwest Publications
Western Ed. Activities, Ltd.
10929-101 St.
Edmonton, Alberta T5H 2S7

Midwest Publications
Educational Resources Ltd.
109-8475 Ontario St.
Vancouver, British Columbia V5X 3E8

Midwest Publications
Kahl's Inc.
Box 126
Kitchener, Ontario N2G 3W9

Milliken Publishing Company
Encyclopedia Britannica Publications
175 Holiday Drive
Cambridge, Ontario N3C 3N4
(519) 658-4621

North Light Books
Prentice-Hall Canada
1870 Birchmont Rd.
Scarborough, Ontario M1P 2J7
(416) 293-3621

Plough Publishing House
Plough Publishing
Crystal Spring
Ste. Agathe, Manitoba R0G 1Y0
(204) 433-7634

Rainfall Inc.
Main Roads Productions
310 Judson Street
Toronto, Ontario M8Z 5T6
(416) 252-9146

Shining Star
Beacon Distributors, Ltd.
104 Consumers Drive
Whitby, Ontario L1N 5T3
(416) 668-8884

Shorewood Reproductions
Access Fine Art Ltd.
66 Portland St.
Toronto, Ontario, M5V 2M8
(416) 861-0606 Fax (416) 861-0444

Summy-Birchard Inc.
Warner/Chappell Music Ltd.
85 Scarsdale Road Unit 101
Don Mills, Ontario M3B 2R2
(416) 445-3131 Fax: (416) 445-2473

Teacher Created Materials
Educator Supplies Limited
2323 Trafalgar Street
London, Ontario N5W 5H2

Vic Lockman
Discount Chsristian Books
12719 126th St.
Edmonton T5L 0X9

Writer's Digest Books
Prentice-Hall Canada
1870 Birchmont Rd.
Scarborough, Ontario M1P 2J7
(416) 293-3621

ENGLAND

Audio Forum
31 Kensington Church Street
London W8-4LL
01-937-1647

Basil Blackwell, Inc.
Basil Blackwell Publisher Ltd.
108 Cowley Rd.
Oxford, OX4 1J5
011-44-865791100

Betterway (U.K. only)
Gazelle Book Services Ltd.
Falcon House, Queen Square
Lancaster LA1 1RN

Conversa-phone Institute, Inc.
L.C.L. Benedict Ltd.
102-104 Judd Street
London NC1H-9NF

Gospel Mission
Gospel Standard Trust
#7 Brachendale Grove
Harpenden Herts AL3 3EL

Milliken Publishing Company
Gemini Teaching Aids
19, Kirkgate
Sherburn-in-Elmet
Leeds, LS25 6BH
0977-684524

North Light Books
Harrap Publishing Group, Chelsea House
26 Market Square
Bromley, Kent BR1 1NA
(1) 313-3484

Plough Publishing House
Plough Publishing
Darvell
Robertsbridge, E. Sussex TN32 5DR
(0) 580 880 626

Rainfall Inc.
New Wine Ministries
P. O. Box 17
Chichester, West Sussex PO206RY
(0243) 543000

Reading Reform Foundation
Reading Reform of England
2 The Crescent, Toftwood
East Dereham
Norfolk NR19-1NR

Rubberstampmadness
Make Your Mark
73 Walmgale
York YO1 2TZ
(0904) 637355

Teacher Created Materials
Gemini Teaching Aids
19 Kirkgate
Sherburn-in-Elmet
Leeds LS25 6BH

Vision Video
West Brooke House
76 High Street
Alton, Hampshire, GU341EN
44-420-891-41 Fax 011-44-420-541160

Writer's Digest Books
Freelance Press
5/9 Bexley Square
Salford Wanshester M3 6DB

WESTERN EUROPE

Betterway Publications
Gazelle Book Services Limited
Falcon House, Queen Square
Lancaster LA1 1RN
ENGLAND

GERMANY

Plough Publishing House
Plough Publishing
Michaelshof, 5231 Birnbach
WEST GERMANY
49 2681 6250

NEW ZEALAND

Rainfall Inc.
Heyes Enterprises
P. O. Box 24-086 Royal Oak
Auckland
64-6-655951

SOUTH AFRICA

Gospel Mission
Good Neighbors Books
Box 4022
Randburg 2125

Vic Lockman
Signposts
PO Box 26148
0007 Arcadia

GENERAL INDEX